A SELECTION FROM SCRUTINY

VOLUME 1

A SELECTION FROM

SCRUTINY

COMPILED BY

F.R.LEAVIS

IN TWO VOLUMES

VOLUME 1

CAMBRIDGE
AT THE UNIVERSITY PRESS
1968

Published by the Syndics of the Cambridge University Press
Bentley House, P.O. Box 92, 200 Euston Road, London, N.W.1
American Branch: 32 East 57th Street, New York, N.Y. 10022

This selection © Cambridge University Press 1968

Library of Congress Catalogue Card Number: 67-24940

Printed in Great Britain
at the University Printing House, Cambridge
(Brooke Crutchley, University Printer)

CONTENTS

Prefatory   *page* xi

4 POST-ELIOT POETS REVIEWED

5 LITERARY CULTURE

CONTENTS

CONTENTS TO VOLUME 2

CONTENTS

PREFATORY

The suggestion that there should be a selection of this magnitude from *Scrutiny* came from the Cambridge University Press. It is not offered as a representative anthology; that was never in question. The idea was that the nineteen volumes contained many things that it might be well to make more accessible; that is, both more easy to turn up than when dispersed through some thousands of pages in the original seventy-six quarterly numbers, and, at the same time, purchasable for a smaller outlay. Work generally current because, since its appearance in *Scrutiny*, incorporated in well-known books, was to be excluded.

This consideration eliminated the main body of criticism of French literature *Scrutiny* had printed—an elimination that, since there seemed no point in a selection from the miscellaneous little that was left, became total. Again, the exclusion of Wilfred Mellers meant the exclusion of music criticism, and the exclusion of the main body of D. J. Enright's work the exclusion of the criticism of German literature. It was easy, then, to arrive at the decision that these two volumes were to be confined to criticism of English literature, with the addition of some matter of closely related interest. Even so, the reader should be reminded—though it is perhaps hardly necessary—how much Marius Bewley, D. W. Harding, L. C. Knights, John Speirs and D. A. Traversi counted for in the critical influence of *Scrutiny*: by reason of the well-known books, it couldn't be suggested in the selection.

The upshot of the initial considerations faced me with a greater embarrassment that I had anticipated. My wife and I bore the major burden of *Scrutiny:* for two decades (including half a dozen years of war) we did the donkey-work and had the responsibility. We wrote more than anyone else—more than we should willingly have undertaken: it was unavoidable if *Scrutiny* was to be kept going. A very large amount of it—all in fact that was written by my wife—has remained unreprinted. Much of it, to judge by allusions, use made, and promptings to reprint, is widely known. My natural self-defensive impulse to keep down, in preparing these two volumes, the proportion of the contents coming under my surname was countered by Mr M. H. Black of the University Press. He had a close acquaintance with the nineteen original volumes, and, having given much thought to what should go into the kind of selection in view, he could back with strong reasons the suggestions he made. I will say no more by way of apology.

The undertaking was a more difficult and exacting one than it had presented itself at first as being, and I have the strongest sense of what I owe to Mr Black's co-operation.

F. R. LEAVIS

Cambridge 1967

I

THE CAMBRIDGE TRADITION

ACADEMIC CASE-HISTORY

Q. D. LEAVIS (1943)

Haddon the Head Hunter, by A. H. Quiggin (C.U.P.)

Everyone knows that A. C. Haddon established the study of Anthropology at Cambridge. How he managed to do so is less common knowledge, so it is fortunate that the biography we have been given is frank about the subject. The facts are recorded with some appropriate though subdued indignation, and it is well that the facts should be put on record, instead of the usual humbug which whitewashes an institution at the expense of the victim. Chapters five and six, called 'Cambridge and Anthropology', provide instructive documentation about how an institution, endowed to promote learning and light, behaves when it is offered the services of a uniquely qualified specialist and teacher who is concerned to break new ground.

Haddon, after leaving Cambridge, became a zoologist, but an expedition he undertook to Torres Straits in 1889 convinced him that while Zoology could wait, the materials for the study of Anthropology must be collected at once before it was too late. Cecil Sharp made a similar discovery about English Folk-song and Dance, but as his materials lay at his back door, so to speak, he was able to collect them and support himself concurrently. Haddon was in a more awkward position—his data existed in Oceania. He was urged to devote his remarkable talents to Anthropology by such eminent pioneers as Frazer and Huxley, and in 1893 Haddon moved from Dublin, where he was professor of Zoology, to Cambridge, in hopes of getting endowment. In 1898, after scraping together funds, he conducted a famous anthropological expedition, the first of its kind, having enlisted the services of W. H. Rivers, McDougall, Seligman and C. S. Myers, whom he made recruits to the new science. This Expedition achieved so much that Frazer and Ridgeway in 1899 sponsored a Memorial urging the University to provide instruction in Ethnology by creating a post for Haddon, pointing out not only his eminent fitness for the post but that he had 'already laid the University and science under great obligations by teaching Anthropology in the University without a salary for three years' and laying stress on his genius as a teacher. Alas,

I

though the Universities were originated by great teachers and are only kept alive by them (not only spiritually but in a very material sense, since it is they who attract students to the schools), yet to arouse enthusiasm as a teacher is not the way to become *persona grata* in the academic world; and though it was well known that the University had resources, and the Memorial was supported by many Heads of Houses and Departments, and by eight professors, all that could be got for Haddon and Anthropology was a lectureship of £50 a year, in 1900. The strength of the opposition behind the scenes may be gauged by the force of the supporting party.

In 1901 Haddon was elected to a fellowship at his own college, and with this nucleus of an income and no facilities except those provided by the generosity of other departments, he settled down to establishing a school of Anthropology. For most of his life he had to make out an income by reviewing, writing and lecturing up and down the country in addition to his university work, and he mostly had to finance from this the equipment, materials and books he needed. In a speech on his seventieth birthday, Haddon observed: 'Our University sometimes seems to behave more like the traditional step-mother than Alma Mater—the Nourishing Mother.' There was indeed a considerable period of his life when the motto of his University must have seemed to him a bitter joke. He had, however, his work, his teaching and his enthusiastic students, and, as time went on, his grateful old pupils all over the world; and he had the support of appreciative scientists everywhere; he was sustained too by the belief that if he 'held on in Cambridge' he might get Anthropology permanently endowed there. As his biographer says, 'he had no selfish aims'; to money and status for their own sake he was perfectly indifferent. The real burden fell on his wife, who had to raise a family under the most difficult conditions of financial and psychological strain.

In 1904, in face of opposition, the Board of Anthropological Studies was officially recognized and Anthropology appeared on the Lecture List, though for ten years longer he had to depend on the goodwill of other departments even for the use of a room for lecturing or teaching. He fought the battle of Anthropology more successfully than his own, for by 1907 future Colonial administrators were being given courses at Cambridge in General Anthropology to suit their particular needs—a scheme Haddon had long urged in various quarters—and the next year a Diploma in Anthropology was established. But it was not till 1909 that Haddon's friends and admirers felt in a position to address a Memorandum to the General Board of Studies recommending that 'Dr Haddon, an enthusiastic and inspiring teacher and an anthropologist of world-wide reputation', should be appointed Reader in Ethnology.

This was successful; £200 a year was actually wrung out of the University for the purpose and Haddon appointed (though insulting opposition 'enlivened the discussion in the Senate', where the proposal was described as 'the most reckless and culpable waste of money that could possibly be imagined'). He held this princely readership till he was over seventy, resigning in 1925, 'having borne the whole burden of teaching in the Department for nearly a quarter of a century'. The chair which he had so richly earned was not established until he was technically too old to be eligible, in 1933.

He died in 1940, in his eighty-fifth year. In spite of everything, or rather everybody, he had achieved much of what he had wanted and more than could possibly have been expected in the circumstances; his life was not tragic, for he was happy, and successful according to any real code of values, and he had all along the recognition of his peers. But why did it have to be 'in spite of'? Haddon was in an innocent sense a good mixer, and had connections and friends in the right places, he was even 'a regular churchgoer' and had the gift of making Anthropology acceptable to bishops and missionaries: he was not the sort of man who is described in the academic world as 'dangerous'. For this reason, no doubt, no campaign of personal calumny and social ostracism was undertaken against him, as is usual in similar cases, and no hostility to his project of establishing the new study was exhibited, as might have been expected, by the contiguous schools of Archaeology, Geology, etc. The general public might well ask, who, if not professors and heads of departments and Houses, supported by the testimony of pupils and outside authorities—who if not these can take action, who in fact runs our universities anyway? It almost looks as though there must be some basis for the belief I have heard expressed, that at the older universities everything is managed by committees and all those committees by a few wicked old men. This is perhaps an extreme statement; at least, the practice of intrigue is not the prerogative of the old. The answer does seem to be that the academic world, like other worlds, is run by the politicians, and sensitively scrupulous people tend to leave politics to other people, while people with genuine work to do certainly have no time as well as no taste for committee-rigging and the associated techniques. (Haddon ignored University politics and was surprised to find that 'what to him was a matter of opinion' would be to some important person 'a matter of offence'—this gives perfectly the temperature of academic life.) And then of course there are the forces of native stupidity reinforced by that blind hostility to criticism, reform, new ideas and superior ability which is human as well as academic nature.[1]

---

[1] Cf. the experiences of an unimpeachable authority, the Oxford historian Mr E. L. Woodward (Domestic Bursar of All Souls, History Tutor of New

These forces are always present to be directed for their own ends by academic politicians, but perhaps they can be trusted to defeat themselves in time. Though material triumph may be lacking, a

College, Proctor, etc.) in his recent autobiography, *Short Journey*: 'I thought of these things when the wife of an elderly don told my wife that it would be nice for me to learn "how the university was run". I am bound to say that I thought it was not well run [1930 circa] and that I was astonished at the incapacity of most of the members of the university council and other bodies of administrative importance... The committee system was overdone...' etc. He gives an instructive account of his few attempts to effect reforms in University affairs. His chief failure was an attempt to get a very obvious reform through—to persuade the authorities to make suitable provision for a modern library instead of the hopelessly congested and unsuitable Bodleian, which it was proposed to supplement by a mere bookstore in the heart of Oxford. He found that all the powers were hostile, having been canvassed by the old librarian, that he wasted a year of his time and energies in trying unsuccessfully to interest likely people in the affair, and that all he and his few supporters could achieve, beyond alienating all the elderly scholars of his acquaintance and incurring a lot of ill will generally, was a bad compromise (and even this was almost wrecked finally by the efforts of the opposition and only saved by the Vice-Chancellor). '...We might have planned, on an open site, with space for future expansion, a building which would stand as a monument to our foresight and our wisdom. And the whole business was botched, in the last resort, because one obstinate old man had not given up his job as librarian at the ordinary retiring age, and because no one had bothered to reform the constitution of the board of curators of the library. *As for me, this experience taught me a good deal about the lengths to which people will go merely to keep things as they are.*' It is hardly necessary to point out the disastrous effects of such an environment on appointments committees, for example; or what rare courage and sense of duty must be required in anyone who refuses to acquiesce in what is, however small the occasion. Obviously such a state of affairs as that outlined in this review can only exist if an innocent or cynical acquiescence in it by everyone can be taken for granted; hence one of the resulting moral obliquities is that it is not the existence of an undesirable situation, but calling attention to it, which is considered offensive and earns censure (to put these matters on record is the last crime, and in fact documents like *Short Journey* and *Haddon the Head Hunter* don't often see the light). A sociological expedition would have a fruitful yield if it undertook field-research into the academic world. And it is a world—the other universities are very largely stocked from Oxford and Cambridge and moreover are closely connected with them by social filaments, so that to be posted at one of these last is to be boycotted all round, the penalty of the *mauvais sujet* which few dare risk incurring. Another relevant point is that intellectual matters are hopelessly overlaid by social life, e.g. the reasons for professorial and other appointments would often repay investigation, as in general the extent to which intellectual standards have in different places been stultified by social factors and academic politics. Outside the sciences, careers founded solely on log-rolling and social contacts are not unknown, and keeping the right company is in many fields the best, if not the indispensable, means of advancement. There is a pretty general recognition that the further the subject is from being a science the less have real qualifications to do with appointments or influential position in the academic world of the humanities; this means that a great disparity commonly exists in such

Haddon comes out on top in the end because it is he and not they who gets results and reputation, and the cause of Anthropology is eventually won. To be sure, he will incur in the process all the malice, thwarting and jealous misrepresentation which the jungle of academic society can produce. It is not surprising that the academic world should be so much like a small town, since human nature is essentially the same in both places; the grounds for indignation are that a university is supposed to be a place where different values reign, and different objects are pursued, than in the outside world. And it is true that in the realm of the sciences there is a tradition of impartial appointment and generous recognition, because in science there are objective standards to appeal to. Haddon was fortunate in having this disinterested world of science behind him; without its backing he could not have found a party to press his claims on the university and would have been wholly frustrated in his work. The real tragedies lie elsewhere.

When Haddon consulted his wife about giving up Dublin and Zoology for Cambridge and Anthropology she replied: 'You might as well starve as an anthropologist as a zoologist.' But there is the specialist of genius who cannot even starve in his own way. There was Haddon's linguistic expert, S. H. Ray, who was the only English authority on Melanesian languages available for the 1898 Expedition. 'Haddon never felt quite happy about Ray. The other members of the Expedition all rose high in the world, and he could feel that their work with him had not been unrewarded. But Ray, who had sacrificed more, had no earthly reward; he remained an assistant elementary school-master to the end of his days. The file of correspondence shows the efforts Haddon made to obtain recognition for him, but all in vain, and this man of genius, one of the world's greatest authorities on Oceanic languages, was compelled to earn his living for forty years by teaching elementary arithmetic to large classes of little East-End London boys, snatching what odd hours he could spare for his linguistic work.' It was impossible to get Ray, with all his qualifications, a foothold in the academic world. He had no college to give him a tardy fellowship. For him not even a lectureship of £50 a year could be secured. All that Haddon could get for him from the academic world was an honorary M.A. degree at Cambridge. When one thinks how much money there was to dispose of in the universities, where comfortable livings seem to have been available for so many insignificant scholars and posts for so many without vocation, where young men have so freely been elected into fellowships on promissory notes that have not by any means

schools between what the body of academics recruited in this way has to offer and the demands of their students, a situation producing discomfort or uglier manifestations of a sense of inferiority on the one side, and lasting resentment on the other. The sociology of the academic world is a sadly neglected subject.

invariably been honoured, and where, in short, the most casual glance round would reveal a number of people who seem to have no reason for being supported with income and status except their strong sense of their right to be—the tragedy of a Ray seems unnecessary.

Haddon's case, even more than Ray's, has the importance of being representative, and it represents a problem which neither Royal nor Statutory Commissions can favourably affect nor any reform that can conceivably follow on the War. If there had not been some elasticity in the departmental system at that time, Haddon could never have established himself (and Anthropology); in those days anyone within the university could give lectures and classes, having extracted some kind of permission, and collect the fees, if he could attract enough of an audience to make it worth while and some kind of a living for himself. This is what Haddon did. (It is through this loophole that Dr Richards, for example, was able while in the Moral Sciences school to give lectures to English students and make his career as a new kind of specialist by publishing the results—*Principles of Literary Criticism*.) Thus even with less than no encouragement from a department an innovator or otherwise obnoxious character has been known to hold on until in the course of time it became apparent that he was in fact a great man and must be admitted, however reluctantly, into the fold, if only to avert scandal. I once heard the late W. E. Johnson, who had taught all the Cambridge philosophers from Russell on, observe that he remembered when some of the most distinguished minds and most influential teachers in Cambridge were free-lances who supported themselves, without fellowships or faculty posts, in this independent way, but that with the tightening-up of things effected by the introduction of the faculty system, such a state of affairs had become impossible.[1] He

[1] Chiefly through the imposition of a substantial composition fee which entitles the undergraduate to attend a number of lecture courses authorized by the faculty. In practice it is levied on every undergraduate, even if he complains that the lectures in his subjects are unprofitable and he has not attended any of them (he still has the right to stay away at the older universities, though not at the modern ones). Thus he could hardly be expected to pay in addition separate fees for free-lance courses of lectures. He must also attend and pay for tuition by a supervisor (Oxford, tutor) selected by his college; though his right to choose his supervisor would no doubt be theoretically granted if it occurred to him to claim it, to claim it often requires considerable moral courage, particularly if the college, when stimulated to the effect by a faculty representative, signifies disapproval of his choice. Thus, as a supervisor also, the free-lance is debarred from competing with the regulars, so that anyone outside the ring can be starved out of the academic world. The composition fee means that the only real check of whether a lecture course is of value to those who pay for it—the size of the regular lecture audience—can be disregarded; and that the good lecturers pay for the inadequate ones. It leads also to obvious abuses, such as repeating a course year after year, even if the substance has been published in book form

considered this unfortunate. And it is easy to see that without such a means of bucking the party machine, so to speak, a Haddon can never again force his way into the stronghold of vested interests that faculties inevitably become. While this makes things more comfortable for the politicians and deadheads, it is not so good for the undergraduates, or for the humanities and sciences, or for the intellectual life of the universities in general, or for the prestige of a school in the outside world. But this brings us to the question, For whose benefit are the universities run? and at this dangerous point we must call a halt to speculation.

'THE DISCIPLINE OF LETTERS'

Q. D. LEAVIS (1943)

A Sociological Note

In the last number of *Scrutiny* we examined the university career of a peculiarly gifted man, the late A. C. Haddon, who combined the abilities of a specialist opening up a new field of knowledge with those of an exceptionally inspiring teacher. It was a career that could hardly be called successful by worldly standards. Chance has given us the opportunity to complete the findings by contrast: we may now inspect the record of a man whom in our time an ancient university has delighted to honour.

It must be said first that this collection[1] of the late George Gordon's letters, made by his widow, seems intended primarily to show that he was an affectionate relative and had many distinguished friends. It is what emerges incidentally that matters, for it is of course in his public and representative capacities, as professor of literature and of poetry, that we are concerned with him here. He has in fact no other importance,

or has been proved useless by non-attendance. These are real grievances which have been expressed by generations of undergraduates without effect. It is not unnatural that they should take more interest than the authorities in whether they are receiving value for their parents' money and their own time. In the last number of *Scrutiny* the review of Dr Löwe's book, *The Universities in Transformation*, quotes him as concluding: 'It may well be necessary first to educate a new generation of university teachers before real headway can be made [in the humanities].' No doubt; and here and there perhaps they are being educated. The difficulty lies in getting them admitted into that closed circle where they should function; how does Dr Löwe propose to find them posts, since the system sketched here is self-perpetuating and even the holes in it have now been blocked? Failing a holocaust of most of the existing personnel and radical alteration of the machinery in their hands, endowment seems the only hope. But Nuffields and Rockefellers endow only sciences.

[1] *The Letters of G. S. Gordon, 1902–42* (O.U.P.)

since there is, as the blurb tactfully puts it, a 'scarcity of more formal monuments to his learning and literary craftsmanship'.

Gordon was the able Scots student who collects Firsts and prizes by cannily directed industry. Coming from Glasgow as already a brilliant Classic, after skimming through History and Greats he saw possibilities, as others have done, in the more recent department of English and transferred his attentions thither—English studies being, apart from the linguist's claims on them, notoriously the prerogative of your Classic (generally of your not-good-enough Classic). So he attracted Raleigh's attention by editing a typically academic collection of essays, *English Literature and the Classics*, to which he himself contributed a piece on Theophrastus; this, he wrote, convinced Raleigh that he would do for the English School. With Raleigh's backing he secured an English fellowship at Magdalen and managed before his fellowship ran out to land with it the Chair of English at Leeds, whence he returned to succeed Raleigh as Merton Professor of Literature in 1922. In 1928 he became President of Magdalen, and subsequently Vice-Chancellor, but his merely academic offices, except as symptoms of success, are beside the point. We must note rather his election to the Oxford Chair of Poetry in 1934, his appointment to the original Selection Committee of the Book Society along with Walpole and Priestley (as to which he wrote, 'I couldn't wish for better company'), his election to the various literary societies that carry social prestige, his undertaking a series of popular fifteen-minute broadcast talks on great literature, his editing a selection of *Times* third leaders, etc. In contrast to Haddon, who achieved so much with so little public assistance, Gordon, in spite of every worldly opportunity in the way of financial endowment, social sanction and professional backing, has left nothing except a few published lectures and addresses. Nevertheless, they have their interest and their place in literary history. For though they are not literary criticism they do give us an insight into the conditions which control literary studies in the universities and are therefore of the greatest value at this moment for us. For if any educational reform as a whole is to be achieved in this country after the War—and everything suggests that attempts in that direction will be made—it must centre on the universities, and there on the humanities. It is impossible to discuss such subjects in the air, without relation to the academic world which conditions them. And that sociology of the academic world which was desiderated in the last number of *Scrutiny* would certainly need to take note of the history of George Gordon. In contrast to Haddon, he was a green bay-tree specimen: what enabled him to flourish? What sources of satisfaction did he provide for his order? we must ask. We may conveniently start by examining his record with respect to literature, for sociology and literary criticism are mutually enlightening.

His chief productions are his two inaugural lectures, *The Discipline of Letters*, delivered before the University of Oxford in 1923, and *Poetry and the Moderns*, delivered in the same circumstances in 1934. Both are professions of belief, with a difference: between them the deluge had occurred, as far as literary criticism is concerned. As late as 1923 Gordon, who evidently lived in a literary backwater, was unaware of any challenge to what he stood for. The discipline of letters, he proclaims, is represented by the Oxford School of English. This is twofold. On the one hand, linguistic-philological studies as an end in themselves. On the other, scholarship—the ideal of perfect editing, that is, a frivolous one which is hostile to any real standards in literature since any text long enough dead is equally meet to be edited, the credit consisting in producing the perfect index etc. to a piece of writing not necessarily worth publishing in the first place. Or in Gordon's own words—and the jargon is characteristic—'In this University Mercury and Philologia, after many deeds of settlement (for the lady has been difficult) are partners, I hope, for life.' He followed this up by an attack on the Royal Commission's *Report on English*, apparently because that proposed that English should take the place traditionally occupied by Classics, and should, in short, be taken seriously as an educational and cultural study. To take literature seriously, he declared, is 'an affront to life'. An inexplicable attitude for a Professor of English Literature to strike in his inaugural lecture? But before we look further into this extraordinary position we will attend his next public appearance on an almost identical occasion.

Poetry and the Moderns, eleven years later, reveals the formerly complacent academic uneasy; if he is dimly aware that he has not a leg to stand on, so to speak, he is still feeling around for a stance to maintain his self-esteem. We note he invokes for support his friends and predecessors Bridges, de Sélincourt, Garrod, Raleigh; with the like-minded to back him he takes up a position of superiority to what he cannot understand and feels as a threat to his prestige. The lecture is nothing but a series of appeals to his audience to respond in the cheapest way, he is out to capitalize the stock responses of the herd, he jeers in order to elicit sniggers of approval, and so on. The lecture is of course only memorable as one contribution to the academic war against contemporary poetry and literary criticism which, raging from about 1925 for a dozen years or more, will in a century or so no doubt become a subject for sanctioned literary research.[1] That campaign looks negligible

[1] Material will be found covering general as well as detailed aspects in the back numbers of *Scrutiny*. Other documents besides *Poetry and the Modern World*

now, but it was conducted with every expression of malice, misrepresentation and personal spite that the academic pen and tongue could command—the scholarly conscience having nothing to do with a critical conscience, or with any other kind, it would appear. We notice in Gordon's lecture that the focus of his ill will is Mr T. S. Eliot, and this was generally so, because as poet and literary critic Mr Eliot represented a challenge which the 'lovers of a continuous literary decorum' could neither overlook nor hope to take up without disaster: some of them envied his success as a poet and all were jealous of his literary influence. Hence the choice of an attack on 'the moderns' as a subject for an inaugural lecture. But even in 1934 it was too late, the tide of public opinion had already turned. Even then Professor Claud Colleer Abbott was editing the letters of Gerard Manley Hopkins (Oxford, 1935) with the implication that they were as important as Keats's—to value highly the poems of Hopkins was another way to incur academic odium, Bridges, in reluctantly and patronizingly editing them, having indicated the permissible degree of admiration. And when in 1937 Mr Humphry House, also of Oxford, produced an expensive edition of Hopkins's Notebooks and Trivia, in themselves of no particular interest, with all the panoply of scholarship including biographies of everyone mentioned in the text and bibliographies of the MSS. etc., well, if the citadel had not actually fallen, at least solidarity had been sacrificed. Or perhaps only consistency, for that section of the academic party which had put on record its opinion that any critic who thought Hopkins a considerable poet was thereby 'certifiable'[1] was at least put out of countenance. But Gordon had an instinct against risking being caught out on a limb: he ends by manoeuvring into the favourite post-diehard academic position. He ends with a profession, not this time of the Discipline of Letters (Mercury wedded to Philologia) but of broadmindedness. He manages to put the critics he is attacking, instead of himself, in the attitude of intolerance by the usual trick of misrepresentation and even invention. We shall return to this later.

Altogether it is a curious history for a professor of English Literature

are John Sparrow, *Sense and Poetry* (1934); F. L. Lucas, *The Criticism of Poetry*, Warton Lecture 1933, and his contribution 'English' to *Cambridge University Studies* (1933); articles and essays by C. S. Lewis, Profs. Garrod and de Sélincourt, Logan Pearsall Smith, G. M. Young, Desmond MacCarthy, Humbert Wolfe, J. C. Squire and other contributors to the Sunday papers and literary weeklies of the period, and of course Dean Inge; papers read to the English Association and such literary societies; and a manifestation of the spirit of the campaign permanently enshrined in *The Concise Cambridge History of English Literature* (ed. George Sampson).

[1] F. L. Lucas, *Cambridge University Studies*, 'English'.

and worth investigating. The *Letters* recently published illuminate it considerably. Gordon succeeded Raleigh at Oxford and was formed by him, so we must go a stage further back, to the case of Raleigh himself. For Raleigh was not only the first professor of English Literature at Oxford, he became a cult. His idiosyncrasies became the mould of form and his prejudices and prepossessions were standardized. We can see that while Raleigh made the Oxford English School he never took literature seriously, apart from its succubus, scholarship. He is an example of the most dangerous kind of academic, the man who hasn't enough ability to set up on his own as a creative artist and bears literature a grudge in consequence.[1] His letters[2] run on humorously about whatever poet he is writing on (Shakespeare, Blake and Wordsworth figure in turn as Bill)—the effect is to place himself on a level with them or whatever literary figure he writes about. His lectures seem to have been dramatic readings studded with epigrams. His professorial writings are all, implicitly or explicitly, about the inferiority of literature to life, an antithesis which he propagated continually, and he is seen perpetually anxious to show that he was not a don, not a professional man of letters, not a serious teacher of literature (though he was quite willing to accept a comfortable living by undertaking to be all three).[3] These characteristics, combined with a denigration of all literary criticism (which did not prevent him from publishing a number of books and resenting adverse reviews of them) when contrasted with his unquestioning belief in the virtues of good mixing in the best company, combine to make an unpleasant impression. A life devoted to teaching literature in this spirit is bound to become uneasy. By 1906 he was declaring, 'I begin to hate criticism. Nothing can come of it,' and he seems before then to have been conscious of the futility of his kind of English studies. 'If I am accused on Judgment Day of teaching literature, I shall plead that I never believed in it and that I maintained a wife and children,' he wrote in 1921. This is an attitude by no means confined to Raleigh or Oxford, and is seen, characteristically, to produce a cynicism about the academic function that is, to put it in the lowest terms, unnecessary (readers may prefer a stronger adjective). It is not necessary to acquiesce, as the Raleighs do, on the ground that there is

[1] The first literary critic, he wrote, was a eunuch, and literary appreciation is an emotion for spinsters.

[2] *The Letters of Sir Walter Raleigh, 1879–1922* (Methuen, 2 vols.).

[3] The comparison that places Raleigh best is with Leslie Stephen. Though earning his living as a free-lance, having given up his fellowship on grounds of conscience, Stephen never wrote without having something to say and worth listening to, worked out a method of literary criticism on a sound basis, and respected his function. He has already been the subject of an article in this journal (Vol. VII, No. 4—see p. 22 in this selection).

no alternative. 'We go to Glasgow about the 10th to get my ridiculous degree,' he wrote once. 'I call it ridiculous because I have been in the kitchen where these things are cooked.' This is not a healthy scepticism, it is an excuse for taking a hand in the cooking as well as for benefiting by it. The next step is to make the P. G. Wodehouses free of the ridiculous degree.

This is Gordon's academic heredity. He shows what happens to ability when it is exposed to the atmosphere of Classical studies pursued without any standards other than those of scholarship and of social snobbishness. One is not surprised to learn from his letters that the important things in life are (1) good mixing—a good man is one who likes a good dinner and knows the right people—and (2) scholarship for its own sake. We see too that one corollary to the latter belief is that ability to edit a text is the only and sufficient test of academic fitness, hence the man who has edited any insignificant text is qualified to practise literary criticism and to direct literary studies. We see Gordon, through his letters, filling all the university posts he can, at home and abroad, with men who have proved their right to 'a senior post' by editing something, and with every conviction of righteousness spreading despair and blight on university students of English throughout the British Commonwealth. We see him believing, as he was taught by Raleigh, that the summit of achievement in modern English is represented by the writings of Charles Lamb and Robert Louis Stevenson —to write on Elia is 'the last test and pledge'; he is 'steeped in the *Letters*...I have read them for fifteen years; and the only fault I find in them is that they make all other Letters seem poor and thin. Even Stevenson must not be read till some time has elapsed; or he seems a green boy'.[1] The other great figure in this gallery is Johnson. I say figure because it is not Johnson's prose writings and poetry whose value is recognized, it is the club figure which can be used for purposes of solidarity (though of course Johnson's club and Johnson's personality were not of that kind). Lamb, Stevenson and Johnson evidently united to form an ideal centre[2] and in so far as Gordon had any particular taste it was for mannered prose with a 'personal' content, while archaizing and pastiches and light verse seem to have been the accepted form for academic *jeux d'esprit*. It was not incompatible with such tastes that he should have sponsored Sir Hugh Walpole's novels and

[1] The whole of this letter (7 September 1920) should be read. He had written an article on Lamb by invitation for *The Times Literary Supplement* and is overcome at his temerity in accepting.

[2] How readily this abstraction of English literature could be assimilated with the Classics is shown by another of the group, R. W. Chapman, who refers to 'the best odes of Horace, the best things in Boswell or Elia' (*Portrait of a Scholar*) in a significant context.

P. G. Wodehouse, joined the former in his anti-highbrow battles, and done his best to keep the academic world clear of the infection of modern literature. That he should reject the real poetry of his time while affecting to find virtue in the academic verse of Bridges also follows. It is not surprising either that he should believe that otherwise poetry has, so to speak, run its race: 'We still have our cellars, with all the old vintages from Chios to Chilswell.' Bridges's 'experiments'—academic tinkering with metrics and spelling, devoid of a personal rhythm—are the kind he can sanction, recognizing in them a respectable ancestry. In this Museum Milton is inevitably, as Leslie Stephen says he was even in Johnson's time, 'a tabooed figure' for criticism.

A bird's-eye view of the culture I have tried to describe is available in the form of an elegant little book of essays published in 1920, R. W. Chapman's *Portrait of a Scholar* (Oxford). Gordon wrote to the author when it appeared, 'I find in these essays not only something that has never been so well expressed, but the flower of a mode of life for you and me seven or eight years old.' Here we find essays on trivial subjects turned with that playfulness which so becomes a scholar ('Silver Spoons', 'Proper Names in Poetry') or serious ones treated in the style of Elia ('Thoughts on Spelling Reform' begins: 'I protest I know little of phonetics'). One is tempted to pause and Veblenize[1] the spectacle. For instance, consider the significance of book-collecting in this culture —it has no more relation to literature than stamp-collecting, but carries a far higher *cachet* in respect to the greater income and esoteric knowledge needed. It would never occur to anyone in this group to refuse to acquiesce in such a merely conventional value, to question it even would be in bad taste. Spoons and furniture are valuable only if they are old, as certain books only because they are rare; hence contemporary poetry could not by definition be any good unless made on strict classical models and in every way reminiscent of them. Modern letters can only have value if they pretend to be old—Elia and R.L.S. will pass but never Dickens, who is deplored for lacking 'style'; the best living writers of English prose, we are told, 'having regard to their manner only' (!) are Bridges, Raleigh, Belloc, E. V. Lucas and Masefield: 'Their prose is good because their models are good . . . seventeenth- and eighteenth-century models [which they] have found adequate to the most exacting demands of their twentieth-century form and invention.' For such a group with such values and preconceptions a live

[1] I am reminded that this trope may not be understood, since Veblen's works are scarcely known in England. The reference is of course to his *Theory of a Leisure Class* in particular. An excellent introduction to and critique of his work is J. A. Hobson's *Veblen* in the *Modern Sociologists* series (Chapman and Hall, 1936).

contemporary use of language such as that of a Hopkins or Eliot, the real art of a Conrad and Henry James, will fall on deaf ears, and the most genuinely witty, urbane and brilliant critic, Santayana, will make no impression.[1] Real literature is necessarily closed to them, and they are aware of it only to resent it.

To look with Veblen's eyes at this 'mode of life', as Gordon rightly called it, is at least to make one point—that its social standards and its conventional literary and cultural values are only different aspects of the same mentality. To threaten its security in any way, by casting aspersions against the genuineness of a literary idol like Landor or Milton or by suggesting that the social structure needs revision, is to get the same reaction. Gordon's letters about the General Strike (that deplorable episode in the history of the universities when under-graduates in plus fours and fellows of colleges marched off in organized gangs to break the workers' strike) are almost unbelievable (see pp. 181-3). Particularly instructive is his gloating over the defeat of Labour and his savage jibes at the ecclesiastics who tried to exert a Christian influence over the middle class (when the bishops called upon educational authorities like Gordon for support he told them to go to hell). He concludes: 'We've had the Great Strike, and in some ways it's going to be as valuable as the Great War . . . We shall feel the benefit of the public object lesson to Labour for the rest of our lifetime at least.' We notice that religion is conceived of entirely as a social institution to which it is necessary to conform (of course one has one's children christened, and goes to Church sometimes because then you get better servants). This fury at the bishops who tried to implement the theoretical implications of the Established Church in an economic crisis exactly corresponds to the emotional reaction to literary critics who refused to

---

[1] Thirty-five years ago Arnold Bennett, then at the height of his powers as a creative artist, was remarking in *The New Age* 'the characteristic inability of the typical professor [of English] to toddle alone when released from the leading-strings of tradition'. 'For their own sakes', he continued, 'professors of literature ought to bind themselves by oaths never to say anything about any author who was not safely dead twenty years before they were born. Such an ordinance would at least ensure their dignity.' It was like Bennett's shrewdness to pick out this key weakness and correlate it with the defects of their professional writings. Raleigh, he declared, had not yet voiced criticism of his contemporaries: 'But wait a few years. Wait until something genuinely new and original comes along and you will see,' for, says Bennett, look at the critical works he has already published—'They are as hollow as a drum and as unoriginal as a bride-cake; nothing but vacuity with an icing of phrases.' In 1911 he was complaining that there did not exist in English that body of criticism which the French artist has to cut his teeth on. For this purpose, he wrote, 'I have no hesitation in de-classing the whole professorial squad—Bradley, Herford, Dowden, Walter Raleigh, Elton, Saintsbury.'—Reprinted in *Books and Persons*.

play the game of letters and actually tried to replace the counters by real values. These forms of behaviour are just as much 'flowers' of that 'mode of life' as *Portrait of a Scholar*. This 'mode of life' has a vested interest in the profession of letters identical with its economic interests. A life devoted to the humanities means not following a vocation but taking up the genteelest profit-making pursuit, one which confers a high caste on its members; literary appreciation must obey the same laws as other expressions of social superiority.[1] The Discipline of Letters is seen to be simply the rules of the academic English club.[2] Only thus can we account for the curious spectacle of a professor of poetry and literature inaugurating his term of office by insulting the greatest living poet (*Ash Wednesday* had appeared four years earlier) and decrying literary criticism, by denouncing State proposals to take seriously the study of literature as an educational process, and by declaring that in his university at least literature should be studied only in its aspects of philology and scholarship, while post-graduate work should be restricted to learning to edit texts. The pusillanimity of the academic character outside the sciences is a matter of common experience, it is a product of the club spirit, no doubt; so that when a Gordon gives tongue so boldly we may be sure he knows the whole pack is ready to yelp with him.

Clearly Gordon had this value for the society to which he belonged, that while he served as a public figure going through the motions expected of a scholar and a gentleman he was also a mouthpiece for its instinctive attitudes of self-protection. What oft was thought but ne'er so well expressed, was the academic reception of his *Poetry and the Modern World*. We noticed, in summarizing this later inaugural lecture, how his position had changed from the complacent insolence of *The Discipline of Letters*. Now he would like to be on both sides at once, and though he cannot conceal his hatred of all that Eliot stood for, he makes a great show of open-mindedness, as in extending cautious (but ludicrously undiscriminating) patronage to the young Oxford poets.

[1] The difference between a vested interest and the dispassionate pursuit of truth is shown by the contrasting behaviour of the humanists and the scientists when faced by similar situations. University schools of science and mathematics did not make fools of themselves about the revolutionary physics, for example, which was accepted without any display of feeling.

[2] A useful index to the constitution of this club is afforded by the prefaces to works of literary criticism and scholarship published in the last decade and a half. Tributes of gratitude therein express no real indebtedness but are advertisements that the author (1) knows eminent persons, (2) wishes to exhibit solidarity with the right people. A third function may often be noted, that of disguising real indebtedness, where ideas, analysis, method or information have been lifted from the 'wrong' quarters to which it would be embarrassing to have to make acknowledgments.

Let us appreciate every dead poet equally (so long as we are not asked to think less highly of, say, Milton and the Romantic movement than we have always understood it to be correct to think), he says, and let us not take seriously any poet now alive (except to raise our hats to our classically sanctioned Bridges and Housman).[1] It is 'the literary groups now vocal' who exhibit 'narrowness and intolerance', he complains and ends on this rather plaintive note.

This was a cunning move, obviously more serviceable than the last-ditch foaming-at-the-mouth attitude. It kept pace with the quiet ratting that was occurring at this time on the Hopkins controversy, and inaugurated the shift of opinion about 'the modern movement' that was noticeable very soon after. For such a social group, though it does not move or alter essentially, has to modify its facial expression from time to time in order to survive. Take the affair of Hopkins, which we have outlined—by the time Mr House had published the fruits of his scholarly labours what bad taste it would have been to suggest that they were superfluous! The critics, that is, had succeeded in persuading the great world that they were right about Hopkins and the academic club wrong, and Hopkins had become a classic in face of the club's persistent blackballing. (This is the mysterious process known in the text-books as 'having stood the test of time'.) Hopkins had to be incorporated into the conventional pantheon. But if the club finds it politic to make concessions, it will only make them on its own terms. In the matter of Hopkins, Professor Abbott's introduction[2] to the letters is a transparent example of its technique of accommodation without reconstitution. Hopkins could not be radically altered, because he was dead; he could only be misrepresented. A more recent instance

---

[1] The sociologist would have to pay special attention to the place of Housman in this society. His claim to be in the Bentley tradition covered his pathological rudeness to other scholars, and as a scholar who had proved his devotion to the ideal by specializing in insignificant texts, he was permitted a degree of privilege otherwise unknown. His soundness in essentials was proved when he delivered the Rede lecture on 'The Name and Nature of Poetry'—its reception and the use made of it are of great interest. Another apparent exception to the general code of the academic order is Mr C. S. Lewis, but the eccentricity of theoretical Christian fervour is permitted to him since he took care to show from the beginning that he held entirely conservative views on the real tests of conformity —Shelley, Milton, Wodehouse, university English studies, and 'modern' critics. He published a book of essays in literary criticism significantly called *Rehabilitations* where all these subjects are treated on orthodox lines. Another necessary test of conformity is represented by Bradley on Shakespeare: though he has been blown upon, some would say blown up, it is *de rigueur* to intimate respect for him by way of showing hostility to the school of Shakespeare criticism which has dared to question Bradley's assumptions and method, to replace the comfortably known by the alarmingly unfamiliar.

[2] See *Scrutiny*, Vol. IV, No. 2.

is Lord David Cecil's *The English Poets* (Cresset Press, 1941), where Hopkins is linked with Patmore, the palm being given to the latter whereas 'Hopkins is difficult not for his thoughts but for his mode of expression'; conversely Bridges is jacked up by pairing him off with Yeats. The opposite process is used to write down Eliot, who is dismissed in the same breath as Auden and Spender; the 'new school led by T. S. Eliot' is pronounced to be a dead end, while 'the main English tradition' in modern poetry, we are told, is kept going by 'Dorothy Wellesley and W. J. Turner' (who oddly enough edit the series in which Lord David's book appears), 'the Sitwells' and Ruth Pitter. It is obvious that these are not judgments of literary criticism but gestures of social solidarity—the only kind of criticism that isn't Bad Form.

But let us consider another example of this principle at work. One of the few entertaining spectacles in this last depressing decade has been that of the academics who had shown themselves most hostile to modern literary criticism recognizing that Eliot had achieved a lasting position in spite of them; but while desiring a place on the platform alongside him they couldn't afford to show too glaring an inconsistency. We may well ask how this came about. Mr Eliot had in fact become respectable for extra-literary reasons (there is no greater proof of respectability than the clerical audiences drawn by *The Rock*), while his poetry and essays had won through to the general educated public on their own merits, assisted by the 'narrow and intolerant critics'. Thus the former literary Bolshevik (*ut* Dean Inge) became fit even to preside over the Classical Association. Mr Eliot has accordingly become incorporated into the canon of accepted Literature—which must be accepted and may not be criticized; and those critics who only recently were outlawed for daring to insist that *The Sacred Wood* and *The Waste Land* were important are now rebuked by the same pens for venturing to disagree with later critical pronouncements of his. The academics, that is, have not changed their skins at all, merely camouflaged them. They still object, as they always have objected, to the practice of real literary criticism, which necessarily menaces their self-esteem and professional reputation. The sociologist would note that for them it is unforgivable to be too far ahead of public opinion; even after public opinion has caught up with, and forced the club to endorse, the discoveries of the pioneering critic, his original offence remains and he will bear always the stigma of harbouring dangerous views. Gordon's protective device has become the modern academic's wear.[1] He does not

---

[1] Cf. *Tradition and Romanticism* by B. Ifor Evans (1940). Our reviewer (*Scrutiny*, Vol. VIII, No. 4) observed: 'The conventional taste of thirty or forty years ago had at least the merit of a consistent view of literary history... Your modern

deny that there may be something in latter-day writers, only, he says, we must be tolerant. This in practice means that you may acclaim Eliot's *Collected Poems* if you will do the same for *The Testament of Beauty;* you may be interested in Kafka and Conrad if you will grant that Wodehouse and Sayers are equally incomparable; you may take Eliot's literary criticism seriously only if you will allow Lamb's to be just as good. Well, isn't that a handsome enough offer?

No, for the literary critic and the educationist will insist that the question they must put to academic authority remains what it always was: are we or are we not to be allowed to apply real standards, to work with real values, instead of currency-counters? Apparently the answer still is that we are not. It was Henry James who declared that 'the confusion of kinds is the inelegance of letters and the stultification of values'.

Gordon's death did not, then, mark the end of the epoch in academic literary history that Raleigh inaugurated. Every university school of English appears to have its Gordons, and they predominate. Mr C. S. Lewis's programme for an English School and his defence of it[1] does not differ from Gordon's *Discipline of Letters* sixteen years earlier, either in tone or in content, nor did he seem aware of the damaging criticisms to which his assumptions and arguments are open. The book was warmly received in academic quarters, where Mr Lewis was credited with brilliant wit and a powerful intellect, and from these came assertions that a blow had been struck for the cause. A really up-to-date intellectual, combining the scholarly virtues with critical genius, had taken service under them, we were given to understand. If there had been the slightest indication of originality in Mr Lewis's outlook or of criticism of the *status quo* in his programme, what outraged bellows would have come from that herd instead! We may conclude that the academic club will go on recruiting its kind so long as it has a stranglehold on appointments in nearly every university, and will continue to put up *à-la-mode* Gordons to maintain its supremacy.[2] It

academic presents a confused and unhappy picture in comparison. While careful to show that he has outgrown the old prejudices, he nevertheless accepts no modern revaluation of the tradition, but tries desperately to make the most of all worlds.'

[1] *Rehabilitations and Other Essays*, 1939. The review in *Scrutiny*, Vol. VIII, No.1, contains the relevant information and the appropriate criticisms.

[2] The sociologist would make some deductions from the terms in which the academic and higher reviewers hailed Mr Geoffrey Tillotson's *Essays in Criticism and Research*. This appeared in 1940 with a preface elevating the claims of scholarship, followed by a number of essays designed to prove that it supersedes the critic's function. Our reviewer had occasion to point out that there are 'many insidious ways in which scholarship can become a mask for critical prejudice'.

is useless, we may deduce and must point out, for state schemes of educational reform at the university level to be broached without considering the realities of the situation. The reforms must be directed to the right quarters.

We started by presenting a question: what does the academic world gain by endowing and countenancing a Gordon and snubbing and starving a Haddon? We can now see that it gains immediately in a psychological sense, because a Gordon enables a bankrupt and decrepit tradition to feel that it can not only stand on its legs but can actually hold up its head and cut a fine figure after all; whereas a Haddon makes it uncomfortable, painfully aware of deficiencies and the possibility of having to return to the Button Mould. The existence on its doorstep of a Haddon becomes a reproach and therefore an intolerable nuisance. No wonder he had occasion to complain of the stepmotherly behaviour of his Alma Mater. But in the long run, we may predict, it will be the Gordons who are the disability. An impatient revolutionary movement in education, the new order that is more than likely to follow the peace, will be tempted to send the whole system down the drain, not only the academic club but the humanistic studies that they have discredited. It would be hard to justify a claim that a university school of English, as described by Raleigh, Gordon, Mr C. S. Lewis, is of value to the community or the individual. There is no future for an order that is incarnated in a Gordon; and it deserves the fate it has invited. But is it not possible to make some attempt to salvage English studies? The first step, clearly, is to take them out of the hands of the old-style academic who, in the name of the discipline of letters, bans any attempted interest by the young in the finest poetry and novels and the most profitable criticism of their own time while welcoming the corrupters of standards, and who forces on the student an intolerably arbitrary view of poetry and the history of our literature. And this is the more indefensible when we look into the authority on which this academic's claims to competence are based.

The claims are ultimately made in the name of the Classical tradition, that your genuine humanist is the familiar Classic, scholar and gentleman that the academic could once claim to be. When English schools were first formed, the Classically trained were the only academics available with which to supplement the philologists. But if the Classic ever was the salt of literary criticism (the evidence for it seems totally lacking), that salt has long since lost its savour. It has long been untrue to imply that the personnel of the academic English club is made up of such legendary people. The caste privileges of the Classic, scholar and gentleman are now claimed, and the prejudices propagated, by those who are rarely the first, often have no real title to the second—and as for

the third, perhaps that need not be discussed. The theory is one employed now by all sorts of intellectual incapables to disguise their
inferiority. Though this is a process of evolution not unknown to the
social historian, I believe, it none the less leaves its supporters in a'
weak position. And even if the theoretical claims are occasionally
substantiable, is there not something more to be said, and urgently in
need of saying, about the fitness of the Classic for directing English
studies? Gordon started with some natural endowment; his career
seems to suggest that his training qualified him for nothing except the
editing of Classical texts. He could bring nothing but prejudices and an
assurance of superiority to his new department, that air of saying
gracefully something profound and final which disguises saying nothing,
the style of *Times* third leaders and *Times Literary Supplement* leading
articles, which are notoriously the work of Greats products and their
Cambridge equivalents. But how much more vicious when higher
English studies are handled in the same spirit! Naturally enough, the
believers in this kind of 'discipline' do not like the criticism that shifts
something, the teaching that stimulates and matures.[1] The natural
reaction of the academic English club, so constituted, has been that
since they are incapable of doing anything themselves as directors and
producers of literary studies, nobody else shall if they can help it (they
are quite willing to help each other to help it, an activity which the
organization of the academic world, as one large club, is peculiarly
fitted to promote).

The stultifying effect on English studies of such a régime has long
been apparent. The moral is that English studies must be cut free from
the classical-scholarly tradition in every respect and at every level;
must point out firmly that the ability to edit texts and make piddling
comments on them is no more qualification by itself for an 'English'
university post than a certificate of librarianship, since it is an ability
that can be readily acquired by quite stupid people with no interest in
literature; and recruit new blood from, and enter into new connections

---

[1] Raleigh wrote to D. Nichol Smith from Oxford (1904): 'They told me in
Liverpool that it was all-important to spend weary hours on diminishing the
incapacity of dull students. I did not contradict them, but I didn't do it: I
wrote a book. No one who understands the real thing cares twopence about
the dull student, except as a man and a brother. Drink with him, pray with him;
don't read with him, except for money.' English in the universities has been a
good deal run on these lines. Whether the dull student is not generally a product
of this convenient practice, and whether his dullness may not disappear in more
favourable conditions—a stimulating environment, good guidance, a suitable
course of study and so on—is a question which hasn't as a rule been allowed to
disturb the comfortable assumption (so unmistakably acted on) that students in
general are dull. It is significant that a Haddon does not find himself surrounded
by dull students.

with, the live studies instead of dead ones. A new deal for English could be initiated at once on the basis of the experimental English college and courses that were long ago outlined in this journal. With the aid of the allied studies—other modern literatures, particularly French, and the social sciences (history, anthropology, psychology, sociology, but cultural history and sociology in particular)—new and uniquely equipped specialists would be turned out whose centre in literary criticism and training in the methods and disciplines of other specialisms would enable them to work further and further into adjacent fields of knowledge with the most fruitful results. And it would equip them to do the work which the mere scholar trained only to edit texts cannot do but which literary criticism must get done. And there is work which other specialisms—psychology, sociology, history—notoriously need done and which only the trained literary critic can safely undertake, work which is waiting to be done because no one who is not a literary critic, in our special sense, can undertake it at all. A simple example lies to hand, in Raleigh's literary remains. Raleigh had most of his life contemplated writing a book on Chaucer. He never wrote it, and we know why. 'The Chaucer has got only so far, that I have mapped out and defined a lot of things that I should like to know and don't. "What the philologists should tell us and don't", "What students of French poetry should tell us and don't";—these are hardly chapter titles' (*Letters*, 1903). Gordon, a much less intelligent man than Raleigh, characteristically comments (Preface to Raleigh's posthumous *On Writing and Writers*, 1926): 'They are the private chapter titles of more than one unwritten book on Chaucer nor can it well be otherwise while the tradition of his text remains uncertain.' Nor could it well be otherwise if the text were as certain as that of to-day's newspaper. What Raleigh wanted the philologist and the French mediaeval scholar to tell him was what only a literary critic could, who was incidentally a philologist and a specialist in early French poetry. Raleigh had come up against questions which no amount of scholarly information alone can determine, they can be 'settled' only by the methods of literary criticism. There is no good book on Chaucer's poetry because no first-class literary critic happens to have had sufficiently intense an interest in Chaucer to go to the immense trouble of acquiring the incidental specialisms and absorbing the masses of 'factual matter' that would equip him to decide *as a literary critic* the critical problems Chaucer raises. And until such a critic does, there will not be the book on Chaucer we all need, let what Bentley of mediaeval studies there ever may be edit the text, or if the authentic text were suddenly revealed from Heaven. There is a similar difficulty about Donne—everyone has had the experience of consulting the great edition—for which we are all deeply grateful to Professor Grierson—and finding that there is no light thrown in the notes, the scholarly and textual notes, on our difficulties. This in my experience is true of all edited texts from the Elizabethan dramatists right down to so apparently straightforward a specimen as Jane Austen's novels. The real difficulties of reading the text, the critical problems, seem to be outside the editor's province, or he is unaware of them because like most scholars he is not a literary critic, too often not even an intelligent reader. That Shakespeare texts cannot be finally determined by 'scientific' editing is now generally admitted. I don't mean that we should send scholarship packing—of course we can't do without it—but that we should insist that scholarship in the narrow sense is recognized for the tool it can only be and a useful tool only when in the right hands. 'I can hire mathematicians but mathematicians can't hire me,' said Edison.

What English studies need then is not more scholarship but fresh contacts, cross-fertilization—a W. H. Rivers of the complex of cultural subjects of which the study of literature forms part, and the intellectual disciplines of which it can profitably draw upon to enrich its method. Failing his appearance, we can at least reorganize English studies on such a basis. Besides being educational in a real sense, so that English studies would be freed from that sense of futility so widely complained of by university students, it would give post-graduate and 'research' students a real field of useful work. And other studies would profit. But can anyone be so optimistic as to believe that any university reform less violent than a bloody revolution would make such a programme possible?

LESLIE STEPHEN: CAMBRIDGE CRITIC

Q. D. LEAVIS (1939)

The reputation of Leslie Stephen as literary critic seems to have been at its lowest ebb when Mr Desmond MacCarthy in his lecture on *Leslie Stephen* (being the Leslie Stephen lecture for 1937) nailed down the coffin. No contrary demonstration was provoked among the audience or the Press. However, some of us may feel that the last word has not yet been said, on our side, and on the other—the corpse's— that these bones can still live. Those of us who can remember the barren state of English literary criticism before *The Sacred Wood* reached the common reader and before *The Problem of Style* and *Principles of Literary Criticism* appeared remember also their debt to Leslie Stephen:

for after Johnson, Coleridge and Arnold who was there who was any help? (Certainly not Pater or Symons or Saintsbury or...) We were grateful to Leslie Stephen not so much for what he wrote—though that was considerable—as for what he stood for, implied and pointed to. He seemed to us to be in the direct line of the best tradition of our literary criticism, to exemplify the principal virtues of a literary critic, and to exhibit a tone, a discipline and an attitude that were desirable models to form oneself on. This, to us, would have seemed the obvious starting-point for any contemporary littérateur speaking on that subject. Mr MacCarthy, however, was entirely apologetic and deprecatory. This—he said, as it were—is what Leslie Stephen was, these were his scraps of abilities (and a poor showing they make, I grant you), of course he had none of the essential qualifications for a literary critic (we know what they are) and he had all these disabilities, but still there it is and I've done my duty by him.

I think it owing to Leslie Stephen to scrutinize Mr MacCarthy's critical values and to state, in greater detail than I have done above, what Leslie Stephen stands for and what his criticism consisted of. For apart from Mr MacCarthy's unfortunate testimonial and the chatty informal *Life and Letters* by Maitland, there is nothing; except Stephen's own *Some Early Impressions*, which even in Cambridge no one seems to read. On the other hand, everyone has read *To the Lighthouse*, and the portrait-piece of Mr Ramsay by Leslie Stephen's gifted daughter elicited immediate recognition from the oldest generation. Yes, that's Leslie Stephen, the word went round; and that brilliant study in the Lytton Strachey manner of a slightly ludicrous, slightly bogus, Victorian philosopher somehow served to discredit Leslie Stephen's literary work. But it is obvious to any student of it that that work could not have been produced by Mr Ramsay. However, Stephen seems fated to be known only as the original editor of the *D.N.B.*

Mr MacCarthy starts by informing us that Leslie Stephen is 'the least aesthetic of noteworthy critics'—meaning, it appears, that Stephen was thereby at a disadvantage. His unfavourable criticism of Sterne, for instance, is due to his inability to enjoy what Mr MacCarthy called Sterne's 'elegant ambiguity' and he does not appreciate that 'Sterne's attitude towards all emotions was playful'. Actually Stephen's last word on Sterne was this: 'Sterne has been called the English Rabelais ... We know that, on clearing away the vast masses of buffoonery and ribaldry under which Rabelais was forced, or chose, to hide himself, we come to the profound thinker and powerful satirist. Sterne represents a comparatively shallow vein of thought... He is too systematic a trifler to be reckoned with any plausibility amongst the spiritual leaders of any intellectual movement.' Mr MacCarthy does not like this kind of criticism, and he consistently but not I think deliberately misrepresents it; you suspect that he finds it uncongenial because it represents a threat to his own existence as a critic. He notes with discomfort Stephen's seriousness, his refusal to compromise or to scale down his standards, and he complains that Stephen's strong sense of character affected his discussion of an author's work. That is, Mr MacCarthy deplores a moral sense in the critic. What he demands instead is easily discovered: 'Stephen was deficient in the power of transmitting the emotions he had derived himself from literature; he seldom, if ever, attempted to record a thrill.' 'As a practising critic he limited himself as far as he could to that aspect of his subject about which it was possible to argue.' Criticism, we are further told, is the adventures of the soul among masterpieces, and the soul of Cambridge, he suggests, had no qualifications for embarking on such adventures 'in a region where reason is at a disadvantage compared with intuition'.

Mr MacCarthy is placing not Leslie Stephen but himself (he might be a vulgarized echo of Arthur Symons). Delivered at Cambridge in 1937, his can only be described as an insolent performance. For if the humanistic side of Cambridge studies has any justification for existing it is in standing in the eyes of the great world—as it does—for a critical position descended from Leslie Stephen's and antagonistic to Mr MacCarthy. Some part at least of Mr MacCarthy's audience must not have been affected as he expected by his recital of Stephen's limitations or failings—that Stephen seemed to think that on the whole books ought not to be written unless they are first-rate of their kind, that mediocrity in peotry is unforgivable, that his studies 'might seem grudging, owing to the number of reservations they contain, until the reader has grasped that praise from Leslie Stephen, which he always strove to make precise, meant a very great deal'. And so on. Actually I suppose the more intelligent section of Mr MacCarthy's audience held these qualities, this outlook, that mode of expression, to be indispensable to the practice of literary criticism. 'I often think that the value of second-rate literature is not small, but simply zero,' Stephen wrote. He was not a Sunday reviewer, we perceive. And unless you are one, or a minor poet, you can hardly be devoted to literature without having reached the same conclusions as Leslie Stephen independently. Again, Mr MacCarthy cannot see the point of Stephen's painstaking examination of Defoe's minor novels (though his essay has the merit of destroying in anticipation the Woolf–Forster claim that Defoe is a literary *artist*) and his similar pieces of critical analysis; he opines that criticisms of this kind (with which 'Leslie Stephens's critical essays are crammed'), while they may 'increase our interest when we think over an author's works', yet 'of course, they do not help us to decide whether the fiction in question is good or bad'. When it comes to judgment, he says, 'the test which Leslie Stephen applied was the relation of a work to life, the extent to which it ministered, in one way or another, to all human good'. This is not the best way of explaining Stephen's critical values, but we can gather the force of Mr MacCarthy's objections. Those of us who do not choose to linger in the aesthetic vacuum of the 'nineties can afford the courage of asserting that we agree with Leslie Stephen and not Mr MacCarthy. Mr MacCarthy's critical position is revealed as the last heritage of the 'nineties (not the Cambridge 'nineties). It is a position which we might well have supposed not merely outmoded but abolished for ever, though I suppose its last recognizable sign of life was as recent as Mr Clive Bell's theory of Significant Form.

Let us recapitulate the grounds of dispute between Mr MacCarthy and Leslie Stephen. Stephen, misguided man, thought the critic should confine himself to what is discussible about a work of art instead of recording his thrill at experiencing it: the youngest hand will have the answer ready that it is the critic's business to advance the profitable discussion of literature, substitute-creation ('transmitting the emotions derived from literature') being indefensible egotism. His detailed analyses of writings, focusing on the writer's idiom and technical devices, do not help us to decide whether the work is good or bad, says Mr MacCarthy; we, on the contrary, who believe that literary criticism can be demonstrated and so argued about find Stephen's procedure—starting from the surface and working inwards to radical criticism— obviously right and convincing. We believe with Stephen that literary criticism is not a mystic rapture but a process of the intelligence. No doubt the environment of Clerk Maxwell and Henry Sidgwick was peculiarly favourable to the development of such an attitude to literature, but we recollect that Arnold and Coleridge also practised this method when they were most effectual. His feeling that the character of an author was a factor in his art to be reckoned with was, we are assured, a demerit in a critic, it interfered with his judgment of a piece of literature. We reply that Stephen had evidently a finer critical sense than Bloomsbury; if we mean by art something more profound than an 'aesthetic' theory can explain we have to agree with Henry James, that in the last event the value of a work of art depends on the quality of the writer's make-up. Art is not amoral and everything is not as valuable as everything else. Stephen did not apply a moral touchstone naïvely. In practice the question at issue is, can we or can we not diagnose Sterne's limitations and George Eliot's only partial success as artists in terms of these writers' make-up? Stephen thought he could and we think he did. The position we share with Leslie Stephen has been admirably stated by Mr L. H. Myers in the Preface to *The Root and the Flower*, where he says that 'Proust, for instance, by treating all sorts of sensibility as equal in importance, and all manifestations of character as standing on the same plane of significance, adds nothing to his achievement, but only draws attention to himself as aiming at the exaltation of a rather petty form of aestheticism. For my part, I believe that a man serves himself better by showing a respect for such moral taste as he may possess.' Unless we adopt this position, says Mr Myers, we 'are likely to be satisfied with art that is petty'. Stephen had no use for art that is petty; Mr MacCarthy wants to be allowed to rebuke him for describing Sterne as 'a systematic trifler' representing 'a shallow vein'. Of course the academic attitude to literature is much the same as Mr MacCarthy's. 'It appears that you prefer some authors to others, Mr Graves' is the classic rebuke of authority to criticism. Stephen was not academic—it is only one of his virtues but it is the fundamental one for a critic—he was not conventional, timid or respectable in his findings. 'It is tempting to try to clear away some of the stupendous rubbish-heaps of eulogy which accumulate over the great men when admiration has become obligatory on pain of literary renunciation,' he wrote. And, again, on Johnson's criticism of Milton:

His independent judgments are interesting even when erroneous. His unlucky assault upon *Lycidas* is generally dismissed with a pitying shrug of the shoulders...Of course every tyro in criticism has his answer ready...The same writer who will tell us all this, and doubtless with perfect truth, would probably have adopted Pope or Johnson's theory with equal confidence if he had lived in the last century. *Lycidas* repelled Johnson by incongruities which, from his point of view, were certainly offensive. Most modern readers, I will venture to suggest, feel the same annoyances, though they have not the courage to avow them freely...Every critic is in effect criticizing himself as well as his author; and I confess that to my mind an obviously sincere record of impressions, however onesided they may be, is infinitely refreshing, as revealing at least the honesty of the writer. The ordinary run of criticism generally implies nothing but the extreme desire of the author to show that he is open to the very last new literary fashion...If Johnson's blunder in this case implied sheer stupidity, one can only say that honest stupidity is a much better thing than clever insincerity or fluent repetition of second-hand dogmas...He had the rare courage—for, even then, Milton was one of the tabooed poets—to say what he thought as forcibly as he could say it; and he has suffered the natural punishment of plain speaking.

Mr MacCarthy evidently thinks that the Cambridge ethos, which everyone including Stephen agrees was the decisive influence in shaping his character, was very inferior intellectually to old Bloomsbury. What sort of environment was it, in fact? The best account of it is in *Some*

Early Impressions (Hogarth Press), where Stephen himself records his debt. Stephen was born in 1832. His family was what he called 'the second generation from the Clapham Sect' (it is interesting to note that Macaulay's was the first generation from it and Virginia Woolf and Vanessa Bell's the third). Stephen did not react against the Clapham inheritance. His admiration for 'the essential Puritan' was derived from his early impressions. He naturally found the Evangelical leaning of Cambridge in 1850 congenial. 'Cambridge has for the last three centuries inclined to the less romantic side of things...We could boast of no Newman, nor of men who, like Froude and Pattison, submitted for a time to the fascination of his genius and only broke from it with a wrench which permanently affected his mental equilibrium. "I have never known a Cambridge man," as a reverent disciple of the prophet said to me, "who could appreciate Newman." Our version of the remark was slightly different. We held that our common sense enabled us to appreciate him only too thoroughly by the dry light of reason and to resist the illusions of romantic sentiment.' It was one of the advantages of Cambridge, he felt, that there was no such spiritual leader as Carlyle or Newman in the place. His mind was formed first by his mathematical tutor, Isaac Todhunter, whose character impressed him as much as his attainments, by the great Whewell (who had no personal charm, and whose character, intellect and influence were markedly opposite to those of Jowett, for whom Stephen felt great distaste) and finally by the pervading influence of John Stuart Mill. 'Pure, passionless reason' was embodied in his works—which was all his disciples knew of him at the time. Stephen speaks of 'that shrewd, hard-headed, North-country type which was so conspicuous at Cambridge' and notes, 'Our favourite antipathy was the "imposter"—that is, the man given to allowing his feelings to override his common sense.' At Cambridge he found a conspicuous absence of interest in the struggle of Church parties then proceeding ('We left such matters to Oxford'), 'the religion of all sensible men' being generally the wear. This Stephen after some years as a don and tutor found dropping away from him painlessly, and he became and remained an agnostic. What Cambridge had to offer him is most clearly seen if we consider the contrasting experience of Mark Pattison, a natural Cantab as it were, who, as Stephen noted, 'fretting under the oppressive spirit of the old Oxford atmosphere' and feeling that Newman represented mere obscurantism, wore himself out in his efforts at educational reform in the university, thwarted by the insufferable Jowett. Stephen left Cambridge without loss of esteem on either side and entered journalism, the higher journalism that was then available to offer a career to talent without degradation. 'I joined the great army of literature because I was forced into the ranks,' he wrote in after life, 'but also with no little pride in my being accepted as a recruit.' The *Saturday Review* succeeded Cambridge and stamped him afresh. He notes that turning over the files many years afterwards to look for his own contributions, he was startled to discover that he could rarely distinguish them by internal evidence. It seems to have been a congenial extension of the Cambridge ethos; he speaks of the 'strong realistic common sense of the Johnson variety' that was practised. The last factor in shaping him as a critic seems to have been the *D.N.B.*, whose editorship he accepted in 1882. There he 'learnt to think that the whole art of writing consists in making one word suffice where other ordinary men use two'. It also assisted him to perfect his dry, unobtrusive irony, thanks to which the Dictionary is, as Maitland said, 'strewn with man-traps'. That impersonal but caustic wit, expressing an outlook characteristically devoid of easy enthusiasm, is most evident in the George Eliot volume he contributed to the English Men of Letters series (of the others— Hobbes, Pope, Johnson and Swift—the two last are admirable). It is a decidedly unsympathetic study, though admirers of George Eliot find to their annoyance that he has said practically all in her favour that there is to say; his critical appraisal of her weaknesses remains an uncomfortable obstacle which they cannot afford to neglect and which is not easily dealt with.

His belief in reason (as opposed to 'intuition'), deplored by Mr MacCarthy, did not lead to crass blindness. He was not ignorant of the fact that a work of art has its own internal logic; but he did not consider that this exempted the author or poet from intellectual scrutiny. He expected a poet who deployed philosophic views to have sound ones, and he realized, in spite of his great 'intuitive' admiration for Wordsworth, that Wordsworth's were not always sound. For Shelley's intellectual lights he had the greatest disrespect, and was able to make a corresponding case against Shelley's poetry—he protests to J. A. Symonds that he cannot agree with his praise of Shelley in the Men of Letters volume, there is 'a certain hollowness' about the Prometheus, an 'insubstantial mist' in much of Shelley's most admired poems. His use of 'reason' is in the Johnson tradition. Since it led him to explode Lamb's sophistical defence of Restoration Comedy and Hazlitt's of Wycherley, it was evidently a useful critical technique. His cautious examination of what a writer has to offer will seem to many of us, in spite of Mr MacCarthy, worth more than a cartload of records of thrills. Do we or do we not find the following kind of criticism more helpful than transmission of the emotions derived from literature?

There are parasitical writers who, in the old phrase, have 'formed their style' by the imitation of accepted models, and who have, therefore, possessed it only by right of appropriation. Boswell has a discussion as to the writers who may have served Johnson in this capacity. But in fact, Johnson, like all other men of strong idiosyncrasy, formed his style as he formed his legs... Johnsonese was, as far as we can judge, a genuine product. Macaulay says that it is more offensive than the mannerisms of Milton or Burke, because it is a mannerism adopted on principle and sustained by constant effort. Facts do not confirm this theory. Milton's prose style seems to be the result of a conscious effort to run English into classical moulds. Burke's mannerism does not appear in his early writings, and we can trace its development from the imitation of Bolingbroke to the last declamation against the Revolution. But Johnson seems to have written Johnsonese from his cradle.

What Swift has really done [in *Gulliver*] is to provide for the man who despises his species a number of exceedingly effective symbols for the utterance of his contempt.

His style was no doubt precipitated by the conditions of working as journalist, editor and biographer, but it is a genuine expression of personality and an effective weapon. Aspects of it were registered in the contemporary *mots*: 'No flowers by request' and 'Stephen's ink was never watery' (or purple, it might have been added). He had the right to come down on Arnold for his rhetoric about the dreaming spires and to object to his mannerisms. Stephen was the type of critic who makes no parade of personality, has no studied attitudes, whose manner consists of an absence of manner but is felt as the presence of a mature personality. He himself described his style modestly as 'short-winded and provokingly argumentative,' and says that whereas X 'can keep up a flow of eloquence' he himself cannot keep on the rhetorical level because he 'must always have some tangible remark to make'. Unlike his contemporaries we cannot consider this in any way unfortunate. His habitual tone and style are represented by this from the essay on Jowett: 'To a distinct view of the importance of some solution he seems to have joined the profound conviction that no conceivable solution would hold water. "He stood," says one of his pupils, in a rather different sense, "at the parting of many ways," and he wrote, one must add, "No thoroughfare" upon them all.' As a critic he stood for outspoken criticism all round; 'I like his [Huxley's] pugnacity—a quality I always admire. The more hard-hitting goes on in the world, the better I am pleased—meaning always hard-hitting in the spiritual sense.' His critical credo is constantly implied in the essays *Hours in a Library* (three volumes), *Studies of a Biographer* (four volumes) and the fragmentary *English Literature and Society in the Eighteenth Century*. It corresponds generally to the position that we hold to-day:

After all, though criticism cannot boast of being a science, it ought to aim at something like a scientific basis, or at least to proceed in a scientific spirit. The critic, therefore, before abandoning himself to the oratorical impulse, should endeavour to classify the phenomena with which he is dealing as calmly as if he were ticketing a fossil in a museum. The most glowing eulogy, the most bitter denunciation, have their proper place; but they belong to the art of persuasion, and form no part of scientific method... Our faith in an author must, in the first instance, be the product of instinctive sympathy, instead of deliberate reason. But when we are seeking to justify our emotions, we must endeavour to get for the time into the position of an independent spectator, applying with rigid impartiality such methods as are best calculated to free us from the influence of personal bias.

Coleridge's specific merit was not, I think, that he laid down any scientific theory. He was something almost unique in this as in his poetry, first because his criticism was the criticism of a man who combined the first simple impulse of admiration with the power of explaining why he admired; and secondly, and as a result, because he placed himself at the right point of view; because, to put it briefly, he was the first great writer who criticized poetry as poetry, and not as science.

Nothing is easier than to put the proper label on a poet—to call him 'romantic' or 'classical,' and so forth; and then if he has a predecessor of like principles, to explain him by the likeness, and if he represents a change of principles, to make the change explain itself by calling it a reaction. The method is delightfully simple, and I can use the words as easily as my neighbours. The only thing I find difficult is to look wise when I use them, or to fancy that I give an explanation because I have adopted a classification.

The phrase 'criticism of life' gave great offence, and was much ridiculed by some writers, who were apparently unable to distinguish between an epigram and a philosophical dogma. To them indeed, Arnold's whole position was naturally abhorrent. For it is not uncommon now to hear denunciations of all attempts to connect art with morality and philosophy. It is wicked, we are told, for a poet, or a novelist, or a painter, to take any moral consideration into account; and therefore to talk of poetry as destined to do for us much that philosophy and religion used to do is, or course, manifestly absurd. I will not argue the point at length... Meanwhile it is my belief that nobody is the better in any department of life or literature for being a fool or a brute: and least of all in poetry. I cannot think that a man is disqualified for poetry either by thinking more deeply than others or by having a keener perception of (I hope I may join the two words) moral beauty... When Arnold called poetry a criticism of life, he only meant to express what seems to me an undeniable truth.

Critics in an earlier day conceived their function to be judicial. They were administering a fixed code of laws applicable in all times and places... There are undoubtedly some principles of universal application; and the old critics often expounded them with admirable common-sense and force. But like general tenets of morality, they are apt to be commonplaces, whose specific application requires knowledge of concrete facts... Criticism must become thoroughly inductive... Briefly, in talking of literary changes, I shall have, first, to take note of the main intellectual characteristics of the period; and secondly, what changes took place in the audience to which men of letters addressed themselves, and how the gradual extension of the reading class affected the development of the literature addressed to them.

I hope I have made it plain not only what Leslie Stephen's strength as a literary critic was, but why I have chosen to describe him as a Cambridge critic. His is not (unfortunately) the invariable kind of criticism practised at Cambridge or by Cambridge products, but it is what the world of journalism and *belles-lettres* means when it refers with respect or malice to 'Cambridge Criticism'. His style, his tone, his mental attributes, his outlook are what are considered the most admirable, or objectionable, or at any rate, whatever your opinion of it, the most characteristic features of the Cambridge school. Cambridge has not by any means produced only Leslie Stephens; it is sufficient to name Rupert Brooke and Housman as evidence that dug-outs exist as refuges from the prevailing wind, that east wind which Elton, I think, says might have done Pater so much good if he had been placed in the other university. In contemporary Cambridge, where one section still holds literary criticism to be a charming parasite and sends its soul, with Mr MacCarthy's approval, adventuring among masterpieces, while another holds semasiology to have superseded literary criticism along with philosophy and the rest—it is high time for those who look back with respect to Leslie Stephen as the exemplar of a sound position and a profitable practice to put it on record why they honour his memory.

HENRY SIDGWICK'S CAMBRIDGE

Q. D. LEAVIS (1947)

Slight and fragmentary as are the reminiscences of Mary Paley Marshall, the University Press must be congratulated on having published them,[1] with their historically valuable photographs, as a more generally available reminder of a very remarkable woman and context than the interesting obituary notice that Lord Keynes contributed to the *Economic Journal* in 1944. As Professor Trevelyan writes in his introduction, 'her intimate personal experience of the very first beginnings of women's education in connection with Cambridge University' is 'historically the most valuable part of the book'. It is a reminder of the most revolutionary period in Cambridge's history, already so remote as to be almost mythical and apparently almost

---

[1] *What I remember*, by Mary Paley Marshall (C.U.P.).

forgotten. Mary Paley, who died three years ago at the age of ninety-four (working daily, till within two years of her death, in the Marshall Library she established in memory of her husband), was one of the first batch of women students at Cambridge, when 'female higher education' was being planted here by Henry Sidgwick and his friends. For he is the key name of this period, as can be seen equally from her memories and from those of many others. To read Mrs Woolf and other feminists one would conclude that university education for girls was actually forced into being by women in the face of the brutal resistance of hostile mankind. In point of fact the initiative was either taken by men or encouraged by them, and in Cambridge at least the experiment depended for its success entirely on the work of a great many distinguished Cambridge men who were impelled by conscience and benevolence alone to give their time and energies and lend their names to the cause (I don't mean what later became known as The Cause).

The indefensible kind of opposition to higher education for women came from the man in the street, to whom the lead was given by women like Charlotte Yonge and Queen Victoria—reinforced by another kind of woman whose motives are suggested in this anecdote of Mrs Fawcett's (I quote her reminiscences from memory): The wife of some important Cambridge figure expressed thankfulness to her that 'that place' [Newnham] was not there in her husband's younger days. 'Why' 'Because if it had been I am sure he would have married one of them instead of me.' It must have been because of such Cambridge ladies that Sidgwick, according to a (probably heightened) story told to Mrs Marshall, 'in those early days of the movement walked up and down wringing his hands and saying: "If it were not for their unfortunate appearance" '—meaning that his young ladies tended to be handsome and well dressed. A respectable opposition came from those dons who saw in Sidgwick's scheme the first steps towards turning a man's university into a co-educational one, an objection that shows to-day as highly prophetic.[1] Even Marshall the great economist, whose early

[1] The fear that Cambridge would be gradually turned into a mixed university if any concessions were made was grounded in the declared ambitions of Miss Davies and her supporters. The one thing all the promoters of women's higher education could agree upon was that they would not have a separate women's university. Royal Holloway College was actually endowed and built on a scale which should enable it to set up as a women's university but the Governors convened a conference (1897) and rejected the idea. 'No one', said James Bryce summing up for them, 'is in favour of having a separate University for Women.' At the outset of her campaign, before anything practical had been effected, Miss Davies wrote (1868) 'The College is intended to be a dependency, a living branch of Cambridge. It will aim at no higher position than, say, that of Trinity

sympathies were entirely with the movement and who worked for it and married into it, dug his heels in at a given point. 'When the great trial of strength came in 1896 over the proposal to grant women's degrees he abandoned the friends of a lifetime and took, whatever his wife might think and feel, the other side.' [1] Similarly Miss Emily Davies found that even academics hostile in theory were prepared to do all they could to help her up to a certain point. When in 1880 she wished to get the University to appoint members to help govern Girton College she wrote, 'I was agreeably surprised at finding people most friendly, and I feel encouraged as to our prospects altogether. I went to see the Vice-Chancellor (Dr Perowne), who was supposed to be unfavourable, and found him very gracious. The Master of Trinity, who I had been told was our great enemy, expressed his willingness to make the proposal for us!' Perowne was the leader of the Conservative party in Cambridge and 'fundamentally opposed to the admission of women in any form'. But he was quite willing to help women to a university education separately; in this he was representative of the opposition.

In 1868 Henry Sidgwick was writing to his sister: 'Do you know I am violently engaged in a scheme for improving female education? A Board is constituted of Oxford and Cambridge men (no end of swells, including the people who have refused Bpcs., etc.).' [2] Next year he reports that his proposals for establishing Lectures for Women that could be examined on met with 'considerable support from members of the University', and in the same year, writing to F. W. Myers 'about female prospects', he said, 'The fact is there is no real conservatism anywhere among educated men. Only *vis inertiae*.' [3] In a widely read letter he contributed to *The Spectator* at the beginning of 1896 he remarks: 'Whatever may be said in favour of a different school education for the two sexes, the present exclusion of women from the higher studies of the University is perfectly indefensible in principle and must

---

College.' 'Such a degree of humility will not be considered excessive,' was the *Times* comment. The rejection in '87 of the proposal to grant women degrees was due to 'the fears of those who, as Dr MacAlister said, felt that they were being asked to adopt a tiger cub on the grounds "that it is such a little one, and can't do any harm, and won't be in the way, and will please the children very much"' (*Emily Davies and Girton College*).

[1] Keynes, *Economic Journal*, June 1944. He continues: 'But Mary Marshall had been brought up to know, and also to respect and accept what men of "strict principles" were like.'

[2] *Henry Sidgwick: A Memoir*, by A. S. and E. M. S. (1906).

[3] When in 1868 Dr Henry Jackson thought it likely that Cambridge could be induced to hold examinations for women, even Sidgwick did not expect immediate success, but 'a memorial, taken round by Mr James Stuart (later Professor of Mathematics), was signed by 74 members of the Senate, including some of the most rigid conservatives'.

sooner or later give way.'[1] His wife and brother make it clear that there was a male genealogy: 'Sidgwick had had his thoughts turned in a general way to the subject of the education of women by the writings of John Stuart Mill and doubtless also by F. D. Maurice, whose interest in it is well known, and who was, as we have seen, at this time Professor of Moral Philosophy at Cambridge.' The outcome of all this was that his proposal that lectures should be organized at Cambridge for women and examined on was sponsored by Henry Fawcett, Professor of Political Economy, and his wife,[2] a committee was formed, Sidgwick took on the secretarial duties and drew up a scheme of lectures, and scholarships were provided for students to take advantage of the opportunity to improve themselves. In 1871 Sidgwick decided that what the movement needed was a Cambridge home, so he took a house for students on his own responsibility, financial and otherwise; he was then thirty-three and a bachelor, with no means but what he earned. He persuaded Miss Clough to take charge of his household, and enlisted such coming men as Alfred Marshall to teach with him there. Thus did Sidgwick initiate Newnham College. For, two years later, after additional houses had been taken, it was decided to build; 'Newnham Hall' was opened in '75 for thirty students, and when Miss Clough died in '92 and Mrs Sidgwick (Arthur Balfour's sister) was called on to succeed her as Principal of Newnham College he cheerfully gave up his house and went to live there for the rest of his life, he being Professor of Moral Philosophy.

One of those who took this newly founded Cambridge Higher Local Examination for women was Mary Paley. Educated like so many Victorian women by mere governesses and fathers, she nevertheless was successful enough to be offered one of the first Cambridge scholarships. Hence the piquant spectacle of the grandson of Paley's *Evidences*, an Evangelical cleric, bringing his daughter up to Cambridge in '71 to place her in the charge of the sister of the infidel poet Clough (her orthodoxy was in fact gradually undermined, by, as she writes, 'Mill's Inductive Logic and *Ecce Homo* and Herbert Spencer and the general tone of thought'). There were four other students that year.

Parallel with all this was the development of Girton College. Miss Emily Davies refused to compromise the principle of identical studies and examinations for women and men by acquiescing in the Cambridge Committee's scheme and against advice she established at Hitchin in

[1] This must have been generally felt, for only four years later 'twenty-two out of the thirty-four Professors then existing opened their courses to women. More followed later, and inter-collegiate lectures also gradually became available.'

[2] Thus making it possible for their daughter Philippa in due course to become Senior Wrangler (13% ahead of the male runner-up).

'69 a rival band of students. But as there were no other instructors available, she had to ask for help from the university. Hitchin was inconveniently placed, 'so that each teacher would have to throw away three hours spent in travelling' each time. Yet Sidgwick, with many more of the Cambridge Committee, was 'interested in this scheme too and was from the beginning and for many years on its staff of lecturers'. It says a great deal for the principles and good nature of the men that though they had reported against Hitchin as a site, and urged Cambridge instead, they gave their services ungrudgingly, and Miss Davies wrote that all the teachers she had in view on opening were 'of the first rank'.[1]

When in a few years a fund enabled building at Girton to be started, a strong objection still held: Sarah Burstall, the future famous Head of the Manchester High School, came up to Girton in '78[2] to take the Maths. Tripos and reported:

All our work was private coaching with such Cambridge men as could be induced to come out three times a week, nearly two dull miles of a long walk along the Huntingdon Road, to take on the teaching of young women, often ill-prepared and unlikely to reflect honour on their teachers. Naturally, first-rate men only came if they were friends of the College and believers in the movement. I was fortunate enough to be taught by three such men (*Retrospect and Prospect*).

More than one Senior Wrangler had taken the trouble to go out to Hitchin in the early days to 'pour an amazing illumination on elementary mathematics'.

One of the great advantages enjoyed by the original women students was that only first-rate men taught them; the inbreeding and consequently much more limited choice of teachers that the development of the women's colleges at Cambridge has brought about is obviously not ideal. Mary Paley and her few fellow students who decided to take the Moral Science Tripos (which then included economics) enjoyed almost individual tuition from such outstanding teachers and thinkers as Sidgwick and Venn and Alfred Marshall, men who were either Professors already or who later held chairs, who were moreover intellectual pioneers engaged in opening up new branches of study. Mrs Marshall says that they had 'practically the same lectures as the men' but given to them separately, so the devoted lecturers 'had to give their lectures twice over' (not to speak of a possible third time at Hitchin). The women had to take their Tripos papers separately from the men, and the papers were brought from the Senate House post-haste by voluntary

[1] *Emily Davies and Girton College*, by Barbara Stephen (1927).
[2] On a scholarship given by a Cambridge man who for many years devoted the income from his Fellowship to this purpose.

'runners', among whom were such eminent (bearded) academics as the logician Venn, Sidgwick, Marshall and Sedley Taylor. The early women students at Cambridge, in spite of their generally irregular education and lack of the advantages inherent in emancipation, seem to have had access to many of the best minds of a great age here— Cambridge stirred to educational and intellectual reform by the large group of gifted men known as the Cambridge Liberals. The other advantage the women pioneers enjoyed was that they had not been through the mill of the examination grind and the other shaping influences of our good girls' schools nor been tested by the 'sieve' of the Entrance Scholarship Examination.[1]

Mrs Marshall's reminiscences give us striking pictures, which can be compared with and supplemented by those quoted in *Emily Davies and Girton College*, of the women students before they became as a regular thing a tamer variety, 'mostly Head Girls of good girls' schools' who superseded them, as Sarah Burstall noted. (Now, in the third stage, about 30% come from the state elementary schools, up the educational ladder, i.e., through the examination sieves.) But the original students were expected to come from the Hall and the Rectory and the homes of professional men and manufacturers, according to Emily Davies. These were not docile, downtrodden or meek-spirited, though they were certainly ladies. In 1872 poor Sidgwick was already complaining: 'This term has been rather a trying one. There is such a strong impulse towards liberty among the young women attracted by the movement that they will not submit to maternal government.' In fact, they were not schoolgirls but 'women of character', even though some of them were but sixteen years old—'really very out- standing people', said Miss Dove, who entered the Hitchin 'College' in '71; 'all people of some force of character, or they would not have been there,' wrote Barbara Stephen. Samples of their conversation and deportment noted by Mrs Marshall are startling. Henry Sidgwick rebuked a young lady who cut his lecture—'You should apologize,' to which she replied: 'Is it a case for two cups of coffee and pistols?' Invited *en masse* to Marshall's rooms in college on Sunday evenings they complained that he had not provided a 'back glass' for their hair, and the poor anchorite (after enquiring what a back glass was) had to buy one. Miss Paley, at a dance at a college Lodge, invited Marshall to dance the Lancers and in spite of his protests of ignorance pushed him

[1] In reviewing Mary Agnes Hamilton's *Newnham* in *Scrutiny* (June, 1936) our reviewer, a Senior Student of Girton, said that 'it is not so easy to share Mrs Hamilton's enthusiasm for present conditions' and remarked, as a schoolmistress herself, that 'a doubt remains as to how far the sieve for the selection of the best-fitted entrants is effective'.

through the figures. Soon after she took her final examinations they became engaged—'Miss Clough pretended to be shocked' but gave them a sitting-room where they collaborated on a text-book which 'contained the germs of much that appeared later in the *Principles of Economics*'. They married and she looked after him and his writing for the rest of his life. Naturally these young women looked down on undergraduates as 'boys', as she writes, and felt that it was for the society of dons that they had come. The women's colleges from the very beginning had evidently two functions. If on the one hand they were to provide Heads for the new girls' schools and women's colleges that began to spring up everywhere, they had an equally important function in providing distinguished academics with suitable wives. The seal was set on this latter activity when Miss Agnata Ramsay, who in '87 was placed alone in the first division of the first class of the Classical Tripos, married the Master of Trinity. Though it was not till '81 that women were permitted to take the examination on exactly the same footing as men and had their names published in class lists, yet they had never suffered for want of countenance and support, and their occasional outstanding successes were received with the greatest generosity. In 1880 the first woman Wrangler appeared; 'the exact places of women candidates were not published, but it was privately known that she was equal to the eighth Wrangler. When the Mathematical Lists were read in the Senate House [to an audience of undergraduates] loud cheers for "Scott of Girton" made it impossible to hear the name of the eighth Wrangler' (*Hertha Ayrton: A Memoir* by Evelyn Sharp).

The advantage that the earlier women students enjoyed then was the difference between being coached for examinations and being educated by liberal minds of a certain stamp. When we enquire what these educators were like we find that they had in common certain characteristics, whatever subjects engaged their particular attention. They were open-minded men of very considerable personal culture who subscribed to an idea of a liberal education and to the highest standard of disinterestedness. To read the life and letters of Sidgwick is to make the acquaintance of a different world from our own. When Sidgwick died there was a rare outpouring of feeling from his many famous old pupils, who included Dr Keynes, Sorley, Arthur Balfour and Professor Maitland. The great Maitland said, 'I believe he was a supremely great teacher,' spoke of his 'rare intellectual virtue' and after describing his lectures as something altogether extraordinary ended: 'We turned to other studies or pursuits, but the memories of Sidgwick's lectures lived on...the method remained, the spirit remained, as an ideal.' One of the undistinguished pupils wrote, significantly: 'The rigid attention necessary to follow him in lecture some found almost too great a strain.' He was incapable of popularizing and lectured and taught always at the highest level. He had started as a Fellow of Trinity by teaching Classics for eight years, but becoming completely sceptical of the value of Classics in education he became interested in subjects which came under the Moral Science Tripos. The year 1868 gives a good cross-section of his character. He was at that time (aet. 29) leading the group of Trinity reformers whose 'thirteen proposals', drafted by himself, included a scheme for awarding scholarships and fellowships for Natural Science, appointment of officials to teach and direct studies in different departments, and the abolition of the religious tests of conformity to the Church of England taken by Fellows on their election, proposals which, as he wrote to his brother, 'open an almost unlimited vista of reform as soon as possible'. Most were carried but not the proposal to abolish religious tests, which would have enabled Dissenters and Roman Catholics and agnostics to hold Fellowships. Whereupon Sidgwick resigned his Assistant Tutorship and Fellowship in protest, risking cutting short altogether his university career for an abstract principle, since he remained a member of the Church. Trinity, however, unwilling to lose him as Trinity Hall had lost Leslie Stephen on almost the same issue, offered him a post as lecturer in Moral Sciences (which carried no dogmatic obligations), so he merely had a much diminished income. Winstanley in his severely legalistic history of Victorian Cambridge is moved by Sidgwick's resignation to the only spark of feeling in the volume: 'It was the purely voluntary act of a high-minded and very scrupulous man who thought no sacrifice too great on behalf of honesty,' he writes. 'It is impossible to exaggerate the moral splendour of his action.' Other Trinity Fellows followed his example and resigned, so that the whole matter came up again for consideration and next year the tests were abolished at Trinity. The following year the religious tests in the universities were abolished by Act of Parliament (1871). Sidgwick's Cambridge was therefore a place where it was possible to be a moral hero and find plenty of backers. A Sidgwick was not isolated, he represented rather the most visible point of growth. Behind him was an intellectual ancestry in which John Stuart Mill and Clerk Maxwell counted for much; he was the friend of George Eliot and her novels owe much to this world.

A similar history surrounds his educational activities. We have seen how the schemes he founded for 'female education' bore immediate fruit. But they were only one section of his plans. In 1868 also, besides working for the women's cause, he was giving a great deal of attention to what could be done for the men. Throughly disillusioned about Classics, he was trying, in common with others at Cambridge, to form a fresh centre for a liberal education. 'We have a new *University Gazette* . . . it is going to contain all the newest educational notions,' he had written. 'I hope the thing will lead to a good deal of healthy discussion.' Sidgwick's contributions were on improvement of Little-Go, reform of the Classical Tripos, the study of English, and revision of the College lecture system, 'including free competition among lecturers. He argued that under a system of free competition bad lecturing would "be driven entirely out of the field".' (Imagine the outrage of an attempt to discuss comparable issues in a University organ to-day!) This is another testimony both to the immense stir of life in the Cambridge of that age and to the liberal atmosphere. In the same year appeared a co-operative enterprise, *Essays on a Liberal Education*, to which Sidgwick contributed an essay of startling modernity called 'The Theory of a Classical Education'. Of this he wrote in a letter to Oscar Browning: 'Curiously, while you half charge me with writing beyond my serious belief, I have not written up to it. If we had only first-rate teachers and text-books of the subjects worth knowing, I should be inclined to pitch the Classics overboard. But one great advantage of literature as an instrument of education is that it supplements a teacher's defects so much. Temple is moving for English, as you probably know.'

Sidgwick was also moving for English, in association with other modern literatures. (Besides his classical training, which he had supplemented with Hebrew and Arabic, he had read and kept up with French, German and Italian literature[1] and seems to have studied history intensively. He became a specialist on moral and political philosophy and delivered papers on sociology, economics and so forth. One might compare the intellectual career of W. H. Rivers.) It was his dissatisfaction with the results of a Classical training that made him opposed to Emily Davies's fanatical insistence on women's taking the Little-Go. He arranged for special terms for his 'house of study' for women; instead of the Previous with its compulsory Latin *and* Greek they could take a local examination 'with its liberal scheme of options', which he thought not only better adapted to the intellectual condition of girls at the time but likely to give a lead to university and school reforms for the men. He declined to join Miss Davies's demand for admission of women to degrees (including the notoriously disgraceful Pass Degree) on the same terms as men because it would have meant their taking Little-Go. As he wrote to her, he was 'not opposed to identity of conditions for the two sexes'[2] but he was 'determined if

[1] He used to give lectures on English and French literature to the Newnham students.
[2] He had written earlier, 'I ask only a fair field and no favour for professional women.'

possible to prevent the University from applying to the education of girls the pressure in the direction of classics that would inevitably be given if the present Previous Examination were made compulsory for female students preparing for Triposes' (1887). Nevertheless, when Miss Davies (who resorted to unpleasant texts from the Bible to describe people like the Fawcetts and Sidgwick if they disagreed with her) met Sidgwick to discuss their differences, she was obliged to admit, '"He certainly is a very engaging man"—an expression of real feeling on her part' (*Emily Davies and Girton College*). She was not a woman to be imposed on by specious personal charm. The special nature of Sidgwick's personality has been described by many well-known men, and just as he expressed his admiration for the personality of Cambridge men like Fawcett[1] in terms of character, so his own was always felt by his pupils and colleagues to be entirely an emanation of character. Maitland, talking of his 'teaching the like of which had never come in my way before', described 'the freest and boldest thinking set forth in words which seemed to carry candour and sobriety and circumspection to their furthest limit. I believe no more truthful man than Sidgwick ever lived. I am speaking of a rare intellectual virtue...a mind that was indeed marvellously subtle but was showing us its wonderful power simply because even in a lecture-room it could be content with nothing less than the maximum of attainable and communicable truth.' Sorley, trying to describe Sidgwick's influence, wrote: 'Sidgwick exerted a powerful influence, both intellectual and moral, upon his pupils. But his temperament was too critical, his intellect too evenly balanced, to admit of his teaching a dogmatic system. What he taught was much more a method, an attitude of mind...candour, self-criticism and regard for truth.' No wonder it has been suggested that Sidgwick was the original of Daniel Deronda, at least as regards the effect Deronda was supposed to have on others. But the point to make is that Sidgwick was not a 'sport' in his time and place. He had been produced by the Cambridge of his youth just as a later Cambridge of men like Maitland was produced from his Cambridge. Leslie Stephen in *Some Early Impressions* (Hogarth Press) gives a good account of this formative ethos. He remarks upon the influence of the 'Apostles', of which the most important member in his time was Clerk Maxwell the great physicist; it was to this society that Sidgwick 'declared he owed a greater intellectual debt than to any other of the influences of his youth'.

[1] When Fawcett died in 1884 Sidgwick wrote in his journal: 'He was a hero of a peculiar type, without any outward air of self-sacrifice or suggestion of idealism in his ordinary talk,' and a year later when Munro (the editor of *Lucretius*) died: 'Two of the most strongly marked figures and characters of Cambridge have gone in Fawcett and Munro, alike in a certain rugged vigour and naturalness, if in little else.'

Stephen says this Cambridge was characterized by a belief in candour, an impatience of humbug, and a suspicion of anything in the nature of affectation in manner. Hence, no doubt, Emily Davies's comment in a letter to her bosom friend in 1886: 'I am well used to the cool Cambridge manner. It is not half so pleasant as the kind, gushing way Oxford men have, but it comes to more.' Stephen says 'Our favourite antipathy was the "impostor"', a Cambridge slang term defined by Sidgwick later as 'a second-rate man who conscientiously thinks himself a first-rate man'. A society that places a high value on character and intellectual virtue instead of on social and intellectual conformity is something that in these days at Cambridge we may look back to with both pride and nostalgia. One is glad to find in it and in Sidgwick's educational work an ancestry or tradition for the enterprise represented by *Scrutiny*. There is no adequate history of Cambridge in the nineteenth century, though abundant materials exist in memoirs, biographies, jottings like Mary Paley Marshall's, letters, and the evidence that is implicit in many a Cambridge man's published works. Winstanley's recent two heavy volumes are really no use at all for the purpose I have in mind, which is to get written not a legalistic history but a cultural one. Instead of being told in terms of statutes, it would have to be revealed in studies of the influential thinkers and great teachers of the university, many of whom still exist in living memory among grateful and often eminent old pupils. It is an act of more than piety to record for posterity the work, character and influence of the Sidgwicks and Haddons and Riverses of the past.

PROFESSOR CHADWICK AND
ENGLISH STUDIES

Q. D. LEAVIS (1947)

It is a pity Chadwick did not live to read the acknowledgment to his work by the younger generation in the last number of *Scrutiny*, and I am tempted by the inadequacy of the obituary notices I've seen to try and put on record, in more detail, just what he did do for English studies, and how his work and personality affected his pupils. Particularly as a lot of nonsense has been put about suggesting that he *harmed* Anglo-Saxon studies by his peculiar views.

I see he started his career as a double-First Classic—what a native endowment he must have had to survive that plaster-of-Paris régime! But the first thing about him one noticed was how unacademic he was, the refreshing absence of that aura of anecdotes, social values and lack of real interest which is so discouraging to the young. His kindly eyes looked at once innocent and shrewd, he retained his Yorkshire accent, and always wore a Norfolk jacket and bicycling breeches costume. When I came up he was one of the very few educational influences a student of English was likely to encounter. It was before the two all-literature English Triposes were invented, and you took one comprehensive Eng. Lit. tripos ('English A') and some other tripos; if you liked, the section of the Archaeology and Anthropology Tripos created by Chadwick, then called 'English B'.

Its conception and the way it was carried out were characteristic of the man. You can read his own account in his invaluable little book, *The Study of Anglo-Saxon* (Heffer, 1941). It's full of good things, written with the disinterestedness, good sense and intelligent insight he brought to bear on all subjects, but it's particularly the last chapter, 'The Future of Anglo-Saxon Studies', which is important for the English student. Here you can see why he so annoyed orthodox academics; starting from observation and his experience as a teacher, he explains with shocking candour that, since few students have any gift for philology, compulsory philology and history-of-language courses are 'futile'. This came with peculiar force from the man who had started his academic career as a classical philologist. He goes on to argue that philology is 'a great hindrance to Anglo-Saxon studies':

The subject appeals to a very small proportion of the students, according to my experience. They should have the opportunity of taking it, at least as a subject for post-graduate study—for which it is best suited. But it is unreasonable to force it upon every student. It is no more necessary for the study of Anglo-Saxon than it is for that of Latin or Greek or a modern foreign language. The connection with (later) English studies has led to a very great increase in the number of people who have at least some knowledge of Anglo-Saxon. English literature is now one of the most popular subjects in our Universities; and in most of them Anglo-Saxon is, or has been, a more or less compulsory element in the course. As to the value of this connection for either subject, my own experience has been that, when Anglo-Saxon is compulsory, it is disliked, and the students gain little or nothing from it. On the other hand, when it is optional, the number who take it is very small—not more than one in ten—but these usually rather like it, if philology is eliminated, and most of them gain thereby. To force it upon a larger number of students is, in my experience, a mere waste of time for both student and teacher. Most of the students regard it as a nuisance.

Worse, he goes on to argue 'in the interests of Anglo-Saxon studies' that

there are serious objections, however, to any scheme which involves an exclusive or even primary connection of Anglo-Saxon with English studies.

The latter do not afford a good training for the former; and in Universities where this connection has ceased it is found that the majority of our best students come from other subjects than English. For Anglo-Saxon studies some inclination for the acquisition of languages and a wider historical outlook are desirable; English studies are too limited in their scope. Indeed, the two subjects appeal to different kinds of mind.

It is all too true, in fact indisputable, but how unprofessional to admit, even to notice, anything of the sort, in what bad taste to announce it from the house-tops! Compulsory Anglo-Saxon, philology and history-of-language courses attached to the popular English Literature degree-studies make jobs for specialists, provide subjects that can be *taught*, lectured and examined on mechanically (no nonsense about education, but just that 'factual matter' which somehow provides 'discipline')—surely that is all the justification needed. But Chadwick was perverse enough to uphold the interests not of professionals but of Anglo-Saxon studies—of which he, after all, held the Chair. He insisted that Anglo-Saxon should be studied in his university in its proper context, in association with the early history and antiquities of the country and in comparison with early Scandinavian studies similarly organized—that is, he made it a study of early civilizations. He wanted to do for our own early culture something comparable to what the Classical Tripos does for the early history of Greece and Rome, to provide a unified study which should be truly educational. 'The number of students who will take such a course as this', he writes, 'will doubtless be small—at least until the importance of our early history is more generally recognized. At present the only way of getting a large number of students to learn Anglo-Saxon is by making it a more or less compulsory subject in a popular course—e.g., by making it impossible to obtain a degree in English without it. I have had experience of both systems, and have no hesitation in expressing my preference for the one which will secure a few keen students, who choose the course of their own free will, and will in all probability derive real benefit from it.'

Well, a lot of 'English' students did opt for Chadwick's scheme nevertheless, and, as he says, got real benefit from it. His tripos opened for us the doors into archaeology, anthropology, sociology, pre-history, early architecture—all beginnings for future self-education; and he saw to it that these subjects, studied with reference to Scandinavia and England, should also extend to the Celtic and Mediterranean areas, opening fresh vistas. The interest and profit were inexhaustible. We didn't, under him and his colleagues, go through the philological grind ('an exercise of memory and faith' as he contemptuously describes it) and we didn't 'get up' Anglo-Saxon as a meaningless adjunct to mediaeval and modern English literature. Nor did we have to study *Beowulf* under the hypocritical pretence that it is great poetry; we used it as an interesting document. Anglo-Saxon literature, studied in connection with Old Norse literature in particular and other early literatures in general, gave us an insight into the origins of literature (his own three-volume work on this subject, *The Growth of Literature*, shows the breadth of his base). And this was only part of the larger scheme, in which the early literatures of Northern Europe and Great Britain were studied, not snatched out of their context as literatures nearly always are, but as part of their inseparable background, the cultures that produced them. This meant that anyone working under Chadwick had to study the history, archaeology, literature, arts, social life and so forth of Northern Europe from the Beaker period to the Norman Conquest; in fact, Northern Europe from the end of the Stone Age to the end of the Dark Ages was conceived and treated as a continuous cultural study. Of course this was a lot even for two years, but it was assumed that the student had special aptitudes. Most students grumbled and groaned when they were launched on two new languages at once, plus a terrifying syllabus which included the entire literatures of Anglo-Saxon and Old Norse, but all retracted later, for Chadwick's method made one take the merely memory work in one's stride—it was not going to be examined on for its own sake—and he was a remarkable teacher as well as a great scholar: the true original mind that can organize knowledge. He got together a good team, too, which included Dame Bertha Philpotts, the authority on the Viking Age. Many look back on the two years they spent with him as the most valuable and formative period of their intellectual life. The effect of such a boldly conceived course of study was evident in the rapid maturing of the students. His system was the opposite of the spoon-feeding method that the modern universities adopt towards their students.

He and his tripos were wonderfully stimulating. There were drawbacks, of course. He was himself a linguistic genius, and as his students used to complain, he apparently thought that everyone is born with a knowledge of runes, Celtic languages and Old High German; but when his attention was drawn to this misunderstanding, he was always very patient and considerate. He was not a theoretical educationist but he could see what is educational and what is not. Nor was he a writer on his special studies who could give them a wide appeal, like W. P. Ker. He was simply a teacher and scholar who had hatched an educational idea and felt its value enough to be stubborn about preserving it. Obviously a strain of the publicist in his composition would have helped to promote his ends, and would have made him able to place his discovery and his methods before the educational world in a more persuasive light. He was too single-minded to be able or willing to grapple with academic politics. He complains: 'An unfortunate feature of University life to-day is that the time and energy which should go to teaching and research has to be spent in committee rooms.' But it is the academic with no vocation for teaching—with nothing to teach—who enjoys the power that can be exercised in committee rooms.

To sum up his achievement: He provided a course of study in itself highly educational. He showed how literary and linguistic studies could be made most profitable, by successfully correlating them with their social background—a very different matter from the scrappy 'Life and Thought' courses which are the inadequate gestures the English Tripos makes in a half-hearted effort to provide a similar organization for mediaeval and modern literature. (Just as his system of comparative study of early literature differs from the oddments of Italian and French set books that the English Faculty Board piously hopes, one supposes, will do the trick for English literature.) After taking Chadwick's 'English B', those who proceeded to 'English A' realized what an opportunity was lost in the handling—or rather, lack of handling—of Mediaeval Literature and 'Life and Thought', even though the English School enjoyed the services of Dr Coulton. Moreover, Chadwick certainly showed how literary studies could be linked up with that school of sociological studies which Cambridge so notoriously lacks. In addition, he of course very considerably furthered Anglo-Saxon studies by getting texts edited and books written, by his pupils and friends as well as himself, and by getting them considered in the larger and more fruitful light he brought to bear on them.

But the professor of Anglo-Saxon who had given evidence before a Board of Education committee that 'it cannot be too clearly recognized that compulsory philology is the natural and mortal enemy of humanistic studies' and that the literary interest of Anglo-Saxon is 'not so great as to repay students of modern literature for the time they will have to spend in acquiring a sufficient mastery of the language to appreciate it'[1]... had to pay the penalty for his disinterestedness. He had insisted on taking his subject seriously and his position as an educationist responsibly, instead of accepting both conventionally, and he was always aware of official opposition. It was true he already had, and so was secure in, the Chair. But an obscure movement, of which we shall never know the exact history, seemed to him to threaten his life-work all along, and it has taken on fresh vigour since his retirement in 1940. In his book on *The Study of Anglo-Saxon* he refers to 'authorities

[1] *The Teaching of English in England* (H.M. Stationery Office, 1921).

responsible for English' who 'wish to acquire control over Anglo-Saxon studies' and that such a scheme as his 'meets with much opposition. The teaching staff may be unanimous in its favour, and the students may be well satisfied and keen, but opposition or interference may come from persons or committees who have no knowledge of Anglo-Saxon studies, but who may think that their own interests may be affected in some way by such a scheme.' Presumably some not very creditable episode of academic history led Chadwick twenty years ago to remove his studies and himself from the English Faculty to the school of Archaeology and Anthropology, which in the person of Dr A. C. Haddon received him with open arms. That great man and he were two of a kind. Haddon must have been a fertilizing influence for him as well as a congenial presence and an ally. One knew what the academic 'English' attitude to Chadwick's scheme was, from the tone in which it was mentioned: resentment. The desire to undo Chadwick's work is one sign of that hatred of life which academic history illustrates in so many ways. For Chadwick was a rare instance of what is supposed to be typical academic disinterestedness but what the academic milieu is instinctively hostile to. No doubt, under the plea of 'getting Anglo-Saxon back into the English Tripos', his work on the other side, as to which he was equally firm, that of freeing 'English' students here from compulsory linguistic and philological cram, will be undone, and, in his own words, 'the herding of masses of students along familiar lines, some of which are barren and useless enough' will be resumed some day—in whose interest? Not the students', assuredly, as Chadwick has shown, at any rate.

T. S. ELIOT

EDGELL RICKWORD (1933)

Selected Essays, by T. S. Eliot (Faber and Faber)

This substantial and comely volume contains the greater part of Mr Eliot's influential criticism. There is about half of *The Sacred Wood*, the three essays from the crucial *Homage to Dryden* pamphlet and the Dante study entire. The additions on the literary side include essays on Middleton, Heywood, Tourneur and Ford; two excellent studies of Senecan influence on Elizabethan drama, a rather discouraged dialogue on Dramatic Poetry and an essay on Baudelaire.

The novelty in the essays on the dramatists and on Baudelaire is the appearance of Mr Eliot as an appreciator of moral essences. In this encroachment on the domain of such verbose critics as Mr Murry and Mr Fausset, he is not, of course, trying to put across an individual conception of morality; tradition governs this as much as it does taste. Mr Eliot's tradition of morality is the most respectable of all, and when he says that 'the essence of the tragedy of *Macbeth* is the habituation to crime', one could do nothing but assent if it were not that the italics show that he is not referring to the man but to the play. Again, he tells us, 'In poetry, in dramatic technique, *The Changeling* is inferior to the best plays of Webster. But in the moral essence of tragedy, it is safe to say that in this play Middleton is surpassed by one Elizabethan alone, and that is Shakespeare.' But even if that is a safe thing to say, the way of saying it is not free from danger. For after subtracting the poetry and the dramatic technique what is there left by which the moral essence may be apprehended? Again, in the essay on Baudelaire he writes: 'In his verse, he is now less a model to be imitated or a source to be drained than a reminder of the duty, the consecrated task, of sincerity.' But is our sensation of the poet's sincerity anything more than one of the reactions attendant on the poem's successful communication? Is anything really clarified by talking of a technical as if it were a moral achievement? It seems a pity that an essay that at the outset affirms the importance of Baudelaire's prose works should not have given some consideration to *L'Art romantique* and *Curiosités esthétiques*, which illuminate Baudelaire's poetic much more than the diaries do. The 'revelations' in the *Journaux intimes*, written later

than the majority of the poems, are perhaps rather specious intellectual-
izations, the violent efforts of a man to whom convictions of that sort
were a novelty, to create a 'strong personality' for himself; their
forthrightness is deceptive, I think. But Mr Eliot 'hazards' an illuminating conjecture when he suggests 'that the care for perfection of form,
among some of the romantic poets of the 19th century, was an effort
to support, or to conceal from view, an inner disorder'. And he goes
on to say: 'Now the true claim of Baudelaire as an artist is not that he
found a superficial form, but that he was searching for a form of life.'
I quote this, firstly because it is a good saying in itself, and also because
the form of expression is comparatively new in Mr Eliot's work. As
it stands it is paradoxical. Not quite so paradoxical as Mr G. K. Chesterton methodically is, but surprisingly near it. It marks a cleavage
between Mr Eliot's earlier and later criticism. It oversteps the conscious
limitations of his earlier method. It must be every ambitious critic's
aim to resolve the dichotomy between life and art; and every superficial
critic does it constantly with negligent ease. Whether Mr Eliot has the
philosophical stamina, as he certainly has the poetic sensitiveness, for
such a task, remains to be seen.

The latter part of this volume is mainly occupied by essays on
attitudes rather than works and here Mr Eliot is heavily engaged with
the Martin Marprelates of to-day and yesterday, some of them within
the Church, like Viscount Brentford, and some outside it. The outsiders,
are, in general, those who believe that art, culture, reason, science, the
inner light or what not, may constitute efficient substitutes for organized
religion. Arnold, Pater, Aldous Huxley, Bertrand Russell, Middleton
Murry and some American humanists who loom more sinisterly in
Mr Eliot's consciousness than seems necessary over here, provide a
variety of scapegoats. His diagnosis of the disease that must ensure the
ultimate instability of all such eclectic systems, built up from 'the
best that has been thought and done in the world', is devastatingly
acute. The antidote is provided in *Thoughts after Lambeth*.

This volume leaves us, then, except for tentative branchings-out,
as far as literature is concerned much where we were after the publication of *Dante*. One should not, perhaps, grumble at that; but the
impression given by this heterogeneous mass is not so profound as
that given by the slim volumes that found their way into the world
more quietly.

The essays on general subjects dilute that impression, for Mr Eliot
is not outstanding as a 'thinker' as he is as a literary critic. His thinking
is adequate to his own emotional needs, as a good poet's always is, but
it has not much extra-personal validity. One may contrast the peroration
of *Thoughts after Lambeth*:

The World is trying the experiment of attempting to form a civilized but non-Christian mentality. The experiment will fail; but we must be very patient in awaiting its collapse; meanwhile redeeming the time; so that the Faith may be preserved alive through the dark ages before us; to renew and rebuild civilisation, and save the World from suicide,

with Berdiaeff's lucid and virile exposition of a similar conviction in his *Un Nouveau Moyen Age*.

I must try and say briefly why Mr Eliot's earlier work seems to me more valuable than his later, or it may seem that I under-rate it just because its conclusions are unsympathetic to me. The intelligence displayed in the later essays might be matched by several of his contemporaries; the literary sensibility of the earlier essays is not matched by any of them. 'Literary sensibility' is a horrible phrase and it does not sound a very impressive faculty, but when one considers how very few people there are actually capable of responding to poetry or word-order generally without prompting from its prestige, or message, or because the objects named evoke a pleasant response, perhaps the possession of this gift may be appreciated at its proper value. It is only the beginning, of course, but its absence vitiates the other critical faculties. Sometimes, when it is present, there is an absence of the co-ordinating faculty and thus the response is deprived of any significance beyond that of a pleasurable sensation. It was the presence of these faculties in unison which differentiated Mr Eliot's earlier criticism from the 'appreciative' convention in vogue at the time. The method at which he aimed, and which he practised with such delicate skill, is perhaps best described by a quotation he used from Remy de Gourmont —*ériger en lois ses impressions personnelles*. If Mr Eliot has for the time being gone outside literature, the loss is very much to literature; no doubt there is a compensation somewhere. But literature, in spite of wireless and cinema, is still the life-blood of the time; we are not sots or sadists by accident and one should not be too fatalistic about the approaching dark ages. If literary criticism is not one of the means Mr Eliot envisages of redeeming the time, nothing can obscure the value of his example. As our writings are, so are our feelings, and the finer the discrimination as to the value of those writings, the better chance there is of not being ashamed of being a human being.

MR ELIOT AT HARVARD

D. W. HARDING (1933)

The Use of Poetry and the Use of Criticism, by T. S. Eliot (Faber and
Faber)

It is clear, and Mr Eliot insists that it shall be clear, that this book is
dominated by its origin as a course of lectures of a not very technical
kind. Inevitably therefore the writing is loose in texture. What is more
regrettable is that the general plan of the course only partially succeeds
in knitting together its parts, and some sections, as for instance that on
Keats, seem to be little more than lecture-making. The material has
been organized partly around a few general themes and partly
chronologically, but the two orders fail to reinforce each other. The
chronological treatment of the criticism of poetry, from Sir Philip
Sidney to Dr I. A. Richards, doesn't effectively illuminate the main
themes: namely, those of the reader's concern with a poet's ethical and
social convictions, of the impossibility of describing poetry as communication, of belief during the reading of poetry, of the attempt to
regard poetry as a substitute for religion. And the concern with
historical material prevents Mr Eliot from carrying very far any direct
attacks upon these problems. Needless to say, what he contributes is
admirable and often suggests a more complete view, but it is seldom
that his probing is deep enough or his formulations accurate enough to
be completely satisfactory.

The most accurate statement of his views is to be found in the brief
remarks on communication. 'We have to communicate—if it is communication, for the word may beg the question—an experience which
is not an experience in the ordinary sense, for it may only exist, formed
out of many personal experiences ordered in some way which may be
very different from the way of valuation of practical life, in the
expression of it. *If* poetry is a form of "communication", yet that
which is to be communicated is the poem itself, and only incidentally
the experience and the thought which have gone into it.' This sparse
and accurate statement of observable fact contrasts strangely with the
following, which the audience presumably preferred: 'What I call
the "auditory imagination" is the feeling for syllable and rhythm,
penetrating far below the conscious levels of thought and feeling,
invigorating every word; sinking to the most primitive and forgotten,
returning to the origin and bringing something back, seeking the
beginning and the end.' In such a passage as this, looseness of texture
becomes almost laxity.

On the most important topic of the book, that of the significance of the poet's motives and beliefs, Mr Eliot's formulated views are less acceptable than those on communication, although his contribution of obvious good sense to a confused problem is exceptionally welcome from such a writer. Combating the view of Dr I. A. Richards he asserts the inevitable importance for the reader of the poet's personal convictions. He supports this less by generalized arguments than by appealing to his own experience in the enjoyment of poetry, by far the most impressive method he could have adopted. But his statement of his own position is not altogether satisfactory. 'When the doctrine, theory, belief, or "view of life" presented in a poem is one which the reader can accept as coherent, mature, and founded on the facts of experience, it interposes no obstacle to the reader's enjoyment, whether it be one that he accept or deny, approve or deprecate.' Although the general meaning of this—as one would grasp it in listening to the lecture—seems sound enough, its exact verbal form, if insisted on, leaves several difficulties unsolved. It must be observed first, of course, that the way is still open for Mr Eliot to maintain that an even fuller enjoyment of the poem is available to those who do share the poet's beliefs, as he asserts at one point in the Dante essay. But if so, belief is an obstacle, or its absence a deprivation of a means, to the *full* enjoyment of the poem; and hence to say merely that a doctrine 'interposes no obstacle to the reader's enjoyment' is to evade, at least verbally, the whole question, which hinges on the *degree* of enjoyment possible. The phrase 'facts of experience' raises a further doubt. If it stands for 'the more obvious facts of experience' the general sense of the passage remains clear. But if it means '*all* the facts of the reader's experience' then it is difficult to see how the reader could fail to *believe* a coherent and mature doctrine founded upon 'the facts of experience'. The difficulty becomes more apparent in the following sentence: 'I can only regret that Shelley did not live to put his poetic gifts, which were certainly of the first order, at the service of more tenable beliefs—which need not have been, for my purposes, beliefs more acceptable to me.' One asks at first how it is that a belief can be more tenable, supposing it possible to have degrees of tenability in belief, without thereby becoming to that extent more acceptable to Mr Eliot. But one then sees that a muddled belief which included some fact of experience regarded by Mr Eliot as essential might be in a sense more 'acceptable' to him than another belief which ignored that fact and yet through its greater coherence was more 'tenable'. This depends, however, on there being a distinction between the 'tenable' and the 'acceptable' belief. At this point I give up, hesitating whether to bequeath the problem to Mr Empson or to an orthodox psychologist.

What from his wider context Mr Eliot seems to suggest is that some views which we regard as heresies, nevertheless bring together enough of the facts of our experience for us to sympathize with them, and to realize that, given certain differences of experience, we could have accepted them as true doctrine. Other heresies are altogether too far removed from anything that might have appealed to us and we are therefore only repelled. This to the simple-minded would seem the natural consequence of the natural view that your like or dislike for a poem or a poet's work is affected by every aspect of his performance and all you know about him. The inevitable conclusion is that in enjoying and in judging poetry one must try to preserve a difficult balance: 'On the one hand the critic may busy himself so much with the implications of a poem, or of one poet's work—implications moral, social, religious or other—that the poetry becomes hardly more than a text for a discourse... Or if you stick too closely to the "poetry" and adopt no attitude towards what the poet has to say, you will tend to evacuate it of all significance.'

In some ways the most valuable parts of the book and those that make it fascinating to read are its glimpses of Mr Eliot's personal opinions on a great variety of topics—Marxist criticism, English literature in a school curriculum, the potential value of the theatre to the poet. Even more interesting are the fragments of personal history that he scatters through the lectures and the comments he makes from time to time upon his intentions and methods in his own poetry. Among the incidental literary evaluations which occur, the most important is the reproof of Herbert Read for having occupied himself too much with 'casting out devils' from the tradition of English literature. As an alternative to the view of daemonic possession in English literature from Milton to Wordsworth Mr Eliot suggests the valuable analogy of the dissociated personality. And he is concerned to recover to the complete tradition those valuable aspects of writing which one line of poets relied upon too exclusively. This concern accounts for Mr Eliot's anxiety to see justice done to the unfashionable poets, from Milton to A. E. Housman. At times, however, the same desire seems to join forces with a readiness to say what can be said—sometimes equivocally —for the merely academically acceptable.

The latter part of the book consists largely in attacks upon the view that poetry can be a substitute for religion. At this point the strength, perhaps, of Mr Eliot's convictions, combined with the effect of a popular audience, seems to make his onslaught a little unfair. His prolonged poking of fun at Dr Richards's sincerity ritual would have been unnecessary with more mature hearers—a quotation or two would have been enough. And his merciless insistence on the literal meaning of Matthew Arnold's 'criticism of life' is in striking contrast with his generous concern to make Dryden intelligible. As for the more positive final contributions, all, coming from him, are valuable and interesting, but, as Mr Eliot would readily agree, a full and definite account of the use of poetry and the use of criticism is still far to seek, if, indeed, it is conceivable.

CRUMBS FROM THE BANQUET

R. O. C. WINKLER (1941)

Points of View, by T. S. Eliot, edited by John Hayward (Sesame Books, Faber)

This selection from Mr Eliot's prose writings is made under four heads—'literary criticism,' 'dramatic criticism,' 'individual authors' and 'religion and society'. Mr John Hayward's efforts at book-making have in the past been attended with considerably more success than is customary in such cases; his achievement in this case is less unequivocal. A circular accompanying the review suggests that the selection might be suitable for use in schools; the shortcomings that I have in mind can best be focused by saying that that is exactly what it isn't. One can sympathize with Mr Hayward's difficulties; he was being asked to fill a non-existent gap. To select passages of 'prose' representative of an author's style and thought is all very well when the author is a C. E. Montague or a Lytton Strachey, whose whole work might have been written with an eye to being selected from; but the essence of Mr Eliot's best critical practice, one might have thought, was its application to the specific situation, its unwillingness to leave a generalization in the air without tying it down to some particular piece of verse or some particular poet. But when you are reconnoitring an author's work for salient points, it is inevitably the generalization that takes the eye and the *ad hoc* criticism that is pruned off. And so we find a series of little gobbets of a page or two or three apiece, headed (titles by Mr Hayward) 'Poetic Imagery', 'Metrical Innovation', 'Dissociation of Sensibility', and the schoolboy or girl who reads this book will find, not the careful scrutiny of language that brought to light a whole age and revealed new possibilities to our own age, but a series of slogans ('tough reasonableness beneath the slight lyric grace') divorced from the situations which they elucidated so brilliantly, like a series of formulae with no experimental data—very few science masters would subscribe to that kind of teaching.

A note at the beginning mentions, though, 'the author's approval'; and one might ask whether there is nothing in Mr Eliot's development to justify Mr Hayward's surgery. No attempt is made to present Mr Eliot's ideas as developing; a quotation about tradition from *After Strange Gods* immediately precedes *Tradition and the Individual Talent*. But this last appears, happily, almost in full; and the other selections are sufficiently diverse to give some bird's-eye view of the shift of Mr Eliot's ideas.

The essay *Tradition and the Individual Talent* is among those demonstrating Mr Eliot's method at its best. '"Interpretation"', he says in *The Function of Criticism*, 'is only legitimate when it is not interpretation at all, but merely putting the reader in possession of facts which he would otherwise have missed.' This is the genuine disinterestedness of science, as opposed to the pseudo-science of the literary-criticism-branch-of-psychology type; and it is this quality that pervades the early essays—*Andrew Marvell*, *The Metaphysical Poets*, and the one I am considering. It controls the ordering of the prose, and is the chief source of its vigour. The sense in reading that every word in every sentence is significant, and that any omission would leave a hole in the structure, derives from Mr Eliot's desire to circumscribe exactly the situation he is dealing with; to use words as a scientist might use symbols, putting the reader in possession of facts which he, Eliot, is in possession of, by reproducing them with as complete accuracy as the language available is capable of. The central ideas, of 'impersonality', and of the 'historic sense', are of the same kind as scientific hypotheses; not critic-as-artist creations, but principles of investigation, armed with which the reader can penetrate without confusion fields of verse hitherto regarded as treacherous and obscure. Mr Eliot reclaimed seventeenth-century verse from obscurity in the same sense in which an engineer reclaims a swamp, or in which Galileo reclaimed the stellar universe from the astrologers.

The author of *Tradition and the Individual Talent* was an empiricist. The apparent large-scale logical cohesion of the essay dissolves away on close inspection. Although the argument has the appearance of being the work of a distinguished theoretician examining the specific case, it turns out to be the great experimentalist turning over his results to the student. Yet the sense that more than *ad hoc* guidance is possible, that there are general principles somewhere anterior, haunts the essay, and haunts its author. He feels he cannot let the matter rest there, and goes in search of underlying assumptions. The direction in which they lie is clear enough; the province of ethics is one from whose bourne very few literary critics return safely. And with the passage of years we see Mr Eliot withdrawing from the hand-to-hand fight with fact, the absorbing attention to the word on the page, and struggling to make his peace with morality.

The shift of attention is marked by a change of subject. The seventeenth century disappears from the field in favour of the nineteenth and twentieth, where, less hampered by exact knowledge, the moralist finds a freer hand. Mr Eliot himself draws attention to the change when it is well under way. 'The lectures', he says in the Preface to *After Strange Gods*, 'are not designed to set forth, even in the most summary form, my opinions of the work of contemporary writers: they are concerned with certain ideas in illustration of which I have drawn upon the work of the few modern writers whose work I know. I am not primarily concerned either with their absolute importance or their importance relative to each other . . . I ascended the platform of these lectures in the role of moralist.' And the avowed object of *After Strange Gods* was to produce a Revised Version of *Tradition and the Individual Talent*. He says, significantly, 'The problem, naturally, does not seem to me so simple as it seemed then, nor could I treat it now as a purely literary one.' And we see something of the extent of the departure from the former practice when we read, 'The chief clue to the understanding of most contemporary Anglo-Saxon literature is to be found in the decay of Protestantism.' The recipe now for comprehension— it is implicit in the whole concept of 'orthodoxy'—is to ask no questions but throw your witches in and see if they drown, and run no risk of endangering your principles: a reversal of the earlier practice. It is no longer possible to say of Mr Eliot what Mr Eliot said of Blake: 'Because he was not distracted, or frightened, or occupied in anything but exact statements, he understood.' Mr Eliot is distracted by the ethical generalizations he wishes to consolidate, and his object is no longer to understand, but to convert. His language now loses its analytic nicety, and masses itself to persuade, cajole, bludgeon, as he attacks the unseen Satanic opponent. 'But as the majority is capable neither of strong emotion nor of strong resistance, it always inclines to admire passion for its own sake, unless instructed to the contrary; and if somewhat deficient in vitality, people imagine passion to be the surest evidence of vitality' (*After Strange Gods*). Failure to agree to the proclaimed principle can only produce an *impasse*: 'I confess that I do not know what to make of a generation that ignores these considerations.' When he returns to the seventeenth century now, the subject he chooses is Pascal's '*Pensées*', and his criteria of relevance have changed remarkably. 'It is no concern of this essay', he says, 'whether the Five Propositions condemned at Rome were really maintained by Jansenius in his book *Augustinus*, or whether we should deplore or approve the consequent decay . . . of Port-Royal.' With this we can readily concur;

but it is unlikely that we should have in mind the reason which immediately follows. 'It is impossible to discuss the matter without becoming involved as a controversialist either for or against Rome.' Even if one accepts this as true, it is hardly the kind of circumstance which one would expect to concern a disinterested critic.

From this time on Mr Eliot's Penelope is in sight. *In Religion and Literature* he makes clear that the time for equivocation has passed. 'In ages like our own...it is...necessary for Christian readers to scrutinize their reading, especially of works of the imagination, with explicit ethical and theological standards.' And the nature of the majority of problems is settled in advance: education, for example (*Modern Education and the Classics*): 'Education is a subject which cannot be discussed in a void: our questions raise other questions, social, economic, financial, political. And the bearings are on more ultimate problems even than these: to know what we want in education we must know what we want in general, we must derive our theory of education from our philosophy of life. The problem turns out to be a religious problem.' One somehow suspected that it would. As Mr Eliot stands with top hat on the table and sleeves rolled at the elbow, it would be surprising if the rabbit failed to emerge. It is not surprising, then, to find that *The Idea of a Christian Society* is almost exclusively preoccupied with generalization, and when the particular judgment occurs its context is prescribed: 'It would perhaps be more natural, as well as in better conformity with the Will of God, if there were more celibates and if those who were married had larger families.' The wheel has come full circle. Mr Eliot has re-emerged from the thickets of ethical controversy and can apply himself to the specific case with complete assurance. To realize the most abstract of ideas through the agency of the immediate occasion has been and is one of the most powerful motive forces in Mr Eliot's verse; but to bring *Marina* or *East Coker* to mind here isn't to convince oneself that Mr Eliot's critical practice has been improved by being brought into conformity with his poetic practice.

The worst, then, that one can fairly say of Mr Hayward's selection is that he has accepted a *fait accompli*. If generalization is to become Mr Eliot's critical métier, then this is merely a fitting garland in his honour; but to those who ten years ago thought him the most distinguished critic that English literature had seen for over a century, it will seem a poor funeral wreath.

'THE FAMILY REUNION'

JOHN PETER (1949)

We do not know very much of the future
Except that from generation to generation
The same things happen again and again.
Murder in the Cathedral

Different compositions require different efforts to read them compre-
hendingly, and it is a peculiar and consistent effort that *The Family
Reunion* demands. This effort is, I should say, towards vigilance—a
vigilance against misunderstanding—and it arises partly from the fact
that the play is deeply personal, partly from the elaboration and intricacy
of the theme. Much denser here than in *Murder in the Cathedral* are the
echoes from Eliot's poems. There is, as so frequently, the obsessive
consciousness of the seasons (very apposite in a play that deals with
similar cyclical phenomena), and there are the very nearly direct
references to poems like *The Hollow Men*, *The Waste Land* and,
particularly, *Burnt Norton*.[1] This in itself argues a degree of self-
implication not found in the earlier play, and the argument is endorsed
when we consider that even as early as *The Waste Land* (1922) Eliot
was already touching on the theme of hereditary misfortune or guilt.
The fact of personal preoccupation having been tentatively established,
however, it is necessary, for the time being, to discard it from the
conscious appraisal of the play: inductive biography or psycho-analysis,
especially of a living writer, is never criticism. I mention it here only to
make a point to which we shall later revert.

As Eliot himself several times remarks in the text, the theme of the
play is 'unsayable', only to be stated obliquely, and it is this fact which
determines the technique he uses. This, the technique, can only be
called algebraic. It is the unfocusing of what one may presume to be a
concrete, personal experience until only its abstract pattern, its 'algebra',
is perceived, and the superimposition of this pattern upon a different
and fictitious aggregate of facts. It is with these fictitious facts that we
are concerned. They have so often been misrepresented that a short
preliminary summary will not be out of place.

Briefly, we may say that *The Family Reunion* is the story of two
generations, and of the interaction of the older upon the younger. We
are given to understand that the marriage between Amy, Dowager
Lady Monchensey, and the deceased Lord Monchensey was not a

---

[1] Characteristically derogatory remarks on fortune-telling and astrology (as in
The Dry Salvages) also figure.

happy one: 'There was no ecstasy.' Also we are given imprecise but substantial suggestions that at some time during the marriage—'a summer day of unusual heat'—there occurred an adultery between the husband and his wife's sister, Agatha. At some time after this Lord Monchensey planned to murder his wife, but was deterred from doing so by Agatha, her reason being that Amy was pregnant. As she later confesses to Harry, Agatha felt then that only vicariously, through Amy's children, would she ever enjoy motherhood. The child is in due course born, and this is Harry, the main figure in the play. There are two more sons and then the father, Lord Monchensey, dies. Harry is from an early age destined by his mother to marry an eligible and conformist cousin, Mary, but this arrangement does not come off. Instead he marries a stranger whom only Agatha is permitted to meet. Seven years after the marriage this younger Lady Monchensey disappears during a voyage across the Atlantic with her husband, and her death is presumed to be accidental. About a year after the voyage Harry returns to his home, Wishwood, for the family reunion that is arranged for his mother's birthday, and, almost upon entering the house, declares that his wife did not fall overboard, but that he pushed her. It is from this point onwards that the main action of the play develops. The problem is to analyse, dramatically, the motive which has prompted this 'murder, and to show how the analysis relieves Harry of some of the burden of guilt under which he is suffering, restoring him from the 'awful privacy of the insane mind' to a place 'somewhere on the other side of despair'.

One preliminary, however, we need to be quite sure about before proceeding with the development, and that is this question of the 'murder'. I have put the term in inverted commas partly because it is never quite confirmed, and partly because it is more of a symbol than a fact. As Agatha later remarks,

> What we have written is not a story of detection,
> Of crime and punishment, but of sin and expiation.

The act is not, that is to say, a physical reality, a push; rather is it to be equated with a whole complex of attitudes, the whole context of that (possibly imaginary) moment of 'murder' on the boat. If it means anything, it is nearer to the concept of unhappiness in marriage than to the concept of killing. I will later endeavour to show what difficulties arise in relation to this treatment of the term. For the moment it is perhaps enough to realize that the act is consistently soft-pedalled. With this in mind we can proceed with the play.

The analysis of Harry's state of mind is naturally complex—a succession of hints, or indirect elucidations, that does not so much conclude in certitude as slowly arrive at a preponderance of it. Two of the characters are principally concerned in helping Harry to explain himself to himself: Mary and Agatha. It might be said in this connection that while Mary diagnoses Agatha cures. It is Mary who, in the second scene of Part I, points out to Harry that his suffering is not an objective thing, but something self-imposed: the subconscious mind's punishment for what it regards as a transgression. This is not, of course, enough by itself to effect a catharsis, and Harry's remorse remains to torture him. In terms of the dramatic symbolism, that is, the Eumenides appear. Later, in the balanced second scene of Part II, Agatha tells Harry of the earlier family history and of the relations between his father and mother. In the light of these revelations Harry perceives that the unhappiness of his marriage, the disposition towards 'murder', is in some sense hereditary and not simply the result of individual, exceptional weakness in himself. His burden of guilt at once begins a metamorphosis. From the negatives of regret, self-mistrust and suffering his attitude shifts round to the positives of repentance and the will to expiate his sin.[1] It is, I think, one of the play's great merits that it so successfully demonstrates how difficult and how far-reaching such a change of attitude may be. Thereafter Harry is free to go on his way— Amy's attempt ('to become a missionary') should warn us that this cannot be paraphrased—

> To the worship in the desert, the thirst and deprivation,
> A stony sanctuary and a primitive altar,
> The heat of the sun and the icy vigil,
> A care over lives of humble people,
> The lesson of ignorance, of incurable diseases.

'Such things are possible,' he adds. And

> It is love and terror
> of what waits and wants me, and will not let me fall.

* * *

[1] Compare C. M. Bowra's comment on Oedipus: 'He is not to be condemned for resisting his destiny, but to be admired for accepting it in all its horror and for being ready to work with the god to see that he makes his full amends. He who has been the victim and the sufferer regains the initiative and takes his destiny into his own hands' (*Sophoclean Tragedy*, p. 185). See also Gilbert Murray's *Aeschylus* (Oxford, 1940), pp. 202 et seq. Harry, we might say, 'follows' the Furies because he realizes that only in the contemplation of his dead wife's suffering, her state-of-being-wronged, can he see his own sinfulness, and thus reach true humility, and so God. I need hardly add that this play is quite as implicitly 'religious' as is *Murder in the Cathedral* overtly.

Such, in outline, is the narrative of the play. It will be appreciated that this is only a basis from which to begin a critical appraisal of the whole. Poetic Drama is in some ways, perhaps, like Programme Music, since in each of these art-forms something relatively abstract and absolute is made to do a menial task. In each case, I would suggest, it is still the generalized references and effects—the poetry, the music—that matter most; and so here. What is important in reading or watching *The Family Reunion* is, in part at least, the sense of the play as an emotional or poetic experience: the sense of being disturbed, confused, lifted as if upon spear-points, and cast down again into the resolution. In part, also, one has to appreciate the texture of thought in the play, the detail with which the original bare idea has been cumulatively invested. It is not the factual *données* of the plot, but the significances and subtleties through which these are made to evolve that matter most. And here one can point out that in this play Eliot has once again succeeded in condensing a theme of the very widest significance into a wieldy and comprehensible unit. I say 'once again' because the technique, operating largely by means of references, invites a comparison, *mutatis mutandis*, with the analogous condensing found in *The Waste Land*, in the minor poems, and in the *Quartets*. There, too, we find a subject-matter which, while it retains a maximum of implication, is nevertheless reduced to a quintessence.

There are, chiefly, two sorts of reference in *The Family Reunion*: those which make connection with psychological theory, and those which make connection with Greek myths and the Greek tragedies in which the myths were used. Eliot has already experimented with both types (I need only instance the 'Mother mother'[1] term in *Difficulties Of A Statesman* and the Aristophanic-cum-Aeschylean touches about *Sweeney Agonistes*) and in this play he sought to integrate them more fully than hitherto. What was the basis for integration will, I think, be obvious if we remember the use of such a designation as 'Oedipus complex' in psycho-analysis. One of the principal preoccupations of the *Oresteia* (Eliot's most specific 'source') is with the idea of the transmissibility of sin. It is the banquet of Thyestes that leaves a curse upon the house of Agamemnon, and it is under the operation of this curse that Agamemnon commits the impious crime of sacrificing his daughter, Iphigenia. This, in turn, generates a curse—or perhaps rather extends the original—and the consequence is that Clytemnestra kills her husband. This, too, is an impure act, and the cycle proceeds. Granted such a belief in the inexorability of fate, it is only by the positing of an intercessionary God that the chain can ever be broken;

[1] A quotation from *Coriolanus*, V, iii; but Eliot is, in the poem, quite clearly using it in his own way and for his own purposes.

and looked at in this light the Athena-Apollo deity in the *Eumenides* can be to some extent likened to the Saviour of the New Testament, who taught that God was not only Jehovah—Vengeance and Punishment—but Love and Forgiveness also. This shadowy identity is indeed something which may help us to understand the present play.

Now this idea of the transmissibility of sin, of the visitation of the sins of the fathers upon the children, is very much the case as it is thought still to obtain in the field of mental conflict. 'The child grown up', says the psychologist, 'is the parent in the next generation, and so neurosis is handed on and on.' To put the matter at its simplest level one might perhaps take the example of children whose parents have been divorced. It is common knowledge that, should this occur during the formative years of the children, they generally find it difficult to make a happy marriage for themselves, and indeed have difficulty with most inter-sexual relationships. But one does not want to simplify the point too much.

It is, then, this parallel, in its religious as well as its intellectual implications, that forms the axis upon which *The Family Reunion* is orientated; and the dramatist is, I think, at pains to keep his co-ordinates plain. Continually in the diction there appear phrases that are simply paraphrases of psychological technical terms. Thus we have 'the loop in time' for the paralysis to which neurosis (sometimes literally) gives rise; and, for therapeutic catharsis, a passage like this:

> The chain breaks,
> The wheel stops, and the noise of machinery,
> And the desert is cleared, under the judicial sun
> Of the final eye, and the awful evacuation
> Cleanses.

Even the chauffeur Downing's vague opinion that Harry 'Suffered from what they call a kind of repression' must be taken to be an intentional reference to the Psychology co-ordinate. On the other hand we have not only the Eumenides but several locutions to remind us of Greek tragedy. Harry's despairing cry about 'the cancer that eats away the self' is surely the λειχῆνας ἐξέσθοντας ἀρχαίαν φύσιν of the *Choephoroe*? And, if this is not enough, we have the line,

> Can't you see them? *You* don't see them, but I see them,

and the specific reference to 'Argos' to preserve the association with Aeschylus.

Eliot, then, has established a fundamental relation between two religious orientations, two cultures, and he has shown a single abiding constant in both. Not only is the process engrossing and valuable *per se*: it has the added merit that it reinforces his choice of the Greek type of drama as a *milieu* through which to attempt the reinstatement of verse drama in English. Method and content, as it were, coalesce. I do not, naturally, wish to imply by this that the corroboration was, after the choice of a theme, anything less than inevitable; but it is not every poet who is able to attain to this degree of unity and consistency. Plots are not ready-made, even when they are derivative, and opportunities for this sort of congruence cannot arise without a very considerable prior effort in planning and construction. It is often by the quality of sheer intelligence that Eliot surprises most.

*   *   *

But it is time to return more specifically to the text, and to make some attempt to isolate and evaluate its particular merits and demerits. Though agreement as to what is good and bad in the play is not, I suppose, likely to be general, no one will presumably wish to deny that it offers grounds both for admiration and for something less. I wish first, very briefly, to consider what seem to me its merits; and then, in conclusion and by way of qualification, to make what I take to be the main criticism that must be lodged against it.

The first positive quality to notice, since it is the simplest, is probably the overall neatness of the construction. As in *Murder in the Cathedral*, there are none but the baldest stage directions—doubtless a reaction from the garrulity of Barrie and Shaw—and this matches the general economy in the writing. 'Insets' to give depth and perspective to what is going on are often of the briefest,[1] and a convention allowing the characters to fall into 'trances' in which they speak their secret thoughts also works admirably in the interests of concentration. At the same time certain recurrent phrases help to give symmetry and stability to the play, holding it together against the centrifugal thrust of the expanding theme. Amy's reference to clocks that may 'stop in the dark', for example, is repeated both at the opening and the end of the play. The reunion is 'a very particular occasion', until at last, with Amy's death, it does indeed become so. Harry's decision ('I must follow the bright angels') is taken up in the refrain of the last chant by Mary and Agatha: 'Follow, follow.' And so on. Wishwood is repeatedly called 'a cold place', except for the occasion when Agatha (and Harry, in a different place) remembers 'A summer day of unusual heat for this cold country'. The previous insistence helps, of course, to give the

[1] One may instance the Doctor's mention of his first patient, the cancer-sufferer, and the admirable passage in which Downing recalls the night of the drowning.

reminiscences the intensity they need. Throughout Part II Harry is given a series of questions about his father; and these, while being, as we might say, an admirable dramatic device for presenting the subjective process of introspection, also help to build up expectation for Agatha's disclosures, which crown his inquiries at the climax of this part of the play. Most palpable of all, perhaps, is the protracted *George and Margaret* device with the younger brothers, Arthur and John. Continually expected, they never arrive; yet the mere reiteration of their names, with the business occasioned by it, helps sensibly to hold the dialogue and the incidents of the plot together.[1]

These—neatness and integration—may seem somewhat formal qualities. Even if we find them so, however, there are others which may be more easily accepted. Consider, for instance, the element of verisimilitude in the play, that is, the touches of authenticity which Eliot has given to the details of his plot. We may find an example of this in Harry's description of the respite he enjoyed after the murder—

> I lay two days in contented drowsiness;
> Then I recovered

—though the precision here is, I think, a little weakened by its being repeated in a later speech by Downing:

> *Charles:* You've looked after his Lordship for over ten years...
> *Downing:* Eleven years, Sir, next Lady Day.

One is also impressed by the circumstantiality with which the background of Harry's childhood is made to unfold. The hollow tree, a symbol of freedom and autonomy, the sense of everything being 'referred back to mother', John falling off the pony ('and always on his head'), 'the low conversation of triumphant aunts'—these memories of an unhappy childhood come naturally and convincingly forward. They are all, moreover, apposite, and help to give correct definition to the picture of Harry's present suffering.

Equally fine, in that it shows a dramatist keenly sensitive to the need for at any rate an apparent credibility, is the touch which makes the

---

[1] There are, of course more substantial reasons for these references to the younger brothers. They are the two sons who have surrendered to their mother's will, thereby earning for themselves the reputation of 'reliability' among the family. To make them miss the reunion which Harry, the runaway, attends, is to comment upon that reliability and so, in an extended fashion, upon the success of their mother's methods. Moreover, there is a parallel between the three sons of each generation, and in this sense John and Arthur are clearly to be identified with, respectively, their uncles Gerald and Charles. Whatever is said about the nephews is accordingly applicable, in part, to the uncles; and thus the device becomes another instrument of economy.

paragraph about Arthur's accident 'not very conspicuous'. Had it been more prominent we might have wondered why Charles had not noticed it before. Again, and more significantly, there is special sensitiveness, both to theme and characters, manifest in that passage in which the 'murder' is so mildly introduced:

> It was only reversing the senseless direction
> For a momentary rest on the burning wheel
> That cloudless night in the mid-Atlantic
> When I pushed her over.

Harry is allowed to speak casually of the act because the suggestion must be that it is not itself intrinsically important; while, conversely, Violet and the others (the representatives of incomprehension) are made to fasten upon the act alone, not on its causes or consequences. It is the same sensitiveness in the playwright that assigns to Harry just the right tone of coolness and unastonishment when he hears that his father once planned to murder his mother.

> In what way did he wish to murder her?

One can, so to speak, hear the next question—'By drowning?'—without its being intruded into the text.

As a study in the implications of personal and family relationships the play is, indeed, necessarily concerned with character, and this close and analytical observation of the chief protagonists is everywhere apparent. Amy is another case. We are made to see how she has substituted a tie with Wishwood for the lost tie with her husband, and how, through Wishwood, she struggles to retain the love of her sons:

> I keep Wishwood alive
> To keep the family alive, to keep them together,
> To keep me alive, and I live to keep them.

Yet this, too, like the proposed marriage with Mary, never comes off. 'Nothing has been changed,' she says, 'I have seen to that.' And Harry, for whom this arrest has been imposed—perhaps because he is himself a neurotic—at once recognizes it as a symptom of neurosis: 'the loop in time,' that is, the wish to linger in the past instead of living forward, into the future. Speaking to Mary he deprecates his mother's attitude:

> It's very unnatural,
> This arresting of the normal change of things:
> But it's very like her. What I might have expected.

Amy is, in sum, the parasite-mother, preying for her life upon the lives of her children, especially Harry. This is why she collapses when she

realizes that Harry's decisions have passed beyond her control. Wishwood, the family, the whole complex, clock-like organization has
'stopped in the dark'.[1]

I have said that the main characters are carefully observed. It would
be true, on the whole, also to say that his observation is sympathetic—
or at least neutral. The characters of the Chorus (Ivy, Violet, Charles,
Gerald), on the other hand, are prosecuted with a consistent irony that
sometimes comes dangerously close to malice. Charles, deploring the
younger generation's proclivities for smoking and drinking, is made
simultaneously to help himself to sherry and a cigarette. It is true that
Gerald is more subtly ridiculed when he replies:

> You're being very hard on the younger generation.
> I don't come across them very much now, myself;
> But I must say I've met some very decent specimens
> And some first-class shots—better than you were,
> Charles, as I remember.

One might say that this comes near to being what Middleton Murry,
speaking of Jane Austen, has called 'a perfect right and left'.[2] But
subtlety is the exception here. Violet is given the merciless line, 'I do
not seem to be very popular tonight'; and Ivy, with her diagnosis as to
the death of Harry's wife ('She may have done it in a fit of temper'), is
also brought down to a level of caricature.

*　　*　　*

On a careful reading I think it does indeed become apparent that the
treatment of the Chorus offers the first intimation of a possible defect
in the play. Cognate with it, a sort of obverse of the same limitation, is
the note of priggishness often to be found in the speeches of Harry and
Agatha. It is irritating time and again to encounter in these the same
stilted tone of omniscience, the same assumption of superiority over the
other characters:

> Thus with most careful devotion
> Thus with precise attention

[1] Only in relation to Amy's death can the play be called a tragedy, and to make
that the pivot of the play is manifestly absurd. One might perhaps contrast
Ibsen's *Ghosts*, where the tragedy is that of Mrs Alving, not of her son.
[2] *The Problem of Style*, p. 63. The trick is, of course, part of the usual stock-in-
trade of a satirist. A cruder example (*Silas Marner*, Part I, chapter xi) may make
it clearer: 'She actually said "mate" for "meat", "appen" for "perhaps", and "oss"
for "horse", which to young ladies living in good Lytherly society, who habitually said "orse", even in domestic privacy, and only said "appen" on the right
occasions, was necessarily shocking.'

> To detail, interfering preparation
> Of that which is already prepared
> Men tighten the knot of confusion
> Into perfect misunderstanding.   (*Agatha*)

> ...I think it is probably going to be useless,
> Or if anything, make matters rather more difficult.
> But talk about it, if you like.   (*Harry*)

> It seems a necessary move
> In an unnecessary action
> Not for the good that it will do
> But that nothing may be undone
> On the margin of the impossible.   (*Agatha*)

There are, of course, inevitabilities here. One of the play's preoccupations is with a concept of 'consciousness'—awareness, more or less, of the complexity, perilousness, even the horror of life—and Harry and Agatha have to be shown more fully 'conscious' than the lesser characters. At the same time it is unfortunate that the playwright has given them a near-oracular intonation to make this point clear. One does not want Othello, so to speak, to insinuate his own nobility and courage. Even if the device is to be thought of as a convention it still contrasts jarringly with the conversational accents of the Chorus. Frequently, too, it grows monotonous. I have heard a rustle of relief and agreement run through an audience at Violet's

> This is just what I expected. But if Agatha
> Is going to moralise about it, I shall scream.

I doubt whether it assists the sympathetic understanding of Harry or Agatha to raise this kind of prejudice against their speech.

There are, then, let us say, uncertainties in the expression which limit its effectiveness. Side by side with the sensitive understanding with which, say, Mary is presented we have these touches of pompousness in Harry and Agatha; and side by side with the excellent dramatic irony that enriches the scene between Harry and Winchell—the adroit play with the ambiguous term, 'her Ladyship'—we have the rather clumsy ironies with which the characters of the Chorus are attacked. An even greater uncertainty (not, I think, unconnected with these former) is to be found if we consider the intensity of Harry's reaction to his 'crime':

> It's not being alone
> That is the horror—to be alone with the horror.
> What matters is the filthiness. I can clean my skin,
> Purify my life, void my mind,
> But always the filthiness, that lies a little deeper...

I was like that in a way, so long as I could think
Even of my own life as an isolated ruin,
A casual bit of waste in an orderly universe.
But it begins to seem just part of some huge disaster,
Some monstrous mistake and aberration
Of all men, of the world, which I cannot put in order.

In and out, in an endless drift
Of shrieking forms in a circular desert
Weaving with contagion of putrescent embraces
On dissolving bone.

The accent is quite unmistakable, an accent of naked revulsion. One may query, however, how much it is supported by the play as a whole. For such an accent of despair to be properly subjugated to the facts of the plot there would have, I think, to be something patently unpleasant about the act of murder itself. Otherwise the effect of the play is to attribute Harry's consciousness of 'filthiness' merely to his general hereditary neurosis: which is no more than to say that it is Harry's distress that causes his distress—to make him a lunatic, obsessed. Eliot has written of the attitudes of Pascal and Swift in a paragraph which furnishes a useful commentary here:

> ...A similar despair [to Pascal's], when it is arrived at by a diseased character or an impure soul, may issue in the most disastrous consequences though with the most superb manifestations; and thus we get *Gulliver's Travels*; but in Pascal we find no such distortion; his despair is in itself more terrible than Swift's, because our heart tells us that it corresponds exactly to the facts and cannot be dismissed as mental disease; but it was also a despair which was a necessary prelude to, and element in, the joy of faith.

This, surely, applied to *The Family Reunion*, helps to bring out a very important point. If, that is to say, Harry's 'despair' is disproportionate, then he is (like Swift) subject to 'mental disease'; and, this being so, his acceptance of religious responsibility must be very much closer to regression than to development, a mere evasion of the pitted struggle in his own consciousness. To make Harry a lunatic, in fact, is to destroy the significance of the play. Some fact in the plot, some *point d'appui*, must be found to support his attitude of horror and disgust, and that fact, when found must provide an *adequate* support. The correspondence of emotion to fact must be preserved.

But the only sufficient support for the despair is, surely, the murder. To attribute Harry's despair to his neurosis is, as I have said, seriously to risk branding him as an irresponsible psychopath; and, in more concrete terms, it is also to locate a prime mover in the play—guilt—outside the compass of 'the facts' as they are presented by the plot.

Had the murder been an act in its nature particularly brutal there would obviously have been a very full and valid 'cause' for the fervour of Harry's emotion. But, as we have seen, while being less than compelling in itself (if anything, a push), the act is consistently glossed over—*has* to be glossed over in order to bring out the real significance of the theme. We are left with the picture of a character who, while speaking of 'filthiness' and 'putrescent embraces', can explain these feelings no more satisfactorily than by referring them to

> The accident of a dreaming moment,
> Of a dreaming age, when I was someone else...

How, one may ask, is this sharp disparity to be explained, and how far does it indicate a defect in the conception of the play?

Inevitably, I would suggest, we are thrown back, for the explanation upon an earlier observation that I made: namely, that the play is, roughly, a transference of emotion from a personal experience to a fictitious setting. From time to time this transference is, through Harry, almost admitted:

> I am not speaking
> Of my own experience, but trying to give you
> Comparisons in a more familiar medium.

Two experiences are present in the play, and even the phantom presence of the personal experience (it is perhaps not fanciful to equate this with the personal experience represented by *The Waste Land*) is enough to blur the story of Harry, its fictitious equivalent.

Explanation is, however, only half the problem. It yet remains to find some standard by which to gauge the seriousness of this insecurity —to see how far it constitutes a failure in the play. And here we can conveniently go back to the essay on *Hamlet* in *The Sacred Wood*. There, it will be remembered, Eliot makes the point that *Hamlet* must be adjudged an artistic failure because there is in it an emotional tone which is not properly supported by the facts of the plot. It is perhaps advisable to quote his own words:

The only way of expressing emotion in the form of art is by finding an "objective correlative"; in other words, a set of objects, a situation, a chain of events which shall be the formula of that *particular* emotion; such that when the external facts, which must terminate in sensory experience, are given, the emotion is immediately invoked. If you examine any of Shakespeare's more successful tragedies, you will find this exact equivalence[1]

---

[1] I may add that examination will also reveal a statement on the matter by Shakespeare himself:
> ...Our size of sorrow
> Proportion'd to our cause, must be as great
> As that which makes it.   (*Antony and Cleopatra* IV, xv, 5–7)

...The artistic "inevitability" lies in this complete adequacy of the external to the emotion: and this is precisely what is deficient in *Hamlet*. Hamlet (the man) is dominated by an emotion which is inexpressible, because it is in *excess* of the facts as they appear.

Here we come, seemingly, to the very heart of the matter. If the objective correlative is 'precisely what is deficient in *Hamlet*', it is, equally precisely, what is deficient in *The Family Reunion*. Two forces are pulling in opposite directions. The requirement of the total theme, on one side, demands that the 'murder' should be as nebulous as possible; and, on the other, the ferment of the personal experience required the murder to be a very real and substantial 'objective correlative'. It cannot, however, be both; and in effect Harry becomes (what Eliot would have us believe Hamlet becomes) no more than a mouthpiece for obsession, disturbing and impairing the play in which he figures. If, in fact, *Hamlet* is to be accounted 'most certainly an artistic failure', then *The Family Reunion* must, I am afraid, be set as low. It is, after all, in that most central of his essays, *Tradition and the Individual Talent*, that Eliot has written the truest criticism of this play: I mean that well-known passage where he says that 'the more perfect the artist, the more completely separate in him will be the man who suffers and the mind which creates'. All the small defects of the play—the rancour towards the Chorus, the occasional hysteria or smugness in Harry's speeches, the general secretiveness—seem to group themselves into one radical deficiency: the lack of what Eliot has taught us to call 'impersonality'. Beyond a doubt there is a failure here, a failure on the part of the poet, a failure that the prescient critic has already diagnosed. One cannot but feel, regretfully, that it is the critic who is right.

SIN AND SODA

JOHN PETER (1950)

The Cocktail Party, A Comedy, by T. S. Eliot (Faber and Faber)

Though the play seems very much closer to *Sejanus* than to *Every Man In His Humour* one cannot feel that it was strange of Jonson to call *Volpone* a comedy. Some such description was usual on the title-pages of his times and of the two chief he chose the least misleading. But when Mr Eliot calls his new play a comedy he seems to me to be closer to the position of a Shakespeare calling *Macbeth* a comedy on the strength of the Porter Scene. Only the incidentals in the play are, in fact, comic and, though on the stage they should be much more effective, on paper they barely deserve the adjective. I suppose that the more perspicacious readers will think of Dante and accept the description in the very limited sense in which it seems intended; the rest are likely, however, to yield to the general chorus of the dramatic critics, to accept the play as 'witty' and 'delightful', and to get little further into it than the title might seem to tempt them to get. If they find it unsatisfactory it will be on the grounds that parts of it are dull and not because—what is surely the real criterion for judgment—it is unsuccessful on the terms that it prescribes for itself.

A good deal of the play, and particularly that part of it that relates to Celia Coplestone, is a development of the ideas handled in *The Family Reunion*, and the reader will be well advised to discard any presuppositions which the use of the term 'Comedy' may raise and to treat the play with the same sobriety that he would bring to its predecessor. Like *The Family Reunion* it is an attempt to discuss religious topics in theatrical terms and, again like that play, it essays this discussion by using situations from modern life. Both plays, that is, attempt something much more difficult than is attempted in *Murder in the Cathedral*, where the remote historical setting allows even the sceptical among the audience to concur in the argument without, as it were, feeling themselves too personally or immediately implicated in it. The difficulty in both the later plays is to effect the necessary emotional synthesis between the world of ideas, of belief, in which the topics discussed may be said to exist, and the mundane world of taxis and boiled eggs which is the *milieu* of the characters. This is not to suggest that there is an inveterate hostility between these two worlds, but rather to indicate how comparatively easily a dramatist seeking to fuse them may be betrayed into, on the one hand, bathos and, on the other, seemingly gratuitous lurches towards sublimity. I think that it is significant that the single (fairly long) quotation in *The Cocktail Party* should be a neo-Platonic passage from *Prometheus Unbound*:

> For know there are two worlds of life and death:
> One that which thou beholdest; but the other
> Is underneath the grave...

That we should be given such lines seems to indicate that the playwright is aware of the dichotomy in his material and apprised of the difficulties inherent in his task. We begin, then, by looking at the play to see whether it has improved upon its predecessor in the handling of these difficulties.

Two improvements can be at once perceived. In the first place, because Sir Henry Harcourt-Reilly is made a professional consultant his analytical probings, comments and advice are given a more than individual authority, and seem far less queerly oracular than do the rather similar speeches of Agatha in the earlier play. This is so, I think, even when he ceases to speak as a doctor and reveals himself as a 'Guardian', intent upon the health of the soul rather than that of the body. His authority tends to pass over with him from the one role to the other, and if we are responding naturally we shall tend not to question it. In the second place the development of Celia Coplestone (we might call her Harry Monchensey in the guise of a young woman) is really only half the play, the other half being concerned with the marital difficulties between Edward and Lavinia Chamberlayne. If not the most important part of the play this other half is at least the most prominent and this has the effect, not only of making the martyr seem more exceptional, more of a departure from the average (as she surely should seem), but also of giving a more balanced picture of religious experience than that given in *The Family Reunion*. The Chamberlaynes are shown as following a religious development of their own which, while quite different from it, is yet supplementary to that of Celia. As Reilly says:

> Neither way is better.
> Both ways are necessary. It is also necessary
> To make a choice between them.

The impression is thus quite different from that given by *The Family Reunion*. There we are left with the sense that virtue is somehow the prerogative of a limited class of 'sufferers', an esoteric quality to which more normal persons cannot hope to attain; here, on the other hand, martyrdom is only one of several varieties of religious experience, and that one of the less common. To an audience composed (let us hope) of non-'sufferers' the latter view is much more likely to recommend itself.

Another difference between the two plays is that there are evidently intended to be no fundamentally bad or trivial characters in *The Cocktail Party*. This may seem so slight a point as hardly to be worth noticing but in fact I think it is crucial. In life, I suppose, we are only aware of virtue negatively, and through knowing the virtuous party for some time. Sobriety is consistent but unaggressive abstaining from drunkenness, charity from malice or unkindness, humility from arrogance or condescension, and so on. As soon as these qualities become too positive or overt, as soon as we have a man who ostentatiously refuses a drink or sententiously refuses to criticize his neighbour, we have, not virtue, but hypocrisy or priggishness. It is by their works that we know the virtuous and not by their professions, and it usually takes time before our knowledge ripens into any sort of assurance. Now where a dramatist means to present a virtuous character he has obviously to work in firmer and more immediate stuff than this and it is understandable that he usually employs his own sort of negative approach by playing the character off against a number of others who are palpably less virtuous. At times, indeed, as in some of the Elizabethan and Jacobean plays, he is content to work almost entirely in negative terms —that is, through a cast of villains—and to allow his moral positives to present themselves merely as implications or inferences. Dramatically speaking, either of these approaches has obvious advantages over the direct approach, where the good characters have to be positively established *as* good, because they do not involve the characters in description or suggestion of one another's goodness, and so give rise to something more convincing than a dull assortment of eulogies. 'Damn braces, bless relaxes,' said Blake: the relevance of this to drama should be self-evident.

In this play Eliot is trying to present virtue directly, without the traditional advantage of a contrast with its opposite, and it seems to me that he is often perilously close to relaxation of the kind I take Blake to have meant. At the end of the play Edward is clearly on the way to regeneration, his relations with Lavinia clearly more unselfish, yet how is this presented? Partly, to be sure, it is a matter of contrast with their previous relationship. But the dramatist does not leave it there. He goes on to give Edward a string of compliments and 'thoughtful' remarks that are as monotonous as they are unconvincing—'I hope you've not been worrying'; 'It's you who should be tired'; 'I like the dress you're wearing'; 'You have a very practical mind'; 'You lie down now, Lavinia.' Even if this is meant to suggest that Lavinia is pregnant it is surely an unhappy way of drawing attention to domestic harmony. Happiness in marriage would inhere in far less definite particulars—a glance, a touch, a tone of voice. Edward is, in fact, in a position analogous to the ostentatious professor of virtue: he has himself to *show* how virtuous he is, and we accordingly at once suspect that he is only mimicking the real thing. This is not charity but solicitude. Yet how else, granted the chosen approach, could the point be made? Celia is another focus for this sort of weakness, though she is at least removed off-stage when her decision is complete. It is true that Alex's laconic narration of her martydom is effective, true also that the reactions of the other characters are at first simple and convincing enough. But very soon they begin to magnify her image into portentousness so that it cracks and allows her validity as a symbol to drain away:

> I've only been interested in myself:
> And that isn't good enough for Celia.

> Do try to come to see us.
> You know, I think it would do us all good—
> You and me and Edward. . .to talk about Celia.

> I cannot help the feeling
> That, in some way, my responsibility
> Is greater than that of a band of half-crazed savages.

It seems to me that the unprejudiced reader will find this insistence almost as tiresome as the muscular Christianity of the foreman in *The Rock*, and will react away from rather than towards the values sought to be embodied in the martyr. His recollections of her pleasantly sensitive normality at the opening of the play will hinder him from seeing her in these large and cloudy terms, and he may even feel that she would have merited more sympathetic attention had she remained the woman she at first sight appears. Skilful acting could doubtless conceal some of these weaknesses but the play is not to be called successful because that is so.

It is not only to Celia, however, that this sort of jar, between an initial and a later character, is confined. Julia and Alex, who with Reilly make up the group of 'Guardians', have an even more striking metamorphosis from their initial selves. This is so palpable that it must be intentional, a sort of deliberate convention, and we are no doubt intended to take Edward's remark about 'the guardian' as a clue showing how to accept the convention:

> The self that wills—he is a feeble creature;
> He has to come to terms in the end
> With the obstinate, the tougher self; who does not speak,
> Who never talks, who cannot argue;
> And who in some men may be the *guardian*...

In the light of this the Julia and Alex of Acts Two and Three are presumably the inner selves of their analogues in Act One, and not real people at all. Yet the contrast between the selves in each case is almost wantonly exaggerated, and most readers or members of an audience must surely find it impossible to accept. Alex is at first vain ('I'm rather a famous cook') and suspicious ('Ah, so the aunt Really exists') and it would appear that he is also not above drinking half a bottle of Edward's champagne. As for Julia, she is vapid ('Lady Klootz'), avaricious ('Are there any prospects?'), featherbrained (see p. 18) and inquisitive, and vain enough to take umbrage when Reilly sings his song. To transform this figure into a 'Guardian' of such potency that she can condescend ('You must accept your limitations') even to her fellow Guardian, the perspicacious Reilly, seems to me preposterous. Are we to infer that no matter how stupidly vicious people may be on the surface they can be spotless within? The human Julia's flippant mention of St Anthony is scarcely sufficient to bridge the yawning void between herself and her *alter ego*, and in fact it is difficult to see how, given two such different quantities, it could be bridged.

Obviously, it will be retorted, Eliot has not tried to bridge it: why impugn him for not doing what it was no part of his intention to do? This is easily said but I do not think that in this instance it is a valid defence. The fact is, as I have pointed out, that there is already some-thing of a tension between the two worlds handled in the play, and to make the contrast between the Julia of the real world and the Julia of the spiritual world so gross is only to increase that tension to a point at which the play begins to tear apart. Where the play should be forcing us to see the interdependence of the two worlds, forcing us to admit that the spiritual underlies and informs the actual, we get instead the impression that they are so distinct, so little related, that to move from one to the other is like putting on an impenetrable disguise. What, after all, besides the name, have these Julias in common? Could we identify the one after being acquainted only with the other? That the deliberate convention of 'inner selves' should at first sight give an impression of simple ineptitude is thus not its chief defect. What is serious is that in another way it is itself inept, and draws attention to a material dichotomy which it was part of the business of the dramatist to dissolve or remove. I have not seen the play and I am aware that it might be argued that this contrast, between the earlier and the later Julia, is less serious on the stage. With a book one can turn back to the early pages and make comparisons; but on the stage there is a temporal progression which leaves us dependent on memory and for this reason we may tend to accept the changed figure more readily. The play's popularity may be evidence that the convention works better in the theatre than in the study, and I should be happy to believe that it does. On the other hand there may be other reasons for its popularity, reasons more properly the province of the sociologist than of the critic. Even in the study do we, after all, *need* to turn back to the early pages for the contrast to be felt, and felt disturbingly?

These might be called structural criticisms. I should like to conclude by observing that the flaccidity of the verse does little to compensate for them. Some of Celia's speeches to Reilly in Act Two are so inexplicit that one is tempted to call them Eliotese. They seem to rely on certain concepts such as 'love' and 'shame' and 'aloneness' (I use this bar-barism because the state is clearly neither loneliness nor solitude), yet they do nothing to make these concepts real. This is at all events what seems to me to be taking place in such a speech as Celia's on p. 123. Again, at other times the verse is so obviously *not* verse that to have printed it as such gives one much the same pause as does the 'Comedy' of the title-page:

Well, Peter, I'm awfully glad, for your sake,
Though of course we...I shall miss you;
You know how I depended on you for concerts,
And picture exhibitions—more than you realized.
It *was* fun, wasn't it! But now you'll have a chance,
I hope, to realize your ambitions.
I shall miss you.

'Anyone who tries to write poetic drama, even today,' Eliot has written, 'should know that half of his energy must be exhausted in the effort to escape from the constricting toils of Shakespeare.' This was well said, and it is to his credit that in *The Family Reunion* and, more particularly, *Murder In The Cathedral* Eliot has written dramatic verse that is both verse and underivative. The impression left by *The Cocktail Party*, however, is rather that the 'constricting toils' have been, if that is possible, too thoroughly cast off. It is not that the dramatist here eschews Shakespeareanisms—no sane reader would throw that in his teeth—but that the verse is of so poor a quality as to make them unthinkable. Even a quotation from Shakespeare rather than Shelley would throw up its context in all too harsh a light. One seems to see the shade of William Archer smile ironically.

MR ELIOT AND SOCIAL BIOLOGY[1]

L. A. CORMICAN (1950)

The most gratifying thing about Eliot's *Notes Towards the Definition of Culture* is that it could be written at all. First of all, it dispels some of its own gloom. Eliot implies in various places that the England of 1948 shows a deterioration from 1900; he indicates nowhere, as far as I can discover, any belief that England shows an improvement in the same time. Yet it is a striking improvement that a great and influential writer can proceed to his diagnosis of social ills quietly assuming that everyone knows the ills to be there. In the second place, it is bound to have good effects along two important lines of modern thinking: the semantic and the agnostic. It will, to some extent, halt the vicious, disintegrating tendency of semantics to turn all discussion of meaning into mere ingenious exercises with words. No one capable of understanding the book could remain quite comfortable in the conviction that all questions in theology, morals, sociology, are games with words. The book also shows that a man, highly cultured, deeply aware of the

[1] This, coming from Ottawa, continues the symposium opened by G. H. Bantock in Vol. XVI, No. 1.

strains and difficulties in our society, capable of quite unusual achievement in art and criticism—such a man can hold a definite religion (or, at least, appear to himself to hold a definite religion). Eliot here represents the point in intellectual history at which the agnostic can no longer flatter himslf that the intelligent people are all on his side. The general excellences are those we have come to expect in Eliot's work— the illuminating *aperçus* on topics we had imagined to be exhausted, the recalling of old but forgotten truths or obscured principles, the calm readiness to follow wherever truth beckons, the constant stimulus to bring our own intellects into free and flexible play.

At the same time, no one who has profited by Eliot's literary criticism is likely to feel quite satisfied with his 'social biology'. To offer any disparaging criticism of Eliot is unpleasantly like quarrelling with one's father. To think at all on culture is for so many of us to be conscious of a large debt to him; if we are able to define our disagreement with him, it is largely because he has supplied us with the critical apparatus necessary to such definition. *Notes*, however, provokes much more than mere disagreement—it points to the conclusion that his work is very uneven in significance. As will be indicated later on, the book lends itself to various interpretations; I am concerned, however (as Eliot would put it) not so much 'with extracting a meaning', but with defining one reader's disappointment with what is undoubtedly a weighty achievement from one of the foremost minds of the day.

For example, an essay of this sort hardly needs all the safeguards Eliot gives it: we find too often the kind of phrase which occurs on p. 48: 'I must constantly remind the reader of the limitations of my subject.' The total effect of these safeguards is to give the essay an unpleasant resemblance to a purely political speech in which all objections and criticisms are forestalled and the speaker commits himself as little as possible. His opening statement of aim, 'to help to define a word, the word *culture*' (p. 13), is an example of playing too safe. Hardly anyone knows better than Eliot that a good book on culture will be good very largely because it is something to argue over; one can hardly argue over the desire of any man that a particular word be defined in a particular way. The book is too long if he aims merely at lexicography; his purpose is too narrow if he avoids all 'outline of social or political philosophy'. Culture can hardly be discussed in this isolated way, since social philosophy is an attempt to be truly wise about the well-being of society—the very aim of Eliot, at least in Chapter II (The Class and the Elite), and Chapter V (Culture and Politics).

As a general weakness, one may note the absence—the annoying, frustrating absence—of the very quality which has made Eliot's literary criticism so stimulating, so influential—the constant recurrence to the concrete case. Without particular illustrations it is difficult either to clarify general ideas or to control one's '*impressions person-nelles*' in such a way that they may be '*érigées en lois*'. In culture as in literature the sensitive intelligent handling of the particular case is more important than any general consideration by itself.

The essay supplies us with evidence that, in the field of social biology, his mind is not the finely adjusted, delicately probing instrument it is in his criticism. On page 89, for example, he presents as distinctly modern the view that 'culture is regarded either as a negligible by-product which can be left to itself or as a department of life to be organized in accordance with the particular scheme we favour'. If the evidence to the contrary were not so overwhelming, one would be inclined to think that Eliot had never heard of Sparta, Augustus or Richelieu: the effort to 'organize culture' is very ancient, very persistent, and obviously it can be organized only in accordance with the scheme someone favours. We are left groping in unnecessary darkness on page 90: 'The differences between the several European nations in the past were not wide enough to make their peoples see their cultures as different to the point of conflict and incompatibility.' 'In the past' is much too vague for a discussion such as this; besides, at *no* time were the *peoples* conscious enough of their culture to be aware of compatibility or incompatibility. Cromwell, the St Bartholomew massacre, the Roman proscriptions are all reminders that 'liquidating enemies' is not an 'alarming development of modern war' (p. 59). We have, of course, become more efficient at liquidating large numbers at once, but that is quite another matter. These are all small points; but if Eliot were to read his essay with the same powers of observation he brings to his reading of, say, Arnold, he would, I am sure, find many more.

This general impression may be reinforced by examining the particular kind of detachment from the practical sphere which is found through-out. The disinterested love of truth for its own sake, detachment from practical convenience to oneself or to one's side or party, this is so rare and so noble a quality that we must salute it and be grateful for it when we find it, especially when it spurs to action so fine a mind as Eliot's. But if we tend to seek only that part of truth which suits us, there is the opposite danger that the pursuit of truth can be detached to the point of an unhealthy aloofness.

For example, he seems to show no consciousness of many important factors which are having a visible effect on culture to-day. He neglects the inevitable impact of material, especially of economic, forces on society. His discussion of Regionalism in Chapter III seems to leave blandly out of account the statement on p. 121: 'In the world of the future, it looks as if every part of the world would affect every other part.' Rapid transport and easy communication which make Europe, in a definable sense, smaller than Wales was two hundred years ago; the constant assimilation which is going on within the English-speaking world; the need for a mobile force of workers with which to maintain activity in our productive machinery: such factors shift the whole basis for regional differentiation. There are needed also public policies which can be made plausible to the voters. (To note such needs is not necessarily to admire them: a doctor may have to give a patient stimulants which he knows to be harmful, but without which, for the moment, the patient cannot survive at all.) Similarly, he shows no recognition of the great changes in the forms of wealth which are basically modifying the relations of classes to each other. To put the point unkindly for the moment, as far as Eliot is concerned, *Culture and Environment* might never have been written.

There is a further unhealthy detachment from facts in the way he expresses his dislike of the dirty, the charlatan side of politics.[1] The evils of politics will continue as they are until sensitive, subtle and flexible minds like Eliot's go into politics; and, however remote the latter possibility may be, perhaps a 'little yeast might leaven the whole mass'. One may cite the footnote, p. 15:

It is only fair to add, that when it comes to talking nonsense about culture, there is nothing to choose between politicians of one stripe or another. Had the election of 1945 brought the alternative party into power, we should have heard much the same pronouncements in the same circumstances. The pursuit of politics is incompatible with a strict attention to exact meanings on all occasions. The reader should therefore abstain from deriding either Mr Attlee or the late regretted Miss Wilkinson.

I find this unpleasantly reminiscent of the schoolboyish antics of Shaw, to whom the 'smart' saying is sometimes more important than fine precision. Eliot's facts may be readily admitted. But the language is distressingly loose, the emphases fall on the wrong places, and the implications are misleading. 'Talking nonsense about culture' is very self-assured for a writer who gives his book so tentative a title: much of what Eliot says in this essay might perhaps provoke the same facile comment in the minds of politicians who have to try to do something in the practical field. 'Politicians of one stripe or another', and 'alternative party' are a weak, patronizing way of saying: 'A plague o' both your houses'; they imply some sort of understanding nod to the reader,

---

[1] Eliot *should* be among the first to see that these evils are particular forms of original sin, and need 'the divine much more than the physician', and much more than the detached observer.

flattering his intellectual snobbery, and indicating: 'Of course, you and I are above the dirty business of politics.' And it is surprising that a man who believes that in a healthy society

> public affairs would be a responsibility not equally borne: a greater responsibility would be inherited by those who inherited special advantages, and in whom self-interest, and interest for the sake of their families (a 'stake in the country') should cohere with public spirit [p. 84]

affirms also that the pursuit of politics is 'incompatible with a strict attention to exact meanings on all occasions'. *Thoughts After Lambeth*, if nothing else, should remind Eliot that no 'pursuit', not even that of the Anglican episcopacy, is compatible with a strict attention to exact meanings on all occasions. And having been so patronizing to the politicians, it is not surprising that he turns to patronizing the reader, and tells him when not to laugh.

The ideas and the attitudes suggested in the footnote just mentioned are, certainly, details; they are, however, symptoms of the peculiar barrenness which belongs to the observer who is under no obligation to make practical decisions. We cannot indeed demand that a man refrain from criticizing till he demonstrates his practical ability to do better; the validity of Eliot's criticism of *Hamlet* is not at all affected by the inferiority of Eliot to Shakespeare as a playwright. But one can demand that, when he writes on politics, he show us a sensitive grasp of the practical realities and complex difficulties in which any political decision is made. The footnote seems to indicate the beginnings of a new monasticism—prompted as the ancient Thebaid was by a conviction that 'all flesh is corrupt', and the good must 'keep themselves unspotted from the world'. What is needed to-day, however, is the monasticism not of the Thebaid but of Monte Cassino—the Benedictine flight from the world which was not only compatible with, but imperatively demanded, every possible effort from the monks to help an ailing world. There is no reason for a man of Eliot's prestige and achievement to hesitate about offering some notes towards the definition of a plan of action. He could, at least, be less embarrassingly brief on the 'ideals and obligations of universities' (p. 123). The universities are not merely opportunities for acquiring the 'unconscious background of all our planning (p. 94); they are focal points for resistance to any engulfing barbarism. With all reverence to Eliot's tact and taste, one could dispense with his history of *The Criterion* to make room for more precise suggestions on what the universities might reasonably hope to do, and also (since Eliot knows the publishing business from the inside) on what the publishers might be expected to do.

There is the same undesirable aloofness in the concluding remark of Chapter V (p. 94):

> Thus we slip into the assumption that culture can be planned. Culture can never be wholly conscious—there is always more to it than we are conscious of; and it cannot be planned because it is also the unconscious background of all our planning.

What he says here is either a truism or misleading. Surely he is hardly denying the elementary principle that the deep unconscious which modifies conscious choice and action is itself largely modified by conscious choice. Even if he has forgotten his Aristotle: 'What end a man considers worth pursuing depends on the character he has (deliberately) built', he cannot have forgotten his Shakespeare:

> Men's judgments
> Are a parcel of their fortunes, and things outward
> Do draw the inward quality after them,
> To suffer all alike'.

The unconscious is hardly any more important in relation to culture than to good literary criticism; in both, what is now unconscious is embedded in the mind because it was for some time deliberately examined and held. Unless he attaches to *planned* some sense which he does not mention, Eliot is simply negating all the efforts of educators from *The Republic* to *Scrutiny* when he says baldly: 'Culture cannot be planned.' If, as he implies in several places, our society is in a crisis, we might apply to it what Napoleon said of a battle: any plan is better than none. As far as Eliot dissociates himself (as he has a right to) from the planners, the planning is bound to fall into the wrong hands, and something like Nazism or Stalinism is much more likely to emerge than culture.[1]

It may be the same wrong aloofness that draws him to the idea of 'constantly dining with the Opposition'. Such dining may result, and has resulted, in the blurring of all important distinctions among the parties, and the consequent reduction of Parliament to a friendly club where sham battles are staged on occasion to edify the uninitiated. Genial readiness to mix with one's political enemies is one of the finest traits of English political life; but it can issue in the detachment from all convictions. The '*trahison des clercs*' may take the form of prostituting intellect to practical politics or to popular vulgarity; it

[1] It is another illustration of the slackness of Eliot's mind in certain sections that the orderly description of culture on p. 120 is phrased throughout in such a way as to fit either Nazism or Stalinism; some parts fit either of these better than they fit what many believe to be the traditional culture of the West.

may take the form (more attractive to the fastidious mind) of refusing, with splendid dignity, to commit oneself to anything practical. If our culture is deteriorating as much as Eliot implies, whose hand is better fitted than his to halt the process, if only by offering us suggestions to argue over? Definitions, even if they run to one hundred and twenty-four pages, are hardly likely to defend the things which Eliot holds really valuable.

He seems to expect (and even to count on) a similar aloofness in the people who will be 'cultured' in the future. There is, I believe, a nest of false assumptions in the remark on p. 120.

The culture of an artist or a philosopher is distinct from that of a mine worker or field labourer; the culture of a poet will be somewhat different from that of a politician; but in a healthy society these are all parts of the same culture.

As far as one can judge from the past, these clear-cut distinctions are undesirable; in any society which could call itself 'healthy', some poets would be politicians, the politicians who could would be poets; mine workers would be philosophers, and some philosophers would work in mines. There is no means of knowing whether Eliot would call the England of the first half of the seventeenth century 'healthy', but surely the blending of occupations and interests in Ben Jonson, in Bunyan, in Milton, indicates that, while brick-laying, fighting, tinkering, politics are distinct things from poetry, the bricklayer, the tinker and the politician need not be distinct from the poet.

From the sociological point of view there are some further serious omissions and over-simplifications. It seems rather disingenuous to put so much reliance on the family to-day with nothing but the brief reference to *The Peckham Experiment* to indicate the problems and difficulties of the family. On the one hand he seems to take as a fact on which we can be easily agreed that we should (p. 104)

do better to admit that we have arrived at a stage of civilization at which the family is irresponsible, or incompetent, or helpless; at which parents cannot be expected to train their children properly.

Since he offers this seriously as better than 'congratulating ourselves when the school assumes another responsibility hitherto left[1] to the parents', it would not seem that he is speaking ironically. Yet (p. 43):

[1] Many sociologists would object to the word *left*; a number of the responsibilities Eliot has in mind were *left* to the parents simply in the sense that no one else bothered about them; the handling of these responsibilities is a complex matter for which parents have seldom received the necessary training.

the primary and the most important channel of transmission of culture is the family . . . When I speak of the family, I have in mind a bond which embraces a long period of time: a piety towards the dead, however obscure, and a solicitude for the unborn, however remote.

He does not indicate how he expects the family to pass from what it is to what it should be; he does not indicate even one condition which is likely to bring the transition about; he offers nothing on the host of conditions which at present are working so powerfully against the family.

From a 'student of social biology' one would have expected some clarification of the distinction between *society* and the *state*. One of the most urgent (and one of the most difficult) problems in social biology is to allow the state all the power it needs to safeguard and foster all that may safely be entrusted to it, while not allowing it to absorb and control every form of communal or social activity. Except for the weakly defined admiration for the family, and the fertile but undeveloped statement on the universities (p. 123), Eliot seems hardly to recognize the problem, much less to help us out of it. The question: What kind of institution is likely in the future to be strong enough to resist successfully the all-devouring state authority, this is the question to which Chapter V (Culture and Politics) suggests no answer. Eliot might, of course, plead that he is not pretending to account for all the necessary conditions for a flourishing culture. But, in the first place, this problem of state and society is really the concrete form of the general problem of individual and group or social culture; and besides, unless we find a means of making our modern Leviathan powerful enough without allowing it to subdue us all, the problems of Chapter V do not arise. The absence of such discussion has the effect of strengthening the general impression of remoteness which clings to so much of the essay; at practically no point does Eliot give the impression of a concrete situation firmly grasped by the writer and clearly presented to the reader. The few references he makes to actual situations are strangely timid and circumscribed.

The most serious omission is the lack of standards either stated or implied. Eliot is far too fine a critic not to know that social criticism, like literary criticism, implies the examination of the particular case in the light of the general consideration. As he puts it himself, for instance, in *The Use of Poetry* (p. 133), one cannot sensibly contemplate 'man's place in the perspective of time, unless one brings to its contemplation some belief that there is a sense and a meaning in the place of human history in the history of the world'. Yet, in spite of keeping so aloof from the practical sphere, he suggests no general principle of discrimination among the various types of culture. This omission of judgments of value is all the more surprising in view of his previous remark:

If...you had no faith in the critic's ability to tell a good poem from a bad one, you would put little reliance upon the validity of his theories [*The Use of Poetry*, p. 17].

There is one point on which the transatlantic reader particularly feels disappointment, and that is the lack of sympathetic reference to America. Eliot is, undoubtedly, entitled to his own opinion and his own conclusions; and there is no reason for turning an article such as the present into an *apologia* for the United States. But it is rather surprising that the two references to the United States (pp. 45, 92) fit so easily into a pattern of thinking which, superficial, misleading and rather mischievous, has become common in England in the last ten years. Eliot's few remarks can do no one any harm, and they can hardly be controverted. But the future of culture will depend to some extent on the degree in which England and the United States influence each other and pool their mental resources. Few Americans would deny that in such an exchange, England has more to offer than to receive. But if England is to be, as we may hope, the 'Athens of the future', there will be needed both a fuller recognition of the generosity (of mind and heart as well as purse) with which Americans handle their dealings with other peoples, and an appreciation of what is healthy and encouraging in the American spirit. If it is assumed, as so many assume (I do not say Eliot himself), that the only developed instincts in the United States are the acquisitive and the sexual,[1] that American scholarship, outside the sciences, is matter for amused contempt, that we must get along with the Americans since they have so much economic power, if these and similar assumptions are uppermost in the minds of Englishmen, then the fruitful co-operation between the two countries becomes impossible—to the detriment of each. One cannot help wishing that Eliot had given, as his special training and position enabled him to give, some positive leadership towards a fuller, more articulated understanding between the intelligent people of both countries. It is not the universities of Europe alone (cf. p. 125) which should have their 'common ideals and obligations'; to put it in the way least flattering to American sentiment, the universities of the United States have much to learn from those of England, and the latter have some obligations in the matter.

The English Government (Conservative, Coalition, Socialist) has for many years been aware of the importance of cultivating friendly relations with America, and of helping Americans to understand

---

[1] To those who have never lived in the United States, Dos Passos' *USA* can be very misleading.

British points of view. It is important then that the channels of cultured exchange should be cleared of obstructions as much as possible. It is only the Beaverbrooks on the one side, and the McCormicks on the other, who imagine that the relations between the two countries can be thought of as clever begging by the English and noisy imperialism on the part of the Americans. It is much to be regretted that the few words Eliot has said could be turned so easily to their own purposes by both the Beaverbrooks and the McCormicks. It is still more to be regretted that, in an essay which insists so much and so rightly on the inter-communion of cultural societies, he should give no indication of how the major economic force in the world is to be integrated more organically into the culture of the West. For few people are better fitted for this than Eliot. The Appendix on The Unity of European Culture was an admirable opportunity to express in terms of culture what is a commonplace in terms of diplomacy, that the borders of the United States lie in Europe; and from the cultural point of view this is only another way of saying that Europe stretches to the Pacific. What Europe becomes in the next fifty years will depend to some extent on what Europe has helped America to become.

The least satisfactory section is that on religion. The whole chapter, Unity and Diversity, leaves us with only the cloudiest notions of what 'faith', 'theology', and 'religion' mean to Eliot. The chapter does indeed contain a refreshingly factual account of the development of the Church of England (p. 79); but he takes even more precautions than Hollywood to ensure that no mention of religion be offensive to anyone, with the result that he commits himself to nothing and appears to be convinced of nothing in particular. He seems also to forget that religion, like culture, lies largely in the unconscious part of one's mind; only an external concept of religion, limited to rites and professed creeds, could lead him to say that 'all Anglican and Free Church lay men are exposed to the same environment of a culture severed from religion' (p. 79). Surely he is aware that the British constitution, property laws, Socialist ideas and ideals, the whole concept of what a government is and what it is for, all these things are what they are largely through the Christianity embedded in them. Even on Eliot's own showing the phrase, *a culture severed from religion*, is inaccurate, since 'an individual European may not believe that the Christian Faith is true, and yet what he says, and makes, and does, will all spring out of his heritage of Christian culture and depend upon that culture for its meaning' (p. 122).

The vagueness of his terms becomes much more unsatisfactory when we come to such a pronouncement as: 'If Christianity goes, the whole of our culture goes' (p.122). Eliot here seems to subscribe to a view which is just as much a matter of intellectual fashion to-day as the opposite was a hundred years ago. Eliot rightly deprecates the nineteenth-century view that religion does not matter; here, however, he attaches more importance to religion than even Christopher Dawson. From the historical point of view it seems strange that a culture which produced a large number of its greatest works of art before the birth of Christ should become so dependent on Christianity that its vitality and fecundity must disappear if Christianity disappears.

The assertion, 'If Christianity goes, the whole of our culture goes', is objectionable also on the grounds that Christianity here must mean any one of the 'various religious persuasions' of those who like to think of themselves as Christians. The sociologist would have no difficulty in proving that quite a number of these might disappear without culture being a whit worse off. Until Eliot tells us which Christianity he means, we can neither agree nor disagree.

From the theological point of view, the statement is also unacceptable. When he tells us that 'it is owing to two thousand years of Christianity'[1] that 'we trace our Christian heritage, the evolution of our arts, our conception of Roman law, our common standards of literature', he makes Christianity a vast cultural and religious bank deposit into which he throws everything he considers valuable. He claims both too much and too little for Christianity; too much, because it is here simply equated with all that is good in the Western world, or at least made the indispensable condition for all these good things. He also claims too little for Christianity; because, if it 'goes' or even can 'go', it might as well be recognized at once as a fake and a humbug. Whatever individual Christians may or may not believe, whatever non-Christians believe or do not believe Christianity to be, Christianity in any of its official definitions of itself up to the beginning of the eighteenth century unambiguously asserts its divine origin and divine power. Unless Eliot is juggling with words, the verb 'go' must mean the same thing in both clauses: 'If Christianity goes, the whole of our culture goes'; unless he is juggling with our minds, the second verb must mean 'disappear'. If Christianity disappears, it will have proved itself to be a colossal deception; if it possibly is such, we can surely contemplate its 'going' without any tremors. In the almost naïve readiness to throw out generalizations and the constant shying away from the definition of key terms, one can hardly recognize the mind which found in one sentence of Swinburne's two misleading assumptions and two misleading conclusions (*Selected Essays*, p. 118).

[1] Here again there is unnecessary inaccuracy. It is only from about the sixth century that Christian institutions can be called, in any definable sense, vehicles for the transmission of culture.

Another tangle of meanings is found in the standard suggested on page 67: 'A higher religion is one in which it is harder to believe.' This is worse even than the communist or agnostic idea that millions believe in Christianity because it is so easy to believe in. As a definition of a 'higher' religion, it is clearly false in the case of Christianity. To Eliot, I presume, and certainly to millions of others (including the 'obscure dead' of almost two thousand years ago) Christianity is much easier to believe in than Zeus, Jupiter, Woden or the Great White Spirit, or any of the beliefs it replaced—and easier not only to people of a 'higher' civilization, but also to African Bushmen and Eskimos. 'Harder to believe' is, however, a phrase which opens so many avenues of thought, suggests so many types of religious experience and introduces so many subjective and variable factors that one could give it almost any meaning one pleases.

It is also difficult to understand why anyone speaking from a 'Christian' point of view, should describe the conflict (pp. 67–8) as *eventually* between Church and State, since Christianity began, unmistakably and confessedly, with such a conflict. From Nero to Henry II and Hitler, the issue is essentially the same as that between Pilate and Christ: are there any fields of conscience in which the State has no jurisdiction at all?

On page 70 *Protestantism* appears as an historical fact; on page 71 as a type of mind or character. We can hardly make sense of the whole passage unless we interpret *Protestantism* as resistance to undue pressure from religious authorities. To call such resistance Protestantism is wanton vagueness and an invitation to loose thinking about the distinction between Protestantism and Catholicism.

Another undesirable simplification occurs in the statement on page 79 that 'the refinement or crudity of theological and philosophical thinking is itself, of course, one of the measures of the state of our culture'. One can only wish that before voicing such ideas Eliot had done what he sets out to do at the opening of the Appendix on European Unity: present his credentials. Both the general method and the particular judgments of *Thoughts After Lambeth* indicate that, in dealing with the refinement or the crudity of the logical thinking, Eliot's credentials are not quite in order. Unless it is fairly easy for the 'layman' to distinguish between refinement and crudity in such cases, it is hardly worth while to make the statement at all. Large numbers of men living in an atmosphere very different from Eliot's have found it easy to conclude, as Shaw does, that Athanasius is crude, Peter impertinent, Paul confused and John suffering from the effects of dope.

The rest of the sentence, 'the tendency in some quarters to reduce theology to such principles as a child can understand . . . is itself indicative of cultural debility', is itself a gross reduction of complex issues to simple terms. Some of the great summaries of Christianity, e.g., the Lord's Prayer, or Paul's 'He who loves his neighbour has fulfilled the law', are precisely statements of religious truth in such terms as a child or an illiterate slave can understand, while remaining statements too profound for any theologian to understand fully.

The most general objection to Eliot's concept of Christianity is that Eliot has so little faith in it; it has apparently brought about many wonderful results in the past, but it is not to be asked to do anything particular in the future. The role he ascribes to it in the past is much too big to be acceptable to the non-Christian, much too vague to please the Catholic.

What is most disquieting about the book is, I have tried to suggest, its symptomatic quality. The accumulative effect of the details I have mentioned is to pose a problem more serious than any explicitly discussed in the book. Coupled with the rest of Eliot's work (e.g. with the inclusion in *Selected Essays* of the nugatory *Marie Lloyd*), the book compels us to wonder whether it has become impossible for intelligent people to absorb, much less circulate, the 'best that is known and thought'. Without such circulation, no organic structure (p. 15) is possible. With every allowance made, *Notes* is as unacceptable in sociology as Belloc's *Milton* in literary criticism. The latter is full of airy assumptions and false conclusions—largely because Belloc had no convictions, no formulable standards; his *Servile State*, on the other hand, is a work of penetrating insight, permanently valuable to anyone who thinks about society and politics. Of penetrating insight into literature, there is an abundance in Eliot: of formulable standards and convictions, there is hardly a trace in *Notes*. It is very unlikely that anyone will find in this essay either a clarification of ideals for the future, or a more exact way of defining one's dissatisfaction with institutions in the present. It was, I suggest, a mistake on Eliot's part to allow his mind, with its range, flexibility and penetration, to be de-routed into a task in which he finds it so difficult to deploy the full resourcefulness of the finest critical powers of the twentieth century.

POET AS EXECUTANT

F. R. LEAVIS (1947)

Four Quartets, by T. S. Eliot. Read by the author (H.M.V. C.3598–3603).

To say that these records must be disappointing even to a listener who approaches them with no high expectation is not to dismiss them or wish they had not been made. For consider the fact: here for posterity is a rendering of some of the indubitably great poetry of our time by the poet himself. And the rendering, as I shall suggest, has some significance for criticism. That, however, is not because of any direct illumination it throws on the poetry. It brings home to us, indeed, how good the verse is; but it does so by not teaching us anything about the rhythms—anything we didn't know already from the printed page. The printed page tells us how they go: the verse is so marvellously exact.

Mr Eliot, if a great composer, is not a great, or good, or even a tolerable executant. His voice, as he uses it, is disconcertingly lacking in body. One wouldn't wish him to elocute in the manner of Mr Robert Speaight (whose *actor's* declamation of Mr Eliot's verse empties it), but a capacity for some strength of tone is clearly desirable. Mr Eliot's reading is of course not unintelligent and insensitive in the actor's way, but it is not positively intelligent and sensitive in the way one would have expected of the poet himself. Judged by that standard it *is* unintelligent. His command of inflexion, intonation and tempo—his *intention*, as performer, under these heads—is astonishingly inadequate. He seems to be governed by a mechanical routine—to be unable to reduce his *clichés* (which suggest the reading of the Lessons) to a sensitive responsiveness.

As for the critical significance of this rendering, with its curious inadequacies, I think they can be related to the striking contrast offered by his later prose to his poetry. In his poetry he applies to himself a merciless standard; it is the product of an intense and single-minded discipline—discipline for sincerity and purity of interest. In his prose he seems to relax from the ascesis he undergoes as composer of verse. The prose-writer belongs to an external social world, where conventions are formidable and temptations are not only often not resisted, they seem not to be perceived. The reader of the poetry would seem to be more intimately related to the prose-writer than to the poet.

These records should call attention to the problem of reading *Four Quartets* out. The problem deserves a great deal of attention, and to tackle it would be very educational.

3

YEATS AND POUND

THE LATEST YEATS

F. R. LEAVIS (1933)

The Winding Stair and Other Poems, by W. B. Yeats (Macmillan)

Those admirers of Yeats who found *Words for Music Perhaps* disappointing will not find this new and larger collection, which includes the earlier, less so. One had, of course, no right to set the standard of one's expectations by *The Tower*, but, naturally, one did.

The present book, in theme and general tone, bears a close relation to *The Tower*, but contains nothing as good as the best of that. The proud sardonic tension—it would be marvellous if it were otherwise—is slackened. It is with a different irony that Yeats here, in *Byzantium*, which corresponds to the *Sailing to Byzantium* of *The Tower*, contemplates the 'artifice of eternity':

> I hail the superman;
> I call it death-in-life and life-in-death.

Soul, though still studying 'monuments of its own magnificence', hardly now 'claps its hands and sings'; what was an astringency in the exaltation is now a sterile bitterness—the 'miracle' is itself 'embittered':

> Miracle, bird or golden handiwork,
> More miracle than bird or handiwork,
> Planted on the starlit golden bough,
> Can like the cocks of Hades crow,
> Or, by the moon embittered, scorn aloud
> In glory of changeless metal
> Common bird or petal
> And all the complexities of mire or blood.

The world of sense, the pride and beauty of life, so potently present in *Sailing to Byzantium*, are now merely (though there is a 'dolphin') 'complexities of mire and blood', and spirit, 'blood-begotten', that would escape the 'complexities', is seen striving in tortured impotence,

> Dying into a dance
> An agony of trance,
> An agony of flame that cannot singe a sleeve.

We are left in the end in bitter contemplation of

> Those images that yet
> Fresh images beget,
> That dolphin-torn, that gong-tormented sea.

The realm of time and sense is elsewhere in the book a more rich and positive presence, but nowhere is there that vital tension between counter-attracting presences which makes the finest poetry of *The Tower*. What is, instead, characteristic of *The Winding Stair* is something (see, for instance, *At Algeciras—A Meditation upon Death*) on which our first comment, 'this is too elliptical,' amplifies itself immediately with 'and too passive'; the constituents are inert. Another way of putting it is suggested by the title of one of the poems; instead of tension we have vacillation. *Vacillation* offers us this dialogue:

> *The Soul.* Seek out reality, leave things that seem.
> *The Heart.* What, be a singer born and lack a theme?
> *The Soul.* Isaiah's coal, what more can man desire?
> *The Heart.* Struck dumb in the simplicity of fire!
> *The Soul.* Look on that fire, salvation walks within.
> *The Heart.* What theme had Homer but original sin?

The relaxed grasp betrays itself most notably, perhaps, in the Crazy Jane poems. The preoccupations of these are Mr Yeats's—Time and the unrealness of the transitory:

> And that was all my song—
> When everything is told,
> Saw I an old man young
> Or young man old?

The 'artifice of eternity' and the 'monuments of unaging intellect' mean nothing to Crazy Jane; they can provide no stay. Nor need she bother about relating things, or about their significance at all; we are certainly not to look to her for coherence. She can be 'mad as the mist and snow'. This, actually, is the refrain, not of one of the Crazy Jane sequence, but of a poem that comes directly from Mr Yeats. Clearly, the resolution, accommodation or *détente* to be arrived at with the help of Crazy Jane (or Tom the Lunatic—a *persona* who, significantly, is sometimes plain Yeats undisguised) has its advantages. There is often, no doubt, a poignant queerness, a pregnant simplicity, a profound naïvety; but in this kind of simplification something is apt to be unsatisfactory in the poignant, the pregnant and the profound. To say that, reading these poems, one has sometimes to repel the thought of Mr G. K. Chesterton would be to make the point far too heavily; nevertheless, something tending that way has to be said.

What is also significant, and can be fairly said, is that Mr Yeats's contemplation, in this book, of Time and the transitory reminds us again and again of Mr De la Mare:

> Behold that great Plotinus swim
> Buffeted by such seas;
> Bland Rhadamanthus beckons him,
> But the Golden Race looks dim,
> Salt blood blocks his eyes.
>
> Scattered on the level grass
> Or winding through the grove
> Plato there and Minos pass,
> There stately Pythagoras
> And all the choir of Love.

The lovely *Parting* might actually pass for Mr De la Mare's.

There is, of course, a great deal in the book that is both good and characteristic, even if the kind of critical attention that is Mr Yeats's due yields a report that may seem ungracious. Need it be said that *The Winding Stair* is, in any case, one of the very few literary events of the year? To be reminded that we have still in this age, honouring the English language, a spirit so austere and fine is an occasion for gratitude.

YEATS AND THE ENGLISH TRADITION

H. A. MASON (1937)

The Oxford Book of Modern Verse, 1892–1935, chosen by W. B. Yeats (O.U.P.)

Someone in *Country Life* writes that 'the Oxford Book of Anything has come to stand happily in our minds for the profit and pleasure of accuracy, scholarship and fine taste'. And without wishing to endorse everything in the other Oxford Books of Verse one can say that they have a high representative value. It is therefore astounding that the present selection should appear in this series. Although, as recent anthologies have made distressingly clear, there seems no longer to be a general consensus of opinion as to which are the better modern poems, so that every choice must seem unduly personal, it does appear a counsel of despair to entrust the selection to one whose taste is merely eccentric. And if the word should appear too severe for the selection, the perverse 'introduction' fully deserves it.

Any observations upon the book bear consequently more on the interests of Mr Yeats than on the problem of an adequate anthology of modern poetry. First of all, it seems probable that the greater part of what has been written between the years 1892 and 1935 just hasn't interested him at all. At any rate, he has reprinted the standard anthology favourites of, for instance, Ralph Hodgson, Gordon Bottomley, Flecker, Newbolt and Julian Grenfell. Wilfred Owen, T. E. Hulme and Isaac Rosenberg do not appear, though they may have been excluded as being 'War Poets'. For 'certain poems written in the midst of the great war' are dismissed on the grounds that 'passive suffering is not a theme for poetry'. At the other end his choice of the younger poets seems to follow the current values (against which various protests have been made in these pages) so closely that it is only charitable to suppose that his interest in them is recent and slight.

Some of his positive preferences remain to me frankly inexplicable. 'I think England has had more good poets from 1900 to the present day than during any period of the same length since the early seventeenth century,' he says in his Introduction. If the number of pages allotted to each poet counts for anything, Edith Sitwell with eighteen and Walter James Turner with seventeen are our most important poets. And that their eminent position in the anthology is not accidental is made clear by the claims made for them in the Introduction. Loyalty to his friends no doubt explains the favourable treatment of Johnson, Dowson and Sturge Moore. But as for the Irish brigade which is given such prominence one can only quote against Yeats his own lines 'to a poet who would have me praise certain bad poets, imitators of his and mine'—

> You say, as I have often given tongue
> In praise of what another's said or sung,
> 'Twere politic to do the like by these;
> But was there ever dog that praised his fleas?

Nothing so much marks the distinction between the ability to criticize in the act of writing a poem and the power of criticizing the poems of others as his remarks on Eliot and Hopkins. It is almost as though he did not understand the tradition of which he is a part. At any rate, he speaks of Eliot's 'rhythmical flatness', and says 'Nor can I put the Eliot of *The Waste Land* among those that descend from Shakespeare and the translators of the Bible. I think of him as satirist rather than poet.' Against Hopkins he seems to hold a temperamental aversion. 'I suspect a bias born when I began to think.' Yeats gives a ludicrous account of 'sprung verse' and prints the lesser poems. The selections from Hardy and Pound (though monetary considerations may have entered here) point the same way. Only one poem of Edward Thomas is given.

Yeats's self-depreciatory remarks on his own position ('I, too, have tried to be modern') recall forcibly what Lawrence had to say about 'art-speech'. His own poems, chosen from his later work, coming between his contemporaries, Arthur Symons

> (And the mandolins and they,
> Faintlier breathing, swoon
> Into the rose and grey
> Ecstasy of the moon)

and Ernest Dowson

> (Wine and women and song
>   Three things garnish our way:
> Yet is day over-long),

accentuate the deficiencies of the chronological method, and provide a criticism (or, at least, another selection could), of the whole period covered by this anthology. He towers over so many schools, or, as he prefers to put it, 'writing through fifty years I have been now of the same school with John Synge and James Stephens, now in that of Sturge Moore and the younger 'Michael Field': and though the concentration of philosophy and social passion of the school of Day Lewis and in Macneice lay beyond my desire, I would, but for a failure of talent, have been in that of Turner and Dorothy Wellesley'.

American Poetry is not represented.

THE GREAT YEATS, AND THE LATEST

F. R. LEAVIS (1940)

Last Poems and Plays, by W. B. Yeats (Macmillan)

This is a saddening volume. That isn't merely because it illustrates once more that slackening of tension which is so apparent in Yeats's work of the past decade—the last. It was remarkable enough that his peak should come as late as 1928, the year of *The Tower*, and he could hardly be expected to keep up through his old age the taut, delicate and difficult complexity that *Sailing to Byzantium* (dated 1927), in that volume, represents supremely. The *Byzantium* (dated 1930) of the succeding collection, *The Winding Stair* (1933), is also a fine poem, and it might appear at first sight to be of the same order; but, actually, comparison exposes a striking loss, and the organization is significantly less rich. And to this inferiority it seems reasonable to relate the large proportion of unsuccessful work—poems that, whatever they were for Yeats, are not poems for other readers: things in which the poet has handed over his job to Crazy Jane, and others in which allusiveness, oracular spareness, esoteric suggestion and familiar types of 'images' and symbols don't produce organization.

There is plenty of this kind of unsuccess in *Last Poems and Plays*. But what makes this volume painful reading is that in it which reminds one of a point about *Byzantium* not yet made. The inferiority of that poem relates to the absence from it of the positives between which the complex tension of *Sailing to Byzantium* is organized. There is, on the one hand, no 'sensual music'—

> The young
> In one another's arms, birds in the trees,
> —Those dying generations—at their song,
> The salmon-falls, the mackerel-crowded seas

—but instead:

> All mere complexities,
> The fury and the mire of human veins.

On the other hand, instead of the 'monuments of unaging intellect', which are felt as a positive presence in *Sailing to Byzantium*, we find the ironic potentialities implicit in 'artifice of eternity' developed into an intensity of bitterness and an agonized sense of frustrate impotence:

> At midnight on the Emperor's pavement flit
> Flames that no faggot feeds, nor steel has lit,
> Nor storm disturbs, flames begotten of flame,
> Where blood-begotten spirits come
> And all complexities of fury leave,
> Dying into a dance,
> An agony of trance,
> An agony of flame that cannot singe a sleeve.

> Astraddle on the dolphin's mire and blood,
> Spirit after spirit! The smithies break the flood,
> The golden smithies of the Emperor!
> Marbles of the dancing floor
> Break bitter furies of complexity,
> Those images that yet
> Fresh images beget,
> That dolphin-torn, that gong-tormented sea.

The bitterness prevails in *Last Poems and Plays*, and takes very unpleasant forms:

> You think it horrible that lust and rage
> Should dance attendance upon my old age;
> They were not such a plague when I was young:
> What else have I to spur me into song?—

There is enough in the book to give point to this comment of the poet's. And we don't need his own explicit prompting to make us ask whether the plight revealed, the terrible barrenness (see in particular the play *Purgatory*), hasn't some critical bearing on his best poetry:

> Those masterful images because complete
> Grew in pure mind, but out of what began?
> A mound of refuse or the sweepings of a street,
> Old kettles, old bottles, and a broken can,
> Old iron, old bones, old rags, that raving slut
> Who keeps the till. Now that my ladder's gone,
> I must lie down where all the ladders start,
> In the foul rag-and-bone shop of my heart.

Certainly 'masterful images' is appropriately suggestive in its application to the mature work, that on which Yeats's status as a major poet rests. The positives erected in it to support his 'ladder' may be said to be pride and an ideal aristocratic beauty, the two closely associated. Here, from *Last Poems and Plays*, is a characteristic image:

> ...Maud Gonne at Howth Station
> waiting a train,
> Pallas Athene in that straight back and arrogant head.

We can rarely forget the straight back and the arrogance in the late Yeats—the great Yeats—and the prevailing notes of the present volume make us remember what inseparable accompaniments scorn and bitterness always were of the positive attitudes. And even the sense of futility associated here with the quest of a strained perfection—

> 'Let the fools rage, I swerved in naught
> Something to perfection brought;'
> *But louder sang the ghost, 'What then?'*
> > (*Last Poems and Plays*, p. 18)

—was always there: we remember *I am worn out with dreams*, *The Collarbone of a Hare* and the rest. So there is an ironic pathos in that last stanza of *Among School Children* (in *The Tower*):

> Labour is blossoming or dancing where
> The body is not bruised to pleasure soul,
> Nor beauty born out of its own despair,
> Nor blear-eyed wisdom out of midnight oil.

> O chestnut tree, great rooted blossomer,
> Are you the leaf, the blossom or the bole?
> O body swayed to music, O brightening glance,
> How can we know the dancer from the dance?

The chestnut tree is a symbol for the fulness of life that is never to be found in Yeats's poetry and the suggestion of which is certainly not the attraction he offers. His heroic achievement—the development out of pre-Raphaelitism through the Celtic Twilight into a poetry quite clear of the Romantic 'poetical' tradition—will remain what it has been for us. The major quality and the element of greatness cannot be denied. But the sense of a heavy price paid and of power wasted and of results incommensurate with effort becomes stronger as we are able to look back and take stock. His pride and beauty, limited and qualified positives as they must in any case appear to us, are not there in any substantial creation. What he has to give us is an attitude, defined in a manner and an idiom.

The valuation I intend may be indicated by saying that he seems to me, while a major poet, to come below Donne, Marvell, Pope, Wordsworth, Byron, Hopkins and Eliot.

There are some interesting things, of course, in this last volume, but the only poem that I find to add to the number of the memorable is *Those Images* (p. 47). To end, however, with a reminder of one of the more admirable aspects of Yeats's pride, here is the final stanza of *The Municipal Gallery Revisited*:

> And here's John Synge himself, that rooted man,
> 'Forgetting human words,' a grave deep face.
> You that would judge me, do not judge alone
> This book or that, come to this hallowed place
> Where my friends' portraits hang and look thereon;
> Ireland's history in their lineaments trace;
> Think where man's glory most begins and ends,
> And say my glory was I had such friends.

PETULANT PEACOCK

W. H. MELLERS (1940)

Letters on Poetry, from W. B. Yeats to Dorothy Wellesley (O.U.P.)

There were, I believe, two dominant motives in Yeats's life as man and artist: a profound faith in Aristocracy, by which he meant the heroic passionate spirit as opposed to the (to him) contemptibly democratic world of 'clerks and schoolmasters'; and a concern for 'custom and ceremony', a social order in which artists believing in and living by that Aristocracy could find subsistence. He stood for these things because the Ireland in which he was nurtured preserved many of the aristocratic virtues of the eighteenth century; and he knew, with the pride and bitterness whence springs the ironic delicacy of poise which is his verse's peculiar distinction, that these virtues were, except in his poetry, doomed. In all that concerned these values—their preservation or destruction—his emotions were as flexible as they were strong, his intelligence as alert as it was magnificent. For the rest, he just wasn't interested: and this is why, his world incarnated in his verse from *The Green Helmet* to *The Winding Stair* and his account of the process of that incarnation completed in his *Autobiographies*, his work was consummated and there was nothing left for him but repetition. His other activities—the Abbey Theatre, his politics ('the seeming needs of my fool-driven land'), his occultism, even the words-and-music campaign which revived so vigorously during his last few years —were in the last resort no part of his world but the refuge of his disillusion.

If it were possible to look at life from the top of the Winding Stair, through the storm-battered ramparts of the Yeatsian Tower, one might see that there is some justification for his condemnation of—it looks like an inability to understand—most contemporary literature. One might see that 'the worst language is Elliot's [*sic*] in his early poems—a level flatness of rhythm,' that Eliot is 'an interesting symptom of a sick and melancholy age' who 'wrings the past dry and pours the juice down the throats of those who are either too busy or too creative to read as much as he does', if one did not reflect that this poet might be, not symptom, but purgative. One might, perhaps, consider Wilfred Owen ('all blood and dirt and sucked sugar stick') to be 'unworthy of the poets' corner of a country newspaper', and one might certainly find in Ezra Pound 'a single strained attitude instead of passion, the sexless American professor for all his violence', if one were willing to ignore the poetry in Owen's 'pity', the tragic implications behind (at his best) Pound's self-knowledge. No doubt, one could also understand why poets who shared certain metaphysical preoccupations seemed for that reason good poets, for it is not so much that Yeats is wrong as that he sees only so much as he wants to see. In so far as he was, and is, a great poet his blindness is of little consequence; but when the roots of that paradoxical austere fertility have begun to wither, it induces a kind of inert despondency to realize how little Yeats had to offer, in his last years, in place of the things he contumeliously abused. For instance, I think this is probably true:

When there is despair, public or private, when settled order seems lost, people look for strength within and without. Auden and Spender, all that seem the new movement, *look* for strength in Marxian socialism, or in Major Douglas; they want marching feet,

but is it very helpful to add:

The lasting expression of our time is not in this obvious choice but in a sense of something steel-like and cold within the will, something passionate and cold?

We have heard of this 'poem cold and passionate as the dawn' often before and in the Byzantium poems it meant something powerfully fine and compelling; but, as applied to his last work, can it be said to signify much except that he knew, but wouldn't admit, that it was time to give up the struggle? Now and again in these letters there is a glimpse of the old heroic fire:

One reason why these propagandists hate us is that we have ease and power. Your tum-ta-ti-tum is merely the dance music of the ages. They crawl and roll and wallow. You say that we must not hate. You are right, but we may, and sometimes must, be indignant and speak it. Hate is a kind of 'passive suffering' but indignation is a kind of joy...

I said when I started my movement in my 25th or 26th year, 'I am going to stiffen the backbone.' Bernard Shaw may have said the same in his youth; it has been stiffened in Ireland with results. I am an old man now and month by month my capacity and energy must slip away, so what is the use of saying that both in England and Ireland I want to stiffen the backbone of the high-hearted and high-minded and the sweet-hearted and sweet-minded, so that they may no longer shrink and hedge, when they face rag-merchants like —? Indeed before all I want to strengthen myself. It is not our business to reply to this and that but to set up our love and indignation against their pity and hate...

but even such passages, since they tell us nothing that the poetry and *Autobiographies* haven't said once and for all, have the ineffectual violence of bombs that explode at hazard long after their premeditated victims have taken refuge in their Anderson shelters.

When we reflect that the first part, at least, of the above quotation is directed merely against certain dolts, idiots, blockheads who had had the temerity to be mildly critical about the *Oxford Book of Modern Verse*, it seems that it wasn't only his poetry that, in these final years, came from 'rage and lust'. Outbursts of petty irascibility, coupled with a self-pity that is none the less morbid for being aggressively expressed, are acutely saddening when they come from a man who, being a great poet, would seem to have attained to wisdom and who, being also a national figure, had received all the honour and homage that the great, in these days, may reasonably hope for. But although this volume tells us little that we didn't know and a few things we'd rather, perhaps, not have known, it would be unfair to close on a carping note. There was a kind of gloomy nobility in the rigour with which, to the end of his days, Yeats lived for poetry, and his great qualities—those which made him a major poet and probably the last representative of the old European Aristocracy—will remain unassailable by war or time. However vast, heterogeneous and international our culture may become, the world is a smaller place for the loss of him, his ancestral houses, the peacock on the stair.

THE CASE OF MR POUND

F. R. LEAVIS (1933)

Active Anthology, edited by Ezra Pound (Faber and Faber)

Serious discussion of this book must address itself rather to the compiler than to the contents. For Ezra Pound, at any rate, is a seriously representative phenomenon. How is it that the author of *Hugh Selwyn Mauberley*, which is indubitably a great contemporary poem, can exhibit himself, in offering us a choice view of the significant contemporary developments in his art, as completely without critical intelligence or perception? *Active Anthology* does indeed contain Mr Eliot's *Fragment of a Prologue*; but one good poem does not make a bad anthology better, nor do two or even three.

The explanation will have to be a potent one, for it is impossible to suppose that the author of *Mauberley* is, as a critic, congenitally impotent. Explanation would seem to fall under two main heads. Both, however, come within the inclusive formula: Mr Pound was faced with doing for himself far more than even great genius can be fairly asked to do. In dedicating himself, as he so gallantly did, to English poetry at such a time and in such an environment, he might well find a certain truculence helpful and even necessary. He might pardonably cultivate the conviction that he, championing his cause and his talent in a world of deaf, malignant and obstructive fools, could never be wrong. The need for some sense of a congenial world, some kind of group solidarity, is irresistible, and he might be excused for choosing to associate with those who encouraged his belief in himself, even if it were by applauding and playing up to his more immature gestures and attitudes of self-encouragement.

A man who, being so placed, is also (and this is the second head) without an elementary apparatus of critical analysis, will be remarkable if he doesn't become to a damaging degree the slave of his confirmed immaturities and of his egotisms more and less subtle. It is no use pointing out to Mr Pound any of the fundamental weaknesses of his critical positions: he will not listen or look. Tell him what is wrong with his conception of technique—explain to him painstakingly, with simple illustrations, just how the inadequacies in analysis that are betrayed by his 'Melopoeia, Phanopoeia, Logopoeia' invalidate most of his subsequent critical offerings—and he will reply to the world at large that certain 'young academes' or 'assistant professors' carp pedantically at his lists of prescribed works or advocate the reading of books about books instead of (like Mr Pound) the reading of poetry. He will never take any notice of the essential points. He cannot; he has become as incapable of disinterested re-orientation as the 'bureaucrats' whom he scorns, and the adolescent audacities of the public antics (and private 'epistolary style') with which he thinks to prove the contrary are as boring and as monotonous as the 'bureaucratic' decorum.

The contents of this anthology corroborate in a desolating way the criticisms one had to make of *How To Read*. The inadequate conception of 'technique' goes with a readiness to take general intentions (if the intentions are such as Mr Pound approves of) for the achieved thing, however remote they may be from realization in particulars. This is the most charitable explanation of the inclusion, for instance, of so much nullity by Mr Louis Zukofsky. The less charitable explanation is that Mr Zukofsky is well known as an approved expositor of Mr Pound. Anyone, it seems, however green and tender or hardened in wordy illiteracy, can become an approved expositor of the *Cantos*. We may expect Mr Pound to find more poets whom he can expect to find interesting in ten years' time.

Further, Mr Pound's notions of good general intentions are both inadequate and out of date. There might, for instance, have been some show of point in presenting William Carlos Williams to the British public fifteen years ago. But it isn't the wordy debility of Georgianism that needs reacting against to-day. As for the inadequacies, they go with the inadequacy, exhibited in *How To Read*, of Mr Pound's notion of what a literature is.

Mr Pound is paid the compliment of this attention because of his past services to literature (not that one can expect from him any but the routine response) and because he looks like becoming a serious nuisance. The difficulty of making a public for modern poetry is desperate enough in any case, and Mr Pound's encouragement of the bogus will, now that the name of the *Cantos* is familiar to the Sunday papers, not tend to make things easier.

But the judgment of one who looks at the *Active Anthology* through bone-rimmed spectacles and over a stiff collar, preserving with academic fastidiousness the creases in his 'lecturer's pants' (see Mr MacLeish in the current *Hound and Horn*), won't worry Mr Pound.

MR POUND'S PROPERTIUS

JOHN SPEIRS (1935)

Homage to Sextus Propertius, by Ezra Pound (Faber and Faber)

It is tempting, and also instructive, to compare Mr Pound's *Propertius* with the original Propertius, but it must be emphasized that it is to *Mauberley* rather than to the Latin verse of Propertius that Mr Pound's *Propertius* is related. Interesting affinities may, perhaps, be detected between the Latin poet and the English poet. A good deal of Propertius (there seems reason to believe) was as much 'translation' from the Greek of Callimachus as Mr Pound's *Propertius* is from Propertius. Only a small proportion of Callimachus has been preserved; but the three poets appear to have this quality as least in common that they are, in a sense I shall return to, 'late'—the Latin poet 'late' in his civilization, our contemporary in his. Nevertheless, it remains the case that the reader who seems to 'appreciate' the Latin will not necessarily appreciate Mr Pound; whereas the reader who already appreciates *Mauberley* will at once appreciate also the *Propertius*. The latter reader is, probably, the 'instructed' reader whom Mr Eliot implies in his Introduction to his selection from which he omits the *Propertius*—'If the uninstructed reader is not a classical scholar, he will make nothing of it; if he be a classical scholar, he will wonder why this does not conform to his notions of what translation should be.' It should be added that nothing in this Introduction sheds so much light on the *Propertius* as certain things in the three essays which appeared as the pamphlet *Homage to John Dryden*. The *Propertius* (though it will only now become generally accessible) first appeared as early as 1918. The three essays belong to 1921 and 1922, so that it is reasonable to assume that Mr Eliot was familiar with the *Propertius* when he wrote them. More significant is the fact that *Mauberley* first appeared in 1920, two years after the *Propertius*.

There is, in addition, the earlier verse and there are, since the *Propertius* and *Mauberley*, the *Cantos*. This is not the place for a detailed consideration of the relative merits of these. I can only testify, here, that the earlier verse and, in spite of Mr Eliot's enthusiasm for them, the greater part of the *Cantos* seem to me very inferior verse in comparison with the *Propertius* and *Mauberley*; and in this I find myself still in agreement with Mr Leavis's judgment in *New Bearings* and also, to this extent, with Mr Blackmur's in the *Hound and Horn* (Jan.–March, 1934). The idea has, however, got about (I think Mr Eliot's Introduction is partly responsible for it) that even if the *Cantos* are in certain respects deficient the younger men may learn an enormous amount from a close study of the versification. But it is precisely because I seldom find in the *Cantos* (in spite of the labour which has obviously been expended on the versification) anything like the varied metrical subtlety I find in the *Propertius* and, especially, *Mauberley* that I find the *Cantos* deficient by comparison. It seems to me, therefore, that it is from the *Propertius* and *Mauberley* rather than from the *Cantos* that whatever of value may be learned from Mr Pound will be learned, and that this is as much as to say that they are the better poems.

It is at this point that I am forced to record a disagreement with Mr Blackmur, the more reluctantly as he was one of the first in America to recognize Mr Eliot and to give good reasons for that recognition. He says (in the article to which I have referred):

For Mr Pound is at his best a maker of great verse rather than a great poet. When you look into him, deeply as you can, you will not find any extraordinary revelation of life, nor any bottomless fund of feeling; nor will you find any mode of life formulated, any collection of established feelings, composed or mastered in new form.

Mr Blackmur agrees that Mr Pound is 'at his best' in the *Propertius* and in *Mauberley*. He agrees also that they are 'great verse'. That 'great verse' seems to me itself the most reliable evidence there can be of the presence of those things which Mr Blackmur, in the passage quoted, says are absent. The 'verse' seems to me 'great' as the result of a pressure of experience against it which it composes and the *Propertius* and *Mauberley* therefore 'great poetry' because 'great verse'.

I cannot, either, accept Mr Blackmur's preference of the *Propertius* to *Mauberley*—

The first [*Mauberley*] is Mr Pound's most nearly, in the ordinary sense, 'original' work, and the second [the *Propertius*] as a translation, the least. The reverse ascriptions are in fact more accurate; and the paradox is verbal not substantial. The substance of *Mauberley*, what it is about, is commonplace, but what the translator has contributed to *Propertius* is his finest personal work.

The *Propertius* and *Mauberley* seem to me to be great in the same kind of way. But because *Mauberley* seems to me to possess in greater degree what the *Propertius* also possesses I consider it the greater poem.

When Mr Eliot said of *Mauberley*, 'It is compact of the experience of a certain man in a certain place at a certain time; and it is also a document of an epoch; it is genuine tragedy and comedy; and it is, in the best sense of Arnold's phrase, a "criticism of life",' he said something which could be said to a lesser extent also of the *Propertius* but which, as Mr Leavis pointed out, could scarcely be said of the earlier verse or of the *Cantos*.

There remains to reinforce these opinions by some more particular consideration of the *Propertius* itself. The sophistication of the verse here is no surface thing. It indicates the deeper sophistication of one who is 'expert from experience'—centuries of experience. A critical self-knowledge is his reward:

> For I am swelled up with inane pleasurabilities
> > and deceived by your reference
> To things which you think I would like to believe

is, of course, said ironically. The constant 'inspection' of his experience is indicated, also, by the frequent employment of non-emotive words.

This is what I meant when I called Mr Pound 'late'. The urbanity of tone belongs to one who is exceedingly (I would not say excessively) civilized. A sense that the experience he is temporarily concerned with is relative to the sum of experience and is not absolute, a sense of proportion, a poise, proceeds from this 'lateness', this sense of centuries of experience. In No. VII, for example, where there is a tendency to passionate excess, the balance is redressed first by the suggestion of satiety, then more particularly by the phrase

> such at least is the story.

There follow magnificent lines, the theme completely traditional, Epicurean, and the poem ends—

> God am I, for the time

—the final emphasis on 'for the time'. No. IX is again completely traditional in theme, and ought on that account to be readily appreciated: also it opens with canorous splendour:[1] it continues—

> I shall live, if she continue in life.
> > If she dies, I shall go with her.
> Great Zeus, save the woman,
> > Or she will sit before your feet in a veil, and tell out the long
> > list of her troubles.

---

[1] 'For the nobleness of the populace brooks nothing below its own altitude. One must have resonance, resonance and sonority...like a goose.' (No. XII)

The intensity of concern in these lines is not mitigated because controlled by the apparent levity of the last two. The poem continues—

> Persephone and Dis, Dis, have mercy upon her,
> There are enough women in hell, quite enough beautiful women
> Iope, and Tyro, and Pasiphae, and the formal girls of Achaia,
> And out of Troad, and from the Campania,
> Death has its tooth in the lot.

These lines have behind them not only Latin poetry (and Greek) but also Provençal poetry and Villon. What transforms the traditional theme, gives it a new body of strength, is that 'hell' and, more especially, the colloquialism at the end.

But this balance between the formal and the informal, between conventional elegance and conversational ease, is not merely a matter of the insertion of contemporary colloquialisms. The diction includes, for example, the 'scientific' Latinisms 'torridity' and 'canicular' (No. VIII).

> The time is come, the air heaves in torridity,
> The dry earth pants against the canicular heat.

It is, rather, a freedom from Poetic Diction which allows of this wide range of selection. The result is that a total variety (and also a complexity) of mood finds its expression, and this is what is pointed to not only by the variety of the diction but by the variety also of the versification (contrast the comparatively monotonous versification of the *Cantos*). The mood modulates between the tragic and the comic. There is broad comedy, broadening in places to farce, in No. IV:

> Damp woolly handkerchiefs were stuffed into her undryable eyes.
> And a querulous noise responded to our solicitous reprobations.

Cynthia's supposed abuse of her rival follows:

> 'She twiddles the spiked wheel of a rhombus,
> She stews puffed frogs, snake's bones, the moulted feathers of screech owls,
> She binds me with ravvles of shrouds.
> Black spiders spin in her bed!
> Let her lovers snore at her in the morning!
> May the gout cramp up her feet!
> Does he like me to sleep here alone, Lygdamus?
> Will he say nasty things at my funeral?'

The poem ends with an ironical comment. In No. X there is again broad comedy. The poet is drunk and loses his way.

'And she has been waiting for the scoundrel
> and in a new Sidonian night cap,
And with more than Arabian odours,
> god knows where he has been.'

He arrives in the early morning instead, curious to know if Cynthia has been faithful or not—'And Cynthia was alone in her bed'—

'You are a very early inspector of mistresses.
Do you think I have adopted your habits?'

I need not labour the contrast between these and any earlier quotations.

Before passing finally to indicate what seem to me the more significant Numbers I ought to stress the element of 'mockery' in Mr Pound's *Propertius* (whether or not, as Mr Eliot thinks, it is present also in the Latin Propertius) for it, perhaps, has its significance in relation to them. It is markedly present in the earlier part of No. XII.

Who, who will be the next man to entrust his girl to a friend?
Love interferes with fidelities;
The gods have brought shame on their relatives;
Each man wants the pomegranate for himself.

It comes (it will be noted) from a knowledge of human—and Divine—weakness. The Olympians are not exempt (No. VIII):

Was Venus exacerbated by the existence of a comparable equal?
Is the ornamental goddess full of envy?
Have you contempted Juno's Pelasgian temples,
Have you denied Pallas good eyes?

nor the heroes from disrespect (No. XII):

and there was a case in Colchis, Jason and that woman in Colchis.

But because no one is without weakness there is a certain tolerance. The poet is disillusioned enough to expect the worst, even of his friend Lynceus, and is therefore not annoyed, or ever surprised, when he finds it. The mockery of Lynceus (No. XII) is playful rather than serious; there is at any rate no question of the termination of the friendship as the result of what has happened. The poet can say also of his mistress (No. XI):

All things are forgiven for one night of your games...
Though you walk in the Via Sacra, with a peacock's tail for a fan.

Numbers I, II, V, VI, XII seem to me the more personal Numbers, in the sense not that they are the less, but the more, significant Numbers.

In these the interests are recognizable, beneath the disguises, as substantially those of *Mauberley*. The poetry seems to derive (as Mr Leavis remarks of *Mauberley*) from a 'recognition of bankruptcy, of a devoted life summed up in futility'. The poet cannot believe in the 'importance' of 'Caesar's affairs', War (the poem was written during the War) and Empire, the things which seem most 'important' and are, of course, not.

(No. I)   Annalists will continue to record Roman reputations,
Celebrities from the Trans-Caucasus will belaud Roman
      celebrities
And expound the distentions of Empire,
But for something to read in normal circumstances?
For a few pages brought down from the forked hill unsullied?
    I ask a wreath which will not crush my head.

(No. II)   Alba, your kings, and the realm your folk have constructed
      with such industry
Shall be yawned out on my lyre—with such industry

(No. V)   And I shall follow the camp, I shall be duly celebrated for
      singing the affairs of your cavalry.

But in spite of the best of intentions, he is in fact not equal, he says, to the 'heroic' (No. II):

And Phoebus looking upon me from the Castalian tree,
Said then 'You idiot! What are you doing with that water;
Who has ordered a book about heroes?
    You need, Propertius, not think
About acquiring that sort of a reputation.'

'Caesar's affairs' and 'everything else of importance' are weighed down in the balance by 'a girl'—'I also shall sing war when this matter of a girl is exhausted.'

(No. V)   Neither Calliope nor Apollo sung these things into my ear,
      My genius is no more than a girl.
If she with ivory fingers drive a tune through the lyre,
      We look at the process
How easy the moving fingers; if hair is mussed on her forehead,
If she goes in a gleam of Cos, in a slither of dyed stuff,
There is a volume in the matter; if her eyelids sink into sleep,
There are new jobs for the author,
And if she plays with me with her shirt off,
      We shall construct many Iliads.
And whatever she does or says
      We shall spin long yarns out of nothing.

He continues, later in the same Number:

> I should remember Caesar's affairs . . . for a background,
> Although Callimachus did without them, and without Theseus,
> Without an inferno.

It amuses him (No. XII) that

> Of all these young women
>   not one has enquired the cause of the world,
> Nor the modus of lunar eclipses
>   Nor whether there be any patch left of us
> After we cross the infernal ripples,
>   nor if the thunder fall from predestination;
> Nor anything else of importance.

The deepest thing in the *Propertius* is this sense of emptiness, of there being nothing whatever left after one has 'looked into the matter'. It is related to the poet's sense of personal failure:

> (No. VI) Nor at my funeral either will there be any long trail, bearing
>   ancestral lares and images;
> No trumpets filled with my emptiness,
> Nor shall it be on an Atalic bed;
>   The perfumed cloths shall be absent.
> A small plebeian procession.

> (No. XII) And behold me, small fortune left in my house.
>   Me, who had no general for a grandfather!
>   I shall triumph among young ladies of indeterminate character,
>   My talent acclaimed in their banquets,
>   I shall be honoured with yesterday's wreaths.

Beneath the surface trifling and frivolity of the poem there is an agonized sense of tragic waste.

It remains only to say that, in my judgment, the *Propertius* will hereafter be recognized along with *Mauberley* and, therefore, along also with the poetry of Mr Eliot and the later poetry of Mr Yeats as one of the few remarkable poetic achievements of the time.

4

POST-ELIOT POETS REVIEWED

WILLIAM EMPSON'S VERSE

H. A. MASON (1935)

Poems, by William Empson (Chatto & Windus)

Publishers in recent years have been generous towards poets. The young aspirant has hardly finished his apprenticeship before he is encouraged to come before the public with a collection of poems. It has been peculiarly exasperating that the work of one of the most interesting of contemporary poets has remained hidden in the comparative obscurity of the 1928 files of the *Cambridge Review* and in undergraduate journals of that period now extinct. Messrs Chatto & Windus have done the public a service in making these poems generally accessible. It is now possible to see on what evidence the general high estimate rests. We have the greater part of these earlier poems revised and polished, together with those written more recently.

Great things have been said of Mr Empson. The dust-cover reminds one that in *New Bearings* he was singled out with one other as the most promising of the younger writers. And in that painfully condensed work he received the most convincing account of his importance that the present reviewer has seen. One can only repeat and paraphrase what is said once and for all in *New Bearings*. But the present volume enables us to state that the number of poems which justify his high reputation is extremely small and almost wholly confined to poems written before 1929. The lesser poems throw light on the successes and reveal the bent which seems to have prevented any further development on the lines of the early good poems.

Not many poems reach the level of *To An Old Lady*. It is a triumph of tone; the subtle sharp fluctuations are impelled on the reader; one is driven breathlessly to respond to the rapid changes of attitude, to bring together the ideas brought from such different spheres. The mental play of resolution, combination and comparison calls for the alertest reading. But the attention required for this and the other good poems is not that of the crossword order. The allusions to unfamiliar bits of knowledge are rare and not essential. What is required is a general sensitiveness and a willingness to open our minds to combinations of thoughts and feelings which would not occur to the ordinary person. It is, in short, the attention demanded by the poetry of Wit. In *Arachne* we come nearest to the traditional sources. Man, 'twixt devil and deep sea',

> King spider, walks the velvet roof of streams:
> Must bird and fish, must god and beast avoid:
> Dance, like nine angels, on pin-point extremes.

The 'surface tension' idea is developed organically out of this. It is used to give biting point to the personal ending of the poem.

> We two suffice. But oh beware, whose vain
> Hydroptic soap my meagre water saves.

Such mastery over technique is extraordinary. What Mr Eliot said of the Metaphysicals on the closeness of feeling and thought could well be repeated here. Whether this is the main stream of tradition in poetry may yet be questioned; the merit of these poems can be shown without elaborate argument by placing them alongside any fair selection of contemporary verse. They have a strongly personal stamp, an independent rhythm.

The characteristics familiar to us from seventeenth century verse —the involved syntax, following the thought in all its windings, the levity enforcing seriousness, the sparse 'Shakespearean' use of language —are combined in the little handful of poems the nucleus of which appeared in *Cambridge Poetry*. What the rest of the book provides is these elements in disassociation. There is the pleasing mockery of *Rolling The Lawn* and the neat *Invitation to Juno*. Such experiments are well worth making. What is disquieting is the great number of poems (especially the later ones) in which neither tone nor rhythm are present. *Sea Voyage* and *High Dive*, for instance, contain a surprising number of ideas brought together, but brought together, it seems, only to show that it could be done. With each new turn of thought the poem—the words—does not leap but drones dully on. *Bacchus* (first published, presumably, in 1933), when compared with *Arachne*, gives the lie to any suggestion of development. What seems lacking in the poem is the 'rich and strongly characteristic life' so noticeable in the earlier poem.

The general fault noticed here (pleasure in subtlety for its own sake) can coexist with vigorous poetic activity. (One might compare the occasional outburst of the same interest in *Seven Types of Ambiguity*.) But when the output is so small the effect is likely to be to render the talent sterile. For lack of material to exercise the technique on, the poet's main interest has become the technique itself in so far as it concerns the manipulation of ideas, the knotting of varied strands of learning, and the playing with word sequences and puns. Let us hope that he will strike a field worthy of his resources. Meanwhile the volume provides us with the material to understand what it is to be a modern poet; how to avoid the wrong kind of imitation; examples of striking success; the exhibition of a fine intelligence applied and misapplied.

MR AUDEN'S TALENT

F. R. LEAVIS (1936)

Look, Stranger! Poems by W. H. Auden (Faber and Faber)
The Ascent of F. 6, by W. H. Auden and Christopher Isherwood (Faber and Faber)

'Since the publication of *Poems* in 1930, which immediately marked the author as a leader of a new school of poetry that has since established itself...' Mr Auden (one may go on, while questioning whether a school that springs up as immediately as the publisher reports is properly to be described as a 'school of poetry') has certainly been a significant and representative figure, a figure to watch. One has watched him for signs of development. His talent was indubitable; one has waited for him to begin to do something with it. Those who open *Look, Stranger!* in hope will be once again disappointed—which doesn't make him the less significant and representative.

The talent, an impressive one, is apparent here in the familiar ways. There are those striking and so characteristic phrases and images. For he certainly has a gift for words; he delights in them and they come. He continues, in a way that would be very promising in a young poet, to be happily in love with expression. But Mr Auden cannot now be far short of thirty, and he is still without that with which a poet controls words, commands expression, writes poems. He has no organization. He hasn't, at any rate, the organization corresponding to his local vitality, to the distinction of his phrasing and imagery at their best. This lack comes out very obviously, as before, in an embarrassing uncertainty of tone and poise, an uncertainty not the less radical and disquieting for his tendency to make a virtue of it. He no doubt knows that he is writing doggerel in XVIII. But he does the same kind of thing in pieces that beyond any doubt ask to be taken seriously—as seriously as anything he offers asks to be taken.

He is, of course, a satirist, and we know that there is such a thing as irony. But his irony is not the irony of the mature mind—it is self-defensive, self-indulgent or merely irresponsible; and his satire is fairly represented by his imitation of Burns (XIV):

> Because you saw but were not indignant
> The invasion of the great malignant
> Cambridge ulcer
> The army intellectual
> Of every kind of liberal
> Smarmy with friendship but of all
> There are none falser.
>
> A host of columbines and pathics
> Who show the poor by mathematics
> In their defence
> That wealth and poverty are merely
> Mental pictures, so that clearly
> Every tramp's a landlord really
> In mind-events.

—Those stanzas might, by themselves, be serious (and they are certainly popular among Cambridge undergraduates). But (not to mention what goes before) they are followed by:

> Let fever sweat them till they tremble
> Cramp rack their limbs till they resemble
> Cartoons by Goya:
> Their daughters sterile be in rut,
> May cancer rot their herring gut,
> The circular madness on them shut,
> Or paranoia.

Mr Auden's irony, in fact, is a matter of his being uncertain whether he is engaged mainly in expressing *saeva indignatio* or in amusing himself and his friends. And there is habitually in him a similar uncertainty.

It is significant that he should in this book borrow the show of a mature poise here from Burns and there from Yeats—see, for instance, III and XXIV. (There are other curious literary reminiscences; among them—though this doesn't illustrate the immediate point—an elaborate echo, in VII, of those sestines from *Arcadia* that Mr Empson quotes in *Ambiguity*.) Since so much of his emotional material and his poetic aura, glamorous or sinister, comes fairly directly from childhood and schooldays, the borrowing can hardly have any other effect on us than that of implicit self-diagnosis. For Mr Auden still makes far too much of his poetry out of private neuroses and memories—still uses these in an essentially immature way. He has, of course, his social preoccupation, and he still habitually makes his far too easy transitions between his private and his public world:

> And since our desire cannot take that route which is straightest,
> Let us choose the crooked, so implicating these acres
> These millions in whom already the wish to be one
>> Like a burglar is stealthily moving,
>> That these, on the new façade of a bank
>> Employed, or conferring at a health resort,
>> May, by circumstances linked,
>> More clearly act our thought.

The sinister glamour that so often attends his premonitory surveys of the social scene is transferred too directly and too obviously from the nameless terrors of childhood or their neurotic equivalent.

But is what is implied here more properly to be called a public world or a private?—

> The Priory clock chimes briefly and I recollect
> I am expected to return alive
> My will effective and my nerves in order
>> To my situation.
> 'The poetry is in the pity,' Wilfred said,
> And Kathy in her journal, 'To be rooted in life,
>> That's what I want.'

'Wilfred', it would seem, is Wilfred Owen, and 'Kathy' Katherine Mansfield. It is a significant habit that is betrayed in this mode of referring to them.

For corroboration of the surmise that the habits of the group world are intimately associated with the failure of Mr Auden's talent to mature we have the new play that he has written with Christopher Isherwood. The talent, the striking gift of expression, appears in the opening soliloquy of Michael Ransom, and here and there in other places. But more generally it is Mr Eliot's gifts that we are aware of, for the play is heavily parasitic upon both the Eliot of *Sweeney Agonistes* and the Eliot of the Choruses. But the hero, Michael Ransom, is not one who can be brought into any comfortable relation with any manner of Mr Eliot's. Ransom says ('*smiling*') to one of his group (the dialogue is in the authors' own style): 'You haven't changed much have you, Ian, since you were head Prefect and Captain of the First Fifteen?' Ian might have retorted in much the same formula. They have none of them, in fact, in Ransom's group, changed much since they were at school—at their Public School. And it is clearly assumed that the audience will not have changed much either. For we are unmistakably expected to feel towards the school hero (the school, of course, being of the class in which mountaineering is a normal interest) the respect and awe felt by his school-fellow followers. How seriously we are to take him we may gather from the Abbot of the Great Glacier who, offering him a place in the Monastery as one of the élite of the earth (Ransom has studied the Book of the Dead), speaks of 'your powers and your intelligence'.

But powers and intelligence cannot be injected into the drama by the mystico-psychological hocus-pocus of the Monastery and of the death-scene. There can be no significance in the drama that is not active in the dramatist's words. Well, the realistic dialogue of *The Ascent of F.6* is simply and unironically Public School, and for the lift into verse we have:

> I have no purpose but to see you happy,
> And do you find that so remarkable?
> What mother could deny it and be honest?
> .   .   .   .
>
> May not a mother come at once to bring
> Her only gift, her love? When the news came
> I was in bed, for lately
> I've not been very well. But what's a headache
> When I can stand beside my son and see him
> In the hour of his triumph?

That is the Tennysonian pathetic.[1] And Ransom at the moment of high tragic realization breaks into the solemn Shakespearian parody of this:

> O senseless hurricanes,
> That waste yourselves upon the unvexed rock,
> Find some employment proper to your powers,
> Press on the neck of Man your murdering thumbs
> And earn real gratitude! Astrologers,
> Can you not scold the fated loitering star
> To run to its collision and our end?
> The Church and Chapel can agree in this,
> The vagrant and the widow mumble for it
> And those with millions belch their heavy prayers
> To take away this luggage. Let the ape buy it

[1] Cf.

> I would you had a son!
> It might be easier then for you to make
> Allowance for a mother—her—who comes
> To rob you of your one delight on earth.
> How often has my sick boy yearned for this!
> I have put him off as often; but to-day
> I dared not—so much weaker, so much worse
> For last day's journey.
> Or the insipid hen. Is Death so busy
> That we must fidget in a draughty world

> That's stale and tasteless; must we still kick our heels
> And wait for his obsequious secretaries
> To page Mankind at last and lead him
> To the distinguished Presence?

It was necessary, in order to make the point, to suggest effectively both the pretensions and the kind of badness of this play. That kind of badness, when a writer of Mr Auden's gifts is led into it, implies not only a complete absence of exposure to criticism, but also a confident awareness of an encouraging audience. In other words, the present is the time when the young talent needs as never before the support of the group, and when the group can, as never before, escape all contact with serious critical standards. In such a time it often seems a hopeless undertaking to promote by criticism the needed critical stir.

F. R. LEAVIS (1940)

Another Time, by W. H. Auden (Faber and Faber)

One of the three parts into which this book is divided is entitled 'Lighter Poems', but it is not in that part that Mr Auden puts his poem on Edward Lear—along with his poem, this one diagnostic, on A. E. Housman (Mr Auden has seen through Housman, who

> Kept tears like dirty postcards in a drawer).

The 'Lighter Poems' should have been kept for private circulation—if for any; for it took no talent to write them and they exhibit a pointless unpleasantness (see notably 'Miss Gee'). Here Mr Auden is still adolescent. Of the rest of the book one has to say that, though the grosser crudities are less obvious than they used to be, he has nothing more like maturity to offer than before (though an exception might be urged in favour of one or two things, e.g. XXXI and 'September 1st, 1939'). The talent is apparent enough, and the inability to organize— to write a poem —equally so. There is the same vigorous mannerism of phrase and the same inability to command an intention capable of justifying the show of vigour. Mr Auden's technique is not one that solves problems; it conceals a failure to grapple with them, or, rather, makes a virtue out of the failure. He has made a technique out of irresponsibility, and his most serious work exhibits a shameless opportunism in the passage from phrase to phrase and from item to item—the use of a kind of bluff.

That poised knowledgeableness, that impressive command of the modern scene, points to the conditions in which his promise has lost itself. We must still feel that he ought to have been a poet, but the possibility of development looks very frail. Perhaps, however, he is more unequivocally conscious of his immaturity than before.

AUDEN'S INVERTED DEVELOPMENT

R. G. LIENHARDT (1945)

For the Time Being, by W. H. Auden (Faber and Faber)

It is becoming apparent that any claim to poetic importance which Auden may have in the future will rest upon effects produced almost casually in his early work. His experiments have been immensely more promising than his achievement, and the fact that his poetry has not profited by them rather indicates that his efforts have not been directed towards improving his poetry, but towards something at the best extraneous to it, and at the worst extremely damaging. It has become increasingly obvious with each new publication that this poet's greatest difficulty lies in determining quite what he wishes to express and in formulating an appropriate attitude towards it, and that, at any time, his equipment for dealing with his matter, in a technical sense, is vastly in excess of what is required. The correct answer to this problem, for Auden, would have been to admit to himself that he could range safely only in a limited field, and to confine himself to saying the comparatively little that he could say personally, and to reduce and refine his effects to the minimum necessary for complete individual expression. Instead of this, he has attempted to assimilate more and more general ideas, to write verse based upon human experience quite outside his individual scope, and hence to write at second hand. His technical facility has been lavished upon the expression of sentimental regrets, boyish fantasies and unbalanced, immature enthusiasms. Few poets can have started writing with such superficial promise of accomplishment, have developed so completely their early weaknesses, and shelved so definitely their early strength. One is thus forced to the conclusion that Auden has occasionally written a few lines worth preserving as a by-product of his conscious application to his task—a view which is supported by a glance through his work. For only such a series of casual successes will explain the absence of any single, successful poem, and yet the appearance throughout of occasional successful passages. Further, it will be noted that those qualities which make for success remain undeveloped throughout—that the better parts of his later work are not an advance on the better parts of his earlier work, whereas his faults develop in a predictable way and connect quite simply with weaknesses already revealed. He has thus undergone an inverted process of development, natural enough in a poet impervious to criticism from outside the group which formed his ideal public, and which existed on a basis of mutual admiration which a more independent poet would have found an embarrassment.

Reading *Paid on Both Sides*, one becomes aware of moral issues suggested but not fully defined or worked out in the poetry—there is a residue which one feels one has not quite grasped, a meaning beyond the literal meaning of the words on the page, suggested, but persistently elusive. Images come to have enormous symbolical significance, an action appears to be in progress between protagonists of immense importance.

> O how shall man live
> Whose thought is born, child of one farcical night,
> To find him old? The body warm but not
> By choice, he dreams of folk in dancing bunches,
> Of tart wine spilt on home-made benches,
> Where learns, one drawn apart, a secret will
> Restore the dead; but comes thence to a wall.
> Outside on frozen soil lie armies killed
> Who seem familiar, but they are cold.

Here there appear to be possibilities; a situation is partly realized in an urgent and supple idiom, and there appears to be a reserve of meaning which might eventually make itself apparent. But as one reads on one discovers that the qualified success of this and later poems depends upon ambiguity—that when a point is reached at which a definite formulation of an attitude or an issue is made, one is confronted with a shallow commonplace, something vaguely defined in terms of 'love', 'beauty' or 'good'. Just as throughout his work the indefinite evil forces, to which he seems extremely sensitive, resolve themselves into nothing more than a succession of images of disease, sterility or cruelty, so his positive values are the merest indications of conventional virtues. In fact, there is no imaginative life whatsoever in Auden's treatment of moral conflict, and it is a verbal fluency, incorporating a number of effectively juxtaposed images, appearing to make a general impression by putting together a number of smaller impressions united at the most by compatible moods, which gives a specious vitality to much of his earlier work. He is consequently at his weakest when he is most explicit, when the suggestiveness of his language has to give way to a bald statement. Then the alarming paucity of idea beneath the surface of his impressionistic facility reveals itself, and in his yearning for

> New styles of architecture, a change of heart

one realizes that Auden is attempting to diagnose the spiritual malady of an age with the experiential equipment of the man in the street. Again, it becomes more and more obvious throughout Auden's work that his morbidity and disillusion, which have always the insecurity of pose, are in fact nothing more than a fashionable accretion, perhaps

unconscious and unavoidable, and that fundamentally he is committed
to an easy materialistic optimism, that somewhere and somehow agents
for good are at work, though what the 'good' is and how these indefinite
virtuous ends are to be achieved is more than he can tell us. We know
that 'It is time for the destruction of error', but after the inevitable,
and sometimes effective, sequence of related images which follow that
announcement in the poem from which it is extracted, all we discover
is that the 'death of the old gang' is a necessary preliminary, and that
after

> The old gang to be forgotten in the spring,
> The hard bitch and the riding master,
> Stiff underground...

we may see

> deep in a clear lake
> The lolling bridegroom, beautiful, there.

What success this has depends upon its lack of explicitness, and it is
therefore not surprising that *For the Time Being*, which is in places the
most explicit work he has produced yet, if in places the most ambiguous,
should also be much the least satisfactory.

For the Time Being consists of two compositions of indeterminate
genre, with a persistent suggestion of having been adapted for broad-
casting. The first, called 'The Sea and the Mirror', is an attempted
extension of *The Tempest* into regions more uncertainly defined, both
geographically and philosophically, than Prospero's island. The second
is the title-piece of the whole and is described as 'A Christmas Oratorio'.
Both are dramatized and have prose inserts of considerable length, in
which the essentials of the situation being treated are discussed very
tediously with the audience. Here, much of the poet's intention, already
apparent from the verse, is unnecessarily emphasized, and much that
remained obscure in the verse is presented with no added clarity in
laboured and ungainly prose. In both works he indulges his increasing
taste for general philosophical propositions, concerns himself with
much deeper issues than he is at all competent to do justice to, and
becomes involved in a complex of ideas which he has neither the
intellectual sweep nor the emotional integrity to assimilate as a poet.
The first poem is much the less explicit of the two, and is accordingly
the more successful; but here the allegorical figures have such a wide
possible field of reference, and the indication of any definite level
at which the poem is to be understood as a whole is so vague,
that the whole point of allegory is lost, the meaning too dependent
on individual construction. (A reviewer in one of the literary weeklies, for example, connected Prospero with Democracy.) Instead of
working out his general ideas in particular and concrete terms
throughout the poem, so that the interplay of concepts and qualities

becomes something accessible to the mind and feelings at once, the poet provides his familiar association of images amd metaphors, but with no suggestion of any coherent imaginative scheme for the whole. In consequence, there is a superficial suggestion throughout that some impressive action is being worked out, but on closer examination the significance of it evaporates, and one is left with the theme of the resolution of the duality of Ariel and Caliban, with other characters from the *The Tempest* who may mean this, that or the other according to the general construction which the reader puts on the main theme. There are occasional passages of pleasant imagery which excite no complaint, unless it be that even here Auden's rhythms are becoming flaccid and his language more reflective than active. Above all, there is a persistent inflated manner which one can trace back without difficulty to earlier work in which the poet permitted himself to preach too unguardedly. Compare, for example:

> Greed showing shamelessly her naked money,
> And all love's wandering eloquence debased
> To a collector's slang, Smartness in furs,
> And Beauty scratching miserably for food...

with his more recent

> O blessed be bleak exposure on whose sword
> Caught unawares, we prick ourselves alive!
> Shake Failure's bruising fist...

There can be few clearer signs of lack of poetic vitality than these automatically produced catalogues of abstract qualities, all doing something conventionally appropriate or with conventionally suitable attributes, but no more vivid or disturbing than if they had remained in the dictionary. At the best, they are dull; at the worst, they are absurd, as when the Star of the Nativity in the second poem invites one to

> Hear tortured Horror roaring for a Bride...

The habit of using capital letters for emphasis, where true emphasis would be achieved by a well-managed sentence construction and rhythm, is one which has grown on Auden. It results not infrequently in an appearance of extraordinary pretentiousness, emphasized by the complete flatness of the straightforward, unambiguous statement, as in the following:

> Sin fractures the Vision, not the Fact; for
> The exceptional is always usual
> And the Usual exceptional.
> To choose what is difficult all one's days
> As if it were easy, that is faith...

'A Christmas Oratorio', from which the last quotation comes, is an example of how bad Auden can be when it comes to treatment of clearly defined moral issues—in this case the theme of the Nativity, with comments by a Narrator who is, presumably, the detached observer of the action, pointing the moral but by no means adorning the tale. There is no place here to quote examples of his lapses of taste, his lack of proportion which makes him self-important when he wishes to be serious, frivolous or even nasty when he wants to be witty. His values, uncertain and unsystematized, represent nothing appreciably solid or coherent. This subject, if it is to be treated tolerably, demands either genuine simplicity or genuine sophistication in the artist. The poet who writes at one end of the scale

> Come to our well-run desert
> Where anguish arrives by cable
> And the deadly sins may be bought in tins
> With instructions on the label...

and at the other

> He is the Way.
> Follow him through the Land of Unlikeness;
> You will see rare beasts, and have unique adventures

has neither qualification. For it is in just that irresponsible spirit, of undefined but 'unique' adventure, that he approaches his material—the Nativity, *The Tempest*, the Oedipus legend in 'The Ascent of F. 6'.

That Auden started his career with apparently unusual gifts cannot be denied; and even this volume displays, in places, snatches of his old accomplishment. But it has no chance when set against his determination to write on a grand scale with the mental equipment only of a minor poet. If his seriousness of purpose were part of his nature instead of yet another, if unconscious, attitude, his tendency to the cheap, commonplace and exhibitionistic might not persist. But it is clear from this volume that his separation from the circle in which that tendency was formed came too late to enable him to discard his public character and see what values of his own he could substitute for those of the group which made his reputation.

THE LATEST AUDEN

R. MAYHEAD (1952)

Nones, by W. H. Auden (Faber and Faber)

'Mr Auden's readers', the dust-jacket informs us, 'know him as an intellectual poet whose technical resourcefulness is always equal to the ceaseless development of his mind and sensibility; a poet who never arrests his progress or repeats himself...' That might seem to be a challenge to those people who have from time to time had occasion to declare their disappointment at the stasis, the failure in fulfilment, of a poet who, amidst an arid literary scene, appeared in his early work to have the virtues of intelligence and vigour and a real, if at times irresponsible, feeling for language. A failure of growth, an absence of anticipated soundness and maturity, have for a number of readers seemed to mark the volumes published since the early *Paid on Both Sides;* yet many must have hoped that Mr Auden might suddenly, somehow, find himself again, might after all justify their early interest and expectation. It is well to say directly that *Nones* does not give evidence of a turn for the good. Indeed, it gives the impression of being in the nature of a full stop; or rather, perhaps, a path from which it seems improbable that Mr Auden will ever wish really to stray.

Perhaps the best way to lend support to this view is to take the hint of the blurb. If Mr Auden's 'technical resourcefulness' is the correlative of his 'mind and sensibility', to what conclusions will an examination of his 'technique' lead us? One may begin by looking at the opening lines of the first poem, 'Prime':

> Simultaneously, as soundlessly,
>   Spontaneously, suddenly
> As, at the vaunt of the dawn, the kind
>   Gates of the body fly open
> To its world beyond

Here, I think it will be agreed, there is a sense of strain, a sense that the poet is trying artificially to inject life into verse that resolutely refuses to leave the ground. For what can the first two lines be said to have achieved? Do the four adverbs, words with a rich potential of associations, signify as much in the context as the attention drawn to them by the alliteration would suggest? Does it not seem as though the choice of those particular words has been dictated less by a concern for precision and rightness than by a preoccupation with alliteration and internal rhyme? To me, at any rate, they seem little more than gestures towards a desired illusion of portentousness. A further source of the lack of conviction one feels behind the lines is a certain rhythmic awkwardness and inexpressivness—not, it must be said, anything like so prevalent in this poem as it is in 'The Managers', or 'Pleasure Island':

> To send a cry of protest or a call for
> Protection up into all
> Those dazzling miles, to add, however sincerely,
> One's occasional tear
> To that small volume, would be rather silly

Those few lines were picked at random from a poem running to some eighty. The monotony of reading verse of that kind, it will readily be appreciated, the effort involved in dragging the apprehension from one line to the next, is such as to make it necessary positively to drive oneself through to the end. The words seem to be strewn haphazardly, tortuously, over a rigid framework which sternly forbids any subtlety of intonation or suppleness of movement. Not that the arrangement of words *has* been haphazard. The first and second lines of the extract end where they do in order that the words 'Protection' and 'all' may receive some sort of stress. I say 'some sort of stress' because the effect obtained is purely ocular. A quite unwarrantable effort of 'interpretation' is required if it is to be brought out in a live reading. Mr Auden ought to know by this time—indeed, I am sure he does know—that one does not obtain effects of speech-stress and rhythm merely by chopping the lines.

Mr Auden, we have already recalled, was distinguished in his early poetry by a feeling for language; that is to say, his language had a pliability, at times a cumulative suggestiveness, that went appropriately with very real, if limited interests. But even then there was a tendency, more insistent as volume succeeded volume, to indulge in verbal virtuosity for its own sake. The results were often striking and amusing, but hardly what one expected from a responsible man growing older in an age growing simultaneously more and more barren and disheartening. His taste for verbal ingenuities persists in *Nones*, though it has become a very feeble sort of juggling:

> Sometimes we see astonishing clearly
> The out-there when we are already in;
> Now that is not what we are here for really.

Or there is the bad, unfunctional use of pun, as in 'Prim':

> Holy this moment, wholly in the right,

Mr Auden has always been fond of coinages and slangisms, a schoolboy habit that one had hoped he would grow out of. *Nones* shows us that he is not tired of them yet. Whereas in the earlier work, however, one tended to regard them as excrescences on more solid substance, they figure here rather as substitutes for genuine verbal vitality. Essentially they are a means of escape from the responsibility of integrating language and experience; of deciding, in other words, exactly what, if anything, the experience amounts to. I do not think that any very convincing case could be made out to justify the following lines, even though the poet might claim the sanction of Browning. The reader who is interested in poetry is likely to feel that his intelligence is being insulted:

> the orchestral
> Metaphor bamboozles the most oppressed
> —As a trombone the clerk will bravely
> Go oompah-oompah to his minor grave—

Such devices, far from being a sign of fertile verbal invention, manifest an essential tiredness, an inability clearly to focus the poetic object. They are protestations of a vitality that does not exist.

'Tiredness' would also seem to be a descriptive word for the staple of Mr Auden's imagery. Much of it has a faded, second-hand air, a suggestion of having been drawn from some property cupboard of modern poetical cliché:

> As disregarded as some
> Discarded artifact of our own,
> Like torn gloves, rusted kettles,
> Abandoned branchlines, worn lop-sided
> Grindstones buried in nettles.

(The passage is an extremely felicitous commentary on itself.) With that kind of thing, as might be expected, there goes a persistent habit of reminiscence. Yeats is a fairly constant presence:

> Speak well of moonlight on a winding stair,
> Of light-boned children under great green oaks;
> The wonder, yes, but death should not be there.

So, in various guises, is Mr Eliot, from echoes of 'Triumphal March' in 'Ischia' to reminiscences of *Four Quartets* in 'The Chimeras'. But the most surprising presence of all is that of Mr Walter de la Mare, whom Mr Auden's would-be ironic surface cannot hide:

> Their learned kings bent down to chat with frogs:
> This was before the Battle of the Bogs.
> *The key that opens is the key that rusts.*

Such 'influences' are not in the nature of the fertile suggestion that leads to fresh poetic creation quite distinct from the original, but rather testify to a want of personal idiom, which in itself is but a local sign of lack of urgency, lack of conviction, lack of real interest.

An air of boredom and lassitude, indeed, broods over the whole volume. Not infrequently Mr Auden seems to be trying to atone for this by indulging in slightly *risqué* side-glances:

> The boiling springs
> Which betray her secret fever
> Make limber the gout-stiffened joint

> And improve the venereal act:

That might be likened to a faintly salacious smile. At other times it becomes a more decidedly unpleasant snigger, like this 'spicing' of the tedious straggle of 'Pleasure Island':[1]

> As bosom, backside, crotch
> Or other sacred trophy is borne in triumph
> Past his adoring by
> Souls he does not try to like;

Disgust, of course, is the impression intended by the poet, but the pleasure taken in enumerating its objects is unmistakable. In any case, that kind of disgust, if genuine disgust it be, can hardly be called healthy or mature. It is little more than the disgust of the sensitive adolescent schoolboy, outraged by his gross contemporaries.

An unresolved ambiguity of attitude, manifesting itself locally in a corresponding uncertainty of tone, has for long been a characteristic of Mr Auden's work. One remembers the satiric gestures at the expense of the Public School ethos, which oddly enough seemed at the same time to be an endorsement of the very prejudices they were apparently intended to undermine. The same kind of ambiguity characterizes such poems as 'The Managers' or 'A Household'. It is hard to say exactly how we are supposed to take the business-man of the latter poem, who, in order 'to disarm suspicious minds at lunch', or to mollify those with whom he has just driven a bargain, paints a false and glowing, picture of his home. Never, '(a reticence for which they all admire him)', does he speak of his early-deceased wife,

> But proudly tells of that young scamp his heir,
> Of black eyes given and received, thrashings
> Endured without a sound to save a chum;

That, in whatever spirit it was offered, could not but be embarrassing.

---

[1] It is apposite to remark here that 'Pleasure Island', in common with other poems in the volume, oddly suggests inspiration from Hollywood. Much of 'Not in Baedeker' could be the commentary of a 'serious' travel film.

It should by now be apparent that *Nones* represents no new departure, no fresh mustering of forces. It is significant that the less tiresome poems in the volume (though they cannot for all that be called good) are mildly amusing squibs in the familiar manner of the earlier Auden, like 'The Love Feast', or 'The Fall of Rome', dedicated to Mr Cyril Connolly:

> Fantastic grow the evening gowns;
> Agents of the fisc pursue
> Absconding tax-defaulters through
> The sewers of provincial towns.

And yet he confesses himself, in 'A Walk after Dark', to be

> already at the stage
> When one starts to dislike the young

The volume shows early irritating mannerisms persisting without even the irresponsible vitality that once went with them. Maturity of years has brought no maturity of outlook, no deepening and broadening of the interests, but merely weariness and boredom. For that is the abiding impression of these poems. Not one of the poems gives evidence of any urgency, any real pressure or personal engagement. The defence could no doubt argue that the volume is a testimony to the variety of Mr Auden's interests. He certainly writes on a number of subjects, if that is the criterion, but his attitude to all of them is external and superficial. The dust-jacket tells us that *Nones* has 'an underlying unity that makes it more than a collection of scattered verse': yet one looks in vain for any dominant impulse controlling the heterogeneous mass. For what has Mr Auden positively to offer? There is, to be sure, a kind of fashionable metaphysical aura:

> Somewhere are places where we have really been,
> dear spaces,
> Of our deeds and faces, scenes we remember
> As unchanging because there there we changed,

Then 'Memorial for the City', with an epigraph from Juliana of Norwich, reminds us that Mr Auden is a Christian. But this lengthy poem has no more vitality than the rest; it does not persuade one that the poet's religious preoccupations have prompted him to live creation any more than his other sources.

Nones, then, is far from being an encouraging volume. Mr Auden has for some time now been academically respectable, and the present volume bears unmistakably the marks of academic enshrinement. It has the right kind of stolidity, and a fundamental inoffensiveness to the comfortably prejudiced but *soi-disant* 'open' mind. That being so, there is little prospect that Mr Auden will in the future choose to alter his course. *Nones* has the variety of deadness that passes very well for 'ripeness' and 'serenity'. But to have pronounced all these strictures on a poet who once evinced such distinct ability, is no laughing matter, no occasion for complacent self-congratulation. To anyone really concerned about the health of contemporary literature, such a spectacle of dissolution must be profoundly depressing, even tragic.

DYLAN THOMAS

ROBIN MAYHEAD (1952)

Collected Poems, *1934–1952*, by Dylan Thomas (J. M. Dent and Sons).

If Dylan Thomas has for some years now been the object of something of a cult, he has at length, to judge from the enthusiastic reception accorded to his last published volume, *Deaths and Entrances*, graduated to the status of a major, indeed a 'great' poet. But although it is now fairly usual for critics to speak of him in the same breath as Eliot, Auden, and Spender,—all four being, one gathers, equally 'great' poets— the kind of distinction commonly made between him and those writers is revealing and important. They, broadly speaking, are designated 'Classical', while Mr Thomas, full of divine imperfection, is the ardent 'Romantic' rebel. A persistent note in the encomiums with which Mr Thomas has been larded has been an insistence on what is generally described as his youthful 'spontaneity' and freshness of response to experience, unspoilt by too much of the 'intelligence' that has perhaps, it is tactfully suggested, made our modern poetical Renaissance rather one-sided; all this going miraculously, it would seem, with a sophisticated mastery of involved verse-forms. The resultant picture is something very like the old familiar one of the Genius, in the total complex of which, one might venture,—without any disrespectful feelings towards the country of the poet's origin—the idea of the Bard counts for not a little.

Both poet and publisher, it must be admitted, give the right kind of critic every encouragement in holding such a view. For good measure this new collected volume includes Augustus John's portrait of Mr Thomas in what one takes to be a characteristic attitude of smouldering inspiration, and the poet's own prefatory note, with its gusty buttonholing protestation of no-nonsense, is the very voice of incandescent Genius:

> I read somewhere of a shepherd who, when asked why he made, from within fairy rings, ritual observances to the moon to protect his flocks, replied: 'I'd be a damn' fool if I didn't' These poems, with all their crudities, doubts and confusions, are written for the love of man and in praise of God, and I'd be a damn' fool if they weren't.

Having thus disarmed criticism by implying that you are a rather inferior creature if you do not share his manly big-heartedness, the poet plunges into a breathless prologue in verse, 'intended as an address to my readers, the strangers':

> This day winding down now
> At God speeded summer's end
> In the torrent salmon sun,
> In my seashaken house
> On a breakneck of rocks
> Tangled with chirrup and fruit

Three words, 'torrent', 'breakneck', and 'tangled', may be detached and isolated as indicating the quality of the volume as a whole. Mr Thomas is characteristically borne on a kind of Shelleyan 'aery surge', through a dazzling flood of image and sensation. To note this, of course, is not necessarily to make a serious charge; such idiosyncrasies may be canalized to serve a positive end, limited though the substance of poetic interest is likely to be. And it would, I think, be hard to deny that Mr Thomas does in some measure possess a capacity for simple sensuous evocation which, without insistence on the evident dissimilarities, may be said faintly to resemble the lesser Hopkins of the 'nature' poetry. The opening of 'A Winter's Tale', quieter and more lucid than the staple of the verse in this collection, is a fair example of this manner at its best:

> It is a winter's tale
> That the snow blind twilight ferries over the lakes
> And floating fields from the farm in the cup of the vales,
> Gliding windless through the hand folded flakes,
> The pale breath of cattle at the stealthy sail,
> And the stars falling cold,
> And the smell of hay in the snow, and the far owl
> Warning among the folds, and the frozen hold
> Flocked with the sheep white smoke of the farm house cowl
> In the river wended vales where the tale was told.

Several criticisms promptly occur to one: the rhythmic flaccidity, the somewhat spineless and irritating repetition of 'and' with the consequent blurring of one image into another, the rather extraneous effect of 'hand folded'. But even when these points have been made, such writing, though not particularly distinguished, might justify one in attributing to the poet an agreeable minor talent—observe the clever concentration of suggestion in 'Flocked'—capable of possible useful exploitation within narrow and frankly accepted limits. The precarious success of these stanzas, however, is unfortunately not sustained. Hints of collapse implicit in the weaknesses just noted are only too surely realized, and before long the poem has modulated, or, more properly, 'lurched', into this kind of thing:

> Look. And the dancers move
> On the departed, snow bushed green, wanton in moon light
> As a dust of pigeons. Exulting, the grave hooved
> Horses, centaur dead, turn and tread the drenched white
> Paddocks in the farms of birds. The dead oak walks for love.

Relation of the stanza to its context imparts no felicity, symbolic or otherwise, to the wilderness of images. Failing to cohere, to build up together into any kind of overall, unified pattern, they consequently fail to make any forceful or even challenging impact.

It is customary for Mr Thomas to begin a poem in full *furor poeticus*, but on the rare occasions when, as in 'A Winter's Tale', he sounds a more steady and considered note at the outset, he soon wrecks the balance by letting his undisciplined and uncritical fancy run away with him. The first stanza of 'On a Wedding Anniversary', for example, despite the histrionic gesture of the opening line, has some subtlety of phrasing and movement:

> The sky is torn across
> This ragged anniversary of two
> Who moved for three years in tune
> Down the long walks of their vows.

The concluding image of the third and final stanza, on the other hand, can only be described, at the most charitable, as hastily conceived and imperfectly grasped, though 'plain silly' might strike one as the more vividly suggestive term:

> Too late in the wrong rain
> They come together whom their love parted:
> The windows pour into their heart
> And the doors burn in their brain.

Mr Thomas's special mannerism, in fact, is just this habit of clutching at the apparently striking image that comes to hand, without a working-out of its implications or a proper consideration of its appropriateness. Violence is substituted for imaginative precision, as though in the hope that the force of the explosion may stun the reader's critical intelligence.

The Thomas enthusiast, of course, will affirm that this is the true fire, the apocalyptic visionary gift of the great poet, and will claim that failure to be impressed is the result of a one-sided estimate of the virtues of controlling critical vigilance in poetry. On the other hand, he will certainly defend Mr Thomas against any suspicion of being a mere poet of intoxication, and will triumphantly point to his 'mastery' of complicated stanza-forms as evidence for the contrary. Nothing, indeed, is more odd about the cult of Mr Thomas than the way in which his admirers alternately praise him now as the spontaneous, 'imperfect' genius, now as the wizard of technique. Such claims have been made for his architectonic skill that it is necessary to devote some special attention to this aspect of his work. If, as has been suggested, the opening of 'A Winter's Tale' faintly recalls the minor Hopkins, there are passages later in the poem that directly challenge comparison with the Hopkins of more distinguished achievement:

> Bird, he was brought low,
> Burning in the bride bed of love, in the whirl-
> Pool at the wanting centre

By no amount of effort to penetrate the poet's intentions can I arrive at a satisfactory explanation of the splitting of the word 'whirlpool'. The conclusion seems to be that Mr Thomas either has not understood the nature of such an effect as the split 'ling/ering', for instance, in Hopkins's 'No worst, there is none', or else sees in the drawn-out 'whirl/Pool' some esoteric felicity inaccessible to the uninitiated reader. The effect of the division would appear to be merely visual, doing nothing to control the tone and movement when one is reading aloud. A similar lack of connection between the disposition of the words in the stanza and the actual pauses and stresses one is obliged to make in order to read the poem intelligibly aloud, turns 'Poem in October', which might perhaps have been quite a pleasant minor success—the tone is not too hectic, and the 'apocalyptic' note is not overworked—into a depressing 'literary' exercise:

> A springful of larks in a rolling
> Cloud and the roadside bushes brimming with whistling
> Blackbirds and the sun of October
> Summery
> On the hill's shoulder,

> Here were fond climates and sweet singers suddenly
> Come in the morning where I wandered and listened
> To the rain wringing
> Wind blow cold
> In the wood faraway under me.

That, to be sure, is not especially striking or original, but it has a certain lucid charm refreshing by comparison with this poet's normal heady wine. It is the more to be regretted, then, that Mr Thomas did not permit his words to seek out and mould their own verse-structure, instead of stringing them brutally—for that, whatever the facts of composition, is the effect produced—across a predetermined system of girders and scaffolding. An examination of 'Vision and Prayer' confirms one's suspicions that Mr Thomas's preoccupation with 'form' is a concern with decoration rather than with poetry. The opening section, presumably 'Vision', is written in stanzas which billow out mathematically from a single word in the first line to a central line of six or seven words and then narrow down once more to the single isolated word, while 'Prayer' reverses the process. That, no doubt, looks very pretty, and perhaps one should be grateful to Mr Thomas for making it clear by pictorial means, for one might well feel a trifle doubtful, from a perusal of the words alone, which part of the poem is 'Vision' and which part 'Prayer'. But one is surely justified in asking for some precise guidance as to the writer's intentions. Does he, in fact, wish his poem to be read or simply to be looked at? If he claims the precedent of 'Easter Wings', one can only beg him to open his Herbert and think again. 'Easter Wings' is not one of Herbert's best poems, but the verse-structure is something more than a way of arranging words to make a picturesque symbolic design on paper.

The feeling informing 'Vision and Prayer', a kind of self-indulgent religiosity as grotesque as the verse-form, is characteristic of much of the later work in this volume. The poet's attitude to life, supposedly, has 'deepened'; or, in other words, a mess of quasi-Christian imagery has been thrown in to swell the broth. This religiosity may take the form of pompous unction, as in 'The Conversation of Prayer', of pseudo-liturgical verbal juggling, as in 'Ceremony after a Fire Raid', or, at its most offensive, of a downright disgusting self-righteousness:

> I shall not murder
> The mankind of her going with a grave truth
> Nor blaspheme down the stations of the breath
> With any further
> Elegy of innocence and youth.

The lines are taken from a poem entitled 'A Refusal to Mourn the Death, by Fire, of a Child in London'. Mr Thomas was doubtless affected by the incident, and intended his poem to be a fitting and dignified expression of his reactions to it. The trouble is that the pronoun 'I', as in the body of his work, is much too conspicuous. But whereas one can tolerate this, however irritating it may be, when the basis of the poem is mere personal rhapsody, it becomes offensive in the extreme when the writer starts to pontificate on matters of common human feeling and suffering.

Mr Thomas's art has not improved with the years. The early poems in the volume, though one could hardly call any one of them successful, have not that kind of gross pretentiousness. And although the imagery is no less tangled than that of the later work, it is not quite the same haphazard welter; Mr Thomas is being less of a genius and more of a poet. If one finds the following lines strained and ineffective, one feels nonetheless that Mr Thomas had some reasonably clear idea of what he was trying to do, even though the experiment did not come off:

> Where once the waters of your face
> Spun to my screws, your dry ghost blows,
> The dead turns up its eye;
> Where once the mermen through the ice
> Pushed up their hair, the dry wind steers
> Through salt and root and roe.

These earlier poems make at least a pretence of coherence, even though the effect is often really the result of a trick. 'A process in the weather of the heart' and 'The force that through the green fuse drives the flower', to take two instances, have the kind of spurious-logical structure of which Shelley's 'Music, when soft voices die' is the classic example.

Superior as they are, generally speaking, to the later productions, the early poems could hardly have given one much hope for the future. Only the strictest self-criticism and self-discipline could have led Mr Thomas to put his exuberant verbal energies to effective poetic use. As it is, his progress has been swift, confident, and disastrous, though 'disastrous' may seem the wrong word to use in speaking of the career of a poet who, spurred on by general acclamation, may be expected to continue to exhibit his mastery of intricate verse-forms for years to come. A cult, in these days, becomes all too easily an institution. But the attitudes implicit in the widespread acceptance of Mr Thomas as a major poet, in the kind of praise with which he has been garlanded, may well give one cause for alarm, may well strike one as potentially disastrous for the future of English poetry.

5

LITERARY CULTURE

T. R. BARNES (1933)

Wyndham Lewis, A Discursive Exposition, by Hugh Gordon Porteus
(Desmond Harmsworth)

Mr Porteus is a disciple. The worship of Wyndham Lewis is his
(inferior?) religion; and one must not expect a devotee to be too
critical of his divinity. He finds adequate praise difficult. Mr Lewis's
satire is better than Dryden's: his style as good as Shakespeare's (p. 118).
'I claim', he says, 'for Lewis, purely on the strength of his *vision*, a
place in art beside the greatest masters of all time.' One can't say fairer
than that.

But though criticism of Mr Lewis is too much to expect from the
ecstatic Mr Porteus, we may test his standard of values, perhaps, by his
remarks about less divine persons. For example: 'Dr I. A. Richards,
with tremendous ingenuity and patience, is attempting to reduce art to
a set of scientific formulae.' Joyce has 'no central vision and a very
limited field of invention'. These two remarks are, I think, sufficient to
show the quality of Mr Porteus's sensibility.

Lewis's admirers usually admit that the master is careless. But, say
they, how much he *knows*. His carelessness doesn't really matter. Mr
Garman in the last number of *Scrutiny* implies that 'slap-dash carelessness...mere transcription of other people's views,...and a proclivity
to follow...any red herring' are 'inevitable adjuncts of a uniquely
vigorous style and a mind more than usually well stocked and inquiring'.
It may be said that 'any red herring' in Lewis's work is far more
frequent than 'any fresh egg'; and such eggs as there are are mostly
foreign—imported from M. Julien Benda.

That Lewis is well informed and intelligent is obvious; but the
exaggerated contemporary estimate of him seems to rest on two things
—the amount he has written, and his own self-advertisement. The
Enemy is simply impresario for Wyndham Lewis; and like most
impresarios, he exaggerates. Lewis, like Shaw, Wells and the Sitwells,
sells his wares. Unlike the Sitwells, he really has something for sale, but
it would be absurd to take him at his own valuation. He is a symptom,
not a leader, of the age. For, like all successful ad-men, he has come to
believe quite uncritically in what he sells: he has become his own inferior

religion: he worships (as Mr Garman notes) Tarr and Pierpoint—a fact which seems to me to invalidate much of his criticism.

Mr Porteus bases his estimate mainly on Lewis's style and his satire.

The first, he says, is visual, imagist, the product of the Painter's Eye. Here I think he may be right; for it seems possible that this explains the strange sterility of Lewis's style. Great emotive writing uses a fusion of many things—vision, sound, rhythm, meaning, etc. To use one of these things in isolation is to limit the possibilities of adequate communication. Mr Porteus himself notes that it is necessary to regard Lewis's style as a translation into the visual. But this is a defect, not, as he supposes, a virtue. It is a misuse, or an inadequate use, of language.

Lewis's satire seems largely self-indulgence. It reminds one of Halifax's dictum: 'Anger, like drink, giveth rise to a great deal of unmannerly wit.' I read recently of a German tailor, who, annoyed with his employer, had the latter's portrait tattooed on his behind. He exhibited it, to the delight of his friends, and the discomfiture of his enemy. Mr Lewis's activity, in the *Apes of God*, and many of his other works, seems to me to be exactly analogous to the tailor's and just as valuable; though he is scarcely the tailor's equal in precision and economy of technique.

THE T. E. HULME MYTH

H. A. MASON (1938)

T. E. Hulme, by Michael Roberts (Faber and Faber)

T. E. Hulme was even in his life-time the object of a cult which the publication of *Speculations* (which contains most of his writings) did apparently nothing to dispel. Perhaps the fragmentary nature of these writings, his untimely death in the war, his support of then fashionable ideas are enough to excuse the special way he was thought of and written about. One must distinguish here betweeen the praises of those personal friends whose opinions in various degrees command respect and the snobs who surrounded his reputation with an atmosphere so close that it was difficult to approach his work without bias.

As a thinker he was essentially an amateur. This quality secured him a hearing similar to that obtained by Dr Richards's *Principles of Literary Criticism.* In *Speculations* we find the same dogmatic 'incisive' style, the refreshingly unacademic contempt for authority, the zest in exposing what Hulme thought charlatanry (two quotations come to mind: 'I consider it a duty, a very pleasant duty and one very much neglected in this country, to expose charlatans when one sees them' and 'There is a tremendous amount of hocus-pocus about most discussions of poetry'), and together with all this an air of many-sidedness, of embracing several disciplines and of escaping from the academic specializations. Not that he was ever smug. In his trenchant distinctions and his welding together of distinctions made in different fields into apparently brilliant positions of startling clarity (the hard dry 'classical vision') he undoubtedly indulged a natural bent. Yet in so doing he actually blurred his meaning and whatever of value can be found in his writings can only be reached by patiently untangling his syntheses and toning down his overstatements.

This work has been admirably undertaken by Mr Roberts. In a careful, but often verbose, exposition of the ideas to be found in *Speculations* he says, 'Most of his assertions are true in their proper field; the problem is to restate them in a way that will make their limitations clear.' Yet he makes two important admissions: that the unity of Hulme's work is temperamental and 'there is scarcely a single statement in Hulme that is not borrowed'. One may then pardonably wonder why he undertook the writing of this book. For the philosophies of Bergson, Husserl and Scheler, etc., if still insufficiently known in this country, are better dealt with technically and by experts; Hulme's aesthetic excursions are on Mr Roberts's own showing unsatisfactory. One may legitimately doubt whether the great work on aesthetics Hulme planned would have been anything but good middleman work for Bergson and Lipps.

In short, I doubt whether Mr Roberts can substantiate his claim that Hulme's great merit is that the ideas he borrowed were important. It seems much more likely from the extensive *ad-libbing* (to borrow a word from the Americans) Mr Roberts allows himself that Hulme's positions were useful to him in working out problems that are preoccupying him. A convenient summary occurs on pp. 252–3. 'Democracy and democratic progress are bound to fail if they do not rest on the religious or tragic outlook; but within the framework of a Christian polity, whose economy reflected the moral principles it professed, a form of democracy would be not only possible but also necessary, for democracy is the form of government that recognizes most openly the responsibility of the individual and the fact that all government rests on the consent of the governed. Progress towards such an end is not impossible. . . ' In reaching this conclusion Mr Roberts is just and frank in pointing out Hulme's limitations. But he himself does not appear to realize how damaging he is to the Hulme myth. It is clear from this book, if it was not so before, that Hulme was of importance almost exclusively as a stimulating influence, and was possibly more valuable in conversations than in his writings. Many of his dicta can be found in different settings in, for example, the work of T. S. Eliot. But these ideas are only valuable when worked out and properly defined. It is by the success of those who are known to have come under his influence that Hulme will be esteemed.

MR E. M. FORSTER

Q. D. LEAVIS (1936)

Abinger Harvest, by E. M. Forster (Arnold)

Apart from the Clark Lectures, reprinted as *Aspects of the Novel*, and the memoir of Lowes Dickinson, this is the only book Mr Forster's eager public has been given since *A Passage to India*, and it is a disappointing book. It is composed of reprinted essays, reviews, articles, etc., divided into sections: one is of literary criticism, another about the East, another on aspects of contemporary England, and one of essays mostly in the popular historical manner (née Strachey) on figures of the Past. The publishers tell us 'the range of outlook is even wider' here than in Mr Forster's previous work, but even his greatest admirers will hardly find anything more than a casual re-statement of Mr Forster's outlook, split up as it were under a spectroscope. *Abinger Harvest* ought to be an occasion for some critic to make a revaluation of the novels too. However, we must be content here with summarizing what this volume alone shows.

It is a mixture of autobiography and criticism. What it chiefly does is to furnish a key to Mr Forster's peculiar poise, that poise which constitutes the individuality of his novels and from which his characteristic irony springs. Under the spectroscope it is seen to be a balance between a critical and a charming stance. He is gifted with impulses in both directions, and, hovering as he necessarily does between the serious and the playful, this makes him unduly concerned to be whimsical. He is often here merely playful and then he tends to become a bore (e.g. the last half of the group of sketches called 'Our Diversions'), or personal in the worst sense. His weakness, felt in the novels as an uneasy wobble in some of the ironic effects, is here revealed as a frequent inability to decide which he wants to be—critical or charming. You get the impression that he is positively unable to resist following out a whimsical train of thought, whatever the business in hand. 'My Wood' is an instance of turning this habit to profit by the use of a serious overtone, but it stands almost alone on this level. Generally his poise in these essays is unstable, he seems, as so rarely in the novels, to be uncertain what he intends to convey or where he means to alight (hence perhaps his liking for Ronald Firbank, who will remain a tiresome fribble to most of us). 'A Flood in the Office' shows a characteristic surrender to the easier current; it starts from a dispute between two eminent engineers about the irrigation of Egypt and continues, at a tangent, about Father Nile. Mr Forster sees from the corner of his eye the real significance of the dispute—the eternal antipathy between the disinterested intelligent man and stupidity allied with vested interests—but it is not the spectacle of integrity struggling to make its voice heard that arrests his imagination: it is the whimsical fancies suggested by 'the unique mass of water'. Of course it makes a more amusing essay this way. The objection is that the consistently whimsical outlook has the effect of making any other appear priggish —exactly as *Punch* does, which Mr Forster very feelingly denounces on other grounds. And you do get the impression that Mr Forster is disinclined to risk being thought too serious, he takes so much care to elicit the 'How amusing' response.

The literary criticism carries us a step further in our analysis. The intuitions are good, there are striking flashes of discernment (some of the critical stuff, such as the essay on Sinclair Lewis, is better than anything in *Aspects of the Novel*), but he doesn't seem to know how to consolidate. As in that book, it is amateur criticism; there is some kind of mental habit that prohibits discipline and sustained effort. The amiably whimsical-personal approach is not made to seem justified as a profitable mode of literary criticism: essays like that on T. S. Eliot are so inadequate that it is surprising that Mr Forster should have thought them worth reprinting. The brief note on Conrad makes the radical criticism of this novelist who has been written and lectured about with so little profit:

This isn't an aesthetic criticism, nor a moral one. Just a suggestion that our difficulties with Mr Conrad may proceed in part from difficulties of his own. What is so elusive about him is that he is always promising to make some general philosophic statement about the universe and then refraining with a gruff disclaimer... These essays [*Notes on Life and Letters*] do suggest that he is misty in the middle as well as at the edges, that the secret casket of his genius contains a vapour rather than a jewel...

And again on Ibsen, how acute, how just:

Although not a teacher he has the air of being one, there is something in his method that implies a message, though the message really rested on passing irritabilities, and not on any permanent view of conduct or the universe... Moral ugliness trespasses into the aesthetic...Poetry might perhaps be achieved if Ibsen's indignation was of the straight-hitting sort, like Dante's.

But for all its sincerity there is something automatic about it, he reminds us too often of father at the breakfast table after a bad night, sensitive to the defects of society as revealed by a chance glance at the newspaper, and apt to blame all parties for them indiscriminately. Now it is the position of women that upsets father, now the lies people tell, now their inability to lie, now the drains, now the newspaper itself, which he crumples up, but his helpers and servers have to retrieve it, for bad as are all political parties he must really see who got in at Rosmersholm.

Yet you feel he is not wholly aware of the force of his criticisms, for he always proceeds to shy away from the point he has made so convincingly and go back on himself—generally out of benevolence.

You go on to conclude that Mr Forster is not so adequate a critic as he might be—as he ought to be, judging by his natural endowments. His blind spots are particularly instructive; they seem to be created by a social environment whose influence would repay investigation. There is the section of essays on The Past. They have none of Lytton Strachey's hateful qualities—the cheap irony, the vulgar prose effects, the assumption of superiority to his historical puppets—but it is significant that he should be sufficiently an admirer of Strachey's to try his hand at this genre, and sad that he should have been encouraged to think the attempts worth republishing (but no doubt many will find them delicious). In these circumstances his personal touch deserts him. 'Presently the old mistress [Hannah More] will ring a bell, Louisa will fail to answer it, there will be horror, disillusionment, flight, the Industrial Revolution, Tolstoy, Walt Whitman, Mr and Mrs Sidney Webb.' This, along with *The Common Reader* 2nd Series, from which it might have come, shows the unfortunate meeting-ground of three writers. It is distressing to see so distinguished a writer sinking to this. From this volume posterity will do some deducing about Mr Forster's background: he feels amiably towards the submerged layers below him ('Me, Them and You,' and there are other indications of a desire, creditable rather than effective, to gear in with the great world); and is critical of those aspects of his economic class which his circle have agreed to consider targets (e.g. '"It is different for me"'), but his most successful achievements here are in a very small way (e.g. 'The Doll Souse' and 'The Scallies'). There isn't much appearance of sharply felt first-hand criticism. Everything points to an uncritical taking-over of group-values. For instance, he boldly confesses to being one of the highbrow minority who can 'make fun' of Wembley, while the next essay displays him revelling in the deliciousness of Mickey Mouse and Co.; anyone who has observed a highbrow film audience relaxing from the effort required to appreciate Russian or surrealist films and preparing to really enjoy themselves when the Walt Disney turn follows must feel this a worthier subject for an ironical pen. A satirist, to command our respect, ought to be aware of his blinkers as well as of his tether. Thus it seems at least somewhat arbitrary to assume that the British Empire is ridiculous whereas Mr Clive Bell isn't; posterity's Bloomsbury (not very long hence) may judge otherwise.

Where suitable subjects occur, when his critical abilities are able to function on important topics that are also congenial, Mr Forster produces his best work. The best section in this volume is that on The East, and the best essay in it on 'The Mind of the Native Indian State'. This is not merely whimsical, merely charmingly witty, but witty to a serious purpose; it is responsible:

The Princes have studied our wonderful British constitution at the Chiefs' Colleges, and some of them have visited England and seen the Houses of Parliament. But they are personal rulers themselves, often possessing powers of life and death, and they find it difficult to realize that the King Emperor, their overlord, is not equally powerful. If they can exalt and depress their own subjects at will, regard the State revenue as their private property, promulgate a constitution one day and ignore it the next, surely the monarch of Westminster can do as much or more. This belief colours all their intercourse with the Government of India. They want to get through or behind it to King George and lay their troubles at his feet, because he is a king and a mighty one, and will understand. In the past some of them nourished private schemes, but to-day their loyalty to the Crown is sincere and passionate, and they welcomed the Prince of Wales, although his measured constitutionalisms puzzled and chilled them. Why did not he take his liegemen aside and ask, in his father's name, for the head of Ghandi upon a charger? It could have been managed so easily. The intelligent Princes would not argue thus, but all would have the feeling, and so would the reader if he derived extensive powers under a feudal system and then discovered that it was not working properly in its upper reaches. 'His Majesty the King-Emperor has great difficulties in these days': so much they grasp, but they regard the difficulties as abnormal and expect that a turn of the wheel will shake them off. However cleverly they may discuss democratic Europe or revolutionary Russia with a visitor, they do not in their heart of hearts regard anything but Royalty as permanent, or the movements against it as more than domestic mutinies. They cannot understand, because they cannot experience, the modern world.

It concludes with a sample of Mr Forster's personal brand of wisdom —a deprecating refusal to be easily wise. The same note is struck elsewhere, as in the capital little sketches 'Advance, India' and 'The Suppliant', which might both have come from *A Passage to India*. It is sustained in the most impressive thing in the book, the courageous and useful address, delivered last year to the International Congress of Writers at Paris, on 'Liberty in England', which contains passages that every civilized person will be grateful to Mr Forster for. (This recalls

Mr Forster's valuable report of that congress in *The New Statesman and Nation*, 6 July 1935.) Along with this goes 'A Note on the Way', which is personal in the best sense. You conclude that Mr Forster's courage—and courage is readily felt to be an important part of this writer's make-up—is not associated with his irony so much as with his delicate emotional machinery. Certainly it is something in the nature of courage which provides the mainspring: courage to assert the virtue of the finer feelings. Compared with the other major novelists of this century Mr Forster exhibits a lack both of personal vigour and of that intellectual strength which impresses as the best source of vitality; you can't imagine him making the kind of personal judgments that Lawrence made nor has his irony anything in common with the refreshing sardonic quality of Lawrence's. Nor has he shown a capacity for such an ironical achievement as *Cakes and Ale*, which, side by side with a sardonic criticism of the writer's environment, exhibits positive values convincingly incarnated. Niceness has its drawbacks apparently, in letters if not in life; Mr Forster in *Abinger Harvest* shows himself to be the nicest kind of person, but so nice as to be somewhat tame perhaps— or else what accounts for the disappointment the book leaves? Though his public work (e.g., formerly as president of the Society for Cultural Relations with Soviet Russia and till recently as president of the National Council for Civil Liberties) is a reminder that it is not necessarily his most ponderable side that is presented to the reader.

LYTTON STRACHEY

T. R. BARNES (1933)

Characters and Commentaries, by Lytton Strachey (Chatto and Windus)

This is a reprint of most of Lytton Strachey's journalism which has not already been collected. The essays and reviews which it contains date from 1905–1931. Most of them are literary (about Horace Walpole, Mrs Inchbald, Fanny Burney, Voltaire); a few are biographical (about Lord Morley, Frederick the Great, the First Earl of Lytton). The Leslie Stephen Lecture on Pope is also included.

The whole book has considerable documentary value; since it reveals clearly (almost naïvely) some of the fundamental characteristics of its author; and, consequently, of contemporary belletrism.

First, for his style. This is, of course, 'impeccable'. It starts by echoing Browne. 'The end of Time is more favourable to epistolary immortality than its beginnings and its maturity: the barbarism of an early age and the unrest of a vigorous one are alike unpropitious to the preservation of letters.' Other people's cadences become less obvious as time goes on; Gibbon is heard occasionally, and Johnson. Here is an example:

His vehemence could be content with no ordinary moderation, either in the callous or the lachrymose; and the same amazing force which made Prussia a Great Power created, in spite of incredible difficulties, in a foreign idiom, under the bondage of the harshest literary conventions ever known, that vast mass of fifth-rate poetising from which shuddering History averts her face.

Look at the 'and' following the semi-colon, and the stock-piling of clauses which follows it. It is very competently done; but it is a mere tasteful (or tasty) pastiche, and nothing more. The first quotation comes from an undergraduate essay, written in 1905. The second was published in the *New Statesman* in 1917.

Next, for the biographical essays. His biographies are Strachey's most ambitious works. They have been accepted as valuable, brilliant, and new. Almost every reviewer of biographical or historical works in, for example, the *New Statesman* compares them with Strachey's. They are either like him, or unlike him; either influenced or uninfluenced by him. Obviously, *Queen Victoria* and *Eminent Victorians* have become a criterion, a touchstone. Also, they sold well; they have imitators; and Mr Philip Guedalla gets published in *Good Housekeeping*, M. André Maurois delivers the Clark Lectures at Cambridge.

This success among the 'middlebrow' public was, I think, based on the fact that Strachey, competently and directly, with judicious subtlety, and appropriately Freudian and free-thinking seasoning, appealed to that desire for fantasy satisfaction through 'characters' or substitute lives, which is the basis of commercial fiction. His attitude flattered post-war up-to-date mechanized amoralism; and he was also skilfully sentimental—'but the future was hidden, and all that was certain was that the past had gone for ever, and that his eyes would rest no more upon the snapdragons of Trinity.' His formula was the familiar Metro-Goldwyn-Mayer heart-throb and mirthquake one. His readers had it both ways.

The literary criticism in this volume is nothing but strings of epithets. Here are a few:

> the originality of his thought: the beauty of his language:
> and the subtle splendour of his emotion
> the polished pomp of —'s sentences
> his brilliant embittered little book
> his exquisite, sensuous, and high-sounding oratory
> the profound obscurity of — and —

The subjects of these remarks are Shakespeare, Donne, La Roche-foucauld, Racine, Gibbon and T. S. Eliot. It doesn't really matter to whom the remarks are applied. When Strachey deals with a period dilettante like Horace Walpole, he creates 'atmosphere' well enough, for what it is worth. Always the patina, not the form, excites him. He never discusses contemporary literature. The only thing he can say of *Satires of Circumstance* is that 'the originality of [Th. Hardy's] poetry lies in the fact that it bears everywhere upon it the impress of a master of prose fiction'.

But the most revealing essay here is that on Matthew Arnold, in which, avoiding any attempt to assess the problem which confronted Arnold—how to keep tradition and value alive in spite of commerce settling on every tree—he contents himself with ridiculing the famous phrase about poetry being 'a criticism of life'. The point is not whether Arnold's proposed solutions (academic and so on) of this problem were right or wrong, but whether his general attitude to literature and the tradition of English culture was or was not worth defending.

These are the concluding sentences of the essay:

He might, no doubt, if he had chosen, have done some excellent and lasting work upon the movements of glaciers or the fertilization of plants, or have been quite a satisfactory collector in an up-country district in India. But no; he *would* be a critic.

It is impossible to read Strachey for long without finding many passages like this, compact of snobbery and querulous inferiority feelings.

Incapable of creation in life or in literature, his writings were his substitute for both. No wonder he has readers. But more surprisingly, he has a following. Though Sitwellism is no longer *chic*, Strachey is an influence in life as well as in letters; he set a tone which still dominates certain areas of the highbrow world—e.g. that part of Bloomsbury which has a well-known annex in Cambridge. The deterioration and collapse represented by Mrs Woolf's latest phase (*Orlando, Common Reader* 2nd Series, *Flush*) is one of the most pernicious effects of this environment.

THE CASE OF MISS DOROTHY SAYERS

Q. D. LEAVIS (1937)

Gaudy Night (Gollancz)
Busman's Honeymoon (Gollancz)

With the above two novels Miss Sayers stepped out of the ranks of detective writers into that of the best-seller novelists, and into some esteem as a literary figure among the educated reading public.

Only D. H. Lawrence (see *Phoenix*) could have reviewed these novels adequately. I confine myself to some incidental observations.

Miss Sayers belongs with Naomi Mitchison and Rosamond Lehmann (see *Scrutiny* for September 1935 and September 1936) and some others who are representative of the new kind of best-seller, the *educated* popular novelist. Like the Ouidas and Marie Corellis and Baron Corvos of the past they are really subjects for other kinds of specialist than the literary critic, but unlike those writers these are to some extent undoubtedly conscious of what they are doing (and so are able to practise more adroitly on their readers). Thus, for instance, the heroine of *Gaudy Night* is a Harriet Vane who writes detective stories, merely for a living and in all modesty, for was she not an Oxford Scholar and a first-class in English? But returning to her Shrewsbury College after many years for an Old Students' celebration, she finds, with what grateful surprise, that not only her coevals but all the best dons clear up to the Warden (Philosophy) are 'fervent admirers' and 'devotees' (in their own words) of her writings. Miss Sayers can hardly be as artless as all that, and it is not surprising that the world has taken her tip and proceeded to talk obediently about her 'artistry' and 'scholarly English'. The hero is of course Harriet's suitor and ultimate husband, and here again I think Miss Sayers has overstepped the limits of what even a best-seller's public can be expected to swallow without suspicion. Lord Peter is not only of ducal stock and all that a Ouida hero was plus modern sophistication and modern accomplishments—such as being adored by his men during the Great War and able to talk like a P.G. Wodehouse moron—he is also a distinguished scholar in history, a celebrated cricketer, an authority on antiques, a musician, a brilliant wit, a diplomat on whom the F.O. leans during international crises, a wide and deep reader and no doubt some other things I've overlooked. Whatever he does he does better than anyone else and he is one of those universal geniuses like Leonardo. Women naturally find him irresistible. Miss Sayers only omits to add like Ouida that 'he has the seat of the English Guards'. He does say, however, to his bride, 'In the course of a mis-spent life I have learnt that it is a gentleman's first duty to remember in the morning who it was he took to bed with him' and Miss Sayers does actually write of him (thus going one better than Ouida, who was a lady), 'He remembered that it had once been said of "ce blond cadet de famille ducale anglaise"—said, too, by a lady who had every opportunity of judging—that "il tenait son lit en Grand Monarque et s'y démenait en Grand Turc".'

I will not comment further on the large part played in these novels by passages such as I have quoted, Miss Sayers being (unlike Mr James Joyce and the late D. H. Lawrence, of whom reviewers could say what they liked with impunity) in such good standing with the respectable. But there is no harm in saying, since it is demonstrably true, that these two passages are fair samples of what Miss Sayers thinks on the one hand witty and on the other daringly outspoken; and we are accordingly in a position to draw some conclusions about the taste of the public which likes such stuff and recommends it with conviction not merely as entertainment but as Good Stuff. For it is not, as you might have thought, as a successor to Marie Corelli and Ouida that Miss Sayers is valued.

This odd conviction that she is in a different class from Edgar Wallace or Ethel M. Dell apparently depends on four factors in these novels. They have an appearance of literariness; they profess to treat profound emotions and to be concerned with values; they generally or incidentally affect to deal in large issues and general problems (e.g. *Gaudy Night*, in so far as it is anything but a bundle of best-selling old clothes, is supposed to answer the question whether academic life produces abnormality in women); and they appear to give an inside view of some modes of life that share the appeal of the unknown for many readers, particularly the life of the older universities.

Literature gets heavily drawn upon in Miss Sayers's writings, and her attitude to it is revealing. She displays knowingness about literature without any sensitiveness to it or any feeling for quality—i.e. she has an academic literary taste over and above having no general taste at all (there can hardly be any reader of Donne besides Miss Sayers who could wish to have his poetry associated with Lord Peter's feelings). Impressive literary excerpts, generally 17th century (a period far off, whose prose ran to a pleasing quaintness and whose literature and thought are notoriously now in fashion), head each chapter. She—I should say Harriet Vane—proudly admits to having 'the novelist's habit of thinking of everything in terms of literary allusion'. What a give-away! It is a habit that gets people like Harriet Vane firsts in 'English' examinations, no doubt, but no novelist with such a parasitic, stale, adulterated way of feeling and living could ever amount to anything. And Miss Sayers's fiction,when it isn't mere detective story of an unimpressive kind, is exactly that: stale, second-hand, hollow. Her wit consists in literary references. Her deliberate indecency is not shocking or amusing, it is odious merely as so much Restoration Comedy is, because the breath of life was never in it and it is only the emanation of a 'social' mind wanting to raise a snigger; you sense behind it a sort of female smoking-room (see the girlish dedication to *Busman's Honeymoon*) convinced that this is to be emancipated. (How right, you feel, Jane Austen was not to attempt male conversation unless ladies are present!)

The patter about value and the business of delving into emotional deeps seems to me more nauseating than anything else in the productions of this kind of novelist, not because anything much is said but because such clumsy fumblings stir up mud in the channels of life that, heaven knows, we all know, it is hard enough to keep clear anyway. And in the matter of ideas, subject, theme, problems raised, she similarly performs the best-seller's function of giving the impression of intellectual activity to readers who would very much dislike that kind of exercise if it were actually presented to them; but of course it is all shadow-boxing. With what an air of unconventionality and play of analysis Miss Sayers handles her topics, but what relief her readers must feel—it is part, no doubt, of her success—that they are let off with a reassurance that everything is really all right and appearances are what really matter. You may be as immoral and disillusioned as Lord Peter, and in fact immorality, etc., are rather fetching qualities and humorous too, but you MUST go to Church and be married in it, and whether you are intellectual, nudist or hard up your frock MUST be well cut—this seems to be the moral burden of these books. It would be unkind to boil Miss Sayers's wisdom down to this and label it What Oxford Has Meant to Me, but evidently Miss Sayers's spiritual nature, like Harriet Vane's, depends for its repose, refreshment and sustenance on the academic world, the ideal conception, that is, of our older universities —or let us say a rationalized nostalgia for her student days.

I think indeed that the real draw of *Gaudy Night* was its offering the general public a peepshow of the senior university world, especially of the women's college, which has been less worked at by novelists than undergraduate life and has the appeal of novelty. (*Dusty Answer* made a similar hit.) It is a vicious presentation because it is popular and romantic while pretending to realism. Miss Sayers produces for our admiration an academic world which is the antithesis of the great world of bustle and Big Business that her readers know. Whereas in their world, she says, everything is 'unsound, unscholarly, insincere'

—the implication being that the academic world is sound and sincere because it is scholarly—you have here invulnerable standards of taste charging the charmed atmosphere ('Thank Heaven, it's extremely difficult to be cheap in Oxford,' says Lord Peter). If such a world ever existed, and I should be surprised to hear as much, it does no longer, and to give substance to a lie or to perpetuate a dead myth is to do no one any service really. It is time that a realistic account of the older universities was put into circulation. Unfortunately for Miss Sayers's thesis the universities are not the spiritually admirable places she alleges. People in the academic world who earn their livings by scholarly specialities are not as a general thing wiser, better, finer, decenter or in any way more estimable than those of the same social class outside. The academic world offers scope for personal aggrandizement much as the business world does, with the results you might expect. No one who has had occasion to observe how people get a footing in the academic world, how they rise in it, how appointments are obtained, how the social life is conducted, what are its standards, interests and assumptions, could accept Miss Sayers's romanticizing and extravagant claims ("" There's something about this place", said Peter, "that alters all one's values. ""). In fact the more one investigates the academic world the more striking appears its resemblance to the business world (I recently met someone who had collected a lot of data showing this; he was distressed).Here, too, to be disinterested or unconventional is to be eccentric and dangerous; here, too, to be materially successful you must be a good herd member; here, too, the trade union and the club spirit obtain. Even assuming that the intellectual virtues Miss Sayers postulates are required by the scholar for his studies, it does not follow that these are carried over into his daily living; in point of fact it is a commonplace of experience that they rarely are. Perhaps we need not call in the psychologist to account for this anomaly. And the academic is even more liable, alas, to be bogus as a specialist or scholar. Of course this is not surprising really, it would perhaps be more surprising if it were otherwise—only best-seller novelists could have such illusions about human nature—but the actual state of affairs everyone must feel to be unseemly, and in fact the accepted pretence is that things are as Miss Sayers relates. Perhaps this accounts for much of her success among the academics themselves; certainly one would rather account for it like this than in any other way. Yet it would surely be healthier from every point of view if the critical winds of the outside world could be let blow through these grimy edifices, and perhaps they would if the facts ever leaked out and left a loophole for criticism to get in by. But popular novelists like Miss Sayers are busy shoring up these hallowed fragments against their ruin; if Miss Sayers were more intelligent you could call it the latest case of *trahison des clercs*, but you suspect her of being a victim of propaganda herself.

But Miss Sayers is after all a product of Shrewsbury College as well as its producer. Who is responsible for this combination of literary glibness and spiritual illiteracy? Are her vices unique and personal? We all know they are not, experience confirms what her style of writing suggests, that she is representative. That inane wit, that unflagging sense of humour, those epigrams, that affectation of unconventionality, that determined sociality, what a familiar chord they strike! 'Are the women at S— College really like that?' someone says she enquired, after reading *Gaudy Night*, of someone on the spot. 'My dear, they are *much worse*!' At any rate Miss Sayers's fictions are clearly the product of a sympathetic *milieu* somewhere and one that pretty evidently had a university education. What is to be said for the female smoking-room that has set its approval on Miss Sayers? How far is Harriet Vane reliable when she reports her dons devoted to her novels? Some of the conversation of the oldest generation of women dons sounds convincing —Miss Sayers has caught the authentic acid note in personal inter-course and the genuine intellectual passion that distinguished them from the succeeding generations—and I don't think they would have had any use for Harriet's lucubrations; but if the younger generation read her novels with pleasure, as she alleges, then the higher education of women is in a sadder way than any feminist could bear to contemplate.

What does seem indisputable is that Miss Sayers as a writer has been a vast success in the senior academic world everywhere. The young report that their elders recommend *Gaudy Night* to them, Miss Sayers has the *entrée* to literary societies which would never have opened their doors to Edgar Wallace, she is canonized as a stylist by English lecturers already, and so on; after all, her reputation as a literary figure must have been made in such quarters. Speculation naturally turns on how anyone can devote himself to the study and teaching of the human-ities (we will let off the scientists in spite of their living in a place that alters all one's values) and yet not be able to place a Dorothy Sayers novel on inspection if it comes his way. Well it does seem queer, but such a lapse is not without precedent. Run your eyes over enough academic bookshelves—not those housing shop but those where they keep what they really choose to read—and you get accustomed to a certain association of authors representing an average taste which is at best negative: Edward Lear and Ernest Bramah's *Kai Lung* (delicious humour), Charles Morgan and C. E. Montague (stylists), Rupert Brooke (or Humbert Wolfe or some equivalent)...we can all supple-ment. Dorothy Sayers can take her place alongside without raising any blushes; these or their kind are the writers she admires herself. But doesn't it raise some awkward questions? What is the value of this scholarly life Miss Sayers hymns if it doesn't refine the perceptions of those leading it? If your work was of any value to you would you want, would you be able to relax on Edgar Wallace (much less on Dorothy Sayers)? Miss Sayers innocently presents her typical admirable scholar and 'English' don engaged on her life's work of what but a History of English Prosody (an all too plausible undertaking)! Apart from the fact that the lady was engaged in perpetrating a sort of public nuisance, think of the effect on the teaching of English in her college of that attitude to the study of poetry. No education could take place there; studying English Prosody will not show anyone why Miss Sayers isn't a good novelist. That kind of scholarship never gears in with life. But is there any other kind? Miss Sayers, however, finds it wholly admirable. By this code, she says, the only unpardonable thing is to be unscholarly; evil consists in producing a popular life of Carlyle without any research. But which is really worse, to be unscholarly or to pass writers like Miss Sayers? Mistakes about Carlyle are not a menace to civilization.

I once conversed on these or similar lines with a Professor of Classics, a man of genuine but diffident literary tastes. He remarked that it seemed unaccountable to him that the writings of a fellow Classic were so highly esteemed by his colleagues. He himself, he said modestly, had an unconquerable aversion to them, they seemed to him empty, the man's 'style' cheap and his wit puerile, but none of his friends agreed with him, it was so discouraging and he felt he must be in the wrong. I said, Not at all, his colleagues' insensitiveness to their native literature seemed to me an illustration of the evident fact that you could spend a lifetime in the study of any language ancient or modern, or any branch of the humanities, without acquiring the rudiments of literary taste or any apparatus for forming a just estimate of a piece of writing. And I added, no doubt brutally, 'What's the good of Classics, what justification for a Classical training can there be if it doesn't form a decent taste?' My friend was taken aback. But he was a conscientious professor and he tried to find an answer. After a bit he brought out hopefully, 'Well, some people are interested in philology.'

I have always tried to bear that maxim in mind. After all, philology is as legitimate a study as mathematics, and every branch of the humanities has its philological aspect, so to speak. I recommend anyone at a loss before the spectacle of the scholar's bedside reading to adopt the above explanation. Miss Sayers, who might evidently have been an academic herself, is probably quite sound on the philological side.

CHARLOTTE YONGE AND 'CHRISTIAN DISCRIMINATION'

Q. D. LEAVIS (1944)

Charlotte Yonge, by Georgina Battiscombe (Constable)
Christian Discrimination, by Bro. George Every, S.S.M. (Christian News-Letter Books)
The Literary Outlook, by S. L. Bethell (Christian News-Letter Books)
Man and Literature, by Norman Nicholson (S.C.M. Press)

There has long been an Amanda Ros vogue of Charlotte Yonge's writings and this biography is chiefly a product of that vogue. Miss Battiscombe has made an attractive book in which information about the life is interspersed with some just comments on the novels and illuminating bits of background. It is perhaps the only kind of book on Charlotte Yonge for which a wide public could be expected now, the popular Lytton Strachey treatment suiting well enough the period and the Amanda Ros aspect of the subject. But to be amused merely by Charlotte Yonge is not the most profitable reaction. Miss Battiscombe wobbles between amusement and a desire to claim literary status of some kind for some of Miss Yonge's novels that she enjoys in some way she can't explain. To see these novels taken at their own and the contemporary valuation we must turn to *Theology* and some recent related publications, where claims for this writer as a serious artist and a very valuable Christian novelist have been made. Evidently these ought to be investigated before the canon of English Literature finds itself permanently burdened with one of the prolific fiction-writers whom time alone has already expelled.

It seems incredible that Charlotte Yonge's novels could be taken seriously as literature except by those of her own way of thinking, and the claims I have referred to seem in fact to be based on the asserted value of her fictions as religious myths. Charlotte Yonge was a day-dreamer with a writing itch that compensated her for a peculiarly starved life. What was pushed out of her is interesting to us not for what it enunciates but for what it reveals and only in so far as a critical apparatus is brought to bear on it. The profitable book on her would be a contribution to the sociological history of literature: an illuminating contrast to Bunyan and a comparison with Jane Austen suggest themselves at once as revealing something about the cultural conditions which nourish a writer or otherwise, the kind of religious outlook that can produce a humane art and the kind that can't. This author had no medium at her command for conveying through literature such moral perceptions as she had, for unlike Bunyan she had no popular inherited art of literary expression to draw on and the personal sensibility of the writer which creates its own artistic language she decidedly had not. Jane Austen, in contrast, shows what the spinster of the previous generation gained by enjoying a real social life of the family and community, the life fed by adult conversation, free play of the mind and character, observation of all sorts and varieties of life and attitudes to it at different social and moral levels appreciated by standards that had arisen out of life itself instead of, like Charlotte Yonge, living only in the ignorant idealization projected by an inhuman theory.

As a moralist she is on a par with pulpit denouncers of short hair and slacks for women—that is, she couldn't distinguish between social conventions and morals of a less superficial quality, and having no sense of proportion she gave as much attention and censure in her novels to the former as to Dissipation and Doubt, the blanket concepts which she used for sin (not being acquainted with any more concrete expression of it). A person for whom evil consists of impropriety and some things she has vaguely heard tell of would seem to be disqualified as a framer of religious myths. And correspondingly she lacked (unlike the fanatic Bunyan or the spinsters Miss Austen and Miss Edgeworth) any sympathy for and even recognition of the natural sources of healthy life. The innocence of the dove is itself hardly an adequate equipment for a novelist, but even the race of doves would have died out soon after the Creation if as lacking as Charlotte Yonge in the instincts that make for survival. This brings us back to her attitude to life, that seems to have determined the interpretation she gave to the Anglican faith imparted to her by Keble. The Church seems to have been less an illumination of life for her than a substitute for living, so we see her selecting the anti-Life elements in Christianity for stress and idealization. The resulting picture of human action is not only impracticable but morbid. Consider the typical pattern of her novels. There is a permanent invalid who is a hero or heroine; tubercular invalids are peculiarly saintly and frequently an idiot is idealized; the most blessed marriages are those in which one party is diseased or physically incapable; the most blessed betrothals are those where the death of one party prevents marriage at all; the most blessed life for a man is to give up the natural field for his abilities in order to become a South Seas missionary, and for a woman to renounce a possible husband in order to devote herself to her relatives, even if they are only imbecile grandparents, or on the mere wish of a parent—self-sacrifice is an end in itself. She makes much play with symbolism but, as was inevitable in so poorly nourished an imagination (the arts meant nothing to her and life gave her no more pregnant experience than the death of a parent, no greater stimulus than a missionary meeting), her symbolism is schoolgirlish. Comparison with any novel where symbols are deployed by an original mind in vital connection with life would illustrate this—*Jude the Obscure*, *Moby Dick*, *Hard Times*, Conrad's *Victory*, one of Hawthorne's or T. F. Powys's works. It is her unconscious symbolism that is more interesting —e.g. the type of admirable wife who is no wife because of an accident to her lower limbs or spine, the saintly clergyman who has either gone blind or developed consumption, the passionate relation between brother and sister in a picture of life where the idea of sex is prohibited. It is understandable that some should find this vision of the good society congenial but that will not convince the majority that it is literature that makes for any kind of health or can offer anything to the mature.

We are entitled to press home this kind of criticism because it has a demonstrable bearing on the failure of Charlotte Yonge's fictions to be of literary value. We are not concerned with her qualifications as a Christian but as a novelist. The lack of roots in first-hand experience for her imagination, of substance for her moral passion, prevent her most cherished effects from conveying what she evidently thought they would. It would have required a genius like Kafka's or Bunyan's with that imaginative pressure which gives body to allegory and that artistic genius for expressing it, to make as literature anything of the new-born infant's baptism and the deferred confirmation scenes she so often stages. Art is a realm where the will can never be taken for the deed, and readers may be forgiven for smiling at places where the utmost solemnity of response is confidently expected by Miss Yonge. Even compared with writers of her own age and class she was deficient in this respect: she had none of that capacity for fable which enabled Kingsley to create in the gist of *The Water Babies* a Christian myth which children readily feel even before they understand it. 'The essence of moral energy is to survey the whole field,' wrote Henry James in his study of the novelist's function. It is certainly something required of the novelist whose claims to our attention are that she staked everything on presenting religious values. But Miss Yonge is so timid and inexperienced morally that her effects are in fact trivial. Religious small-change is handed us on every possible occasion; if, for instance, anyone is disappointed in some trifling matter, mamma or elder sister is sure to remark: 'I dare say it is very good for us not to have our ambition gratified. There are so many troubles worse than these failures, that it only shows how happy we are that we should take them so much to heart.' Surely such inflation lowers the value of the moral currency. The limitations that produced moral triteness are paralleled by her worldly ignorance that cripples her fictions: meeting the mass of humanity only as Sunday scholars—she never set foot in a cottage—she yet undertook, with the best-seller's confidence, to treat the largest social and ethical questions in a China-to-Peru setting of real life, so that 'there is a bad Chartist spirit among the colliers' is the only recognition of something wrong that she makes in a novel explicitly dealing with the social problem.

The Yonge type of moral fervour impresses one as amounting to nothing more than a refusal to allow anyone else moral or spiritual privacy or freedom. She has therefore no basis for the moral drama essential to the novelist's art. We think in contrast of Richardson, who subscribed like her to the antediluvian theory of parental control of a daughter's hand and the submission of the daughter as a religious duty. In *Clarissa* where this theory is the mainspring of the action it is checked by the novelist's deeper feeling that if we look at the particular instance the theory won't do because it outrages human sympathies. The interplay between the theory (accepted as morally right) and the test case (appealing to another source of values) produces the tragedy: Clarissa can act only as she does, in duty to herself, but from the moment she violates the theory by taking the only means of escape in her power—accepting Lovelace's offer of assistance—she is doomed; yet after suffering every form of degradation she commands respect and triumphs. Richardson's conviction of the importance of his theme informs with power the smallest details of his setting. There is no such drama in Miss Yonge's novels because she was incapable of perceiving that moral theory may require revision or reinterpretation in the light of experience or in consequence of a change in the sensibility of a society. In her fictions moral lesson is deduced from theory as mechanically as in a Sunday-School story of the last century. Apart from the ideal of Christian living described, as to the desirability of which there can evidently be more than one opinion, she has nothing to present but a moral ethos where everybody's first duty is to give up everything for everybody else and where no one can enjoy anything without feeling guilty and obliged to justify himself at a moral bar, where every impulse is suspect and made to seem sinful, and where the only sanctionable activities unconnected with religion are parlour games and a form of lively conversation where humour is restricted to thoroughly harmless puns. As representing a religious culture these novels are not impressive and it cannot do the Anglican cause a service to resurrect her fictions as propaganda.

It remains to ask, why should anyone want to resurrect them? Charlotte Yonge was logical as only a simple-minded fanatic can be, pressing her theory to its extreme conclusions. Thus she held, and bases the action of novels upon the argument, that there can be no secular art (not by inclusion but by rejection—no secular music should exist, only Victorian Sacred Music), she objected to any higher education for women because only by being in a religious order could they justify it, and so on. She shows, says a contributor to the current number of *Theology*, how far a clearly conceived dogmatic outlook will carry a writer. And it is on these grounds that she is put forward as a valuable author by the critics of a new school who seem to derive, as they acknowledge inspiration, from Mr T. S. Eliot's *After Strange Gods*, where 'the standard of orthodoxy' was explicitly brought to bear on literature. This school of Anglican criticism has already produced its text-books, its poetry (discussed elsewhere in this issue), its drama, and has in *Theology* its organ. It therefore calls for consideration here, like the Marxist literary movement of the 'thirties which we discussed at the time and which it in many respects resembles. It offers to perform two critical functions. First, to improve the orthodox by opening up access for them to the literature of the age, in which we have only to offer them our best wishes for success. Second, there is a very evident assertion that what Bro. George Every calls Christian Discrimination has a superior light by which literary criticism should be directed, which can by innate virtue short-circuit literary criticism.

We have to insist, as we did with the Marxists, that the essential thing in undertaking literary criticism is that you should be a literary critic concerned, with complete disinterestedness, to demonstrate by the methods of literary criticism exactly what it is that a piece of literary art is doing. This is often quite different from what it alleges it is doing or undertakes to do, and we have to repeat to the dogmatic Christian discriminator the warning we gave to the Marxist critic, that before certifying a work on the grounds of content or apparent orthodoxy it is as well to be sure that its actual 'message', what it inevitably and essentially communicates, is what you thought it was. By not applying the method of literary criticism to Charlotte Yonge's novels the Christian discriminator has undertaken to endorse something that many Christians of all kinds would agree, one imagines, to deplore and disown. Miss Sayers provided a similar test in her novels and drama, and we see the principle at work exposed in *Blackfriars*, where an ecclesiastic recently declared that her literary productions are valuable art *because* she is orthodox. The avowedly Christian critic would have to be a saint indeed to be capable of the disinterestedness necessary to expose the writings of a pillar of his orthodoxy as bad art. (Catholic critics have before now incurred animus in their own community by suggesting that Chesterton and Belloc, for instance, were not only not good poets but have an undesirable aspect.) Though Bro. George Every does allow that a Christian artist is not necessarily always better

than a freethinking one, he is nevertheless generally seen in the position
of the Evangelical preacher who condemned Maria Edgeworth's novels
because they insidiously showed perfect happiness and virtue without
religion; thus he values highly Charlotte Yonge's novels because she
shows that you cannot be good and have no right to be happy unless
you are a High Anglican. Similarly, we see Mr Bethell concerned in
his book not to be a literary critic but to make an appearance of literary
criticism for his own purposes—to prove that he may enjoy best-sellers
and detective stories and the rest without any loss of face as a Christian
soul, that his tastes in fiction and poetry, those of *l'homme moyen
sensuel*, are not inconsistent with alleged possession of the finest
perceptions in life and art and the realm of the spirit (thus his book in
the same series). If the Christian critic of literature is not a literary
critic he is nothing, and having become one he will hardly be content
to cease to be one, to exercise some 'standard of orthodoxy' or to
indulge in special pleading. For in examining a piece of literature as a
literary critic he is inevitably appraising it and the appraisal is a process
much more subtle than the application of any standard of orthodoxy or
the extraction of any moral lesson or the discovery of some panacea for
a situation producing works of art that don't answer to his doctrinal
specifications. Grant a position of privilege to the Christian as a
literary critic and we must admit the equivalent claims of the Marxist,
the agnostic, and the subdivisions of Christian critics, each with his
own standard of orthodoxy and each concerned to push the claims of
his equivalents of Miss Sayers and Miss Yonge and his sect's Georgian
poets (and to denounce the other parties' literary productions). Sec-
tarian literary criticism would lead to a variety of subjective criticism
where little if any common agreement as to value would be possible. At
present we have, the inheritance from a long tradition, a centre of merely
literary critics whose disinterested evaluations have made possible some
recognition of poets and novelists who subscribe to no orthodoxy, that
is, nearly all creative artists of the last two centuries; this centre, moreover, provides an atmosphere and *milieu* where value-judgments can be
discussed with some freedom. When Bro. George Every published a
piece in *Theology* some years ago mentioning the work of *Scrutiny* in
this field, Mr C. S. Lewis promptly wrote up invoking anathema on
him and *Scrutiny*, and when Mr Turnell eight years ago founded *Arena*
as a focus for Catholic discrimination and argued (at a very much more
impressive critical level than the Anglican critics) that Catholics lost
something by cutting themselves off from the live tradition of contemporary literature, *The Tablet* made a response similar to Mr Lewis's.
The violence and narrowness of Marxist dogmatism are too generally
known to need illustration. Perhaps what a work of literature has to

offer us is not best discovered in an atmosphere in which the spirit of theology is given play, in which (as in *After Strange Gods*) the direct inspiration of the Devil is imputed to any artist who runs counter to our prejudices, in which access to the one source of absolute truth is confidently claimed by the critic, and anathema invoked on dissentients.

The method of literary criticism, as repeatedly defined in these pages, is to secure the maximum general agreement for evaluation by starting with something demonstrable—the surface of the work—and through practical criticism to proceed inwards to a deeper and wider kind of criticism commanding assent (or giving an opening for disagreement and discussion) at every step. It may well be shocking to the mere literary critic that Christians and even professional maintainers of standards of orthodoxy should be unable to read what is in front of them, should be unable, for example, to discover for themselves, even if they cannot point to the evidence in the texture of her writings, that Miss Sayers unconsciously incarnates a very inferior set of attitudes and values, or (conversely) cannot, because of theological differences, see that *The Pilgrim's Progress* is great art. It seems to follow that a specialist non-theological training is necessary to make sure what it is we are discussing when what we want to discuss is a poem or a novel. Bro. George Every looks forward (in *Theology*, September 1940) to a company of Christian critics who, being trained in theology as well as what he calls our grammar and rhetoric, will be able to provide literary criticism that he has no doubt, he says, will be better than the criticism of *Scrutiny*.[1] This seems too sanguine. There is no reason to suppose that those trained in theology, or philosophy for that matter, are likely to possess, what is essential to the practice of literary criticism, that 'sensitiveness of intelligence' described by Matthew Arnold as equivalent to conscience in moral matters. A theological training seems to have a disabling effect and has subsequently to be struggled against when literary criticism is the concern. And there are other dangers. When theology is made a substitute for literary criticism or is tacked on to bad criticism the result is disastrous. In *Man and Literature* Mr Norman Nicholson, following up *After Strange Gods*, is seen at work, armed with a few theological themes, on all kinds of recent authors. Though no doubt of interest to those of his own outlook who cannot

[1] It seems that in self-protection we should point out that *Scrutiny* critics come from all kinds of social and religious backgrounds, and that we have repeatedly published contributions from at least four Roman Catholic critics. It would be interesting to know whether these could be picked out on internal evidence alone, and if Bro. George Every could indicate exactly in what way he thinks their criticism of say, *Le Misanthrope*, *As You Like It* and other Shakespeare plays could be improved by the addition in some way of theology.

begin to read for themselves, the results are quite useless for any other purpose, one would have thought, for this writer has no fineness of perception and no corresponding critical idiom and method. The chapter on D. H. Lawrence is particularly gross and therefore mis-representing. (The assumption that they are all addressing a W.E.A. kind of audience would account for the crudeness of Mr Bethell's and Bro. George Every's arguments too, but the tone of Christian know-ingness they all employ does not improve matters, nor add grace to their pillaging of other writers without acknowledgment.) It was in the palmy days of *The Criterion* that theology became the latest *chic* in the fashionable intellectual's outfit, and we can observe in some members of the *Theology* group the point where the Christian discriminator and the Bloomsbury exhibitionist do not merely meet but overlap; if theology is going to be aired for these purposes the gravest suspicions of its value to literary criticism will be confirmed. The method of *After Strange Gods* is temptingly easy, and particularly adapted to further individual and group complacency, it is evident.

The line for a Christian apologist for literature to take is surely that in the work of considerable poets and novelists—few of whom were or remained churchmen, and we may well ask why this is so—the finest and keenest perceptions of an age show themselves, communicated in the language by which we live as social beings; and that to deprive oneself of them, in the name of religious orthodoxy or anything else, is to deprive oneself of full life and real understanding of the world we are part of. The tendency of orthodoxy is to repress these perceptions for its own convenience and cause a moral cramp in the developing consciousness—an effect very obvious in Charlotte Yonge's novels so that these might justly be described as undesirable literature.[1] The spontaneous explosive reaction of artists to this kind of pressure is as inevitable as a drowning man's struggle for air: Blake, Samuel Butler, the early Shaw and Lawrence among others bear violent witness to the

---

[1] There is a quotable instance, in one of her most esteemed novels, that localizes the general effect described above. A small child decorating the room with holly has climbed on a chair by the fire, forgetting this was forbidden, and a moral and emotional scene at the child's expense is staged on the subject of transgression, ending with the curate's reporting with emotion:

'Wilmet recommended not taking the prize prayer-book to church [as punishment], and she acquiesced with tears in her eyes. A good child's repentance is a beautiful thing—

> "O happy in repentance' school
> So early taught and tried".'   (*The Pillars of the House*)

The determination of the educated that a secular school system should take children out of the clutches of the religious is understandable.

force of a repressive moral environment and the waste of energy exerted to lever it off. When Lawrence wrote:

> It is the way our sympathy flows and recoils that really determines our lives. And here lies the importance of the novel properly handled. It can inform and lead into new places the flow of our sympathetic consciousness, and it can lead our sympathy away in recoil from things gone dead.

he indicates the most important part of the novelist's function, and suggests how much more delicate and complex that is than the work of the moralist or theologian, enjoying his clearly conceived dogmatic outlook and ordering his final judgments by the 'standard of orthodoxy', can be. The novelist, unlike the theologian, works in terms of concrete particularity.

If Christian discriminators wish to gain a respectful hearing they must jettison their Charlotte Yonges instead of trying to thrust them on us, and show themselves in opposition to that tendency of all orthodoxies for which some phrase needs coining to express the converse of what Arnold called 'the dissidence of Dissent'. They must possess a finer sensibility in their own province as well as in ours. 'Brother Every, discriminating Christianly', as Mr Bethell puts it, states dogmatically of the maintenance of standards and work of the literary critic, that this 'capacity is certainly a matter of intelligence and not virtue' and therefore inessential for a Christian (though possibly an added grace); Mr C. S. Lewis made a similar statement even more vehemently in the attack in *Theology* cited above. The virtue that does not include this kind of intelligence, we reply, can be only a very qualified variety and contains an element of danger to itself. When Charlotte Bronte in *Villette* records the recoil of a Protestant conscience from a professedly Christian society which seemed to her to have 'gone dead', when Stendhal diagnoses the seminary world of the day in *Le Rouge et Le Noir*, when Henry James and Edith Wharton examine the values by which a society lived, they are doing in a sharp local way what all good novelists are doing, the work of the critic and maintainers of standards; and Bro. George Every's idea that if only general education could be stopped (and he hopes it may[1]) the need for literature and criticism would disappear shows how shallow his recognition of the uses of literature must be. If the Christian discriminators singled out for recognition the art of the Stendhals and Conrads and Tolstoys and showed they could understand and utilize such novels as *Nostromo*, *Middlemarch*, *Anna Karenina*, *Darkness at Noon*, *Portrait of a Lady*, *The Root and the Flower*, instead of deploring George Eliot, claiming Jane Austen as a 'Christian novelist' because they know she was a

[1] *Theology*, September 1940.

clergyman's daughter, and displaying superiority on theological grounds to Thomas Hardy, their own intention would be advanced as well as the cause of literature. That they should desire to make literature 'the handmaid of theology', as Mr Bethell says, is natural, but when supported by so very poor a showing of first-hand literary criticism their efforts to prove that they can make it so, let alone that it should be so, are peculiarly unimpressive.

D. H. LAWRENCE PLACED

A note by F. R. LEAVIS *and a letter by* H. COOMBES (1949)

The following letter to the Editors is timely: it will serve instead of the note that was to have been printed under *Comments* in this issue—a note provoked immediately by a dismissal of D. H. Lawrence in *The New Statesman and Nation* (the critic being the Literary Editor) as a 'clinical case', and by this passage which appeared in *The Times Literary Supplement* for 18 December (1948—the occasion being a review of Maupassant's *Bel Ami* in translation): 'He accepted without reserve the large part that sex has played in life—not least, in French life—and in French literature from the time of Rabelais and Ronsard. But his acceptance never sinks to the anatomical crudities of D. H. Lawrence, nor becomes, as with Lawrence, an obsession and a gospel.'

To this admirer of Maupassant it may be replied that, while there is only one *Lady Chatterley's Lover* in Lawrence's *œuvre*, even in the special undertaking of that book he is preoccupied with the assertion of spiritual values: it is Maupassant whose attitude to sex is crude. But the critical *florilegium* presented by Mr Coombes shows how little such a reply is likely to abash the offender, who enjoys the consciousness of having with him a consensus of the *élite*. It would be easy, with a very little research, to extend the anthology to fill a whole number of *Scrutiny*. A year of the higher journalism would provide flowers enough to occupy many pages.

It is a disgraceful state of affairs, bearing out to the full Lawrence's diagnostic severities about the contemporary civilized mind. To hope that any appeal to the facts and the truth can avail against prepossession, conceit and insensibility so potently banded is perhaps vain. All the same, it had been intended to return to Lawrence in these pages. As Mr Coombes says, the business of appraisal presents many complexities. But some critical treatment will be attempted in an early number of *Scrutiny*.

F. R. L.

Dear Sirs,

Though from time to time there have been highly appreciative references to D. H. Lawrence in the pages of *Scrutiny* (and in the works of *Scrutiny* writers, notably in *The Great Tradition*), there has never been a full article on Lawrence in your Review. The subject is a complex one, and the *Scrutiny* writers are busy people. But such is the nature and quality of the great bulk of criticism on Lawrence that *Scrutiny* could undertake nothing more valuable, I believe, than a 'Revaluation'.

I give below a number of quotations which, if taken all together, would come roughly to the impression of Lawrence that is current in 'educated' circles. Among the authors are one or two respected names, and to them I apologise for including them in this company. And some of the articles, etc., from which the quotations are taken are, on the whole, 'pro-Lawrence'; it is a pity that respected critics do not always make it clear that they are not bringing grist to the mills of the stupid or the nasty when dealing with such a profound and complex theme as Lawrence. All the quotations seem to me sufficiently unambiguous to justify my use of them in this connection.

Roger Dataller, in *The Plain Man and the Novel*:

'Since he had dismissed the brain for the belly-worship of his creed, the vision of a peaceful and rational society could have no attraction for him. He was an enemy of the mind; and though somehow he might have repudiated this as shrilly as he repudiated all accepted standards, he remained a mouthpiece of reaction in contemporary letters. The "mindless, eyeless, hysterical mass-consciousness" with which his work is identified has become the bane of modern Europe.'

D. S. Savage, in *The Personal Principle*:

'The significance of Lawrence lay in his life rather than in his works'...'his refusal to allow art its due rights and to be himself the considerable artist which he potentially was'...'Lawrence's abandonment of all that we understand by the spiritual heritage of the West and his turning to vital primitivism'...'Because Lawrence was not a thinker'...'Lawrence's view of life, his "biologism", which is a similarly retrogressive dissolution back into primary life, implies a refusal of spiritual values.'

V. S. Pritchett, in *The Living Novel*:

'Lawrence's teachings are interesting because they are a compendium of what a whole generation wanted to feel, until Hitler arose, just after Lawrence's death, and they saw where the dark unconsciousness was leading them. Seen in this light, Lawrence represented the last phase of the Romantic movement: random, irresponsible egotism, power for power's sake, the blood cult of Rosenberg. And Lawrence was representative, because tens of thousands of people in England and Europe were uprooted people, like himself.'

F. Swinnerton, in *The Georgian Literary Scene*:

'My belief is that the reputation of this author will decline. As men and women learn more about their own minds, his remarkable pioneer work will fall in importance...We shall be forced back upon his books as literature; and this test, without considerable reservation, they will not pass.'

Legouis and Cazamian, in *A History of English Literature*:

'But it would be futile to try and lay the chief stress upon the artist in him: the artist in him is neither very great nor of the finest quality; Lawrence indeed would not rank so high as he does, but for the sombre enthusiasm that raises him above his own self.'

Norman Nicholson, in *Man and Literature*:

'In *St Mawr* Lawrence the critic sets out with the Freudian interpretation in his mind to make up a story about a horse. But the symbol has not really caught fire in the mind of Lawrence the creator. As a result, the horse never takes on real symbolical significance, but becomes a sort of grotesque caricature of Lawrence himself. In his identification of himself with the horse Lawrence even goes so far as to make the wretched animal have no foals *because it doesn't want to* [Mr Nicholson's italics]. Lawrence, it should be remembered, had no children, nor did many of his characters.'

Compton Mackenzie, in *Literature in my Time*:

'...but for Lawrence, married to a German wife, pressed for money, and in poor health, the war annihilated reality. It plunged him into a miasma of morbid dreams'...'It is not absurd to suggest that Walt Whitman was a happier D. H. Lawrence, the happiness being conferred by the physical vigour fate denied to Lawrence.'

Henry Miller, in *The Cosmological Eye*:

'Lawrence's animal natures, just because of their irreducible obscenity, are the purest bodies in our current literature. Animated by a metaphysical conception they act through obedience to fundamental laws of nature. Of these laws Lawrence admits his complete ignorance. He created his metaphysical world by faith; he proceeds only by intuition. He may have been utterly wrong, but he is absolutely consistent.'

Hugh Kingsmill, in *D. H. Lawrence*:

'Though without any of Nietzsche's nobility of character and capacity to endure neglect and solitude, Lawrence in his slight way, often recalls Nietzsche, another poet enmeshed in the will, and solacing his impotence with dreams of new forms of life in which he would be the master.'

W. Empson, in a review of W. Y. Tindall's *D. H. Lawrence and Susan his Cow*:

'It is fair enough to laugh at Lawrence, who got into some absurd personal and intellectual positions, and no doubt for some people was a harmful leader. Hugh Kingsmill has done it recently very well, but he was funny with the human breadth that the subject requires.' [I may say here that though Mr Kingsmill's book is probably not the 'repulsive little book' that Mr Empson finds Mr Tindall's to be, it is not, in my opinion, distinguished by 'human breadth' in its humour or in anything else.—]   F.R.L.

Rex Warner, in *The Cult of Power*:

'And it seems to us now that his system, for all its fervour, was largely negative, a mere assertion of his denial of the system of his upbringing. His God, for instance, must be the exact opposite of the "gentle Jesus" of his childhood'. . . 'Fascism finally succeeded, at least temporarily, in making the synthesis that eluded Lawrence.'

Stephen Spender, in *The Destructive Element*:

'There are two ways of regarding Lawrence. The first is, qualitatively, as I have done here, regarding especially the descriptive passages in his novels, and the Nature poems in *Birds, Beasts, and Flowers*. The other and more disappointing way is to consider him primarily as a preacher.'

There they are then. The fact that some of them are comical is little compensation. Though some of the critics are comparatively unknown, their works are in public libraries and their influence spreads.

Scrutiny writers are of course aware of the desperate state of affairs to be inferred from the quotations, but I don't feel that that makes this 'public challenge' superfluous. If *Scrutiny* doesn't do something about it, who else is likely to? 'One must speak for life and growth, amid all this mass of destruction and disintegration.'

                                                                H. COOMBES

6

THE LITERARY WORLD

THE LITERARY RACKET

F. R. LEAVIS (1932)

> things rank and gross in nature
> Possess it merely. That it should come to this!

In discussing the state of reviewing with people of experience—reviewers, editors, publishers and authors—we were commonly, when illustrative anecdote had begun to accumulate into monotony, presented with the conclusion: 'But everybody knows all about it. And anyway, there's nothing you can do.' In a sense everybody does know. Yet if we could print (as for sufficiently obvious reasons we cannot) some of the choicer of the instances we collected, most of the readers of *Scrutiny* would have a shock. For the fact is that the cultivated in general do *not* realize how completely reviewing has ceased to have anything to do with criticism: honest and intelligent reviews still occur, but the function of reviewing (the legitimate function) has lapsed.

Even observing the discretion necessary to escape legal revenge (the law of libel is not as an outraged sense of decency would have it) we might yet surprise the reader with histories and other data illustrating the value of advertising, the reach and thoroughness of the Literary Racket, and the power and vindictiveness of the gangs. But it would still be felt that, while all this was no doubt representative of the classy Sunday papers, the dailies and the more hearty weeklies, yet it had little bearing on—well, on the only weekly (whichever it is one may have chosen) that an intelligent person can read. And to bring the bearing home would require a particularity that is obviously precluded.

This is not to deny that there are honourable exceptions (again particularity would be indiscreet). But it would be in any case a mistake to stress exclusively racketeering and the grosser forms of abuse. What is meant by saying that the function of reviewing has lapsed may be best put in this way: though the need for intelligent reviewing is greater than ever it was before, no intelligent critic can hope to find steady employment in the exercise of his qualifications.

Why this is so may be indicated by considering the problem that faces a conscientious literary editor. In the first place the problem is one of dealing with the sheer bulk of reading-matter that comes to the office for review. He would be a gifted person if he could decide offhand which of some scores of books are worth serious criticism. Moreover, even if he could, intrinsic value could not be the final criterion determining space and treatment: publishers are clients of the Advertising Manager, as the most conscientious editor can never be allowed to forget. To rescue him from this predicament—that is, to spirit away the obscene fact of its existence—there is to hand the fraternity of Higher Reviewers, themselves products and victims of the situation. Some of them may once have been potential critics. But they, like the editor, have livings to make, and in the process of making a living they have inevitably left behind what critical qualifications they may have had.

Nevertheless, they are distinguished critics and authorities, with pretensions to maintain and self-esteem to cherish. The inevitable outcome, as indicated in the first number of *Scrutiny*, is solidarity. See them fall upon the rash outsider who undertakes to remind the world what serious standards are. As for the traitor from within, anyone inclined that way does not need the comradely warning that revolt means extinction. But we will not, by instancing melodramatic cases of this kind, give them a disproportionate emphasis. Comradely feeling (and there is a great deal of it) has in general much pleasanter functions. There are those little dinners at the Berkeley, those cocktail parties, and so on, where authors and reviewers learn to 'get together'. Mere sense of decency makes unkind reviews or reviews in the wrong spirit impossible.

And so what might appear to be the problem facing the conscientious editor disappears. As for that pamphlet called *Have with you to Great Queen Street* which came out some time ago—well, pamphlets—or episodes—of that kind don't often come out.

But social pressure and the pressure of the Advertising Manager are, after all, symptoms rather than causes. The radical fact is the advance of civilization. The supply of literature has become an industry subject to the same conditions as the supply of any other commodity. For many firms publishing is a business like the manufacture of 50s. suits, and the methods of Big Business are accordingly adopted. The market is raked for authors—for potential profit-makers—the wares are boosted by the usual commercial methods. The gigantic advance in output that makes good reviewing more than ever necessary has been its destruction—by asphyxiation in various forms.

Are we, then, beating the wind? Those who tell us so, tell us at the same time that these things are commonplace. They may be. But we do not believe that the greater number of clients of the 'higher journalism' realize how preponderantly the reviewing they read is what it is—oil for the cogs of the publishing machine. To get this fully recognized by those capable of recognizing it has never been whole heartedly attempted. It is worth attempting. And there is certainly somewhere a public—if it can be mobilized—that will support criticism—if it is offered.

THE BACKGROUND OF TWENTIETH CENTURY LETTERS

Q. D. LEAVIS (1939)

A Number of People, by Sir Edward Marsh (Heinemann)
Unforgotten Years, by Logan Pearsall Smith (Constable)
Enemies of Promise, by Cyril Connolly (Routledge)
Modern Poetry, by Louis MacNeice (O.U.P.)

Sir Edward Marsh was the patron of the Georgian poets, Mr Connolly is the co-mate of the post-war literary gang, Mr MacNeice is a contributor to the contemporary poetic renaissance. Each has recently published a book about his circle. We have the socio-literary history of three phases for inspection, and may take the opportunity to draw some conclusions about the literary *milieu* of our age, the background of twentieth-century letters. If you are inclined to think this a norm, read the history of the same period in American letters, as recorded by Malcolm Cowley in *Exile's Return* and Lincoln Steffens in his autobiography. Sir Edward Marsh's picture has nothing in common with Steffens's, MacNeice's case-history of self and partners in no way resembles Cowley's. No one could deny that the American history represents a healthy development, an evolution out of chaos and futility to a general recognition of standards and an agreement as to abiding values, in literary criticism. The 'critical' sections of the two later English books are depressing reading. Mr Connolly's list of who's who in modern literature, his choice of the hopes for English literature and those who he thinks are reviving imaginative writing, has to be read to be believed, and Mr Connolly is an exceptionally able and bright-minded member of our higher journalism. However, the third section of his book, 'A Georgian Boyhood', should be read carefully by literary critics as well as educationists: his account of the Eton education and its effect on taste and character—Eton standing for the English public-school system generally—offers a comprehensive answer to the questions raised by a comparison of these books with their American equivalents. The information he unconsciously gives about the relation between knowing the right people and getting accepted in advance of production as a literary value is even more useful than the analysis he consciously makes of the stultifying effects of an exclusively classical education conducted in an exclusively upper-class and male establishment.

Sir Edward Marsh's book raises all the questions. He is a beautiful specimen, a perfect litmus-paper without, as a literary critic, any individuality, personal taste or character. A Classic at Westminster, he passed second in the Civil Service examination, and thereafter, mixing as intensively as possible with the best people, he became an innocent blotting-paper to all literary aspirants he met in the right company, particularly good-looking young men with fetching manners. He was overwhelmed by Rupert Brooke, and after meeting Ivor Novello he became so impressed with the talents of the author of *Keep the Home Fires Burning* that he even took a passionate interest in musical comedy. It was his representative quality that enabled him to produce in the Georgian Poetry-Books something that went like hot-cakes (the second volume sold nineteen thousand). And as his classical education gave him an unshakable conception of what poetry ought to be, so his environment gave him no occasion to doubt his rightness of judgment. He still believes that 'Rupert Brooke is destined to remain as a considerable figure in English Literature', that Gordon Bottomley's and Lascelles Abercrombie's poetic dramas are great poetry, that Georgian poetry will soon be rehabilitated, and is confident of his own place beside Tottel (predicted by Gosse) for anthologizing it. He still feels how right he was to refuse in 1925 to have anything to do with the 'new directions' of English poetry (the only reference to Eliot's poetry is a silly joke) and it never occurs to him, any more than to Mr Connolly, to question Mr Desmond MacCarthy's right to refuse anyone else the right to criticize Milton—for both of them it is enough that he himself is an Etonian.

The same complacency, an inability to apply purely literary criticism because of an unconscious acceptance of social values in this as in all other fields, is visible in Connolly almost equally, even though he sets out to account for his feeling that something is wrong somewhere. *The Waves* is a supreme work of art, Isherwood and Orwell are the coming great writers, 'the prose of Spender is also unusual, and in his critical book *The Destructive Element*, he makes a study of that great Mandarin, Henry James, which must affect the values of any contemporary who reads it'. I suppose it is because, instead of knowing Mr Spender personally, I have been reading Henry James's novels for fifteen years that the only way in which his study affected me was as a botched-up piece of journalism by someone who had not only no capacity for examining James's novels critically but who had not even read them with ordinary care and intelligence. Though Mr Connolly attacks the classical culture of Eton as 'by nature sterile' and though he protests against the College literary values of his time—the Victorian Romantic and the facetious in verse, Pre-Raphaelite prose—he does not think of questioning the social foundation of the world of letters. He ends his case-history: 'Since I was unable to write in any living language when I left Eton I was already on the way to being a critic. My ambition was to be a poet, but I could not succeed when poetry was immersed in the Georgian or neo-Tennysonian tradition . . . I was, however, well grounded enough to become a critic, and drifted into it through unemployability.' He does not apparently think this a criticism of the state of our literary journalism. But this does explain what has always puzzled some of us. Contemplating the literary reviewing we cannot help wondering how it is that these reviewers, who know all the literary figures of their world, have had the most expensive education, and are not so overworked that they have no time to think if they wanted to, are not only unable to make first-hand judgments but are also completely ignorant of informed opinion. Where did Mr A get his reputation for brilliant wit, how is it that B's stuff is counted devastating satire, why does Miss C get respectful reviews, on what grounds could anyone assert Mrs D's latest novel is worth serious attention? are questions that regularly recur to many readers of our literary weeklies, monthlies and even quarterlies. Mr Connolly early on in his book observes: 'Critics in England do not accept bribes, but they discover one day that in a sense their whole life is an accepted bribe, a fabric of compromises based on personal relationships.' Sir Edward Marsh is incapable of such a reflection, but even as aware a man as Mr Connolly does not seem able to see its full implications for literary criticism. He tells us how when he and his Eton set were faced with leaving College for the University the prospect seemed 'exhilarating and cosy, for, subject to a little permutation, the sentimental friendships from College continued unabated with undergraduates from other schools forming an audience, who, at a pinch, would contribute new blood to the cast'. A parable of the structure of our little world of letters. Skip a step and you see how it is that these elegant unemployables get into the higher journalism, and even the academic world, and how reputations are made—you have only to get the right people, whom you already know or can get introductions to, to write the right kind of thing about you in the right places. The odious spoilt little boys of Mr Connolly's and so many others writers' schooldays—their education surely no less strange than that of the Nazi aristocracy as described by Erika Mann in *School for Barbarians*—move in a body up to the universities to become inane pretentious young men, and, still essentially unchanged, from there move into the literary quarters vacated by the last batch of their kind. Rupert Brooke in 1906 at Cambridge 'was in the set which filled the place that mine had held when I was "up"', writes Sir Edward. Mr Connolly and his set expected to succeed Rupert Brooke's, and are now seeing to it that the literary preserves are kept exclusively for their friends. We who are in the habit of asking how such evidently unqualified reviewers as fill the literary weeklies ever got into the profession need ask no longer. They turn out to have been 'the most fashionable boy in the school', or to have had a feline charm or a sensual mouth and long eye-lashes. And in the creative field the same process is seen at work. The Oxford group moved naturally into the place left by Sir Edward's Georgians, to create the latest poetic renaissance, almost straight from school; and having no critical standards to reckon with, as we have seen, they have remained what they were at school. Hence Mr MacNeice's account of his friends and their work reads like a book written by a schoolboy for schoolboys. 'Going to Germany soon after leaving Oxford, Auden took readily to post-War Germany's intellectual curiosity and spirit of heroic or idyllic Kameradschaft. He admires the cinema's unrivalled capacity for rapportage; Auden has always believed that a good writer must be first a good reporter. His poetry is obviously conditioned by his background and experiences, and also by his not unfriendly contempt for the female sex, whom he regards as still precluded from civilization by circumstances.' It is no use looking for growth or development or any addition to literature in such an adolescent hot-house. The one literary artist of serious performance, vitality and worth in the period covered by Sir Edward and Mr Connolly was D. H. Lawrence. He imports the only jarring note into the former's memoirs, otherwise so happily studded with affectionate anecdotes of the best people in society and the arts. Lawrence is reported to have said that Eddie Marsh ought to have his bottom kicked (for his impudence in telling Lawrence that his poetry didn't scan—see the Lawrence *Letters*). Eddie records it serenely, for Lawrence was an outsider. The tone taken by the literary reviews at the time Lawrence required obituary notices is a testimonial to the success of the public-school–university hold over literary criticism. No one who ever read Lord David Cecil, for instance, on Lawrence can fail to appreciate that the achieved reputation of an outsider was felt as a personal insult by the people who run our literary world. Order is revealed among a chaotic puzzle of memories: we read in the paper that two young men are the likely candidates for the something literary prize or poetry medal, one being sponsored by Sir Edward Marsh and one by some other bigwig—neither would be sponsored by the literary critic; we could never before account for Mr Connolly's write-up of Naomi

Mitchison's embarrassing bestseller *We Have Been Warned*; Sir Edward himself tells us how he was asked by the authorities whether Henry James ought to be given the Order of Merit, and instructed to find out whether Joyce ought to be given a Civil List Grant. Henry James got his O.M. on his death-bed after some trouble, but suppose it had been Lawrence (D. H.) or someone as unconventional and society-shunning as Walt Whitman! The gulf between disinterested opinion on contemporary literature and fashionable esteem is for a variety of reasons deplorable.

Mention of Walt Whitman brings us to the other book listed here, the memoirs of Logan Pearsall Smith. Mr Smith was an American Quaker in the distant days before he settled down to become an English *littérateur*. Unlike Henry James and Mr T. S. Eliot he sold his birthright for a mess of pottage, or more precisely for the Paterian tradition of fine writing and the English social tradition of letters. The earlier parts of his book are good reading, for his origin provided him with a point of view and a fruitful background. His reminiscence of Walt Whitman is something that no one else in this galley could have been capable of setting down, and his criticism of the Balliol ethos of his time is correspondingly refreshing. But that was long ago. He is now as convinced as Eddie Marsh that modern poetry and modern prose are no good, and as sure as Rupert Brooke that style means decoration and stilts. 'This draught of Shakespeare's brewing—the potent wine that came to fill the great jewelled cup of words he fashioned,' he writes, and even in unimpassioned argument: 'There are two main methods of attaining excellence in writing, two ways of attempting to reach the peaks of Parnassus.' Responsibility for failure to develop his initial endowment must lie with the company he kept, which though it has always reviewed with extravagant praise his literary criticism and his creative efforts will never convince posterity that the *Trivia* are not boring or the monograph on Shakespeare not empty fine writing. The advantages Americans enjoy in having no public-school system, no ancient universities and no tradition of a closed literary society run on Civil Service lines, can hardly be exaggerated.

'UNDER WHICH KING, BEZONIAN?'

F. R. LEAVIS (1932)

It would be very innocent of us to be surprised by the frequency with which we are asked to 'show our colours'. But the source of the command does sometimes surprise us. Indeed, this very formulation came first from Mr George Santayana, and others whom we respect have repeated it, in substance, since. We should have thought that we had amply made out our case (if that were needed) for holding the assertion and application of serious standards in literary criticism to be an essential function, and one disastrously inoperative now.

Not that we suppose the service of this function to be the whole duty of man, or our own whole duty. The more seriously one is concerned for literary criticism the less possible does one find it to be concerned for that alone. *Scrutiny* has not, as a matter of fact, confined itself to literary criticism. But to identify *Scrutiny* with a social, economic or political creed or platform would be to compromise and impede its special function. This, in its bearing on the challenge now in view, has already been glossed by: 'the free play of intelligence on the under-lying issues'. More, of course, needs saying. What is immediately in place is to insist that one does not necessarily take one's social and political responsibilities the less seriously because one is not quick to see salvation in a formula or in any simple creed. And it is unlikely that anyone actively and sympathetically interested in *Scrutiny* (whether as a reader or otherwise) will exhibit this kind of quickness. On the other hand, those of us who are particularly engrossed by the business of carrying on *Scrutiny* should perhaps resolve (though it seems unnecessary) to warn ourselves now and then against making the perception of the complexity of problems an excuse for complacent inattention: special duties are not ultimately served by neglect of the more general. But the special function of *Scrutiny* is an indispensable one, and there appears to be no danger of its being excessively attended to.

Supporters of *Scrutiny*, then, are, we suppose, of varying social, political and economic persuasions. But the function indicated would hardly have been fully realized if its bearing on such persuasions were left at this, no more immediate and particular than has yet been suggested. If there seems to be no reason why supporters of *Scrutiny* should not favour some kind of communism as the solution of the economic problem, it does not seem likely (there is no thought here of Mr Middleton Murry) that they will be orthodox Marxists. The efficiency of the Marxist dialectic, indeed, makes it difficult to determine what precisely orthodoxy is (we do not find even Mr Maurice Dobb, whom Mr Eliot singles out for commendation, very lucid). But there can be no doubt that the dogma of the priority of economic conditions, however stated, means a complete disregard for—or, rather, a hostility towards—the function represented by *Scrutiny*.

Why the attitude expressed in the varying formula that makes 'culture' (a term to be examined) derivative from the 'methods of production'—why this attitude must be regarded as calamitous Trotsky himself brings out in his *Literature and Revolution*. This book shows him to be a cultivated as well as an unusually intelligent man (which perhaps has something to do with his misfortune). But he too, unhappily, like all the Marxists, practises, with the familiar air of scientific rigour, the familiar vague, blanketing use of essential terms. He can refer, for instance, to the '2nd of August, 1914, when the maddened power of bourgeois culture let loose upon the world the blood and fire of an imperialistic war' (p. 190). This, however, is perhaps a salute to orthodoxy. And it would not be surprising if he had thought it wise to distract attention, if possible, from such things as the following, which uses 'culture' very differently, and is hardly orthodox: 'The proletariat is forced to take power before it has appropriated the fundamental elements of bourgeois culture; it is forced to overthrow bourgeois society by revolutionary violence, for the very reason that society does not allow it access to culture' (p. 195). The aim of revolution, it appears, is to secure this accursed bourgeois culture for the proletariat. Or, rather, Trotsky knows that behind the word 'culture' there is something that cannot be explained by the 'methods of production' and that it would be disastrous to destroy as 'bourgeois'. To assert this un-Marxian truth is the aim of his book. 'The proletariat', he says (p. 186), 'acquires power for the purpose of doing away with class culture and to make way for human culture.' And he insists that the necessary means to this consummation is to maintain continuity. That is, he knows, and virtually says, that 'human culture' at present is something covered by 'bourgeois culture', the Marxian blanket.

But even Trotsky, although he can speak of the need to 'turn the concept of culture into the small change of individual daily living' and can say that 'to understand and perceive truly not in a journalistic way but to feel to the bottom the very section of time in which we live, one has to know the past of mankind, its life, its work, its struggles, its hopes...', cannot (or may not) realize the delicate organic growth that 'human culture' is. Otherwise he could not so cheerfully contemplate fifty years (p. 190) of revolutionary warfare, during which everything must be subordinated to proletarian victory, and assume, without argument, that the result will be a society in which 'the dynamic development of culture will be incomparable with anything that went on in the past' (p. 189). But perhaps, and 'dynamic' strongly suggests it, 'culture' again means something different.

Indeed, Trotsky at this point in the argument, like all the Marxists, becomes indistinguishable from Mr Wells. Neither of them has faced the problem, though Trotsky, unlike Mr Wells, appears capable of seeing it if it is put. A Marxist intelligent enough and well enough educated to speak of a 'human culture' that must, if it is to exist at all, carry on from what orthodoxy dismisses as 'bourgeois culture', can hardly have failed to divine that, if he thought too much, not only his orthodoxy but his optimism would be in danger. Nothing brings out more strongly that orthodox Marxists (like most other publicists) use the word 'culture' uncomprehendingly than their failure even to perceive the problem—the problem that their dogma concerning the relation between culture and the 'methods of production' confronts them with in a particularly sharp form.

It confronts us all. For it is true that culture in the past has borne a close relation to the 'methods of production'. A culture expressing itself in a tradition of literature and art—such a tradition as represents the finer consciousness of the race and provides the currency of finer living—can be in a healthy state only if this tradition is in living relation with a real culture, shared by the people at large. The point might be enforced by saying (there is no need to elaborate) that Shakespeare did not invent the language he used. And when England had a popular culture, the structure, the framework, of it was a stylization, so to speak, of economic necessities; based, it might fairly be said, on the 'methods of production', was an art of living, involving codes, developed in ages of continuous experience, of relations between man and man, and man and the environment in its seasonal rhythm. This culture the progress of the nineteenth century destroyed, in country and in town; it destroyed (to repeat a phrase that has been used in *Scrutiny* before, and will be, no doubt, again) the organic community. And what survives of cultural tradition in any important sense survives in spite of the rapidly changing 'means of production'.

All this seems fairly obvious, and what should be equally obvious is the new status and importance of leisure. Leisure (however much or little there might be) mattered less when work was not, as it is now for so many, the antithesis of living. (See, e.g., George Bourne, *Change in the Village*, pp. 200–216.) Now, unless one is unusually lucky, one saves up living for after working hours, and for very few indeed can the bread-winning job give anything like a sense of fulfilment or be realized as in itself a significant part of a significant process. Marxists do not contemplate any reversal of this development; nor is enthusiasm for Five-Year Plans, the sense of a noble cause, or romantic worship of mechanical efficiency to be permanently the sanction of labour in itself unsatisfying. 'The Revolution', writes A. L. Morton, a Marxist, in the October *Criterion*, 'neither creates nor is intended to create a new leisure class. It is intended rather to create a leisure community...' The Marxist, then, who offers his Utopia as anything better than Mr Wells's must face the problem that we should all be facing. For any reasonable hope for civilization must assume that the beneficent potentialities of machine technique will be realized, and there seems no reason to doubt that the material means of life might be assured to all at the cost of small labour to each.

The problem is suggested by Mr Morton here: 'The state of poetry is largely dependent upon the connection of the leisure class with the productive powers. The connection must be close and vital, though that of the individual poet need not be, since he expresses less himself than his social environment. The great ages of poetry have been those in which the poetry-producing class was young and vigorous and was breaking through existing productive relationships. Conversely, a class without social functions tends to produce decadent poetry.' Without being uncritical of Mr Morton's generalizations one may ask: What will 'social functions' be in a leisure community—a community, that is, in which the 'productive process' is so efficient as no longer to determine the ordering of life? Mr Morton speaks of a 'leisure community integrally associated with the productive forces in a way in which no one class has ever been before'; but there is surely no particular virtue in being 'associated' with productive forces so mechanically efficient that 'integrally', here, seems to mean very little? No doubt when we are all leisured the special moral disadvantage of belonging to a leisure class will be gone, but 'social function', it is plain, means so much more in the generalizations about culture and the productive process that it is inapplicable here, or, if applied, becomes a mere arbitrary counter. It is a comment on the Marxian dialectic that it can take a man in this way up to the problem and leave him unable to see it.

The problem faces us all, and not hypothetically, but practically and immediately. It is a more difficult one than Trotsky, that dangerously intelligent Marxist who has some inkling, suggests in his statement of it (p. 193): 'The main task of the proletarian intelligentsia in the immediate future is not the abstract formation of a new culture regardless of the absence of a base for it, but definite culture-bearing, that is, a systematic, planful, and, of course, critical imparting to the backward masses of the essential elements of the culture which already exists.' The problem is, rather, not merely to save these 'essential elements' from a swift and final destruction in the process that makes Communism possible,[1] but

---

[1] 'Industrialization is desirable not for itself, but because Communism is only possible in an industrial community.'—A. L. Morton, *The Criterion*, October 1932. Cf. 'The essential point is that agriculture ought to be saved and revived because agriculture is the foundation for the Good Life in any society; it is, in fact, the normal life...And it is hardly too much to say that only in a primarily agricultural society, in which people have local attachments to their small domains and small communities, and remain, generation after generation, in the same place, is genuine patriotism possible...'—T.S.E., *The Criterion*, October 1931.

to develop them into an autonomous culture, a culture independent of any economic, technical or social system as none has been before. Whether such a rootless culture (the metaphor will bear pondering, in view of the contrast between the postulated communist society—in constant 'dynamic' development—and any that has produced a culture in the past) can be achieved and maintained may be doubtful. If it cannot, we have nothing better to hope for than a world of Mr Wells's men like gods, and have rather to fear that the future has been forecast in California.[1] If it can, it will be by a concern for the tradition of human culture, here and now, intenser than Trotsky's (the Marxist excommunicate); a concerted and sustained effort to perpetuate it, in spite of the economic process, the triumphs of engineering and the Conquest of Happiness, as something with its own momentum and life, more and more autonomous and self-subsistent. And in its preoccupation with this effort *Scrutiny* does not find itself largely companied.

This plea, however, will not bring us off; we have illusions. There is a choice; we must speak or die: Stalin or the King by Divine Right? And the Marxist dialectic, with its appearance of algebraic rigour, stern realism and contemptuous practicality, has great advantages—in dialectic—over those who are pusillanimous enough to let themselves be bothered by the duty and difficulty of using words precisely. The rigour, of course, is illusory, and, consequently, so are the realism and the practicality. 'In general,' says Mr Edmund Wilson approvingly in the *New Statesman and Nation* for 15 October, 'it is surprising how promptly the writers are lining up in one or other of the camps, and how readily their antagonisms are developing.' When people line up so promptly one suspects, not only that the appeal of the *chic* has something to do with it, but that the differences are not of a kind that has much to do with thinking; and the ready development of antagonisms among those whose differences are inessential should surprise only the very innocent.

Trotsky's use of the term 'culture' has already been noted. It is part of what Mr Wilson calls the 'Marxist technique'; he himself speaks of the 'old bourgeois culture' and the 'culture of Marxism'. 'Bourgeois' and 'class', likewise, are primary indispensables of the technique. Prince Mirsky, in his celebrated essay in *Echanges* (December 1931), dealing with 'la poésie bourgeoise', takes as 'le poète bourgeois' Mr T. S. Eliot. He exhibits less acuteness—or (and very naturally) more orthodoxy—than Trotsky, who would hardly have been naïve enough to pronounce (though he does contradict himself, and is capable, he also, of sentimentality): 'La bourgeoisie est vide de valeurs, toutes les valeurs

[1] See *Stardust in Hollywood*, by J. and C. Gordon.

vivantes sont du côté de la classe ouvrière.' The 'values' of the working class (though, of course, one never knows what definitions the Marxist, when challenged, will produce from under the blanket) are inevitably those induced by the modern environment—by 'capitalist' civilization; essentially those, that is, of the 'bourgeoisie' and of most Marxists. Mr Wilson (to illustrate this last point), a critic intelligent enough at his best to have written the best parts of *Axel's Castle*, was capable of resting the structure of that book on the values of the 'man who does things', and, seeing that he had thus proclaimed himself a contemporary of Dr John B. Watson, we ought not to have been surprised when he came out as an admirer of Kipling and innocently assumed that Lytton Strachey was a great writer.

Prince Mirsky, although, presumably, he does not enjoy Mr Wilson's advantage of having been born to the English language, has over Mr Wilson the advantage of living in London. He would not, as Mr Wilson has (see the *New Statesman and Nation*), have solemnly endorsed the collocation of 'Dostoevsky, Cervantes, Defoe and E. E. Cummings ...' And he may have a good critical sensibility. But that is not proved by his exposition, intelligent and adroit as it is, of Mr Eliot's poetry. What he certainly shows is unusual skill in applying the 'Marxist technique', and the way in which in explaining *The Waste Land* he seizes on the 'structural symbols,' *l'Humide, le Sec et le Feu*, and over-stresses their function, paying little attention to the essential organization, betrays the influence of the Marxian training. But the significantly betraying thing is the footnote: 'Les lecteurs d'Edith Sitwell sont en grande partie les mêmes que ceux de Bertrand Russell dont les *Principles of Mathematics* sont l'évangile des logistes.' Mathematicians are often illiterate, and Bertrand Russell wrote *The Conquest of Happiness*, and Prince Mirsky might as aptly have said that the readers of Edith Sitwell are in great part the same as those of Ernest Hemingway.

The relevance of this further appeal to performance in literary criticism should not need urging. To be concerned, as *Scrutiny* is, for literary criticism is to be vigilant and scrupulous about the relation between words and the concrete. The inadequacies of Mr Wilson and Prince Mirsky as literary critics are related to their shamelessly un-critical use of vague abstractions and verbal counters. What is this 'bourgeois culture' that Mr Eliot represents in company, one presumes, with Mr Wells, Mr Hugh Walpole, *Punch*, *Scrutiny*, Dr Marie Stopes and the *Outline for Boys and Girls*? What are these 'classes', the conflict between which a novelist must recognize 'before he can reach to the heart of any human situation'? (See *Literary Criticism and the Marxian Method* by Granville Hicks in *The Modern Quarterly* for Summer 1932.) The Marxist, of course, is pat with his answer: he will define class in terms of relation to the 'productive process'. The concept so defined—how usefully and how adequately to the facts this is not the place to discuss—will at any rate engage with its context. But when one comes to talk of 'bourgeois culture' the context has changed, and only by virtue of the Marxist dogma and the Marxist dialectic is it possible to introduce the concept here and suppose one is saying anything. Class of the kind that can justify talk about 'class culture' has long been extinct.[1] (And, it might be added, when there was such 'class culture' it was much more than merely of the class.) The process of civilization that produced, among other things, the Marxian dogma, and makes it plausible, has made the cultural difference between the 'classes' inessential. The essential differences are indeed now definable in economic terms, and to aim at solving the problems of civilization in terns of the 'class war' is to aim, whether wittingly or not, at completing the work of capitalism and its products, the cheap car, the wireless and the cinema. It is not for nothing that Trotsky's prose, when he contemplates the 'dynamic development of culture' that will follow the triumph of Revolution, takes on a Wellsian exaltation (see e.g. pp. 188–9), and that, when he descends to anything approaching particularity, what he offers might have come from *Men Like Gods* (see p. 252). And the title of Prince Mirsky's essay, *T. S. Eliot et la Fin de la poésie bourgeoise*, should have been one word shorter.

The rigour of the Marxian dialectic, then, is illusory, and the brave choice enjoined upon us the reverse of courageous, if courage has anything to do with thinking. Must we therefore take the other alternative offered us: 'si le poète—l'idéologue—bourgeois veut opposer à la Révolution quelque chose de positif et de convaincant (de convaincant pour son propre esprit) il ne peut avoir de recours qu'à la résurrection de quelque revenant médiéval...'? Must we be Royalists and Anglo-Catholics? In the first place reasons have been advanced for doubting whether those who find Marxism convincing, for their own minds, are applying minds in any serious sense to the problems that face us and them. So if, while agreeing that the recovery of religious sanctions in some form seems necessary to the health of the world, we reply that they cannot be had for the wanting, the Marxist had better not start to think before he twits us with ineffectiveness. And as for Anglo-Catholicism and Royalism, those who may find these, *pour leurs propres esprits*, convincing do not convince us that they are taking up an effective attitude towards the problems. The impressive statement, in the abstract, of a coherent position is not enough. And the main reply to the gesture that bids us, if we respect ourselves, line up

[1] Prince Mirsky refers to 'la classe où appartenait Donne'; but what has that 'bourgeoisie' in common with that of the Victorian age or that of to-day?

there, as the logical and courageous alternative, is not that *The Principles of Modern Heresy* and *The Outline of Royalism* have not yet, after all, been given us, but: 'Look at *The Criterion.*'

The Editor's spare—too spare—contributions almost always exhibit the uncommon phenomenon of real thinking turned upon the 'underlying issues', though, in their bearing on concrete problems, they show no signs of coming any nearer than before to effective particularity. But we must not, under Marxian incitement, suggest unfair tests. The effective particularity we can fairly demand would involve maintaining in *The Criterion* high standards of thinking and of literary criticism. The point that it is necessary to make is, in view of our own enterprise, a delicate one, but only the more necessary for that. Let us suffer the retort when, and as much as, we may deserve it, and express now the general regret that the name of *The Criterion* has become so dismal an irony and that the Editor is so far from applying to his contributors the standards we have learnt from him.

The relevance of the point may be enforced by remarking the particular weakness of *The Criterion* for the dead, academic kind of abstract 'thinking', especially when the 'thinker' (incapable of literary criticism) stands in a general, abstract way for 'order', 'intelligence' and the other counters, all of which are worth less than nothing if not related scrupulously to the concrete.

The Marxist challenge, then, seems to us as heroic as Ancient Pistol's and to point to as real alternatives. And we do not suppose that, in *Scrutiny*, we, more than anyone else, have a solution to offer. But, looking round, we do think that, without presuming too much, we can, since there seems no danger of too great an intensity of concern for them, make it our function to insist on certain essential conditions of a solution. Nor, inadequate as our insistence may be, does it appear superfluous to insist that the essential problems should be faced.

Nothing more (if it lived up to this account) should be needed to justify *Scrutiny*. But if some more immediate engaging upon the world of practice would reassure, then we can point to it. We have a special educational interest, and the association of this with the bent already described is unprecedented and has already shown its strength.

RETROSPECT OF A DECADE

F. R. LEAVIS (1940)

In opening our ninth year at such a time as this, the mere bringing out of the new issue, with the implied intention to carry on while that remains possible, seems manifesto enough. The importance of the function that *Scrutiny*, in its own necessarily modest way, exists to serve is to-day generally granted. Eight years ago, we recall, things were different. The purpose of *Scrutiny*, as we conceived it, was plainly enough set forth in the first issue, but that didn't inhibit the chorused and reiterated 'Show your colours!' There was a simple choice to be made, and not to make it and proclaim it was to be guilty of pusillanimity. We remember as representative of the prevailing assumptions and indicative of the pressure of the environment at that time, this comment on our 'political attitude', made with malicious intent by an eminent young intellectual: 'Well, of course, you're as little Communist as you dare be.'

The assumption that not to be Communist required courage was at that time a natural one. The pressure was certainly tremendous—to wear red, or some colour recognized as its opposite. But that had been a reason for starting *Scrutiny*, and could only be one for continuing to feel that the undertaking was worth persisting with. There was never, as a matter of fact, any hesitation or inexplicitness about our anti-Marxism, this negative being a corollary of our positive position. And our positive position was that, though without doubt the human spirit was not to be thought of as expressing itself in a void of 'freedom', unconditioned by economic and material circumstances, nevertheless there was a great need to insist on the element of autonomy and to work for the preservation of the humane tradition—a tradition representing the profit of a continuity of experience through centuries of economic and material change. Further, it was an essential part of our position, as we conceived it, *not* to be as positive as some people— possible sympathizers—would desire: we intended *Scrutiny* to stand for the humane tradition as something to be fostered apart from any particular religious creed; and the fostering of a free play of critical intelligence we thought of as essential to the tradition. In this sense *Scrutiny* invites the description 'liberal'.

Such a position could hardly be stigmatized as Fascist. But we got a good deal of free advertisement in young-intellectual organs, which used to attack *Scrutiny* for 'playing into the enemy's hands' by encouraging 'irresponsibility' in the intelligent young and distracting from a clear perception of the clear-cut issues. As the decade wore on we got less advertisement of this kind: Marxist intellectuals became more and more occupied with explaining that Marxist criticism was not what in these attacks it had very militantly represented itself to be. And then, of course, quite recently the Marxist decade came to its sharp close: that chapter ended before the chronological period was quite out.

But Marxist the decade decidedly was. It was also, in literature, as a reviewer in the following pages notes, a very barren decade. Compare it with the nineteen-twenties. The nineteen-twenties were the decade of Joyce, Eliot, D. H. Lawrence, Virginia Woolf, E. M. Forster, T. F. Powys, the effective publication of *Mauberley*, the discovery of Hopkins and the advent of Yeats as a major poet. The nineteen-thirties started with a Poetic Renascence. Now at their close one is driven to judge that the making accessible of Isaac Rosenberg (who has not yet been 'discovered', in spite of his great superiority in interest over Wilfred Owen) was a more important event in English poetry than any emergence of a new poet. In the novel there was *The Root and the Flower*; but what else is there to mention—at any rate, of cis-Atlantic origin?

The prevalent Marxizing and the barrenness might well seem to be in obviously significant relation, Marxist doctrines about literature and art being what they are. But it would, of course, be unsubtle to insist much on the suggestion of simple cause-and-effect. If the young intelligentsia yielded so readily to the satisfactions of an easy salvationism, explanations may no doubt be reasonably looked for in the menacing state of the world. Politico-economic problems filled the prospect, and unless you supposed you knew of a very simple solution, you could hardly suppose you knew of one at all. Certainly, the kind of political distraction that characterized the decade was very bad for creative work.

But there is one aspect of the unfavourable state of civilization that especially concerns *Scrutiny* and its specific function. In all ages, no doubt, there have been cliques and coteries, and young writers have founded mutual-admiration societies and done their best to make these coincident with the literary world—the world that determines current valuations. But has there ever before been a time when the young aspirant, graduating from his university group, could immediately and without any notable sense of a change find himself in a fraternity that effectively 'ran' contemporary letters—'ran' them so effectively that he could make a name and a career without even coming in sight of adult standards? The existence of such a state of affairs will be found amply recorded and documented in the eight volumes of *Scrutiny*. The disastrous consequence may be pointed to in the representative career of W. H. Auden, distinguished by his promise at the beginning of the decade.

No one would expect reminders of the nature of standards to be received with gratitude. It seems worth noting, however, in further illustration of the decade, that a little research in back files will reveal the young, predominantly Left-inclined *élite* incongruously cocking their snooks at *Scrutiny* from the pages of *The Criterion*—the only attention *Scrutiny* ever got in that promisingly styled organ. It may perhaps be permissible to record too that, because of such performances there, where we had once looked for judicial criticism by more philosophical standards than ours, we have on occasion thought it necessary to abstain from reviewing books that certainly ought otherwise to have been reviewed: we were anxious not to give the least colour of countenance to the prevailing gang-warfare notion of critical exchange. But to have to confess failure to that extent was a disappointment, for without a serious critical interplay there can hardly be said to be the beginning of a functioning contemporary criticism.

On the other hand we feel that the history of the decade has justified the intentions with which we started. And, conscious as we are of many inadequacies, it would be dishonest to pretend that, so far as one organ can hope to maintain the function of criticism, *Scrutiny* appears to us, when we turn over the back volumes, to have fallen discreditably short in its attempt at maintaining it. Moreover, to have brought and kept together something of an intellectual community, however small, seems to us to have been worth the labour. We shall carry on while we can.

HENRY JAMES AND THE ENGLISH ASSOCIATION

F. R. LEAVIS (1946)

Henry James, we know, had oddities that grew upon him in his later years. So, if we care to take it, we have an easy explanation to hand when we read the letter he wrote to John Bailey on 11 November 1912, declining the offered chairmanship of the English Association:

It is out of my power to meet your invitation with the least decency or grace. For me, frankly, my dear John, there is simply no question of these things: I am a mere stony, ugly monster of *Dis*sociation and Detachment. I have never in all my life gone in for these other things, but have dodged and shirked and successfully evaded them—to the best of my power at least, and so far as they have in fact assaulted me: all my instincts and the very essence of any poor thing that I might, or even still may, trump up for the occasion as my 'genius' have been against them, and are more against them at this day than ever, though two or three of them (meaning by 'them' the collective and congregated bodies, the splendid organizations, aforesaid) have success-fully got their teeth, in spite of all I could do, into my bewildered and badgered antiquity...I can't go into it all much—but the rough sense of it is that I believe only in absolutely independent, individual and lonely virtue, and in the serenely unsociable (or if need be at a pinch sulky and sullen) practice of the same; the observation of a lifetime having convinced me that no fruit ripens but under that temporarily graceless rigour, and that the associational process for bringing it on is but a bright and hollow artifice, all vain and delusive. (I speak here for the Arts—or of my own poor attempt at one or two of them; the other matters must speak for themselves.) Let me even while I am about it heap up the measure of my grossness: the mere dim vision of presiding or what is called, I believe, taking the chair, at a speechifying public dinner, fills me, and has filled me all my life, with such aversion and horror that I have in the most odious manner consistently refused for years to be present on such occasions even as a guest pre-assured of protection and effacement...I have at such times let them know in advance that I was utterly not to be counted on, and have indeed quite gloried in my shame; sitting at home the while and gloating over the fact that I wasn't present.

How regrettable was this unnecessary scruple, or moroseness or timidity, in James. Surely he could see that it was his duty to lend his prestige to the work of an Association whose explicit aims are 'to uphold the standards of English writing and speech' and 'to spread as widely as possible the knowledge and enjoyment of English Literature'. The advantages of associating the maintenance of the essential standards with the cultivation of others for which recognition is more readily got are surely plain: if social solidarity can't be promoted for good ends, what hope is there? Good mixing has its uses.

But perhaps James offered himself the excuse that his backwardness was unlikely to set a dangerous example. And had he been able to project himself forward some decades and then look back he would no doubt have felt that his expectations had been justified. And in *News-Letter No. 2* of the English Association (September 1946)—which might all the same have surprised him—he would have read the appreciative announcement of yet another willing President elect:

The recent publication of the two first volumes of Sir Osbert Sitwell's autobiography, *Left Hand, Right Hand* and *The Scarlet Tree*, besides being a literary event of the first magnitude, has gone some way towards satisfying the interest felt by all lovers of wit, poetry, and 'fine writing' in the person-ality of the head of the Sitwell family. Among members of the English Association this interest is naturally heightened by the knowledge that he will be next year's President.

Eighth holder of a Baronetcy created on the eve of the Regency and scion of a house whose roots strike deep into the ancient earth of England, Sir

Osbert's tastes and activities have never been those of the typical Derbyshire squire—though, to be sure, one of his forbears *did* hunt a tiger in the woods about Renishaw. In the realm of letters our President Elect has left hardly any province uninvaded, and he has cultivated each separate field with characteristic energy, originality and distinction.

We are told (in his own words) that 'he has conducted, in conjunction with his brother and sister, a series of skirmishes and hand-to-hand battles against the Philistine' and that he instituted '"Joy through Intelligence Campaign" (Inc.)'. And the *News-Letter* proceeds to cull for us the vivacities that stand against Sir Osbert's name in *Who's Who*: 'Students of that instructive annual have long since perceived with delight that [his] recreations assume a different form every year.' 'Among his self-recorded activities perhaps the most fascinating is the Rememba Bomba League, "founded in 1924: reconstituted, 1927". But, alas, the badge of membership is not described.'

The English Association, it will be seen, goes ahead wholeheartedly, but without undue solemnity, with its work of upholding standards. The nature of those standards may be gathered from any number of *English*, the quarterly it publishes. The ethos of *English* is fairly suggested by the passages quoted above from the *News-Letter*. Some years ago we commented on the Association's official statement that it 'lived on the earnings' of *Poems of To-Day* (an educational work on which Mr T. S. Eliot made some blunt remarks in *The Criterion*). The Association has been true to its traditions, as both the reviews and the verse in *English* bear witness. And it is all in keeping that the hundreds of teacher members who have instructed their pupils in *Poems of To-Day* should now teach them to admire, not only Sir Osbert's prose and wit, but also Miss Edith Sitwell's poetry.

All those who have ever been concerned in any attempt to make university literary studies minister to life would find a file of *English* worth glancing through—for the evidence so abundantly exposed bears even more significantly upon universities than upon schools. It must suffice here to say that if such investigators looked up a 'Sociological Note' that appeared in *Scrutiny* under the title 'The Discipline of Letters' (see above p. 7), they might agree that the analysis given in that Note was strikingly confirmed: in *English* the associational spirit prevails completely and complacently—prevails as a defence, certainly *not* of living literature, or of the kind of life of mind and spirit that makes literature a living influence.

MR PRYCE-JONES, THE BRITISH COUNCIL
AND BRITISH CULTURE

F. R. LEAVIS (1951)

A booklet was published last year for the British Council under the title *The Year's Work in Literature, 1950*, edited by Mr John Lehmann. The report it offers on 'Literary Periodicals' is by Mr Alan Pryce-Jones. He mentions this review in the first sentence, and repeatedly thereafter: no one is to suggest that *Scrutiny*, this time, has been ignored or slighted. In fact, he relates his main argument to a 'diagnosis' that he has extracted, his readers are to understand, from the manifesto that appeared in the first number.

At first sight, it looks as if the editors of *Scrutiny*, in this opening manifesto, had hit on the reason for a decline in literary journalism. What was wanted, they suggested, was a review not purely literary but conscious of the larger contemporary world of which literature forms one part. By implication, therefore, no consistent standards of criticism were discernible in the early 1930's, and so the public lay open to the blandishments of rival cliques, none of them strong enough or coherent enough to impose accepted values upon the rest. Furthermore, a literature divorced from everyday stresses of civilized life must naturally find it impossible to attract enough supporters to maintain a healthy number of literary reviews.

About this 'diagnosis' he is urbanely ironical:

Oddly enough, though, such reviews, when later they came into being in accordance with the precepts of *Scrutiny*, held their own no better than the rest...

The Editors, it is true, do say that, while finding their centre in literary criticism, they intend also to print articles and reviews dealing with other than literary subjects. But a reader who carried away the impression that, in saying this, they were offering their 'diagnosis'—diagnosis of the disease that made a calculated and resolute effort to assert the function of criticism timely—must have given the manifesto a very small part indeed of his attention (if 'attention' is a word that applies at all). The 'diagnosis' actually offered had been enforced by a great weight of marshalled evidence in *Fiction and the Reading Public*, a work of research published just before the first number of *Scrutiny* came out. Mr Pryce-Jones will perhaps say that he has not heard of *Fiction and the Reading Public*. He has, however, heard of *Scrutiny*, and even had, apparently, the first volume in front of him. If he had looked at the second number in that volume he would have found an article called *What's Wrong with Criticism?*

That article gives a developed statement of the 'diagnosis' in a survey of the contemporary situation. Its argument is that, when, as a result of the process that may be indicated by references to the Education Act of 1870, and the name of Lord Northcliffe, the appeal to the Common Reader—representative of a coherent cultivated public—can no longer be made, the control of the currency of accepted valuations, the organs of critical authority and the positions of advantage for the influencing of taste will get into hands the business of which is not to promote the function of criticism, but to replace it by something else. And the article shows with some particularity that the contemporary literary world is controlled by a system of personal and institutional relations that, pursuing its own ends, is inevitably hostile both to the play of criticism and to the emergence and recognition of the new and significant.

Mr Pryce-Jones could not, of course, be expected to point out that in the twenty years since *What's Wrong with Criticism?* was written the system has become much more formidable in its comprehensiveness and its power—a fact so signally illustrated by the circumstances of his report. This, presumably, was commissioned by Mr John Lehmann, the editor of *The Year's Work in Literature, 1950* which is published for the British Council—which is financed out of public funds and has the august and authoritative impersonality of an institution. How, and by whom, we ask, are its literary policy determined and its literary jobs distributed? Three years ago, another British Council publication, *Prose Literature since 1939* (by Mr John Hayward), evoked this comment in *Scrutiny* (December, 1948):

It would of course be 'hypercritical' to suggest (though Americans and foreigners in the present writer's hearing have said it) that nothing could be worse for the prestige and influence of British Letters abroad than Mr Hayward's presentment of the currency values of Metropolitan literary society and the associated University milieux as the distinctions and achievements of contemporary England.

Who can doubt that this suggests fairly enough the way in which the promotion of cultural ends by instruction and guidance 'published for the British Council' must, in sum, inevitably work? A perusal of the booklet in which Mr Pryce-Jones's article appears will hardly tend towards any other conclusion. The valuations, the ethos and the criteria promulgated through the weeklies, the Sunday papers and the B.B.C. are provided by the British Council (financed out of public funds) with further means of imposing themselves and with a kind of institutional authority. And these British Council guides and surveys, it is to be noted, are not for foreign consumption only; they are to be found prominently displayed in the bookshops here, and clearly enjoy a considerable sale in the home market—along with that growing series of essays on authors past and present which is commissioned by, and published for, the British Council.

Mr Pryce-Jones—who, after all, can express his view of things in the Third Programme, and may well feel that the editorial policy of *The Times Literary Supplement* is in good hands—does not glance at this aspect of contemporary letters. Instead, he reflects that criticism has always been in a bad way, and that even if it should really be in a bad way, there would be no cause for worrying. The process of his argument, as a matter of fact, is not clear, but this, at any rate, is where it leads him: ' . . . the exact kind of crisis which hits the literary world in each generation is not very important. What is important is whether there are the writers to put it to use. And between the existence of such writers and the prosperity of literary reviews there is no connection whatever.'

This faith might be found touching—if only one could think that it *was* faith and not indifference or cynicism. It offers us the pure Romantic conception of the creative individual. How does the great work come into the world? The individual of genius is born; taking the impact of Life, he finds himself inspired; the great work emerges. But even if it did emerge, it would still need to get published and recognized and sold; and if Mr Pryce-Jones supposes that the system represented by the publication in which his survey appears has any overmastering tendency towards recognizing and fostering and backing the new stir of life—the original and significant and truly distinguished—a perusal of the contents of that publication, along with those of the other British Council publications, will show him to be under an illusion. The essential spirit and effect of such a system—which has for *raison d'être* the emancipating of literary distinction (a matter of kudos and prestige) from all dangerous relation to standards—must inevitably be inimical to the real thing, the new and living.

But it is inimical, further, in a more radical way, the possibility of which Mr Pryce-Jones's Romantic innocence declines to perceive: it tends against the development and maturing of the talent, and so against the very conception of the significant work. For Matthew Arnold, when in the famous first essay of the First Series he deals with the dependence of the creative mind on the 'atmosphere' of 'ideas' and valuations in which it lives, is stating the obvious truth. And to bring up the young potential writer in a world in which, from school-days on, he is exposed to the unanimous and authoritative suggestion that the chart of contemporary significances offered him by the Sunday papers will direct him to the sources of life and light is serving him worse than asking him to do for himself more than the individual talent can be hopefully asked to do.

It is perhaps not surprising that an ability to display crude ignorance of the nature of criticism should go with Mr Pryce-Jones's indifference to the function. Only the most elementary instruction meets the case. When one read in Mr Noel Annan's *Leslie Stephen* (see chapter IX) an astonishing travesty of the idea and the practice of criticism as they are to be found in *Scrutiny* one reflected that the author's training had not been in the literary-critical field—though it was still disconcerting that the presumable qualifications to discuss Stephen's thought should be divorced from an elementary understanding of the nature of literary criticism. But where, one now has to ask,—where among the professionals in the literary-critical field—is such elementary understanding to be counted on? Mr Pryce-Jones is reputed to occupy the editorial chair of an augustly institutional critical weekly; this passage (confirming the effect of what has been quoted above) gives the measure of his enlightenment about the function he has it in charge to promote: 'There is, in other words, no desirable life of which literary reviews are an essential component and in which fixed standards of criticism gain a kind of legal backing...'

'Fixed standards', 'impose accepted values',—no one who knew what 'standards' are could talk about 'fixed standards' or 'imposing them' or providing them with a 'legal backing'. A judgment is a real judgment, or it is nothing. It must, that is, be a sincere personal judgment; but it aspires to be more than personal. Essentially it has the form: 'This is so, is it not?' But the agreement appealed for must be real, or it serves no critical purpose and can bring no satisfaction to the critic. What his activity of its very nature aims at, in fact, is a collaborative exchange or commerce. Without a many-sided real exchange—the collaboration by which the object, the poem (for example), in which the individual minds meet and at the same time the true judgments concerning it are established—the function of criticism cannot be said to be working. Without a wide coherent public, capable of making its response felt— capable, that is, of taking a more or less active part in that collaboration —there is, for the critic, no effective appeal to standards. For standards (which are not of the order of the measures in the Weights and Measures Office) are 'there' only in and by the collaborative process that criticism essentially is.

These elementary truths, surely, are not in themselves difficult to grasp. The actual business of criticism, on the other hand, cannot be well performed without a special training, developing natural aptitude. A glance round at the contemporary scene—or a brief study of *The*

Year's Work in Literature, 1950—will establish the point of insisting on that truism. The classic's training (or the historian's), however assiduously supplemented by brilliant talk among choice spirits, does not—the evidence is distressingly clear—qualify a writer for the intelligent discussion of literature. Literary criticism is a special discipline: to get that recognized must be an essential part of any serious concern to restore the function of criticism. And the insistence is the more necessary because the qualities of the 'literary mind' (to give that description the force it ought to have) are badly needed outside the literary-critical field. (For a recent illustration of the way in which they can tell in extra-literary work one may point to the critique of the Kinsey Report in Lionel Trilling's *The Liberal Imagination*.)

'*Scrutiny* reads like the laboratory report of a small, but efficient laboratory.' If serious literary criticism (of very varied kinds) 'reads like' that to Mr Pryce-Jones, it does; but there can be no excuse for suggesting, as *The Times Literary Supplement* did on a notorious occasion some eighteen months ago, that *Scrutiny* is associated with the view that criticism can be a science, or has done anything but discountenance the ambition to make it one or to win credence for the pretence that something of the nature of laboratory method can have a place in it. Mr Pryce-Jones grants, encouragingly, that the 'results' (of a 'purely local work') make 'good serviceable reading'. And it is indeed the fact that British Council representatives all over the world where the work is done—the work 'in the field'—testify that they have found *Scrutiny* uniquely serviceable ('I make my living out of *Scrutiny*' is the way one of them put it). For the 'purely local work' has effected a revaluation of an immense range of English literature of the past, from the fourteenth century on, as well as an appraisal of the output of the last twenty years. And the results (if 'plain fare at the best') have been found incomparably usable (as some appropriate department of the British Council may have registered, or at any rate can, if it wishes, for inquiry will bring in the evidence in profusion)—as well as very good to steal from.

It is an ironical memory that when the British Council first proposed to export *Scrutiny* officially it asked that it might have 'surplus' copies free of charge. When informed that there were no surplus copies, and, further, that all work in connection with *Scrutiny* (except the printer's and the distributor's) was unpaid, and that losses had been met out of private and ill-furnished pockets, the British Council proposed to pay half-price for such copies as it might require. Some insistence was needed from the *Scrutiny* side before the British Council agreed to pay the full price.

Possibly Mr John Lehmann's team, and the other commissioned authors who help the Council to promote the cause of British culture, perform *their* services free, out of a sense of public duty.

KEYNES, SPENDER AND CURRENCY-VALUES

F. R. LEAVIS (1951)

World Within World, by Stephen Spender (Hamish Hamilton)
The Life of John Maynard Keynes, by R. F. Harrod (Macmillan)

> 'I *am* damned critical—for it's the only thing to be,
> and all else is damned humbug.'—Henry James

World Within World, the publisher's advertisement tells us, is in its thirtieth thousand, and has been highly praised by Cyril Connolly, Harold Nicolson, Christopher Isherwood, V. S. Pritchett, Walter Allen, Edgar Anstey, Raymond Mortimer, T. C. Worsley, Phyllis Bentley, Edmund Blunden, Richard Church, Leonard Woolf, John Connell, and *The Times Literary Supplement*. Nothing, then, said about it in *Scrutiny* can matter much to the author—a reflection that helps one to say what has to be said; for this is peculiarly a case where one wants it to be plain that all that one says, when constating the facts (which seem to be very important), is necessary to one's concern for general and impersonal significances.

What, then, makes Stephen Spender's autobiography worth attention is the extraordinary contrast between the account of the book conveyed by the reviewers and the patent enough reality. The reviewers (like the book) assume that the book is of great importance because of the established literary distinction of the author, and they find the high distinction of a gifted writer brilliantly present in the book itself. Yet any competent reviewer knowing nothing of the author would have been bound to deduce from the book that, of all professions, the literary was one for which he was certainly not intended by nature. The flatness of the writing is hard to convey by description, because it is an absence of character—unless one may say that it expresses the innocence that the reviewers (while concurring in the judgment that he is a 'born writer'—Mr Leonard Woolf's phrase) all remark as a personal quality of the author. But as a literary quality this 'innocence' amounts to an essential lack of literary gift, and a bent for cliché and ineptitude.

She was one of those girls whom the universities excite to a peculiar degree. She seemed literally bathed in the warm admiration of young men.

It always seemed to me that the Great War had made singularly little impression on him. He believed that we lived in an age of improvements, and not even that holocaust had shaken him in his belief.

She talked with many underlinings, in that way which is so consciously verbal with some women that it is their special idiom, as a special timbre of blank verse distinguishes each Elizabethan dramatist.

Yet her [Virginia Woolf's] interest in royalty was largely due to the fact that royalty, surrounded by an atmosphere of radiant adoration as though bathed in a tank of lambent water, were peculiar and exotic in precisely the way in which people are luminous and strange in her writing.

The 'innocence', as the reviewers note it, is what we have in the quality of his ambition to 'be a poet'—his answer, he records, when Mr Eliot asked him what he wanted to do; to which Mr Eliot replied, 'I can understand your wanting to write poems, but I don't quite know what you mean by "being a poet".' The meaning, or the significance, is perfectly plain to us; Mr Spender, with an admirable simplicity, has made it so. This is representative:

When I realized that the desire to be Prime Minister was in itself only a thirst for notoriety, I shifted my ambition. Instead of wanting the fame that makes people discussed in the news, I looked to that which lasts for many years. I turned back to poetry. But although I wanted a truer fame, I cannot deny that I have never been free from a thirst for publicity very like that of my father. Even to-day it disgusts me to read a newspaper in which there is no mention of my name.

The desire to become famous as a poet (and, if possible, as a statesman—and a soldier too) is one that many are familiar with, or will recall if they look back far enough. The astonishing thing about Mr Spender's case is that he has achieved his desire—astonishing, because at no time has he given evidence of a more specific compulsion to poetry or to literary creation. And the passage is not, as a reader taking it in isolation might suppose, recording an outlived naïveté. The conversation in which Mr Spender told Mr Eliot that what he wanted to do was to 'be a poet' took place after he had published a book of poems, and 'begun to lead a literary-social life of luncheons, teas, and week-ends at country houses', and he reflects in recalling that conversation: 'My problem is what this book must make apparent: what I write are fragments of autobiography: sometimes they are poems, sometimes stories, and longer passages may take the form of novels.' Describing how he differed from the other leaders of The Poetical Renascence, 'as for me', he says, 'I was an autobiographer restlessly searching for forms in which to express the stages of my development'.

That the autobiographical bent is not a sign of creative power, but the reverse, we do not need Coleridge's authority for believing, and why Mr Spender was driven back on autobiography, and how little conducive to creative strength this autobiographical material was calculated to be, he has already told us in an extract from his journal (given on p. 104):

My own work is to write poetry and novels. I have no character or will power outside my work. In the life of action, I do everything that my friends tell me to do, and have no opinions of my own. This is shameful, I know, but it is so. Therefore I must develop that side of me which is independent of other people. I must live and mature in my writing.

The absence of creative power or impulse needn't mean lack of literary intelligence. But Mr Spender would seem never to have achieved even the beginnings of what can in any strictness be called an interest in literature.

Some of the writers who now came to interest me were T. S. Eliot, Virginia Woolf, Robert Graves, Laura Riding, Ernest Hemingway, Osbert, Edith and Sacheverell Sitwell, Ezra Pound, Henry Green, Herbert Read—to name a few. What I admired was their hard clear imagery, their boldness of experimentation and their search for expressing complicated states of consciousness.

This was in his Oxford days, but the innocence is never transcended. He tells us that 'Day Lewis to some extent corrected the blurred quality of the Georgians by introducing images drawn from factories and slums and machinery into his poetry'. He can give as an anthology of supreme things: 'A sentence of Virginia Woolf's, beginning, "A great beast stamps its foot", a line of Eliot, "The awful daring of a moment's surrender", and, at a later date, a description of a rock pool by Cyril Connolly—all these seemed to be beyond the writers themselves, as the sceptre and the crown lie beyond the man who is a king.' He can tell us that Connolly is 'the best living parodist'—Connolly, who is capable of lumping James and Pater together under the head of 'mandarin prose', and of betraying the radical influence of Pater in his own consciously post-Joycean and post-Eliotic alembications. E. M. Forster is 'the best English novelist of this century'. Remembering that Mr Spender has in the past felt bound to write about James (to whom so many commentators have paid attention without being, properly speaking, acquainted with him), we are not surprised to find that James suffers a number of mentions in *World Within World*. Speaking of Mr Isaiah Berlin, Mr Spender says: 'Human behaviour was for him a subject of fantastic inquiry into motives and actions, reminding me of Henry James's many-branched speculations over the characters in his novels.' Of his Aunt Mary he tells us: 'She hated any tender emotions with a thoroughly English intensity only understood by novelists like Trollope and Henry James.' In a phrase clearly reminiscent of H. G. Wells's notorious assault, he refers to 'the later manner' as resembling 'a steam-roller spinning out filigree'.

There is no need to multiply illustrations. The point they enforce makes itself as unanswerably when one turns over the pages of *World Within World* as it did when one looked at a page here and there in *The Destructive Element*, the critical work in 'which', says Mr Spender, 'I analysed the deep consciousness of destructive forces threatening our civilization, which was to be found in the work of Henry James, James Joyce, T. S. Eliot, and some more recent writers...'. How, then, comes the question, did Mr Spender, with such disadvantages, achieve his confidence in himself as a poet, a critic, and an intellectual? Or how (to put it another way) did he achieve recognition as such, so that for years now he has been an established value, and a major British Council export?[1] 'There was a sense of fulfilment [he says] in meeting these people. I was accepted by writers whose names were still surrounded for me by a sacred glow.'

The answer, of course, must be partly a tribute to Mr Spender's personality. More generally, it brings up in a very impressive way a theme that has been a great deal canvassed in these pages: the fact that the present age in this country is characterized by a literary world in which, whatever principles and criteria prevail, they are not the principles and criteria of literary criticism. Mr Spender's account of his Oxford years, the most interesting part of his book, is significant in relation to the development of that phase of those conditions ('the literary world') which determined his own portentous success. It was the late 'twenties, and 'calling on Auden was a serious business'. 'For his Oxford contemporaries the most impressive thing about Auden was that, at such an early age, he was so conscious and confident a master of his situation.' Mr Spender's view of Auden is still essentially undergraduate—but then so is that which one may expect to find any week in *The Times Literary Supplement* (to note which is to make a quintessential observation about the present state of English letters). 'Sometimes he gave the impression of playing an intellectual game with himself and with others, and this meant that in the long run he was rather isolated.' But his attitudes and intellectualities are reported with awe—and they did, in fact, we know, have a most effective influence. 'Such lectures by one young writer to another, with their mixture of

[1] See the discussion *The Progress of Poesy* in *Scrutiny*, Vol. XV, No. 4. A companion booklet to Mr John Hayward's *Prose Literature since 1939* was written by Mr Spender on Poetry, and is published for, and circulated by, the British Council.

sense and nonsense, fun and portentousness, malice and generosity, compose a secret language among a circle. They are the witches' brew from which a literary movement is made.'

The Auden we are shown was intent on making a literary movement, and, conditions in the world of letters being what they were, we can see that he had formidable qualifications:

He thought that the literary scene in general offered an empty stage. 'Evidently they are waiting for Someone,' he said with an air that he would soon take the centre of it. However, he did not think of himself as the only writer of the future. He had the strongest sense of looking for colleagues and disciples, not just in poetry but in all the arts. He looked at a still life on the wall and said: 'He will be The Painter.' This was by Robert Medley. His friend Isherwood was to be The Novelist. Chalmers was another of the Gang. Cecil Day Lewis was a colleague. A group of emergent artists existed in his mind, like a cabinet in the mind of a party leader.

*   *   *

I took to showing Auden my poems...After I had known him six weeks he must have approved of as many of my lines. Therefore it was rather surprising to discover that he considered me a member of 'the Gang'. Once I told him I wondered whether I ought to write prose, and he answered: 'You must write nothing but poetry, we do not want to lose you for poetry.' This remark produced in me a choking moment of hope mingled with despair, in which I cried: 'But do you really think I am any good?' 'Of course,' he replied frigidly. 'But why?' 'Because you are so infinitely capable of being humiliated. Art is born of humiliation,' he added in his icy voice—and left me wondering when *he* could feel humiliated.

The conditions were even more favourable than Auden could have known. So far as literary fashions were concerned, it was the right moment. Eliot had done the work; the time was ripe for Modern Poetry to be 'in'; the advantage was reaped by the Gang. Dons at Cambridge who had resisted Eliot till they were beginning to feel that resistance was possible no longer jumped with relief at Auden's *Poems*, and one heard of margins annotated black. Auden began to appear on Tripos papers. What! not able to appreciate Eliot?—*His* admirers, it was intimated, were sadly in the lag: Auden had superseded him. Here was Modern Poetry of a difficult intellectuality, the difficulty of which, all the same, was hearty and encouraging, and did not demand of the reader that he should question in any radical way his everyday attitudes. It proposed instead the easy acceptance of a guaranteed rightness. For among the favourable conditions, we have to note that the Slump had happened and the days of Public School Marxizing and Fellow-travelling had begun. And 'if Auden is the satirist of this poetical renascence,

Spender is its lyric poet. In his work the experimentalism of the last two decades is beginning to find its reward...Technically, these poems appear to mark a definite step forward in English poetry.'

Who, one wonders painfully, wrote that blurb to Stephen Spender's *Poems*, published by Faber and Faber? One knows, at any rate, who must have passed it. And Faber and Faber were publishers also, it is in place to note, of *The Criterion*. The movement that commanded the reviewing in *The Criterion* and the *New Statesman and Nation* would command the effective voice of contemporary criticism. But Anglo-Catholicism, Royalism, Classicism on the one hand, and, on the other, Shaw, Wells, Russell, Joad?—not a possible consolidation? A brief survey of the review pages of both organs will show that differences of philosophy and ethos were easily transcended; in a short while the new movement ('the Gang') had both the Left-inclined weekly and the Right-inclined quarterly unambiguously at its service.

The processes of mass civilization that, by 1930, had so drastically reduced the number of critical organs and thus virtually abrogated the standards of criticism (for standards of criticism can have their effective existence only in an educated public that can make itself felt, as none can if there are not a considerable number of reviews, maintaining a large corps of intelligent and disinterested critics)—these reductive processes need not be discussed here. (Consider how different from what we have to contemplate now was that past state of affairs which we can deduce from R. G. Cox's article in the present (Vol. XVIII, No. 1) *Scrutiny*.) But it may still be wondered that there should have been, apparently, so little sense of what was happening, no protest, no note of scandal; certainly no resistance in places where one might have expected to find it. Can, for instance, so distinguished an intellectual as the Editor of *The Criterion*, assisting at the stultification of his work as poet and critic, have been as unaware as all that? Was it unawareness, or a sense that resistance was vain, and acquiescence a natural and inevitable course? In such a state of things the distinction is not a sharp one.

And about the 'state of things' it has to be said further at this point that, in the literary world, there was already an established tradition of coterie power, and of coterie power as a dazzling, creditable and proper thing. It was a tradition that, in ways more and less subtle, tended to countenance the intrusion of social and personal values into the field of criticism. In fact, not only conscience, but consciousness, in these matters had been gravely weakened. For an editor to attempt, in his review, to vindicate the function of criticism would have been to deserve the odium due to a gratuitous and most offensive moral heroism.

It is here that a consideration of the second book given at the head of this review becomes immediately relevant. Keynes, as Mr Harrod shows us, had a major share in the formation of 'Bloomsbury', belonged to it throughout his life, and was a main source of its strength. In fact, Mr Harrod shows us a Keynes who was the most formidable promoter of the coterie spirit that modern England has known. To say this of Keynes is to pay tribute to the great gifts that made him formidable. These are not in question—his gifts as economist, logician and financial speculator. But Mr Harrod credits him also with an all-round distinction; with gifts that qualified him to be a shaping and determining influence in the field of the humanities, and to be trusted, as a supreme intelligence, judging confidently and authoritatively, with the responsibilities of an enormously powerful patron. In this Mr Harrod pays an unconscious and revealing tribute to the power of the coterie influence, to which, as he tells us in his Preface, he enjoyed an early exposure:

By good luck...I was brought into touch with a number of members of the 'Bloomsbury' circle when I was a young man in the 'twenties. They made a sharp and indelible impression on my mind.

He is—and in the very arts he practises in his book—an artless and admirable witness to what 'Bloomsbury' essentially was. He tells us, for instance (and it is an interesting minor contribution to English cultural history), that Lytton Strachey went before going to Cambridge to Liverpool University, drawn by the presence of Sir Walter Raleigh,[1]

whose influence was important. It is pleasant to think that Raleigh's beautiful dry humour was not lost upon Strachey. Raleigh was in the van of a shift of critical values [he asserted, we recall, Shakespeare's moral neutrality]. Cultivated persons of the late-Victorian period were no doubt well-read in our earlier masterpieces, but they were inclined to be over-zealous in their admiration of the Victorian pontiffs...

—it is plain that Raleigh's notion of style, too, was not lost upon Strachey.

But the point to be made is that Keynes's distinction was confined to the field in which he was a professional. Where he was an amateur, though he took with him his characteristic high confidence, he was a mere amateur; as critic, man of taste and humanist he reflected the taste, idiom and assumptions of the very inferior coterie *milieu* to which he belonged.

And they gained, too, from his resources of knowledge and worldly contact. He was their main pillar of strength, their financial adviser, their patron. He was always ready to help, in one way or another, to promote their material interests.

[1] Raleigh's significance was discussed by Q. D. Leavis in *Scrutiny* Vol. XII, No.1 under the title '*The Discipline of Letters': a Sociological Note.* (See above p. 7.)

That so distinguished and influential a man should have been formed by such a *milieu*, and should have used his power and his prestige to confirm its dominance and propagate its ethos, is a fact of some historical importance in relation to the matters discussed in the first part of this review.

We can see it to have been a significant moment in the history, not only of Cambridge, but of modern English culture, when, at the turn of the century, at the time of Keynes's going up to King's from Eton, the coterie had its start, and the character of the *milieu* began to define itself. It might be asked why the coterie should have been so inferior. Without offering to explain in any ultimate sense, one may say something about the nature and conditions of the inferiority. The group of young men, mainly King's and Trinity, that Mr Harrod describes, a group having in its connection with the famous 'Society', intimate contacts at more senior levels, and a continuity with an illustrious intellectual tradition, obviously contained some real distinction as well as a good deal of academic—and academic-social—brilliance. But there is something about the constitutive ethos of the *milieu* that the intellectual distinction and the continuity from the past make the more ominous. We have it here, in Keynes's attitude to a representative great Cambridge man of the immediate past (the letter is dated 1906):

Have you read Sidgwick's Life? Very interesting and depressing... He never did anything but wonder whether Christianity was true and prove that it wasn't and hope that it was...

I wonder what he would have thought of us; and I wonder what we think of him. And then his conscience—incredible. There is no doubt about his moral goodness. And yet it is all so dreadfully depressing—no intimacy, no clear-cut boldness.

We can guess well enough what Sidgwick would have thought of Lytton Strachey. And an *élite* of young Cambridge minds that could find the ethos of Lytton Strachey more congenial than that of Henry Sidgwick was certainly a significantly new thing. But of course the name to be set over against Sidgwick's is that of G. E. Moore (the following was also written in 1906):

It is *impossible* to exaggerate the wonder and *originality* of Moore; people are already beginning to talk as if he were only a kind of logic-chopping eclectic. Oh why can't they see!

How amazing to think that we and only we know the rudiments of a true theory of ethic; for nothing can be more certain than that the broad outline is true...I even begin to agree with Moore about Sidgwick—that he was a wicked edifactious person.

That Moore was, in his very limited way, a disinterested mind and innocent spirit made him the more irresistibly the very sanction they needed. 'The supreme values of life', writes Mr Harrod, summarizing Moore's teaching, 'were the states of consciousness involved in human relations and in the appreciation of beauty.' This congenial doctrine (Keynes himself in the late 'Memoir'[1] notes what it left out) was enforced in an austere logic which lent itself to deployment in a kind of coterie dialectic. Thus the apostles were able to take a fixed and complacent immaturity in themselves for something very different; to associate an inveterate triviality with a suggestion of intellectual distinction and moral idealism—with, in fact, a kind of unction.

Their devotion to their 'specific image of what is meant by the idea of the good life' was 'sustained, no doubt,' says Mr Harrod, 'by certain elements of unearned income'. The immediate point to be made is that it was sustained by other 'unearned elements'; by an unrecognized legacy of other than money-values (essentially unrecognized, as comes out in the attitude to Sidgwick). It is all in the natural course of things that a 'civilization' of this kind ('it was certainly a civilization,' says Keynes in that late 'Memoir'), conscious of a high distinction of refinement, should run not only to thinness and 'brittleness' (Keynes's word for a characteristic kind of coterie talk), but to pretentious cheapness and to something one can only call vulgarity (consider, in their different ways, Lytton Strachey and Rupert Brooke).

As for the 'elements of unearned income', they need not, we know, of themselves have involved the Bloomsbury idea of the good life. Quite different moral, intellectual and practical habits ('civilizations') have been sustained by 'elements of unearned income'. And a glance may be given here at Mrs Keynes's recent very interesting account of Maynard's education.[2] When he went to Eton, it was arranged, she tells us, that he should be supplied with white ties by the gross, so that he should be able to wear a new one every day, and when he was elected to College Pop, an order was placed with a local florist to deliver daily a fresh button-hole. A small matter, perhaps, but highly significant. It tells us a great deal about one aspect, at least, of what may be called his ethical education. The significance becomes the more apparent when we recall that Mrs Keynes's father was the minister of the Bunyan chapel (and the descent on the other side was in the same religious tradition). With such a background, an education in the belief that one belongs to a highly privileged oligarchy, and has a natural right to the best of

---

[1] *Two Memoirs by J. M. Keynes*, reviewed in *Scrutiny* Vol. XVI, No. 3, under the title *Keynes, Lawrence and Cambridge*.
[2] *Gathering up the Threads*, by Florence Ada Keynes (Heffer).

everything ('best' being interpreted as it is in Vanity Fair), inevitably tended to produce in Keynes the result that we actually see.

Explaining why Keynes devoted his genius to financial speculation, and 'went deeply in' ('on a narrow margin of cover'), Mr Harrod tells us:

He was determined not to relapse into salaried drudgery. He must be financially independent. He felt that he had that in him which would justify such independence. He had many things to tell the nation. And he wanted a sufficiency. He must be able to take stalls at the Russian ballet whenever he wished—and entertain the dancers, if that struck his fancy. He must be able to buy his friends' pictures—and pay them handsomely. These other dealers in money merely squandered their earnings on banal conventional luxuries. He must use his brains to put some of their money into his pocket, where it would fructify not only financially, but in supporting the people who really mattered, and in giving his own powers scope.

The rejected 'salaried drudgery' was university teaching. Ah! but with the harvest of speculation he supported the arts, bought his friends' pictures, and bought other pictures too—with great acuteness for (though Mr Harrod reports the suspicion that he 'was never deeply moved by visual art') he left what turned out to be an extremely valuable private collection. And here what is to-day widely known as the Puritanic note has to be struck (a note of simple matter-of-fact moral observation to the minister of the Bunyan chapel). It regards an inevitable relation between the use for 'good' of the resources so amassed and the spirit of the amassing, the conception of the good life that encouraged it and throve on it.

'This exclusive Cambridge circle', writes Mr R. H. S. Crossman, reviewing the book in the *Universities Quarterly* for May, 'gave him the poise of an intellectual oligarch, who could afford to be condemned as inconsistent and irresponsible by the vulgar, so long as his peers recognized that he was acting according to their esoteric code.' That is an admirable way of describing Keynes's peculiar formidableness as a promoter of the coterie spirit. Even in the field of economics, where Keynes's relevant authority and his informed concern for standards are unquestioned, this spirit had, as Mr Harrod recognizes, some unfortunate consequences. 'The formation of a coterie', Mr Harrod ventures, 'may be valuable to sustain the courage of those whose work is in the realm of the imagination. But [he adds] 'Keynes may have tended to apply a helpful expedient in a sphere where it was inappropriate.' The evidence that Mr Harrod gives is of a spirit that has to be resisted as mischievous anywhere; that it should have got even into the sphere where Keynes was a specialist has a sinister significance for the present inquiry: '"But there isn't anyone else," they said.' Mr Harrod intimates, deferentially, that this conviction was ill founded, and worked harm for economics.

'Really, you know, there isn't anyone else': a good deal earlier in the book he has reported this as the note of 'Bloomsbury' ('outsiders were neglected'). How could something of that spirit, and of the stultifying confusion of values that, at best, it must involve, *not* manifest itself in the patronage and the influence, the use of financial resources for 'good', made possible by Keynes's addiction to speculation?

'He maintained', says Mr Harrod of the (then) Bursar of King's, 'his interest in the quest for choice spirits in each new generation, for young men of intellect and sensibility who would carry on the traditions of his own undergraduate days...and he gave them an *entrée* into Bloomsbury.' Though we are left in no doubt that the recruitment referred to here is not to be understood as having been merely of economists, we are not forbidden to suppose that it may have entailed academic status: in this region Mr Harrod sees no need to insist on distinctions, and the completeness with which he assumes that the criteria of 'Bloomsbury' are the unquestioned criteria of 'intellect and sensibility' reflects the completeness of the identification he found in the milieu on which Keynes conferred such power and influence. (If only one might quote —but no! one mustn't—Mr Harrod's account of his own introduction at Keynes's college! But there is much amusing and eloquent evidence of that kind in the book.)

To revert now to the questions provoked by the consideration of Mr Spender's book: How could there be such an absence of protest, of apparent resistance and sense of scandal, when the Fellow-travellers of the Poetical Renascence, in the early 'thirties, took possession of the organs of criticism? How could the illustriously edited *Criterion* lend itself so easily (it would appear) and so incongruously?

Considering these questions we can see what there is to be said with immediate relevance about Keynes's place in history. It is not (at least, it is not there the stress falls at the moment) that he promoted, in the cultural realm, the 'Bloomsbury' idea of the good life, or the ethos of any particular milieu, but that he promoted in enormously influential ways the habit of substituting the social-personal values for the relevant ones. If, on the one hand, belonging to a highly dominant intellectual and social milieu, you use your power and prestige to slight the essential intellectual standards and to discredit the notion of critical conscience, and, on the other, to give respectability and sanction to the natural human weakness for replacing the real standards by personal and coterie considerations, then you may be fairly credited with having helped substantially to bring about the state of things revealed in Mr Spender's autobiography. And it has to be remembered that the literary-intellectual 'world' was a small one, and that the parts of it not dominated from the axis Eton-King's-Bloomsbury-and-the-relevant-weekly couldn't matter much.

To-day the triumph of the social-personal (or 'club', we may now call it) principle is complete. The club is not narrowly exclusive, but you must belong (and keep the rules) if you are to be recognized to exist. And if the club is not narrowly exclusive, the system of relations by which it controls the organs and institutions through which the currency-values are established and circulated is comprehensive and complete. The completeness with which the notions of criticism, critical principle and critical standard have been superseded was demonstrated when, a year or so ago, a note was printed in this journal pointing out the lack of obvious suitability in the judges for the Festival of Britain Poetry Prizes: there was genuine scandalized indignation in many quarters, including some that couldn't be thought of as being anything but disinterested. *That* kind of thing is inexcusable and unpardonable.

Yet now the prizes have been awarded, we find as respectable a newspaper as the *Manchester Guardian* reporting discouragement and dismay, and asking whether, with such a lack of obvious felicity in the appointment of judges, awards more calculated to promote life in English Poetry could have been expected. But the question that should be asked is whether, when things have got into the state in which they are now, the kind of encouragement of the arts from which Keynes hoped so much, that represented by the Arts Council, can really, in sum, do anything but encourage and strengthen the system referred to above—the system that, in literature at any rate, makes the restoring of the critical function (and so the recovery of a public) impossible.

REFLECTIONS ON THE
MILTON CONTROVERSY

JOHN PETER (1952)

Despite uneasy truces and despite the desultory nature of the campaign, guerilla warfare rather than pitched battle, no one can fail to see that the war between Criticism and Scholarship still continues. It is clear, too, that no corner of the field is more exposed or more hotly contested than that occupied by Milton. This does not mean, of course, that it is a deserted corner: the scholars, particularly, still tramp about in it and many of them, by dint of ignoring the shrapnel-bursts around them, have contrived to behave as though nothing were amiss. Such self-possession can hardly be commanded by anyone who, like myself, has tried to lend an honest ear to both sides, and it is bound to be with a good deal of reluctance that he ventures out under the bullets. At the same time there would seem to be almost an obligation upon neutrals who are interested in Milton to come forward with as honest a report on the battle as they can presently make, rather than to retire into non-committal security. It is many years since Dr Tillyard found it 'extremely salutary that the present age should have begun questioning [Milton's] right to eminence'[1] but I think the remark still epitomizes the attitude of most of us who, while being outside the controversy, are necessarily implicated in it and concerned to see it argued to its conclusion. And, this being so, it can only be with regret that we observe the tendency among so many writers to presume that it is, in fact, concluded, that the scholars have won a resounding victory, and that the critics' attempts to analyse some of Milton's deficiencies, always wrong-headed, have now been revealed as disreputable also. To shy away from an argument is not to win it and, more important still, is bound to leave the bewildered onlooker (that is, the student) in a greater state of bewilderment than ever. Yet in a matter like this no one has a stronger right than the student to be considered. Having watched several groups of students both in England and in Canada torn this way and that in their attempts to form an estimate of Milton, I am convinced that unless the argument is allowed to run its course, unless it is persevered with responsibly and in the open, it can be of no use to them. If it is allowed to go underground they are left only with a dim sense of taboos and smouldering resentments and may easily conclude, in self-defence, that the assessment of this poet is an improper activity, something that decent people don't talk about. Indeed, I believe this attitude is already distressingly general—distressingly, because surely nothing could be more pernicious in the field of literary criticism.

As I say, it seems to be assumed that the battle has been won, with the scholars triumphant, and since this is so I want here to consider a number of points from the vindications that have been advanced on Milton's behalf. To consider every vindication in detail is obviously quite impracticable in an essay of this kind but I hope that if a few key arguments are carefully scrutinized, and found wanting, the effect will be to encourage a student to review the whole controversy without his snatching at the paralysing assumption that it is all over and already, seen in historical perspective, rather unreal. In my eyes there is nothing unreal about it and indeed many of the issues which it raises seem to me

[1] *Milton* (London, 1946), p. 355.

so vital to a healthy sort of criticism that to refuse to acknowledge them points presumptively to disingenuousness. In this instance I am prepared, with the lawyers, to equate *suppressio veri* and *expressio falsi*. I am of course well aware that to join issue with the defenders of Milton, even in the interests of a common settlement, is likely to be misinterpreted. There are always a few individuals who, having a vested interest in the poet, and one that is peripheral or bigoted enough to be insecure, will cry out at once that I am preaching sedition. To make allowances for such reactions is beyond the powers of any critic (to say nothing of his patience) and I shall not attempt it. On the other hand I am loth to agree with the Fool that truth's a dog must to kennel and I feel sure that the author of *Areopagitica* would himself have approved of any attempt to pursue the whole question of his poetry in a candid and forthright way. The jealous spirit which in our time so balefully presides over literary arguments is a grasping demon and if it is encouraged it is bound in the end to strangle all our attempts at judgment. Writing recently in the *Review of English Studies*,[1] Mr J. B. Leishman had occasion to remark that of the poems contained in *England's Helicon* 'not more than twenty, and probably rather less, would positively require to be included in an anthology which sought to represent Elizabethan lyrical poetry at its best'. There is nothing very disturbing about so sane and indeed generous an estimate; what is disturbing is the fact that the writer found it necessary at the same time to declare (twice) that he is 'a man of many crotchets'. This suggests plainly enough the stage at which, unless we are prepared to be less egotistic and sulky in our judgments, criticism is destined to arrive. *Any* fresh judgment, however reasonable, will have to be proffered as the quirk of amiable and irresponsible eccentricity, lest it should call up anathema from some somnolent authority who once ventured a more orthodox opinion, and in course of time the whole notion of a normative judgment will disappear, to be replaced by heaven knows what elaborate and apologetic systems of hypothetical assumptions, putative rebuttals and quasi-conclusions. In many ways we are well along that road already. It is one that I do not propose to follow here. I shall make my points as trenchantly as I can, trenchancy being a virtue that argument can ill dispense with, but I shall make them without animosity, in the hope that if they are provocative it will rather be of a rejoinder than of a spasm of resentment. I make no pretence to the scholarship of the writers from whom my extracts will be taken, but since the extracts present the findings of criticism rather than those of scholarship I shall rely on the common right of all readers of Milton to dispute those findings.

[1] New Series, Vol. II, pp. 381–2.

To begin with a generality, we might say that it is no disparagement of the work of critics like F. R. Leavis and A. J. A. Waldock to claim that, if to-day their verdict on *Paradise Lost* as a poem at best only partially successful seems irrefutable, that is partly because those who admire the poem have done so little to meet this verdict in anything like a cogent way. It seems to me that between them the two critics mentioned have established a quite formidable case against Milton's claim to pre-eminence, and that it can only be a false buoyancy which leads apologists for Milton to expect (as many of them appear to) that vague commendations of the epic will be enough to divert the critical reader from that case. Milton has, it is true, a customary or prescriptive title in this matter—as I recall Peacock even went so far as to call him our greatest poet—but in the field of criticism custom has no force whatever when it has to be set against demonstration and convincing argument. Neither Dr Leavis nor the late Professor Waldock has, after all, branded Milton as worthless. What they have done is to draw attention to certain positive weaknesses, both in the verse and in the general structure or conception of his epic. If my own experience is at all representative it seems to me likely that what the general reader now awaits, though perhaps with less and less expectancy, is an equally pertinent rejoinder from the other side, a persuasive critical demonstration of the merits of Milton's verse and an account of the structure of his epic which will reveal such strength and propriety in it as to set Waldock's criticisms at a substantial discount.

In Professor Waldock's case, though it is now five years since his book appeared, no real rejoinder has been entered. So far as I know, the only advocate of Milton who has had occasion to deal with *Paradise Lost and its Critics* is Dr Tillyard, in his Studies in Milton, but his treatment of it is far too indirect to be accepted as a careful refutation. At least this seems to me true of the essay on *The Crisis in Paradise Lost* where, I suppose, he has Professor Waldock's arguments most in mind. Elsewhere he cites the book, as often as not, merely to corroborate minor interpretations of his own and, though he does set Waldock right on the intention of six lines in Book III (p. 56), and disagrees with one of his remarks about Satan (p. 58), he seems hardly concerned with the significance of the general thesis of the other book and the gravity of its implications. Only once, in commenting on a passage in Book IX (pp. 28–9), does he draw near to this central thesis, the confusion and inconsistency that vitiate the poem, and here it is only to set the criticism, having agreed with it, discreetly on one side. He admits that in the passage in question 'we have to do with a discrepancy with which Milton was powerless to deal except by faking', a remark that paraphrases Waldock's comment on it, but adds at once, with a startling blend of haste and complacency, 'And if we follow the lead of the poetry, we can only admire him for doing as well as he does.' This is not refutation; it is not even disagreement. Yet surely some attempt to come to terms with Waldock's objection, not only to this passage but to the whole poem, is necessary if Dr Tillyard's position as an advocate is not to be precarious? He himself speaks highly of *Paradise Lost and its Critics* in the same volume and in this he will surely have most readers on his side. Where the reader and he part company is, I think, in his assumption that Waldock's findings can be somehow left in abeyance, not directly challenged but tacitly and rather stealthily encroached upon. The reader's retort is likely to be that, Waldock's book being what it is, he accepts its criticisms of the poem with very few reservations, and that if this is ill advised it is for the admirers of Milton to show him why, just as it has been for them to show why Dr Leavis's earlier criticisms of Milton's verse should not be accepted.

In Dr Leavis's case the position is different, at least to the extent that refutation has been attempted. It is difficult to feel, however, that the attempts have done much to diminish the assent with which, after fifteen years, one still reads his essay. Other writers who, in his own phrase 'came out' against Milton during the 'thirties have, for one reason or another, come to seem much less persuasive than they may then have seemed. Ezra Pound's vigorous attack, in the course of which he spoke of 'the donkey-eared Milton', of 'the coarseness of his mentality' and of 'the abominable dog biscuit of Milton's rhetoric', now appears not merely cantankerous but vague; Professor Dobrée's praise of Dryden at Milton's expense has been persuasively countered by Sir Herbert Grierson; Middleton Murry's invocation of certain passages in Keats's letters against Milton has met with objections from Dr Tillyard which one feels should be accepted; and T. S. Eliot, referring to his own earlier deprecations, has lately been at some pains to point out, in the words of *Prufrock*, 'That is not what I meant at all; That is not it, at all.' But the chapter in *Revaluation* still holds its ground and no amount of harping on its over-sanguine opening can alter the fact that what follows is a reasoned and, in the absence of confutation, compelling analysis of deficiency. Indeed, even to speak of the opening as 'over-sanguine' may be a distortion. 'Milton's displacement' may perhaps in view of the tenacity with which his admirers have rallied to his assistance, be a little optimistic; but 'displacement' is surely a relative term and to accept it, as many readers seem to have done, as a casting out of Milton from even the lower ranks of poetry is simply absurd. Here again an argument cannot be neutralized if we are only concerned with a parody of it. To disagree with Peacock it is hardly necessary to set Milton lower than Cowley or Gray or Rupert Brooke.

I say that Milton's admirers have rallied to his assistance and it is a fact that they have done so in such numbers as to give, at first sight, an impression of strength. On examination, however, it seems to be no more than that—an impression rather than a proof. In a case such as this mere numbers prove nothing, as my mention of Ezra Pound and the rest will already have suggested, and one has only to take particular and *seriatim* stock of the defences to see how vulnerable many of the arguments upon which they rely turn out to be. It is plain, of course, that at the lowest level—Pearsall Smith for instance—they reveal only a rather idiotic self-assurance (something from which even a co-belligerent like C. S. Lewis has felt it necessary to dissociate himself). But even where the writer avoids this kind of irresponsibility we find, I think invariably, that in at least one respect or on at least one occasion he has gone out of his way to advertise his own personal unfitness for the task he has proposed to himself. Rajan attempts to answer Dr Leavis's case without once mentioning him, and thus as it were deliberately confines himself to what is vague and general, and C. S. Lewis, though he at least has courtesy enough to recognize his opponent, after finding himself obliged to concede that Dr Leavis's account of Milton's verse is much the same as that which he would himself present, concludes that between them there is only a temperamental difference, one 'loving' what the other 'hates'. The implications for criticism of such an admission seem to have escaped him altogether; or if they have not, at least he has refused to pause over them. These are general objections and may seem vague, but I think they are just and that they tend to be corroborated by the particular lapses that disfigure the work of both critics. Lewis writes of Homer—

Once the diction has been established it works of itself. Almost anything the poet wants to say, has only to be turned into this orthodox and ready-made diction and it becomes poetry. 'Whatever Miss T. eats turns into Miss T.'[1]

—after which it is something of an effort to feel that he can have a very profound conception of poetry; and Rajan's examination of Milton's verse keeps turning into Sitwellian clap-trap, as here:

Thus *m* and *n* occur thirteen times in the first four lines and on all but two of these occasions they occur in conjunction with an *i* or an *o*. Such combinations backed by the predominant current of meaning convey irresistibly the terror of Satan's downfall.[2]

[1] *A Preface to Paradise Lost* (London, 1942), p. 23.
[2] *Paradise Lost and the Seventeenth Century Reader* (London, 1947), p. 113.

I do not myself believe that 'style' (even Homer's) can be hypostatized like this, treated as though it were a mould into which thoughts and feelings can be poured and then turned out like jellies as poetry, nor do I find terror implicit in a conjunction of *m*'s, *n*'s, *i*'s and *o*'s, and when a critic's attention is so relaxed that he can countenance either pro-position it is without enthusiasm that I find myself awaiting the value-judgments that he will offer. In fact, however, both writers tend to eschew value-judgments of a direct kind, and evidently feel that to explain *why* a poet wrote as he did is all that a critic can attempt. Yet the austerity of this view and the propriety of their explanations are (as usual in such cases) continually threatened by their own relish for Milton's verse and by the value-judgments which this relish implies, and at times the two contentions—(i) that if Milton's verse is limited it is limited by the conception of poetry that prevailed in his time and (ii) that his verse is not limited—become hopelessly overlaid. It seems impossible that unprejudiced readers should be impressed by arguments where the basic assumptions are as hazy as this, and obvious that the haziness arises, not from any vital concern about the poetry, but from a desire to vindicate the individual, John Milton, as though he were a personal friend—that is, as it might be with a friend, by deliberately or unconsciously distracting attention from his faults. But it was those very faults with which Dr Leavis was concerned, and no rebuttal which is chary of a meticulous consideration of them can properly be said to have 'answered' his criticisms. And I think that here Dr Leavis has an added advantage over his opponents in that he himself, as in the chapter called *Mr Eliot and Milton* in *The Common Pursuit*, has demonstrated his readiness to deal with a counter-argument in a very close and specific way, point by point as it were. In the light of this it seems the more significant that his own arguments have received no comparable treatment nor, with one possible exception, even an attempt at it.[1]

In offering these objections to defences of Milton's verse I have admittedly so far made little mention of the two writers who are probably, by virtue of a special concern with the poet or general eminence in the field of seventeenth-century scholarship, most often regarded by the public as his most indomitable champions: I mean Dr Tillyard and Sir Herbert Grierson. Dr Leavis has himself dealt

---

[1] The possible exception is Sir Herbert Grierson—see *Milton and Wordsworth* (C.U.P. 1937), pp. 125–131—though it will be observed that he avoids citing such remarks as '[Milton] exhibits a feeling *for* words rather than a capacity for feeling *through* words' and the converse applied to Shakespeare: 'The total effect is as if words as words withdrew themselves from the focus of our attention and we were directly aware of a tissue of feelings and perceptions.'

with these two advocates of Milton and it would be impertinent for one outside the controversy to repeat his replies.[1] There are, however, perhaps two points which a general reader like myself may be allowed to make, points which must have occurred to other readers in going through the comments of Dr Tillyard and Sir Herbert Grierson, and if only to suggest that the objections one feels to the work of Rajan and Lewis have their parallel in the case of these apologists also, they seem worth making here. I should like to consider a short passage from each of the two.

The first passage comes from an essay on *L'Allegro* and *Il Penseroso* by Dr Tillyard. He is considering Milton's use of words in these poems as it is represented in a typical couplet from *L'Allegro:*

Apart from a couple of minor syntactical difficulties the language is extremely lucid. This does not mean that the poems are shallow. Take the couplet

> Hard by, a Cottage chimney smokes,
> From betwixt two aged Okes.

This is simple language, but as poetry the lines are not negligible. We all know that cottage, but the picture we each make is different from our neighbour's. And it is Milton who makes us our picture. His outline compels us to fill in the detail. His means—and I doubt whether they they can be called simple—are drastic economy of detail and musical suggestion. The heavy beat of the first line has nothing to do with the smoke; it suggests squatness, and the quality of being solidly based, in the cottage. Statement and rhythm are doing different jobs of work. The rhythm of the second line rises a little at the end—the oaks are tall—and has something carelessly solid in it—the oaks know their own dignity. (I am well aware of the dangers of talking in this strain; I merely wish to say with some emphasis that the couplet has substance.)[2]

Here surely most readers must have felt that for one 'well aware of the dangers of talking in this strain' Dr Tillyard has been uncommonly reckless. In what sense the rhythm of a line may be said to have 'something carelessly solid in it', and indeed in what sense *rhythm* may be said to *rise*, is difficult to determine, and when these assertions are applied to an unusually metrical trochaic line like 'From betwixt two aged Okes' they seem even more meaningless. Whatever 'emphasis' the comments involve is surely hopelessly false, and it would seem from the writer's own exculpatory afterthought that he is himself at any rate partly aware of their falsity. But even if we set aside these remarks about rhythm, and the dubious procedure followed in presenting them (assertion to persuade, followed by retraction so as to remain

[1] See the essay 'In Defence of Milton' in *The Common Pursuit*.
[2] *The Miltonic Setting* (C.U.P. 1938), p. 9.

uncommitted), is there anything else in the comment that deserves to be called critical? Look at the other means that Milton is supposed to be using, 'drastic economy of detail'. As Dr Tillyard puts it, he implies that there is something subtly artistic in Milton's use of bare outlines in his picture here. He seems to me to be saying that the couplet is good because, being not quite sufficient in itself, it obliges us to enter into its sense and add to it; and his approach ('it is Milton who makes us make our picture') plainly suggests that we are to give due credit to the poet for making us use our imagination in this way. Yet what status as criticism, when we pause over it for a moment like this, can the argument claim? Setting aside the question whether we do as a matter of fact 'fill in the detail' of the scene for ourselves as we read, and disregarding the assertion, which depends upon it, that 'the picture we each make is different from our neighbour's'—assuming, that is, for the moment that these things do happen as Dr Tillyard says they do—to what extent can a claim for dexterity in the poet be founded upon them? I submit that in so far as these visualizations do take place as one reads the couplet they have to be attributed simply to a general property of language, and even of single words, and that to use them as evidence for poetic ability, as *positive* evidence, is simply perverse. When I. A. Richards says that 'the more simple the object contemplated the more varied the responses will be which can be expected from it'[1] he offers a statement which, whether true or not, is not in itself absurd. But to twist such a statement, as Dr Tillyard does here, to sustain a value-judgment, is to invite absurdity, for one begins then to appraise a poem in terms of what its author has *not* put into it and can feel free to claim that any simple line (even those in Dr Johnson's 'As with my hat upon my head I walk'd along the Strand') is a masterpiece of implication, inviting the reader to 'fill in the detail'. Literary criticism is admittedly not an exact science but it is not, I hope, as bedevilled as this.

It is only natural that an extract of this kind should suggest certain general reflections on the type of defence that has been tendered to Milton but perhaps it will be best if I defer these until the second extract, from Sir Herbert Grierson, has been given. It is taken from *Milton and Wordsworth* and relates to the first four books of *Paradise Lost*:

In these books one 'stroke', as Addison would call it, of creative and surprising genius follows another—Satan and the angels prostrate on the floor of Hell, Satan's dialogue with Beelzebub, his progress across the burning marle, . . . the rousing of the angels, and that tremendous 'stroke' which one might hardly

[1] *Principles of Literary Criticism* (London, 1938), p. 9.

have expected from Milton, Satan shaken with remorse as he surveys the
fallen followers of his pride:

> Thrice he assay'd, and thrice in spite of scorn
> Tears such as angels weep burst forth; at last
> Words interwoven with sighs found out their way.

Is there even in Shakespeare a greater moment? And Shakespeare might have
marred it by a touch of bombast or wit.[1]

The slighting reference to Shakespeare here is no doubt intended to be
provocative, but I think it is clear, too, that Sir Herbert's question is a
perfectly honest one and that it is intended to make a quite serious
comparison. Yet how many readers will grant the comparison? For
myself I am quite unable to, and I am bold enough to doubt whether
others familiar with the two poets will not feel the same. Two fairly
obvious points about any such 'stroke' in Shakespeare at once suggest
themselves. First, I believe that in Shakespeare a 'stroke' of this kind
would usually and perhaps invariably involve distinctively *poetic* means,
so that the resultant effect would be inseparable not only from the
statement contained in the words chosen but from their connotations also
—consider for example the force of the simile, at once enhancing and
ironic, in

> If you have writ your annals true, 'tis there,
> That, like an eagle in a dove-cote, I
> Flutter'd your Volscians in Corioli:
> Alone I did it.

Secondly, I feel that in Shakespeare the effect would often be to con-
centrate a whole mass of impressions we had already received and
bring them poignantly and vividly home to us—as in Lear's

> Do not laugh at me;
> For, as I am a man, I think this lady
> To be my child Cordelia.

But Milton in the lines quoted is really doing neither of these things.
In the first place we have only just met the Satan of the poem, so that
for all we know it may be Milton's intention to present him as lachrymose: the poetic *context* does nothing to make his tears either moving
or wonderful. Moreover, as I shall show in a minute, even if we were
reading the poem for the second time, so that Satan's weeping could be
more imaginatively related to the rest of his history, we should probably
lose in another way what we had gained in this. In the second place
there is nothing in the poetic effect of the lines that can be compared
with Coriolanus's 'like an eagle in a dove-cote', or even with the

---

[1] *Milton and Wordsworth*, p. 107.

simple delicacy of the counterpointing of 'lady' and 'child' in the example from *King Lear*. Someone may indeed perhaps point to 'Tears such as angels weep' as being in its way an equivalent for these Shakespearean effects (there is certainly nothing else to point to) but will such a claim bear examination? Sir Herbert himself does seem to assume that the phrase is a touch of sublimity and that Milton wants us to feel how precious celestial tears must be. But if we had been through the poem once we should know how frequently Milton strays from his main themes to tell us about the substance and properties of angels and we might well feel that these words contained only a simple prosaic qualification—'the tears that angels, like men, can weep (for they can)' rather than 'celestial tears'. Thus if in fact we were re-reading the poem we might on the one hand have the advantage of seeing Satan's weeping as a striking variation from his habitual demeanour but on the other hand our reaction to the phrase describing his tears would almost certainly be much cooler and less immediate than Sir Herbert would appear to allow. The definitional sense of the phrase would have shrivelled its connotations of sublimity and we should be able to see how little there actually is in common between it and the other simile in *Coriolanus*. Though it is disagreeable to have to say so, it seems to me that Sir Herbert here seems almost idolatrously partial to Milton and rather insensitive to Shakespeare. There are at best only one or two 'strokes' in *Paradise Lost* that can be compared with Shakespeare like this, and perhaps only one: the four magnificent lines (two of which, by the way, Addison wanted to omit) with which it ends.

The two points to which I have been leading up and which I think these two extracts may suffice to confirm can now be stated.

The first point concerns the comparison with Shakespeare. Anyone who has really read the essay on Milton's verse in *Revaluation* will have seen that it is this comparison that Dr Leavis is chiefly concerned to make, and they will have inferred that a good part of his intention in writing as he did was to question the loose bracketing of the two poets as though they were pretty well equally balanced when measured by the quality of the poetry that they wrote. It is true that many of Milton's defenders have tried to suggest that it was really Donne who was involved in Dr Leavis's comparison but—since he only refers to Donne once, quoting him to illustrate 'the Shakespearean usage of English'—this is so patent an attempt to shift the basis of the argument to their own advantage that with the ordinarily attentive reader it is bound to defeat its own purpose. If, then, much of the debate is really rooted in the comparison with Shakespeare, it is safe to say that, in order to yield to a critic soliciting his agreement, a reader will demand from him at least as much sensitivity to Shakespeare's verse as to Milton's. And when he finds, among those repudiating Dr Leavis's arguments, even so judicious a Miltonist as Sir Herbert Grierson falling short in this sensitivity he is surely justified in wondering to what extent those arguments have been properly understood—to what extent there *is* an argument, and not simply an instinctive response to what is vaguely sensed as a threat. Moreover, when he has not only the analysis offered in the essay but also the testimony of a convinced admirer of Milton like Mr C. S. Lewis to assure him of Dr Leavis's sensitivity to *Milton's* verse his wonder may quite properly begin to harden into a conviction that Dr Leavis is a more dependable guide than any of the opposing voices. I cannot see what, unless it be prejudice, there is to bar such a conclusion.

Again (and this is my second point) when we come upon an apprecia-tive but sophistical commentary on Milton's writing like the one I have quoted from Dr Tillyard (it is not the only example of its kind, though admittedly striking) we must surely begin to wonder why such an account should ever have been conceived. The fault does not lie with Milton, for there are undoubtedly a number of passages in his work—passages where, as Dr Leavis has said, 'the verse glows with an unusual life'—that offer themselves for critical approval. Some of these have been dealt with by Dr Leavis and that there are others he himself would be, I imagine, the first to grant. I shall take two that seem to me appropriate. Consider for instance (though here we have something rather different from a glow of vitality) the passage in the first book in which we are shown Satan calling upon his fallen host to arise:

> Nathless he so endur'd, till on the Beach
> Of that inflamed Sea, he stood and call'd
> His Legions, Angel Forms, who lay intrans't
> Thick as Autumnal Leaves that strow the Brooks
> In *Vallombrosa*, where th' *Etrurian* shades
> High overarch't imbowr; or scattered sedge
> Afloat, when with fierce Winds *Orion* arm'd
> Hath vext the Red-Sea Coast, whose waves orethrew
> *Busiris* and his *Memphian* Chivalrie,
> While with perfidious hatred they pursu'd
> The Sojourners of *Goshen*, who beheld
> From the safe shore their floating Carkases
> And broken Chariot Wheels, so thick bestrown
> Abject and lost lay these, covering the Flood,
> Under amazement of their hideous change.   (299–313)

This, with its encrustation of similes, seems to me characteristic of Milton. But the similes are not merely encrusted—they are organized with extraordinary skill. He begins simply, by likening the fallen angels lying on the lake to autumn leaves thickly scattered on water flowing darkly under trees. Then, keeping the core of this image but altering its surface slightly, he compares them to sedge floating on the sea. With a smoothness that precludes the suspicion on our part that our attention is being manipulated, we are told that it is the Red Sea on which the sedge is floating, and this diplomatic shift allows us to move on naturally and unobtrusively to the recollection from the book of Exodus, the destruction of the army with which Pharoah was pursuing the children of Israel. And suddenly, seeing now the wreckage and flotsam of the Egyptian army on the surface of the sea, we realize what has happened, how beautifully the images have been turned back upon themselves and resolved, leaving us back where we started, with the picture of myriads of soldier-like forms stretched in defeat on the sea of fire. No apologetic qualifications need be resorted to by the critic who claims that such a passage is impressively contrived, and it seems to me that even a critic who claimed that there were few more skilful handlings of simile in English poetry might find many readers prepared to allow his claim. On the other hand, if it was a specifically rhythmical effect that Dr Tillyard wished to adduce in Milton's favour, he might well have had recourse to such a passage as this, from Book II, where the rhythm and movement incontestably *do* contribute to the meaning:

> At last his Sail-broad Vannes
> He spreads for flight, and in the surging smoak
> Uplifted spurns the ground, thence many a League
> As in a cloudy Chair ascending rides
> Audacious, but that seat soon failing, meets
> A vast vacuitie: all unawares
> Fluttring his pennons vain plumb down he drops
> Ten thousand fadom deep... (927–934)

This is not, however, the procedure that he adopts. Instead of taking (as we should expect him to take) an unusually successful passage, and demonstrating its merits, he takes a quite ordinary passage and tries to squeeze out some kind of virtue from it. I may say in all seriousness that I appreciate his difficulty. Dr Leavis's criticisms were not directed against particular passages but against the general run of the verse, the Miltonic average so to speak, and since this is so the critic who adduces one or two demonstrably good passages can hardly feel that he has disposed of those criticisms. It seems to me that Dr Tillyard has this fact in mind, for whereas in his treatment of *Paradise Lost* in an early book like *Milton* he did not attempt demonstration, and was content merely to throw out assertions about the quality of some passages ('the incomparable description in Book Eleven of the corruption of eternal spring', for instance), in his later books (my extract comes, it will be remembered, from *The Miltonic Setting*) he has tried to deal analytically with particular excerpts—even, as we see, from the minor poems. And nobody could deny that in the example I have given he has chosen to deal with an average rather than an exceptional couplet. But to what effect? The writer who found it 'extremely salutary' that Milton's eminence should be questioned appears now, in the exaggeration and speciousness of his defences, a resolute bardolater, with an itch to prove that there is 'substance' everywhere in Milton. So invidious an impression is obviously unfair and in reading paragraphs in his writings which seem, like that I have quoted, to insist upon it—as also in reading a passage like the one I have quoted from Rajan—I find myself asking whether these aberrations would not have been avoided if the writers had taken more careful stock of the nature of the adverse judgments with which, however remotely, they were engaged. If Milton's average *is* a rather dull one, if we have to stretch and strain in order to pretend otherwise, would it not be better to admit it and pass on? When one turns up Dr Leavis's essay again one is often surprised, after this wild championing, to find him speaking of the 'consummate art of *Lycidas*', the 'exquisite achievement' of the songs in *Comus*, quoting as a 'felicity' Tennyson's phrase about Milton's 'God-gifted organ voice', and analysing passages from *Paradise Lost* to illustrate what, at his best, Milton can do. Yet in the context of the essay these things are not at all surprising—seem indeed, to judge by results, to go quite unheeded. I am not of course denying that the general effect of the essay is critical—adversely critical, that is. What I am trying to suggest is that the criticisms which it offers are particular and definite, and that it is in no sense the sort of baby-plus-bathwater throw-out that would account for the overwrought loyalty with which defenders of the poet have so often attempted to answer it. And here my two points seem to me to converge: to what extent is there an argument? to what extent have Milton's advocates understood the case against him? to what extent are their wilder defences simply the result of flurry and misunderstanding? When I regret the lack of a meticulous and specific consideration of Dr Leavis's case from the other side I am not, then, I believe, demanding from his opponents more than would seem to be required of them already by the nature of disputation itself. Had there been such a reply in the past, disputing what was disputable, conceding what had to be conceded, the argument could have been a very different affair, a matter of critical co-operation towards a wholly useful end rather than an occasion for polemic and hyperbole. Far from cowing the student into a nervous silence it might instead have given him a truly just and sensitive attitude to Milton, and shown him also the sort of discovery, fresh in each age, that literary criticism can achieve.

I suppose it is a little late in the day to be pointing all this out. But my excuse must be that the transition from the controversy itself, such as it was, to the present situation, in which most Miltonists are prepared to close their eyes and behave as though it had never occurred, has been a gradual one, and that only lately has it become patent enough to make necessary the sort of caveat I have tried to develop here. Besides Dr Tillyard's *Studies in Milton* I am thinking particularly of two other recent publications in the field of Milton criticism, the one a reprint of the 1645 edition of the minor poems with appended 'essays in analysis' by Cleanth Brooks and John Edward Hardy and the other a symposium, evidently with some pretensions to being thought comprehensive, of articles on the poet by modern critics. No adverse critic has found his way into the symposium, nor is there any mention of the controversy in Brooks and Hardy's volume. Indeed, of all the writers who have probed for limitations in Milton's poetry these two most recent critics refer only to T. S. Eliot—the reference, in itself very brief, being to his 'retraction' rather than to anything written earlier. With Brooks and Hardy's own sort of criticism, and its reliance upon formal 'patterns', 'resurrection images' and the New English Dictionary, I am not here concerned. What does concern me is that their book (like the others) is intended for students. I have already observed that in my eyes the premature termination of the controversy is an unnecessary victimization of the student, something that is bound to leave him perplexed and uneasy rather than enlightened; but this new tendency, as it were, to censor any murmuring against Milton's reputation, to withhold from the student opinions that might conflict with those of a teacher whose regard for Milton bordered on adulation, is much more serious, and even a little sinister. In saying this I am not, of course, merely agreeing with Coleridge that 'the very act of dissenting from established opinions must generate habits precursive to the love of freedom'— though that is an opinion which, in my view, experience tends to verify. Rather I am objecting to the introduction into the sphere of education of a kind of bias and authoritarianism which to anyone, like myself, engaged in teaching can only appear vicious. With Milton, I cannot praise a fugitive and cloistered virtue, nor yet an opinion which depends upon a selection of all the relevant facts. Where that selection is the outcome of imposition rather than choice, moreover, it surely needs to be even more peremptorily condemned. The controversy may indeed, as it stands, be a victimization of the student but to make this an excuse for further victimization, by neglecting to mention it or hugger-muggering it, is quite indefensible. Is the aim of our education henceforth to be conformity? And, if so, conformity to what? I ask, with Juvenal, *quis custodiet ipsos custodes?*

7

JUDGMENT AND ANALYSIS: NOTES IN THE ANALYSIS OF POETRY[1]

'THOUGHT' AND EMOTIONAL QUALITY

F. R. LEAVIS (1945)

Notes in the Analysis of Poetry (i)

When we look at *Heraclitus*[2] we see that the directly emotional and personal insistence distinguishing it is associated with an absence of core or substance: the poem seems to be all emotional comment, the alleged justifying situation, the subject of comment, being represented by loosely evocative generalities, about which the poet feels vaguely if 'intensely' (the 'intensity' of this kind of thing is conditioned by vagueness). Again, the emotion seems to be out there on the page, whereas in reading *Proud Maisie* we never seem to be offered emotions as such; the emotion develops and defines itself as we grasp the dramatic elements the poem does offer—the data it presents (that is the effect) with emotional 'disinterestedness'. For 'disinterestedness' we can substitute 'impersonality', with which term we introduce a critical topic of the first importance.

Someone may comment that, on the one hand, for Scott, whose poetic impulse clearly came not from any inescapable pang experienced in his immediately personal life, but from an interest in ballads and in the ballad-convention, the impersonality of his poem was an easy achievement, while, on the other hand, absence of impersonality in the handling of poignant emotion needn't be accompanied by the self-cherishing emotionality, the wallowing complaisance, of *Heraclitus*. These matters can be carried further, and the essential distinctions given force, only by close and varied reference to the concrete. Here is a contrast analogous to the last, but a contrast in which the 'impersonal' poem unmistakably derives from a seismic personal experience, while the obviously emotional poem is not suspect, like *Heraclitus*, of being a mere indulgence in the sweets of poignancy:

[1] Constituting part of a book.
[2] *They told me, Heraclitus.*

(a)   A slumber did my spirit seal;
    I had no human fears:
She seemed a thing that could not feel
    The touch of earthly years.

No motion has she now, no force;
    She neither hears nor sees;
Roll'd round in earth's diurnal course,
    With rocks, and stones, and trees.

(b)   Break, break, break,
    On thy cold gray stones, O Sea!
And I would that my tongue could utter
    The thoughts that arise in me.

O well for the fisherman's boy,
    That he shouts with his sister at play!
O well for the sailor lad,
    That he sings in his boat on the bay!

And the stately ships go on
    To their haven under the hill;
But O for the touch of a vanish'd hand,
    And the sound of a voice that is still!

Break, break, break,
    At the foot of thy crags, O Sea!
But the tender grace of a day that is dead
    Will never come back to me.

No one can doubt that Wordsworth wrote his poem because of something profoundly and involuntarily suffered—suffered as a personal calamity, but the experience has been so impersonalized that the effect, as much as that of *Proud Maisie*, is one of bare and disinterested presentment. Again, though the working this time doesn't so obviously prompt to a diagrammatic schematization, the emotional power is generated between the two stanzas, or between the states represented by the stanzas: 'she was, she is not'—the statement seems almost as bare and simple as that. But the statement is concrete, and once the reading has been completed the whole poem is seen to be a complex organization, charged with a subtle life. In retrospect the first stanza takes on new significance:

> A slumber did my spirit seal;
> I had no human fears

—the full force of that 'human' comes out: the conditions of the human situation are inescapable and there is a certain *hubris* in the security of forgetful bliss. Again, the 'human' enhances the ironic force of 'thing' in the next line:

> She seemed a thing that could not feel
> The touch of earthly years.

In the second stanza she *is* a thing—a thing that, along with the rocks and stones and trees with which she is

> Roll'd round in earth's diurnal course,

cannot in reality feel the touch of earthly years and enjoys a real immunity from death. The 'diurnal', chosen apparently for its scientific nakedness and reinforcing as it does that stating bareness with which the diction and tone express the brutal finality of the fact, has actually, at the same time, a potent evocative force: it puts the fact in an astronomical setting and evokes the vast inexorable regularity of the planetary motions, the effect being analogous to that of the enclosing morning–night contrast of *Proud Maisie*.

In *Break, break, break* we again have the poem that offers emotion directly—the poem in which the emotion seems to be 'out there' on the page. If we read the poem aloud, the emotion, in full force from the opening, asserts itself in the plangency of tone and movement that is compelled upon us. We do not, however, this time feel moved to a dismissing judgment. The poet is clearly one of distinguished gift, we cannot doubt that behind the poem there is a genuinely personal urgency, and we are not ready to accuse him of being moved primarily by the enjoyment of being poignantly moved—though we *can* very readily imagine a rendering of the poem that should betray too much enjoyment of the poignancy.

And here, in this last suggestion, we glimpse a way of getting beyond a neutrally descriptive account of the differences between the two poems. We can say that Wordsworth's poem is a securer kind of achievement. If someone should comment that to make it a point against a poem that it lends itself more readily to abuse is to assume a great deal, it will perhaps be best not to take up the challenge directly but to advance another proposition: an emotional *habit* answering to the mode of *Break, break, break* would need to be regarded critically. The poet, we can say, whose habitual mode—whose emotional habit—was represented by that poem would not only be very limited; we should expect to find him noticeably given to certain weaknesses and vices. Further, the reader who cannot see that Tennyson's poem, with all its distinction and refinement, yields a satisfaction inferior in kind to that represented by Wordsworth, cannot securely appreciate the highest poetic achievement at its true worth and is not very likely to be at all strong or sure in the kind of judgment that discriminates between *Break, break, break* and *Heraclitus*.

'Inferior in kind'—by what standards? Here we come to the point at which literary criticism, as it must, enters overtly into questions of emotional hygiene and moral value—more generally (there seems no other adequate phrase), of spiritual health. It seems best not to say anything further by way of immediate answer to the challenge. By the time we have closed the discussion of impersonality, a theme that will come up in explicit form again, a great deal more will have been said to elucidate, both directly and indirectly, the nature of the answer. The immediate business is to push on with the method of exploration by concrete analysis—analysis of judiciously assorted instances.

The pairs of poems that we have examined as yet have presented strong and patent contrasts. It is time to pass on to a comparison where the essential distinction is less obvious:

(*a*) Softly, in the dusk, a woman is singing to me;
     Taking me back down the vista of years, till I see
     A child sitting under the piano, in the boom of the tingling strings
     And pressing the small, poised feet of a mother who smiles as she
       sings.

     In spite of myself the insidious mastery of song
     Betrays me back, till the heart of me weeps to belong
     To the old Sunday evenings at home, with winter outside
     And hymns in the cosy parlour, the tinkling piano our guide.

     So now it is vain for the singer to burst into clamour
     With the great black piano appassionato. The glamour
     Of childish days is upon me, my manhood is cast
     Down in the flood of remembrance, I weep like a child for
       the past.

(*b*) Tears, idle tears, I know not what they mean,
     Tears from the depth of some divine despair
     Rise in the heart, and gather to the eyes,
     In looking on the happy Autumn-fields,
     And thinking of the days that are no more.

     Fresh as the first beam glittering on a sail,
     That brings our friends up from the underworld,
     Sad as the last which reddens over one
     That sinks with all we love below the verge;
     So sad, so fresh, the days that are no more.

     Ah, sad and strange as in dark summer dawns
     The earliest pipe of half-awaken'd birds
     To dying ears, when unto dying eyes
     The casement slowly grows a glimmering square;
     So sad, so strange, the days that are no more.

Dear as remember'd kisses after death,
And sweet as those by hopeless fancy feign'd
On lips that are for others; deep as love,
Deep as first love, and wild with all regret;
O Death in Life, the days that are no more.

Neither of these poems answers to the description of 'bare present-ment'. Both of them look pretty emotional: that is, they make an insistent direct offer of emotion; they incite patently to an immediate 'moved' response. Tackling that most dangerous theme, the irrevocable past, each flows 'from the heart' in swelling and lapsing movements that suggest the poignant luxury of release, the loosing of the reservoirs. At first sight (*a*), with its banal phrases—'vista of years', 'the insidious mastery of song', 'the heart of me weeps', 'the glamour of childish days', its invocation of music, and the explicit 'I weep like a child for the past' with which it concludes—might seem, if either of the poems is to be discriminated against as sentimental, to be the one. But even at a first reading through of the pair it should be plain that there is a difference of movement between them, and that the movement of (*a*) is, by contrast, the subtler. Against the simply plangent flow of (*b*) we feel it as decidedly complex.

When we examine this effect of complexity we find it is associated with the *stating* manner that, in spite of the dangerous emotional swell, distinguishes (*a*) from (*b*). And when we examine this effect of state-ment we find that it goes with a particularity to which (*b*) offers no counterpart. For the banalities instanced do not represent everything in the poem; the 'vista of years' leads back to something sharply seen— a very specific situation that stands there in its own right; so that we might emend 'stating' into 'constating' in order to describe that effect as of prose statement (we are inclined to call it—but the situation is vividly realized) which marks the manner. The child is 'sitting under the piano, in the boom of the tingling strings' and 'pressing the small poised feet' of its mother—we note that 'poised', not only because of its particularity, but because the word seems to be significant in respect of an essential, though unobtrusive, quality of the poem. The main immediate point, however, is that in all this particularity we have something quite other than banal romantic generality: this is not the common currency of sentimental evocation or anything of the kind. The actuality of the remembered situation is unbeglamouring, becoming more so in the second stanza, with the 'hymns' and the 'tinkling piano'. Something is, we see, held and presented in this poem, and the pre-senting involves an *attitude towards*, an element of disinterested valuation. For all the swell of emotion the critical mind has its part in the whole; the constatation is at the same time in some measure a placing. That is, sensibility in the poem doesn't work in complete divorce from intelligence; feeling is not divorced from thinking: however the key terms are to be defined, these propositions at any rate have a clear enough meaning in this context.

But to return to the 'tinkling piano': we note that it stands in contrast to the 'great piano appassionato' of the last stanza, and, along with the 'hymns', to the music that started the emotional flood:

> So now it is vain for the singer to burst into clamour
> With the great black piano appassionato.

We note further that in the ordinary sentimental poeticality inspired by the 'insidious mastery of song' it would not be 'vain': the poet would be swept away on the flood of the immediate, represented by the emotional vagueness into which the 'music' would be translated.[1] It is a remarkable poet who, conveying the 'insidious mastery' and the 'flood' so potently, at the same time fixes and presents with such specificity the situation he sharply distinguishes from the immediate. It is unusual, and suggests lines on which we might explain our finding the 'poised' of the first stanza a word to underscore.

But of course we have passed over a phrase in the second stanza corresponding to the 'vain', and marking a correlated though different distinction—one tensely counterpoised with the other: 'In spite of myself'—

> In spite of myself the insidious mastery of song
> Betrays me back . . .

Here we may profit by a comment on this poem made by D. W. Harding in his *Note on Nostalgia*:[2]

The fact of experiencing the tendency towards regression means nothing. It is the final attitude towards the experience that has to be evaluated, and in literature this attitude may be suggested only very subtly by means of the total context. In *The Grey Land* and in *Piano* the writer's attitude is clear. Shanks obviously finds a tranquil pleasure in the thought of throwing up the sponge. In Lawrence's poem the impulse seems to have been equally strong and is certainly expressed more forcefully, but the attitude is different. Lawrence is adult, stating the overwhelming strength of the impulse but reporting resistance to it and implying that resistance is better than yielding.

That 'heart of me', we see, is no mere sentimental banality. For the poet his 'heart' is not his; it is an emotional rebellion that he fights against and disowns. *He* is here, and his emotion there. Again, the 'glamour of childish days' is a *placing* phrase; it represents a surrender that his 'manhood' is ashamed of.

---

[1] Cf. J. C. Squire's *To a Musician*.
[2] *Determinations*, p. 70 (ed. F. R. Leavis).

No more need be said about the elements of this kind in the poem. It is a complex whole, and its distinction, plainly, is bound up with its complexity. This complexity, to recapitulate, involves the presence of something other than directly offered emotion, or mere emotional flow—the presence of something, a specific situation, concretely grasped. The presentment of this situation involves a disinterested or 'constating' attitude, and also a critical attitude towards the emotion evoked by the situation: here we have our licence for saying that, however strong an emotional effect the poem has, that is essentially conditioned by 'thought': the constating, relating and critical mind has its essential part in the work of sensibility. We can say further that the aspect of disinterested 'presentment' is not confined to the situation seen at the end of the 'vista of years'; the collapse upon the 'flood of remembrance' is itself, while so poignantly and inwardly conveyed, presented at the same time from the outside. It is a kind of object for contemplation, though one that isn't 'there' except in so far as we are also inside it. We are immersed in the flood enough to feel, as immediate experience, its irresistibleness; at the same time it is as much 'out there' as the 'child sitting under the piano'. And in these observations we are making notes that are very relevant to the theme of 'impersonality'.

Complexity, we can see at once when we pass on, is not a marked characteristic of Tennyson's poem, which is what at the first reading its movement seemed to indicate. It moves simply forward with a sweetly plangent flow, without check, cross-tension or any qualifying element. To give it the reading it asks for is to flow with it, acquiescing in a complete and simple immersion: there is no attitude towards the experience except one of complaisance; we are to be wholly in it and of it. We note, too, the complete absence of anything like the particularity of (a): there is nothing that gives the effect of an object, or substantial independent existence. The particularity of 'the happy Autumn-fields', 'the first beam glittering on a sail', and the casement that 'slowly fades a glimmering square', and so on, is only speciously of the kind in question. No new definitions or directions of feeling derive from these suggestions of imagery, which seem to be wholly *of* the current of vague emotion that determines them. We note that the strong effect of particularity produced by (a) is conditioned by the complexity—by the play of contrast and tension; but (b) seems to offer a uniform emotional fluid (though there are several simple ingredients, represented by 'sad', 'fresh', 'strange', 'sweet' and so on—the insistent explicitness of which is significant).

And the relation between 'thought' and 'feeling' as illustrated by Tennyson's poem?—A note of Yeats's on his own work comes to mind here: 'I tried after the publication of *The Wanderings of Oisin* to write of nothing but emotion, and in the simplest language, and now I have had to go through it all, cutting out or altering passages that are sentimental for lack of thought.'[1] This has an obvious bearing on *The Lake Isle of Innisfree*. *Tears, idle tears*, in the main respects dealt with in the last paragraph, may fairly be classed with *Innisfree*. Whether we are to call it 'sentimental' or not, it certainly bears to *Break, break, break* a relation that gives force to the suggestion made in regard to this last poem. The poet who wrote the one wrote the other: they are both highly characteristic; and it is plain that habitual indulgence of the kind represented by *Tears, idle tears*—indulgence not accompanied and virtually disowned by a critical placing—would be, on grounds of emotional and spiritual hygiene, something to deplore. There is nothing gross about the poem; it exhibits its author's highly personal distinction; but it unquestionably offers emotion directly, emotion for its own sake without a justifying situation, and, in the comparison, its inferiority to Lawrence's poem compels a largely disparaging commentary.

The comparison is not gratuitous, a puritanic intrusion of critical righteousness; readiness to make the kind of judgment that the comparison enforces is implicit in any sound response to Tennyson's poem. The grounds for this insistence could, if necessary, be demonstrated pretty conclusively from the case—the clinical suggestion applies—of Shelley. Shelley, whose genius is not in dispute, preaches, in the *Defence of Poetry*, a doctrine that makes the writing of Poetry as much a matter of passive submission to the emotional tides, and as little a matter of active intelligence, as possible. Consistently with this doctrine, a representative expression of his genius such as the *Ode to the West Wind* depends for its success on our being so carried along in the plangent sweep of emotion that we ask no questions. To the questions that propose themselves when we do stop and consider—Can 'loose clouds' really be 'shed' on the 'stream of the wind' 'like earth's decaying leaves'? What are the 'tangled boughs of heaven and ocean'? and so on—there is no better reply than that the questions don't propose themselves when we are responding properly (as it requires an effort *not* to do). The thinking mind is in abeyance, and discrepancies assume an inevitable congruence in the flood of plangency.

There is, then, an obvious sense in which Shelley's poetry offers feeling divorced from thought—offers it as something opposed to thought. Along with this characteristic goes Shelley's notable inability to *grasp* anything—to present any situation, any observed or imagined actuality, or any experience, as an object existing independently in its

[1] *Early Poems and Stories*, p. v.

218

own nature and in its own right. Correlatively there is the direct offer of emotion—emotion insistently explicit—in itself, for itself, for its own sake: we find our description merging into criticism. For, reading Shelley's poetry, his best, the finest expression of his genius, there is demonstrable force and point in saying that a due acceptance will have in close attendance on it the at any rate implicit qualification: 'But these habits are dangerous.' It is significant that the example of gross sentimentality examined at the beginning of this chapter[1] was produced by Shelley. And it is not an exceptional lapse. Shelley's works, indeed, provide much more serious occasions for criticism; criticism that is far more damaging because it goes deeper. Here we have the reason for adducing him at this stage of the argument: in the examination of his poetry the literary critic finds himself passing, by inevitable transitions, from describing characteristics to making adverse judgments about emotional quality; and so to a kind of discussion in which, by its proper methods and in pursuit of its proper ends, literary criticism becomes the diagnosis of what, looking for an inclusive term, we can only call spiritual malady.

There would be no point in offering here an abridged critique of Shelley in demonstration. To be satisfactory, the treatment must be fairly full, and I have attempted such a treatment in *Revaluation*. But it may still be worth insisting, by way of developing a discussion opened above, that if one finds it a weakness in Shelley's poetry that feeling, as offered in it, depends for its due effect on a virtual abeyance of the thinking mind, one is not appealing, as seems so often to be assumed, to a criterion represented by the seventeenth-century Metaphysicals.

The possibilities are not as limited as that; the problem cannot be reduced to that choice of simple alternatives which the Shelley–Donne antithesis suggests. And perhaps there is more to be said about the presence of 'thought' in Metaphysical poetry than those who resort so readily to the antithesis recognize. The obvious presence, we know, is in the ratiocination and the use of intellectual material (philosophical, theological and so on). In following the argument and appreciating the nature and relevance of the ideas invoked one has, reading Metaphysical verse, to make something of the kind of sustained intellectual effort demanded by a closely reasoned prose treatise. That, of course, isn't all: in good Metaphysical poetry the analogies that form so large a part of the argument introduce imagery that is concretely realized and has powerful imaginative effects—effects that depend, though, on our following the argument.

The vices to which the Metaphysical habit inclines are antithetical to those attendant on the habit represented by Shelley and the Tennyson of

[1] *That time is dead for ever, child!*

Tears, idle tears: they are a matter, not of the cultivation of emotion for its own sake, but of the cultivation of subtlety of thought for its own sake; we find ingenuities of analogy and logic (or quasi-logic) that are uncontrolled by a total imaginative or emotional purpose. And in a great many successful Metaphysical poems the emotion seems to have a secondary and ancillary status: without some *fulcra* of emotional interest the ingenious system of tensions—the organization of 'wit'—couldn't have been contrived; and that says pretty much all there is to say about the presence of emotion. But when a poet of Metaphysical habit is personally moved and possessed by something profoundly experienced, as, for instance, Donne in the *Nocturnall*, then we have poetry of very exceptional emotional strength.

The part of 'thought' in this strength deserves more consideration than it usually gets under the head of 'Metaphysical wit': there is more to it than subtle ratiocination—the surprising play of analogy. The activity of the thinking mind, the energy of intelligence, involved in the Metaphysical habit means that, when the poet *has* urgent personal experience to deal with it is attended to and contemplated—which in turn means some kind of separation, or distinction, between experiencer and experience. 'Their attempts were always analytic'—to analyse your experience you must, while keeping it alive and immediately present as experience, treat it in some sense as an object. That is, an essential part of the strength of good Metaphysical poetry turns out to be of the same order as the strength of all the most satisfying poetry: the conceitedness, the Metaphysicality, is the obtrusive accompaniment of an essential presence of 'thought' such as we have in the best work of all great poets. It can be said in favour of the Metaphysical habit that it favours such a presence.

These points may be enforced by considering, in comparison with a representative piece of Victorian verse, a passage of Marvell:

(*a*) Sombre and rich, the skies,
Great glooms, and starry plains;
Gently the night wind sighs;
Else a vast silence reigns.

The splendid silence clings
Around me: and around
The saddest of all Kings,
Crown'd, and again discrown'd.

* * * *

Alone he rides, alone,
The fair and fatal King:
Dark night is all his own,
That strange and solemn thing.

Which are more full of fate:
The stars; or those sad eyes?
Which are more still and great:
Those brows, or the dark skies?

Although his whole heart yearn
In passionate tragedy,
Never was face so stern
With sweet austerity.

Vanquished in life, his death
By beauty made amends:
The passing of his breath
Won his defeated ends.

  *   *   *   *

Armour'd he rides, his head
Bare to the stars of doom;
He triumphs now, the dead,
Beholding London's gloom.

Our wearier spirit faints,
Vex'd in the world's employ:
His soul was of the saints;
And art to him was joy.

King tried in fires of woe!
Men hunger for thy grace:
And through the night I go,
Loving thy mournful face.

Yet when the city sleeps,
When all the cries are still,
The stars and heavenly deeps
Work out a perfect will.

(*b*)   What Field of all the Civil Wars,
Where his were not the deepest Scars?
   And Hampton shows what part
   He had of wiser Art.

Where, twining subtile fears with hope,
He wove a Net of such a scope,
   That Charles himself might chase
   To Caresbrooks narrow case.

That thence the Royal Actor born
The Tragick Scaffold might adorn:
   While round the armed bands
   Did clap their bloody hands.

He nothing common did or mean
Upon that memorable Scene:
But with his keener Eye
The Axes edge did try:

Nor call'd the Gods with vulgar spight
To vindicate his helpless Right,
But bow'd his comely Head,
Down as upon a Bed.

To forestall the possible comment that the comparison is arbitrary, it had better be said at once that Johnson's stanzas are offered as a foil to Marvell's. And, actually, *By the Statute of King Charles at Charing Cross* may fairly be taken as representative of the tradition, to which it belongs, the main nineteenth-century tradition, and it is highly characteristic for a poet of that tradition to centre his interest in a hero of the past and to exhibit towards him Johnson's kind of attitude. On the other hand, we can say of Marvell that, had he chosen to deal with a figure from the past he would have treated him as a contemporary, and that it is highly characteristic of Marvell to express so sympathetic an attitude towards Charles in a poem of which Cromwell is the official hero.

It must be plain at once that such impressiveness as Johnson's poem has is conditioned by an absence of thought. This is poetry from the 'soul', that nineteenth-century region of specialized poetical experience where nothing has sharp definition and where effects of 'profundity' and 'intensity' depend upon a lulling of the mind. The large evocative-ness begins in the first stanza, so that we needn't press the question whether 'clings' in the second—

The splendid silence clings
Around me

—is the right word: we know that if we have lapsed properly into the kind of reading the poem claims such questions don't arise, and that, absorbed in the sombre richness, the great glooms, and so on, we merge without any question at all into the sadness of 'the saddest of all kings'. If we are in a mood to ask questions, the process by which all this evocation is made to invest the 'fair and fatal king' hasn't the needful potency, and reading

Dark night is all his own,
That strange and solemn thing,

we may perhaps comment adversely on the conditions of vague impressiveness in the poem and alcoholic lack of focus in the reader that make 'thing' an impressive rime. How complete an abeyance of the questioning mind is called for becomes still more obvious when the poem itself asks formal questions:

> Which are more full of fate:
> The stars; or those sad eyes?
> Which are more still and great:
> Those brows, or the dark skies?

Taken as real questions, requiring answers, they are merely ludicrous. Again, the essential absence of thought—the absence that is essential to the emotional effect—is apparent when (as the right reader doesn't) we try to relate what look like key statements, focusing the significance of the poem. We are told that

> The passing of his breath
> Won his defeated ends

and then, in the next stanza but one, that

> He triumphs now, the dead,
> Beholding London's gloom

—nothing more at all seizable is conveyed regarding the nature of his triumph except that he became a legend and a symbol adapted to the purposes of the Lionel Johnsons. And here, of course, we make our critical point: it is his purpose that Johnson is really concerned with, not Charles, who is merely an excuse, a cover, and opportunity. We may note in Marvell's

> He nothing common did or mean

an apt implicit comment on the suggested royal triumph of saintly *Schadenfreude* that gratifies Johnson, but we know that criticism needn't bother itself with a solemn comparison of Johnson's attitude towards Charles with Marvell's. There is no Charles *there* in Johnson, who is not preoccupied with anything in the nature of an object, felt or imagined as existing in its own right.

> Our wearier spirit faints,
> Vex'd in the world's employ:
> His soul was of the saints;
> And art to him was joy.
>
> King, tried in fires of woe!
> Men hunger for thy grace:
> And through the night I go,
> Loving thy mournful face.

—It is plain that the hunger comes first, the appetite for a certain kind of religiose-emotional indulgence, and that Johnson goes straight for this, uninhibited by any thought of reality—or any thought at all; and that what he loves is his love, his favourite vague and warm emotions and sentiments, which Charles (the thinking and judging mind being in a happy drunken daze) can be taken as justifying. The curious show of thought and logic necessary to Johnson's purpose is well illustrated in the final stanza, with its opening 'Yet'. We can say easily enough what that stanza does, but we cannot say what it means.

It takes no great critical acumen to see all this. The poem is offered for the obviousness of its illustrative significance. It shows in their essential relations vague evocativeness, the absence of anything grasped and presented, the absence of imagery that will bear any closer attention than that given by the rapt and passive mind in its gliding passage, the absence of constating and relating thought, the direct aim at emotion in itself, the grossness of sentimentality. We do not, of course, argue from the poem to Lionel Johnson's personal qualities. It merely shows what an unfortunate tradition can do with a mind of some distinction.

Tradition served Marvell very differently. Though the *Horatian Ode* is not one of his Metaphysical poems, the Metaphysical element perceptible in it goes so perfectly with the actual Horatian mode as to reinforce very neatly a point made above—the point that conceitedness and the other distinctively Metaphysical qualities are, in good Metaphysical poetry, obtrusive manifestations of an essential presence of 'thought' such as we have in some non-Metaphysical poetry. The contemplating, relating and appraising mind is unmistakably there in the characteristic urbane poise of the ode. There could hardly have been a directer or more obviously disinterested concern with objects of contemplation: the attitudes seem to be wholly determined by the nature of what is seen and judged, and the expression of feeling to be secondary and merely incidental to just statement and presentment. These qualities, which are exemplified on so impressive a scale and in so developed a way in the ode as a whole—in the cool, appraising poise of the eulogy of Cromwell, the delicately ironic survey of contemporary history, the grave aplomb of the close, and in the very fact of Charles's appearing to such advantage in such a context—are apparent enough in the passage on Charles as it stands by itself. And it is plain that its strength as feeling and attitude, its unassertive command of our sympathy, depends on them.

It may be well to repeat that there is no question here of solemn comparative appraisal of the two poems—or of weighing Johnson's poem against Marvell's fragment. The point of the juxtaposition is that it gives us an illustrative contrast of modes. An antithesis so extreme, some one may comment, as to leave the bearing of the comparison in doubt: it is in the nature of Marvell's ode not to be a product of strong personal emotion (there is no evidence in it that Marvell had any to control), but to be the poised formal expression of statesmanlike wisdom, surveying judicially the contemporary scene. That is so; nevertheless, no one will contend that feeling has no part in the effect. Much as the ode seems to be a matter of explicit statement, its judgments are conveyed concretely, in terms of feeling and attitude. In fact, if it were a question of choosing the more potent piece of propaganda for the 'fair and fatal king', the more deeply moving evocation, sympathetic and sympathy-winning, wouldn't even the devotee do well to prefer Marvell's lines? And it should be plain that qualities of essentially the same order as those which justify us in talking of the presence in the *Horation Ode* of the contemplating, relating and appraising mind can co-exist with the evidence, in tone and feeling, of greater personal urgency—a presence that needn't be at the same time, as it is in the ode, one of very definite and conscious tradition in the attitudes and valuations. Indeed, it would be possible to arrange poems in series in such a way as to make the classification of the *Horatian Ode*, *Proud Maisie* and *A Slumber did my spirit seal* together, as against the contrasting poems of Lionel Johnson, Tennyson and Shelley, obviously reasonable.

By way of exploring these matters further let us now consider briefly a poem in which Shelley makes what looks like an insistent offer of thought:

> Music, when soft voices die,
> Vibrates in the memory—
> Odours, when sweet violets sicken,
> Live within the sense they quicken.
>
> Rose leaves, when the rose is dead,
> Are heap'd for the belovèd's bed;
> And so thy thoughts, when thou art gone,
> Love itself shall slumber on.

The poem has an effect of sharp insistent logic. A series of ostensibly parallel propositions leads up to the 'And so' of the inevitable-sounding conclusion. It is characteristic of the poem that we take the effect without asking whether this 'And so' clinches an analogy or a syllogism. When we do set ourselves resolutely to reading with full and sustained critical attention we find that the effect combines the suggestion of both, and is able to do so only because it is neither, except speciously, by a sleight that depends upon an abeyance of the demand for logic.

> Music, when soft voices die,
> Vibrates in the memory

—that seems merely to state the simple fact that we remember music when it has ceased. The second couplet—

> Odours, when sweet violets sicken,
> Live within the sense they quicken

—seems merely to translate the proposition of the first into terms of the sense of smell; though we note that the 'live', developed by the equivocal 'quicken' ('make lively'—'impart life to'), reinforces the potential equivocation of 'vibrates'.[1] But when we consider the third couplet—

> Rose leaves, when the rose is dead,
> Are heap'd for the belovèd's bed

—we find that it is only by a kind of bluff that it has the effect of being another equivalent proposition. The implicit assimilation of the 'rose leaves' to the status of remembered sounds and scents throws back on these (already by suggestion something more than memories) a material reality, or, rather, produces in us a vague sense of a status that combines material reality with non-material persistence: so here they are, the petals, physically impressible by the 'belovèd', and yet the clinching effect of the final couplet—

> And so thy thoughts, when thou art gone,
> Love itself shall slumber on

—involves something more than a clean one-way passage from mere things to mere 'thoughts', and is a completing of the process of legerdemain (for the working of the poem depends on something closely analogous to optical illusion—'the quickness of the hand deceives the eye'). We have in 'thy thoughts' the clinching equivocation: 'thy thoughts' are ostensibly the petals that remain 'when Thou art gone', and this implication of persistence evokes (while we are reading currently) the ghost of a significant force because, without telling ourselves so, or distinguishing between the two senses, we take 'thy thoughts' as being at the same time 'thoughts of thee'.

What kind of status the bed has that 'Love itself' 'slumbers on' there would be no profit in inquiring, or what kind of being 'Love itself' is or has. The proposition has a metaphysical air, but, clearly, any significance it may claim is merely a ghost. The difference between this kind of effect, which depends on an absence of attention and a relaxing of the mind, and, say, Marvell's *Definition of Love*, which demands a sustained intellectual effort in the following-through and following-up of the thought, needn't be laboured. Exploration may be

[1] Cf. the opening of *Burnt Norton*.

more profitably pursued through another kind of contrast, that provided by this characteristic poem of Blake's:

O Rose, thou art sick!
The invisible worm,
That flies in the night,
In the howling storm,

Has found out thy bed
Of crimson joy;
And his dark secret love
Does thy life destroy.

It is a commonplace of academic literary commentary that Blake and Shelley are related by peculiar affinities; but what most strikes the reader whose attention is upon the poetry they wrote is their extreme unlikeness. In Blake's best verse there is something corresponding to the 'wiry bounding line' he demanded of visual art. It is not merely that he is strong on the visual side—a truth that lends itself to a misleading overstress. If we are to associate his essential strength with the 'thing seen' it must be in the full consciousness that the phrase here has more than its literal sense. The essential objects in its preoccupation with which his poetry exhibits such purity of interest—such disinterestedness—are not susceptible of visualization; they belong to inner experience, emotional and instinctive life, the inner life of the psyche. It is Blake's genius that, dealing with material that could be present to him only as the most intimate personal experience—the very substance of his appetites, desires, inner urgencies, fears and temptations—he can write poetry that has virtues analogous to those of the 'wiry bounding line'. Its intensity is not one of emotional insistence; there is none of the Shelleyan 'I feel, I suffer, I yearn' there is no atmosphere of feeling and no I.

In his essay on Blake (one of his finest) Mr Eliot, discussing the 'peculiar honesty' (or 'unpleasantness') of Blake's poetry, says: 'None of the things which exemplify the sickness of an epoch or a fashion has this quality; only those things which, by some extraordinary labour of simplification, exhibit the essential sickness or strength of the human soul.' Again: ' *The Songs of Innocence and of Experience*, and the poems from the Rossetti manuscript, are the poems of a man with a profound interest in human emotions, and a profound knowledge of them. The emotions are presented in an extremely simplified, abstract form.' I quote these remarks by way of enforcing the point that what distinguishes Blake's poetry from Shelley's may fairly be said to be a presence of 'thought'. The seeing elements of our inner experience as clearly defined objects involves, of itself, something we naturally call 'thought'. And it will be noted by the way how inevitably we slip into the visual analogy, the type and model of objectivity being the thing seen (there are bearings here on the visualist fallacy in criticism); and, further, that there is the significant linguistic usage by which to 'see' is to understand ('I see!'). In any case, the 'extraordinary labour of simplification' behind Blake's best things is a labour of analysis—analysis that he can present in direct statement, as well as implicitly in the resulting 'simplified form'. Again it is convenient to resort to Mr Eliot's essay:

His philosophy, like his visions, like his insight, like his technique, was his own. And accordingly he was inclined to attach more importance to it than an artist should; this is what makes him eccentric, and makes him inclined to formlessness.

> But most through midnight streets I hear
> How the youthful harlot's curse
> Blasts the new-born infant's tear,
> And blights with plagues the marriage herse,

is the naked vision;

> Love seeketh only self to please,
> To bind another to its delight,
> Joys in another's loss of ease,
> And builds a Hell in Heaven's despite,

is the naked observation; and *The Marriage of Heaven and Hell* is naked philosophy, presented. But Blake's occasional marriages of poetry and philosophy are not so felicitous.

By 'direct statement' I mean the kind of thing that Mr Eliot calls 'the naked observation', and it should be plain that there can be cases where the 'observation' is pretty manifestly present in the 'naked vision'. *The Sick Rose* is surely such a case.

The aspect of 'vision', of course, is the more obvious. We hesitate to call the Rose a symbol, because 'symbol' is apt to imply something very different from the immediacy with which Blake sees, feels and states in terms of his image—the inevitableness with which the Rose presents itself to him as the focus of his 'observation'. We have here a radical habit of Blake's; a habit on which the remark made above regarding objectivity and the thing seen has obvious bearings—and a habit, it might be added, that shows the strength it was to Blake as a poet to be also a visual artist. Yet, after all, how much of Blake's Rose do we cover with 'visual' and 'thing seen'? The vocative establishes the Rose 'out there' before us, so that it belongs to the order of visible things and we don't question that we see it; but does its visual presence amount to much more than that?

'Crimson', of course, makes an undoubted visual impact, but of the total work that it does, in its context, that visual impact is only one element. What 'crimson' does is to heighten and complete the clash of association set up by the first line:

O Rose, thou art sick.

To call a rose 'sick' is to make it at once something more than a thing seen. 'Rose' as developed by 'thy bed of crimson joy' evokes rich passion, sensuality at once glowing, delicate and fragrant, and exquisite health. 'Bed of crimson joy' is voluptuously tactual in suggestion, and, in ways we needn't try and analyse, more than tactual—we feel ourselves 'bedding down' in the Rose, and there is also a suggestion of a secret heart ('found out'), the focus of life, down there at the core of the closely clustered and enclosing petals.

The invisible worm,
That flies in the night,
In the howling storm,

offering its shock of contrast to the warm security of love ('She's all States, and all Princes, I, Nothing else is') conveys the ungovernable otherness of the dark forces of the psyche when they manifest themselves as disharmonies. The poem, we can see, registers a profound observation of a kind we may find developed in many places in D. H. Lawrence—an observation regarding the possessive and destructive element there may be in 'love'.

There is, then, much more solid ground for attributing 'thought' to this wholly non-ratiocinative and apparently slight poem than to that ostensibly syllogistic, metaphysical piece of Shelley's. And the presence of 'thought' goes with the focused and pregnant strength, the concentration of significant feeling, that makes the poem so unlike the characteristic Shelleyan lyric. Blake, of course, didn't confine himself to such pregnant brevities as *The Sick Rose;* he aspired to give developed and extended expression to his 'profound interest in human emotions' and his 'profound knowledge of them'. I am thinking of his long poems. Of the long poems Mr Eliot says that their weakness 'is certainly not that they are too visionary, too remote from the world. It is that Blake did not see enough, became too much occupied with ideas.' Just what such 'ideas' are would be an interesting and fruitful inquiry. It is enough to say here that their weakness as poetry is their weakness as thought. Their generality is of a kind that makes them illusory and inefficacious. They are lacking in grip on the data they are supposed to organize, and they betray a lack of grasp in the poet for such undertakings. Instead of serving as instruments of clarification, they tend to function as a kind of ritual, rote, or game—a game that could have given no satisfaction to the poet if they hadn't blurred the experience they were meant to interpret.

That such strength as is represented by *The Sick Rose* isn't necessarily a matter of the inspired *instantané*, the lyrical flash, but *can* be exhibited in a systematic exploration of experience, Mr Eliot's own poetry very strikingly testifies. I am thinking above all of the *Four Quartets*. Though the procedure is not one of logical discourse, the labour behind these is as much a labour of thought, and of thought in the same sense, as the labour is that goes to a philosophical treatise. And they owe their virtue as thought, analytic and constructive, to their being distinctly poetic in method: they are essentially and intensely poetic poetry, and can only be understood if their utterly unproselike character is recognized. This unproselike character means the reverse of a relaxed discipline of thought. It is not for nothing that the opening Quartet, *Burnt Norton*, is largely an analysis (by strictly poetic methods—and one can imagine no other by which an analysis so effectively radical could have been conducted) of the nature of conceptual thinking, or of the nature of thought in relation to experience. More generally, it can be said that the essential undertaking of the *Four Quartets* as a whole involves a radical inquiry into the nature of language, the analysis being the indispensable ancillary to construction or re-creation. Dissatisfaction with the relations of thought to experience that are imposed by current linguistic usage—by the conceptual currency as it is ordinarily taken over into poetry—forms an explicit corollary of the positive aim.

The examination of T. S. Eliot's later poetry that attempts to enforce these observations is to be found in my *Education and the University*, and I will attempt no summary here: a particular critique of the necessary length hardly fits the scheme of the present book. Yet that poetry represents a case of great immediate relevance. It is quite unlike Donne's, and, when arrived at by the exploratory path we have pursued, it constitutes a more patently clinching and justifying conclusion to the line taken about 'thought' in poetry than a critical expositor could have reasonably hoped to find. For while it is different from Blake's too, the passage to it from Blake's involves, in respect of the present interest and argument, no great jump; there is an easy, obvious and cogent continuity.

A strength patently recognizable as of the same kind as that which led us to speak of the presence of 'thought' in Blake's poetry is there in Eliot's in more developed form, integral with a sustained and complex process, exploratory, analytic and organizing, that is unquestionably thought in the same sense as the thought of the metaphysician. The great difference between the thought of the metaphysical treatise and the thought in *Four Quartets* lies in the genius that enables the poet to refuse with such hardly credible rigour and success the ready-made, the illusory and the spectral in the way of conceptual apparatus, and to keep his abstractions so fully charged with the concrete of experience and his thinking so unquestionably faithful to it. Such precision and efficiency of thought are possible only to a great poet, and this poetry brings vividly home to us that to think effectively about experience is to think with it and in it (which is why no amount of intellectual drill in itself, however responsive and athletic the trainee, and no mere acquisition, however thorough, of technique, method and apparatus, can generate vital thinking, or are likely to conduce to it).

These, of course, are not new truths, but we realize them with a new force in coming to terms with *Four Quartets*, from which we bring away an enlivened understanding of the nature and conditions of vitality of thought in general. Here, in this poetry of Eliot's, intensely poetic as it is and related, in the ways suggested, to what is strong in other poetry, we have an admirably demonstrative enforcement of the point that the critical discipline capable of justifying formal literary study is a discipline of intelligence, and one that no one who is committed to using language for disciplined thought can afford to forgo.

IMAGERY AND MOVEMENT

F. R. LEAVIS (1945)

Notes in the Analysis of Poetry (ii)

Shakespeare, of course, has his own miraculous complexity. Nevertheless, the effects just examined[1] serve in their striking way to enforce a general point. What we are concerned with in analysis are always matters of complex verbal organization; it will not do to treat metaphors, images and other local effects as if their relation to the poem were at all like that of plums to cake. They are worth examining—they are there to examine—because they are foci of a complex life, and sometimes the context from which they cannot be even provisionally separated, if the examination is to be worth anything, is a wide one.

But to return now, after the caveat of this extreme instance, to something simpler. There is nothing of the complexity of 'Pity, like a naked new-born babe' about the eighth line of the following stanza:

[1] The part of the chapter upon which the present extract follows gives an analysis of the context of 'Pity, like a naked new-born babe' (*Macbeth*, I, vii).

> Busie old foole, unruly Sunne,
> Why dost thou thus,
> Through windowes, and through curtaines call on us?
> Must to thy motions lovers seasons run?
> Sawcy pedantique wretch, goe chide
> Late schoole boyes, and sowre prentices,
> Goe tell Court-huntsmen, that the King will ride,
> Call countrey ants to harvest offices;
> Love, all alike, no season knowes, nor clyme,
> Nor houres, dayes, moneths, which are the rags of time.

The metaphor in

> Call countrey ants to harvest offices

would seem to answer pretty well to the notion of metaphor as illustrative correspondence or compressed descriptive simile. To the lovers the virtuous industry of the workday world is the apparently pointless bustle of ants and as unrelated to sympathetically imaginable ends. But already in this account something more than descriptive parallel or the vivid presentment of an object by analogy has been recognized. We might easily have said 'the silly bustle of ants': it is plain that the function of the metaphor is to convey an *attitude towards* the object contemplated—the normal workday world—and so to reinforce the tone of sublimely contemptuous good humour that is struck in the opening phrase of the poem,

> Busie old foole...

The function, in fact, parallels that, in the last line of the stanza, of 'rags', the felicity of which metaphor clearly doesn't lie in descriptive truth or correspondence.

So elementary a point may seem too obvious to be worth making, but, at any rate, it is now made. To put it generally, *tone* and *attitude towards* are likely to be essential heads in analysing the effects of interesting metaphor or imagery. And we may now go on to make another elementary point: unlikeness is as important as likeness in the 'compressed simile' of

> Call countrey ants to harvest office.

It is the fact that farm-labourers are not ants, but very different, that, equally with the likeness, gives the metaphor its force. The arresting oddity or discrepancy, taken by us simultaneously with the metaphorical significance (the perception of which is of course a judgment of the likeness), gives the metaphor its evocative or representational felicity and vivacity—for that it has these we may now admit, on them depending the peculiarly effective expression of the attitude. It is from some such complexity as this, involving the telescoping or focal coincidence in the mind of contrasting or discrepant impressions or effects that metaphor in general—live metaphor—seems to derive its life: life involves friction and tension—a sense of arrest—in some degree.

And this generalization suggests a wider one. Whenever in poetry we come on places of especially striking 'concreteness'—places where the verse has such life and body that we hardly seem to be reading arrangements of words—we may expect analysis to yield notable instances of the co-presence in complex effects of the disparate, the conflicting or the contrasting. A simple illustration of the type of effect is given in

> Lilies that fester smell far worse than weeds,

where 'fester', a word properly applied to suppurating flesh and here applied to the white and fragrant emblems of purity, brings together in the one disturbingly unified response the obviously disparate associations. For a more complex instance we may consider the well-known (probably, owing to Mr Eliot, the best-known) passage of Tourneur:

> Does the silkworm expend her yellow labours
> For thee? For thee does she undo herself?
> Are lordships sold to maintain ladyships
> For the poor benefit of a bewildering minute?
> Why does yon fellow falsify highways
> And lays his life between the judge's lips
> To refine such a one? Keeps horse and men
> To beat their valours for her?

The key word in the first line is 'expend'. In touch with 'spin', it acts with its force of 'spend' on the 'yellow', turning it to gold, and so, while adding directly to the suggestion of wealth and luxury, bringing out by a contrasting co-presence in the one word the soft yellowness of the silk. To refer to silk, emblem of luxurious leisure, as 'labours' is in itself a telescoping of conflicting associations. Here, then, in this slow, packed, self-pondering line (owing to the complex organization of meaning the reader finds he cannot skim easily over the words, or slip through them in a euphonious glide[1]) we have the type of the complexity that gives the whole passage that rich effect of life and body. An interesting analysis of the passage in relation to the themes of the plays, for it is closely wrought into the dramatic context, will be found in an essay by L. G. Salingar, '*The Revenger's Tragedy*'

---

[1] Cf. the admired couplet:

> Lo! where Maeotis sleeps, and hardly flows
> The freezing Tanais thro' a waste of snows.

and the Morality Tradition.[1] But there is a rich vitality that is immediately apparent in the isolated extract, and we are concerned here with taking note of its obvious manifestations.

In the second line, 'undo' has in it enough of the sense of unwinding a spool to give an unusual feel, and an unusual force, to the metaphorical use. This metaphorical use, to mean 'ruin' (developing 'expend') makes the silkworm more than a mere silk worm and leads on to the next line,

> Are lordships sold to maintain ladyships,

where the specious symmetry of 'lordships' and 'ladyships' gives both words an ironic point. There is a contrast in sense between the substance of the one and the nullity of the other; and 'lordships', as we feel the word, gets a weight by transference from the 'yellow labours' and the laborious 'expending' and 'undoing' of the silkworm. And the weight and substance in general evoked by the first three lines, in the labouring movement of their cumulative questions, sets off by contrast the elusive insubstantiality evoked as well as described in that last line, with the light, slurred triviality of its run-out:

> For the poor benefit of a bewildering minute.

The nature of the imagery involved in

> lays his life between the judge's lips

might perhaps not be easy to define, but it is certainly an instance in which effectiveness is not mainly visual. The sense of being at the mercy of another's will and word is focused in a sensation of extreme physical precariousness, a sensation of lying helpless, on the point of being ejected at a breath into the abyss. In 'refine' we probably have another instance of a double meaning. In the first place 'refine' would mean 'make fine' or 'elegant' (the speaker is addressing the skull of his dead mistress). But the gold image, coming through by way of 'sold' (and the more effectively for never having been explicit), seems also to be felt here, with the suggestion that nothing can refine this dross. In this way the structure of the last sentence is explained: horse and men are represented by their 'valours', their 'refined' worths, which are beaten for 'such a one', and so the contrast of the opening question is clinched—'her yellow labours for *thee?*'

The point has been by now fairly well illustrated that, whatever tip the analyst may propose to himself for a local focusing of attention, the signs of vitality he is looking for are matters of organization among words, and mustn't be thought of in the naïve terms that the word

---

[1] See *Scrutiny*, Vol. VI, No. 4.

'image' too readily encourages. Even where it appears that some of the simpler local effects can be picked like plums out of their surroundings, it will usually turn out that more of the virtue depends on an extended context than was obvious at first sight. Consider, for instance, this characteristic piece of Keatsian tactual imagery:

> Then glut thy sorrow on a morning rose,
>> Or on the rainbow of the salt sand-wave,
>> Or on the wealth of globèd peonies...

The 'globèd' gives the sensation of the hand voluptuously cupping a peony, and it might be argued that this effect can be explained in terms of the isolated word. But actually it will be found that 'globèd' seems to be with so rich a palpability what it says, to enact in the pronouncing so gloating a self-enclosure, because of the general co-operation of the context. Most obviously, without the preceding 'glut', the meaning of which strongly reinforces the suggestive value of the alliterated beginning of 'globèd', this latter word would lose a very great deal of its luxurious palpability. But the pervasive suggestion of luxury has a great part, too, in the effect of the word; for what is said explicitly in 'wealth' (and in 'rich' in the next line) is being conveyed by various means everywhere in the poem.

The palpability of 'globèd'—the word doesn't merely describe, or refer to, the sensation, but gives a tactual image. It is as if one were actually cupping the peony with one's hand. So elsewhere, in reading poetry, one responds as if one were making a given kind of movement or a given kind of effort: the imagery the analyst is concerned with isn't (to reiterate the point) merely, or even mainly, visual. *As if*—the difference between image and full actuality is recognized here; a difference, or a distance, that varies from image to image, just as, where poems as wholes are concerned, the analogous difference varies from poem to poem. For images come somewhere between full concrete actuality and merely 'talking about' as poems do—their status, their existence, is of the same order; the image is, in this respect, the type of a poem. In reading a successful poem it is as if, with the kind of qualification intimated, one were living that particular action, situation or piece of life; the qualification representing the condition of the peculiar completeness and fineness of art. The 'realization' demanded of the poet, then, is not an easily definable matter; it is one kind of thing in this poem and another in that, and, within a poem, the relation of imagery to the whole involves complex possibilities of variety.

In fact, in more than one sense it is difficult to draw a line round imagery (which is why the tip, 'scrutinize the imagery', is a good one). The point has already been made that even what looks like a sharply localized image may derive its force from a wide context. Here is imagery of effort:

> *Macbeth*:　　　If we should fail,—
> *Lady Macbeth*:　　　　　　We fail!
> 　　　　　But screw your courage to the sticking-place,
> 　　　　　And we'll not fail.

A certain force is immediately obvious in the line as it stands here. The *Arden* editor of *Macbeth* comments (p. 41):

> The metaphor is in all probability derived, as Steevens thought, from the screwing up of the chords of stringed instruments.

Yet, after confirming Steevens, as he thinks, with other passages from Shakespeare, he can conclude his note:

> Paton and Liddell think the metaphor was probably suggested by a soldier screwing up the cord of his cross-bow to the 'sticking-place'.

To take cognizance of this suggestion and pass it by in favour of the analogy from tuning—that is a characteristic feat of scholarship. An effect of tension can be urged in favour of either of the proposed analogies, but beyond that what peculiar appropriateness can be found in the tuning of an instrument? On the other hand, the dramatic context makes Paton's and Liddell's probability an inevitability. It is the murder of Duncan that is in question; the menace and a sense of dire moral strain vibrate through the scene from its opening, and the screwing up of resolution to the irretrievable deed ('If it were done, when 'tis done'...) is felt bodily as a bracing of muscles to the lethal weapon ('screwing' here is no job for the finger-tips). Besides tension, there is a contrasting sense of the release that will come, easily but dreadfully (a finger will do it now), when the trigger lets the cord slip from the sticking-place and the bolt flies—irretrievably. When twenty lines farther on, at the end of the scene, Macbeth says

> 　　　　I am settled, and bend up
> 　Each corporal agent to this terrible feat

the *Arden* editor this time notes, justly: 'The metaphor of course is from the stringing of a bow.' The cross-bow has been replaced by the long-bow.

In the following lines of Donne the most notable effect of effort, equally inviting the description 'image', is not got by metaphor:

> 　　　　On a huge hill,
> 　Cragged, and steep, truth stands, and hee that will
> 　Reach her, about must, and about must goe;
> 　And what the hills suddenness resists, winne so...

Here the line-end imposes on the reader as he passes from the 'will' to the 'Reach' an analogical enactment of the reaching.[1]

We might perhaps say 'a metaphorical enactment', though what we have here wouldn't ordinarily be called metaphor. The important point is that it provides the most obvious local illustration of a pervasive action of the verse—or action in the reader as he follows the verse: as he takes the meaning, re-creates the organization, responds to the play of the sense-movement against the verse structure, makes the succession of efforts necessary to pronounce the organized words, he performs in various modes a continuous analogical enactment. Such an enactment is apparent in

> about must, and about must goe;

and, if less obvious, sufficiently apparent in

> What the hills suddenness resists, winne so,

where the sense-movement is brought up abruptly as by a rock-face at 'resists', and then, starting on another tack, comes to a successful conclusion.

There is no need to multiply illustrations, though a great variety could easily be mustered. The point has been sufficiently made that in considering these kinds of effect we find 'imagery' giving place to 'movement' as the appropriate term for calling attention to what has to be analysed. That we cannot readily define just where 'imagery' ceases to be an appropriate term need cause no inconvenience, and there seems no more profit in attempting a definition of 'movement' than of 'imagery'. The important thing is to be as aware as possible of the ways in which life in verse may manifest itself—life, or that vital organization which makes collections of words poetry. Terms must be made means to the necessary precision by careful use in relation to the concrete; their use is justified in so far as it is shown to favour sensitive perception; and the precision in analysis aimed at is not to be attained by seeking formal definitions as its tools. It is as pointers for use—*in* use—in the direct discussion of pieces of poetry that our terms and definitions have to be judged; and one thing the analyst has to beware of is the positiveness of expectation (not necessarily, even where fixed in a definition, a matter of full consciousness) that may make him obtuse to the novelties and subtleties of the concrete.

The term having been introduced, it will be best to proceed at once

---

[1] Cf. Keats's *To Autumn*:

> And sometimes like a gleaner thou dost keep
> Steady thy laden head across a brook...

to an instance in which the useful pointer would clearly be 'movement'.
Suppose, then, one were asked to compare these two sonnets of
Wordsworth's and establish a preference for one of them:

It is a beauteous evening, calm and free,
　　The holy time is quiet as a Nun
Breathless with adoration; the broad sun
　　Is sinking down in its tranquillity;
　　The gentleness of heaven broods o'er the Sea:
　　　　Listen! the mighty Being is awake,
　　　　And doth with his eternal motion make
A sound like thunder—everlastingly.
Dear Child! dear Girl! that walkest with me here,
　　　　If thou appear untouch'd by solemn thought,
　　　　Thy nature is not therefore less divine:
Thou liest in Abraham's bosom all the year;
　　　　And worshipp'st at the Temple's inner shrine,
　　　　God being with thee when we know it not.

Surprised by joy—impatient as the Wind
　　　　I turned to share the transport—Oh with whom
　　　　But Thee, deep buried in the silent tomb,
That spot which no vicissitude can find?
Love, faithful love, recalled thee to my mind—
　　　　But how could I forget thee? Through what power,
　　　　Even for the least division of an hour,
Have I been so beguiled as to be blind
To my most grievous loss?—That thought's return
　　　　Was the worst pang that sorrow ever bore,
Save one, one only, when I stood forlorn,
　　　　Knowing my heart's best treasure was no more;
That neither present time, nor years unborn
　　　　Could to my sight that heavenly face restore.

One might start by saying that, though both offer to be intimately
personal, the second seems more truly so, and, in being so, superior;
and might venture further that this superiority is apparent in a greater
particularity. Faced now with the problem of enforcing these judgments
in analysis one would find that imagery hardly offered an opening at
all. On the other hand there is a striking difference in movement, a
difference registered in the effort of attention required of the reader
as he feels his way into a satisfactory reading-out, first of one sonnet,
then of the other. An effort, as a matter of fact, cannot properly be said
to be required by *Calais Beach*; it contains no surprises, no turns
imposing a readjustment in the delivery, but continues as it begins,
with a straightforwardness at every point and a continuity of sameness

that make it impossible to go seriously wrong. *Surprised by joy*, on the contrary, demands a constant and most sensitive vigilance in the reader, and even if he knows the poem well he is unlikely to satisfy himself at the first attempt, such and so many are the shifts of tone, emphasis, modulation, tempo, and so on, that the voice is required to register ('movement' here, it will be seen, is the way the voice is made to move, or feel that it is moving, in a sensitive reading-out).

The first word of the sonnet, as a matter of fact, is a key word. The explicit exalted surprise of the opening gives way abruptly to the contrasting surprise of that poignant realization, now flooding back, which it had for a moment banished:

> —Oh! with whom
> But Thee, deep buried in the silent tomb...

Then follows a surprise for the reader (the others were for the poet too):

> That spot which no vicissitude can find.

It is a surprise in the sense that one doesn't at first know how to read it, the turn in feeling and thought being so unexpected. For the line, instead of insisting on the renewed overwhelming sense of loss, appears to offset it with a consideration on the other side of the account, as it were—there would be a suggestion of 'at any rate' in the inflection. Then one discovers that the 'no vicissitude' is the admonitory hint of a subtler pang and of the self-reproach that becomes explicit in the next line but one. There could be little profit in attempting to describe the resulting complex and delicate inflection that one would finally settle on—it would have to convey a certain tentativeness, and a hint of sub-ironical flatness. Then, in marked contrast, comes the straightforward statement,

> Love, faithful love, recall'd thee to my mind,

followed by the outbreak of self-reproach, which is developed with the rhetorical emphasis of passion:

> But how could I forget thee? Through what power,
> Even for the least division of an hour,
> Have I been so beguiled as to be blind
> To my most grievous loss?

The intensity of this is set off by the relapse upon quiet statement in

> That thought's return
> Was the worst pang that sorrow ever bore,

—quiet statement that pulls itself up with the renewed intensity (still quiet) of

> Save one, one only,

where the movement is checked as by a sudden scruple, a recall to precision (particularity, intensity and emotional sincerity are critical themes that present themselves to the reader in pretty obvious relation here). The poignancy of the quiet constatation settles by way of the 'forlorn'

> Save one, one only, when I stood forlorn

into a steady recognition of a state of loss, the state, the unending privation, being given in the flat evenness of the concluding lines, in the expressive movement of which the rime-scheme plays an important part:

> when I stood forlorn,
> Knowing my heart's best treasure was no more;
> That neither present time, nor years unborn
> Could to my sight that heavenly face restore.

This is the kind of analysis—a kind where the pen is peculiarly at a disadvantage as compared with the voice—by which one would back the judgment that in *Surprised by joy* we have deeply and finely experienced emotion poetically realized, the realization being manifested in a sensitive particularity, a delicate sureness of control in complex effects, and, in sum, a fineness of organization, such as could come only of a profoundly stirred sensibility in a gifted poet.

Of the movement of *Calais Beach* one can give only a negative description; it yields no analysis to pair with that given of the movement of *Surprised by joy*, and seems, in the contrast, to have no life. Nor can anything be found in imagery, or in any aspect, to offset this disparaging account. *Calais Beach*, in fact, in spite of the offer of intimate personal feeling, must be judged to be, in an unfavourable sense, wholly general. By this I mean that it gives the reader nothing better than the soothing bath of vague religiose sentiment that, without Wordsworth's help, he might enjoy any serene summer's evening, watching the sun go down over the sea. We might say that the sonnet gives us 'the sunset emotion'. To say that, of course, isn't necessarily to damn it. But if a poet invokes a stock experience of that order he must control it to some particularizing and refining use; and refinement and particularity are what we look for in vain in *Calais Beach*.

We might clinch the case against it by bringing up as a third term in the comparison the sonnet *Upon Westminster Bridge*, which comes conveniently just before it in the *Oxford Book* (No. 520):

> Earth has not anything to show more fair:
>   Dull would he be of soul who could pass by
>   A sight so touching in its majesty:
> This City now doth like a garment wear
> The beauty of the morning; silent, bare,

> Ships, towers, domes, theatres, and temples lie
> Open unto the fields, and to the sky;
> All bright and glittering in the smokeless air.
> Never did sun more beautifully steep
> In his first splendour valley, rock, or hill;
> Ne'er saw I, never felt, a calm so deep!
> The river glideth at his own sweet will:
> Dear God! the very houses seem asleep;
> And all that mighty heart is lying still!

So far as the distinction between 'general' and 'particular and personal' is in question, *Upon Westminster Bridge* looks as if it ought to stand with *Calais Beach*. Need we, in fact, do more than replace 'sunset' by 'sunrise', and say that *Upon Westminster Bridge* gives us 'the sunrise emotion'? That would suggest the difference between that sonnet and the highly 'particular and personal' *Surprised by joy*. And yet surely there is another principle of distinction by which these two sonnets would be bracketed as good poems (though not equally fine) over against *Calais Beach*. What is it that makes this last so positively distasteful to some readers (for I have discovered that others besides myself dislike it strongly)? In any case, *Upon Westminster Bridge*, when compared with it, exacts a decided preference, and the question is perhaps best answered by asking why this is so.

The opening looks unpromisingly like that of *Calais Beach*; the key words, 'fair', 'soul', 'touching' and 'majesty', suggest the same kind of solemn unction, and a glance at the closing lines seems to confirm the suggestion:

> Ne'er saw I, never felt, a calm so deep!
> The river glideth at his own sweet will:
> Dear God! the very houses seem asleep;
> And all that mighty heart is lying still!

And the first point that, as we read through from the beginning, calls for particular comment seems also corroborative—the simile here:

> This City now doth like a garment wear
> The beauty of the morning

—isn't that a very loose simile? It was inspired, one suspects, by an easy and unscrupulous rime to 'fair', and its apparent first-to-hand quality suggests a very facile concern for 'beauty'. The particularity that follows we put, without enthusiasm, but duly noting a superiority over *Calais Beach*, on the credit side of the account:

> silent, bare,
> Ships, towers, domes, theatres, and temples lie
> Open unto the fields, and to the sky;
> All bright and glittering in the smokeless air.

It seems a very generalized particularity, one easily attained. And yet we should by now be aware of a decided superiority in this sonnet that makes it a poem of some interest; so that some further inquiry is necessary. The clue presents itself in the unobtrusive adjective 'smokeless'. Though unobtrusive, it is far from otiose; obvious as it looks, it does more than it says.[1] It conveys, in fact, both its direct force and the opposite, and gives us locally in its working the structure of the poem. For this poem, unlike *Calais Beach*, has a structure, and what this is now becomes plain.

Looking back, we realize now that 'like a garment' has, after all, a felicity: it keeps the City and the beauty of the morning distinct, while offering to the view only the beauty. Any muffling or draping suggestion the simile might have thrown over the 'ships, towers, domes, theatres, and temples' is eliminated immediately by the 'bare' that, preceding them, gets the rime stress (so justifying, we now see, the 'wear' that it picks up and cancels). They

> lie
>
> Open

—the fact is made present as a realized state in the reader's consciousness by an expressive use of the carry-over (the 'lying open' is enacted) and by a good rime which, picking up the resonance of 'lie' with an effect of leaving us where we were, enhances the suggestion of a state:

> silent, bare,
> Ships, towers, domes, theatres, and temples lie
> Open unto the fields, and to the sky.

The suggestion is further enhanced by the unenergetic leisureliness and lack of tension (as if giving time for two large indicative gestures) of that last line, which, giving metrically and in sense structure so much room to its two nouns, also reinforces by contrast the evocative strength of the packed preceding line. Then comes the key adjective, 'smokeless'—

> All bright and glittering in the smokeless air

---

[1] Contrast Bridges' *From high Olympus and the domeless courts*, and Hopkins's comment, *Letters*, XLVI.

—revealing the duality of consciousness out of which this sonnet is organized: the City dosen't characteristically 'lie open', and the 'garment' it usually 'wears', the pall of smoke, is evoked so as to be co-present, if only in a latent way, with the smokelessness.

> Never did sun more beautifully steep
> > In his first splendour valley, rock, or hill;
> Ne'er saw I, never felt, a calm so deep!
> > The river glideth at his own sweet will:
> Dear God! the very houses seem asleep
> > And all that mighty heart is lying still!

—Ships, towers, domes, theatres, and temples are invested, in this sonnet, with the Wordsworthian associations of valley, rock and hill, and the calm is so preternaturally deep because of a kind of negative co-presence (if the expression may be permitted) of the characteristic urban associations. 'Calm' hasn't the obvious ambivalence of 'smokeless' but beyond question the stillness of the 'mighty heart' is so touching because of a latent sense of the traffic that will roar across the bridge in an hour or two's time; just as 'sweet' (along with 'glideth') owes its force to the contrasting associations of the metropolitan river.

The structure analysed is not a complex one, and perhaps may be thought too obvious to have been worth the analysis. The point to be made, however, is that *Calais Beach* hasn't even this measure of complexity; it has no structure, but is just a simple one-way flow of standard sentiment. Consider the key words: 'beauteous', 'calm', 'holy,' 'quiet', 'Nun', 'adoration', 'tranquillity', 'gentleness', 'broods', 'mighty Being', 'eternal', 'everlastingly', 'solemn', 'divine', 'worshipp'st', 'Temple', 'shrine', 'God'—there is nothing to counter the insistent repetitious suggestion; nothing to qualify the sweet effusion of solemn sentiment. In fact, the cloying sameness is aggravated by an element not yet noted: instead of the kind of complexity introduced by 'smokeless', we get the sestet, which, with its 'Dear Child! dear Girl! and 'Abraham's bosom', adds saccharine to syrup and makes the sonnet positively distasteful.

There are, of course, innumerable ways in which 'movement' may come up for consideration. *Surprised by joy* was chosen as an extreme instance, in which 'imagery' hardly gave the analyst an opening at all. Commonly 'movement' and 'imagery' demand attention together. The following is a simple instance:

> The gray sea and the long black land;
> And the yellow half-moon large and low;
> And the startled little waves that leap
> In fiery ringlets from their sleep,

> As I gain the cove with pushing prow,
> And quench its speed i' the slushy sand.

The first two lines suggest a preoccupation with pictorial effects, and they invite a languorous reading—or would, if we didn't know what follows. Actually, an approach might be made by asking how it is that, though the stanza is so clearly Victorian, we could have said at once, supposing ourselves to have been reading it for the first time, that it is clearly not Tennysonian or Pre-Raphaelite. The first brief answer might be that it has too much energy. We are then faced with the not difficult task of saying how the effect of energy is conveyed. To begin with,

> the startled little waves that leap
> In fiery ringlets from their sleep

clearly don't belong to a dreamy nocturne. The 'startled', itself an energetic word, owes some of its force to the contrast with what goes before (even though the first two lines are not to be read languorously) —a contrast getting sharp definition in the play (a good use of rime) of 'leap' against 'sleep'.

It is an energetic couplet. The energy is active, too, in 'fiery', which is apt description, but doesn't reveal its full value till we come to 'quench' in the last line, the most interesting word in the stanza. That fire as well as thirst shall come in with the metaphor is ensured by the 'fiery', and in 'quenching' the speed the poet betrays (he probably couldn't have said why 'quench' came to him) how he has projected his own eagerness—his ardour and desire for the goal—into the boat, pushing on with his will, in a way that must be familiar to everyone, that which is carrying him forward. The nature of the energy that thrusts forward through the tranquil night has defined itself concretely by the time the second half of the poem has been read (it must now be given):

> Then a mile of warm sea-scented beach!
> Three fields to cross till a farm appears;
> A tap at the pane, the quick sharp scratch
> And blue spurt of a lighted match,
> And a voice less loud, thro' its joys and fears,
> Than the two hearts beating each to each!

Neither of the stanzas, it will have been noted, has a main verb, a lack intimately related to the mood and movement of the poem. The absence of main verb, it might be said, is the presence of the lover's purpose and goal: his single-minded intentness upon the goal and the confident eagerness with which he moves towards it are conveyed by the overtly incidental, by-the-way, nature of the sensations and perceptions, and the brisk, businesslike succession in which, from the beginning of the poem on, they are noted and left behind. Though incidental, they are vivid, as in a moment of unusual vitality and receptivity, and that this vividness—it is at the same time a vigour of report—should carry with it no attribution of value suggests the all-absorbingness of the purpose and focus of attention. The succession of notes, in fact, conveys a progression. And the effect of energy observed at the outset derives from this particular kind of movement— the particular sense of movement that has just been analysed. The movement, of course, derives its peculiar energy from the local vividness, but even such energetic imagery as

> the quick sharp scratch
> And blue spurt of a lighted match

owes something to the general movement as well as contributing, and it can hardly be said that 'quench' in the first stanza (an effect of the same order—it works along with 'slushy' as well as having the metaphorical value already discussed) contributes more than it owes.

The movement, it might be commented, isn't very subtle, nor is the total effect; and that is true. But the simplicity has its illustrative value, and the poem is an unmistakable instance of a strong realization. Vigour of that peculiar kind, obviously involving limitations, is characteristic of Browning, but is rarely manifested so decidedly as poetic virtue, and so inoffensively to the sensitive.

To proceed, by way of concluding this chapter, to another comparison:

(a)
> Wake; the silver dusk returning
> Up the beach of darkness brims,
> And the ship of sunrise burning
> Strands upon the eastern rims.
>
> Wake: the vaulted shadow shatters,
> Trampled to the floor it spanned,
> And the tent of night in tatters
> Straws the sky-pavilioned land.

(b)
> Out of the wood of thoughts that grows by night
> To be cut down by the sharp axe of light,—
> Out of the night, two cocks together crow,
> Cleaving the darkness with a silver blow.
> And bright before my eyes twin trumpeters stand,
> Heralds of splendour, one at either hand,
> Each facing each as in a coat-of-arms:
> The milkers lace their boots up at the farms.

Suppose one were asked to compare these in respect of metaphor and imagery, which they both use with striking boldness—a boldness of poetic stylization that might be thought to constitute a similarity. If we look at the first stanza of (*a*) we might be inclined to say that the decorative effect there was the main purpose. Certainly there is a sense in which the metaphorical imagery is offered for its own sake and (apart from being beautiful and striking) not for anything it does; it demands immediate approval, in its own right, as something self-sufficient and satisfying—we mustn't, for instance, ask what becomes of the burning ship as the silver flood mounts (or does it?) and full daylight comes. The function of the imagery here, in short, is to hold the attention from dwelling in a realizing way on the alleged sanction—the actuality ostensibly invoked. It demands attention for what it immediately is, but only a very limited kind of attention: the reader takes in at a glance the value offered; it is recognized currency; the beauty is conventional and familiar.

And 'decorative', after all, is not altogether the right word. It might do for the opening of Fitzgerald's *Rubaiyat* (which was possibly at the back of Housman's mind as he wrote the stanza); but there is an emotional drive here that would prompt the accepting reader with 'lyrical'. That drive expresses itself in the urgent movement, which is intimately related to the qualities noted in the imagery. In fact, an admirer of Housman might say that the imagery, like the movement, expresses a passionate indocility to experience, along with a wilful hunger after beauty. A return comment would be that (unless some justifying significance emerges later in the poem) the kind of beauty offered values itself implicitly at a rate that a mature mind can't endorse.

When we come to the second stanza the comment must be that the 'indocility' has become a violence—a violence to common experience, and the relation of the imagery to observable fact a gross and insensitive falsity. The tempo and the whole nature of the passing of night into day are outrageously misrepresented by 'shatters' and the picture of the land strewn with rags of dark. The 'shatters' is reconciled with the 'tatters' (the 'vault' to the 'tent'), it will be noted, only by the bluff of the rime, a kind of bullying or dazing effect; and the stamp of the movement, hobnailed with alliteration, emphasizes the insensitiveness. The movement, in fact, provides the most convenient index of the quality of the poem. To have cut off the two first stanzas from the rest does Housman no injustice, as the reader may confirm by turning up VIII (*Reveille*) in *A Shropshire Lad*. And in confirming he will be verifying also that a challenge to a reading-out would be a good introduction to the analysis: even an ardent admirer would, after the second stanza, find it difficult to declaim the poem convincingly, so embarrassing is the patent inadequacy of the substance to the assertive

importance of movement and tone, the would-be intense emotional
rhetoric.

It is a difference in movement that strikes us first as we pass from
(a) to (b). Associated with this difference there is, we become aware,
a difference in the imagery: whereas Housman's depends on our being
taken up in a kind of lyrical intoxication that shall speed us on in
exalted thoughtlessness, satisfied, as we pass, with the surface gleam
of ostensible value, Edward Thomas's invites pondering (we register
that in the movement) and grows in significance as we ponder it:

> Out of the wood of thoughts that grows by night
> To be cut down by the sharp axe of light,—
> Out of the night two cocks together crow,
> Cleaving the darkness with a silver blow.

—Of the use of metaphor here too it might be said that it seems to be
decorative in intention, rather than dictated by any pressure of a
perceived or realized actuality. To present a 'wood of thoughts' as
being 'cut down' by an 'axe of light' looks like a bold indulgence
in the pleasures of stylization. Yet we have to recognize that 'wood',
with its suggestions of tangled and obscure penetralia, stirring with
clandestine life, is not an infelicitous metaphor for the mental life of
sleep. And when in re-reading we come to 'silver blow' we have to
recognize a metaphorical subtlety—that is, a subtlety of organization—
that distinguishes (b) from (a) (it is subtlety of organization, of course,
that produces the effect, in Thomas, of a pondering movement).
'Cleaving' identifies the effect of the sound with that of the axe, the
gleam of which gives an edge to the 'silver' of the blown trumpet.
The 'silver-sounding' trumpet is a familiar convention, and the
element of wilful fantasy in this translation of the cock-crow becomes
overt in the heraldically stylized twin trumpeters:

> And bright before my eye twin trumpeters stand,
> Heralds of splendour, one at either hand,
> Each facing each as in a coat-of-arms.

We are prepared so for the ironical shift of the last line, where daylight
reality asserts itself:

> The milkers lace their boots up at the farms.

The poet, aware as he wakes of the sound and the light together,
has humoured himself in a half-waking dream-fantasy, which, when
it has indulged itself to an unsustainable extreme of definiteness,
suddenly has to yield to the recognition of reality.

Returning to the comparison between (*b*) and (*a*), we can now make another point, one that has been covered under the term 'movement'. Housman's proffer of his imagery is simple and simple-minded: 'Here is poetical gold; take it! Here is radiant beauty; be moved.' What we are aware of from the first line in Edward Thomas's little poem is, along with the imagery, an attitude towards it; an attitude subtly conveyed and subtly developed.

REALITY AND SINCERITY

F. R. LEAVIS (1952)

Notes in the Analysis of Poetry (iii)

The following comes from an exercise in critical comparison involving three poems: Alexander Smith's *Barbara*, which is [was] to be found in the *Oxford Book of English Verse*; Emily Brontë's *Cold in the earth*; and Hardy's *After a Journey*. The challenge was to establish an order of preference among these poems. But only two of them are seriously examined below.

About which of the three poems should come lowest in order of preference there will be ready agreement. Alexander Smith's *Barbara* has all the vices that are to be feared when his theme is proposed, the theme of irreparable loss. It doesn't merely surrender to temptation; it goes straight for a sentimental debauch, an emotional wallowing, the alleged situation being only the show of an excuse for the indulgence, which is, with a kind of innocent shamelessness, sought for its own sake. If one wants a justification for invoking the term 'insincerity', one can point to the fact that the poem clearly *enjoys* its pang: to put it more strictly, the poem offers a luxurious enjoyment that, to be enjoyed, must be taken for the suffering of an unbearable sorrow. The cheapness of the sentimentality appears so immediately in the movement, the clichés of phrase and attitude, and the vaguenesses and unrealities of situation, that (except for the purposes of elementary demonstration) there would be no point in proceeding to detailed analysis: the use of the poem for present purposes is to serve as a foil to Emily Brontë's—which it does by the mere juxtaposition.

Its quality as foil to Emily Brontë's is plain at once. The emotional sweep of the movement, the declamatory plangency, of *Cold in the earth* might seem to represent dangerous temptations; but in responding to the effect of passionate intensity we register what impresses us as a controlling strength. It remains to be seen just what that is:

Cold in the earth—and the deep snow piled above thee,
    Far, far removed, cold in the dreary grave!
Have I forgot, my only Love, to love thee,
    Sever'd at last by Time's all-severing wave?

Now, when alone, do my thoughts no longer hover
    Over the mountains, on that northern shore,
Resting their wings where heath and fern-leaves cover
    Thy noble heart for ever, ever more?

Cold in the earth—and fifteen wild Decembers
    From these brown hills have melted into spring:
Faithful, indeed, is the spirit that remembers
    After such years of change and suffering!

Sweet Love of youth, forgive if I forget thee,
    While the world's tide is bearing me along;
Other desires and other hopes beset me,
    Hopes which obscure, but cannot do thee wrong!

No later light has lighten'd up my heaven,
    No second morn has ever shone for me;
All my life's bliss from thy dear life was given,
    All my life's bliss is in the grave with thee.

But when the days of golden dreams had perish'd,
    And even Despair was powerless to destroy;
Then did I learn how existence could be cherish'd,
    Strengthen'd and fed without the aid of joy.

Then did I check the tears of useless passion—
    Wean'd my young soul from yearning after thine;
Sternly denied its burning wish to hasten
    Down to that tomb already more than mine.

And even yet, I dare not let it languish,
    Dare not indulge in memory's rapturous pain;
Once drinking deep of that divinest anguish,
    How could I seek the empty world again?

The poem does unmistakably demand to be read in a plangent
declamation; in, that is, a rendering that constitutes an overt assertion
of emotional intensity. If we ask why, nevertheless, the dangers such
an account might suggest don't seem at any point disturbingly present,
we can observe for answer that what is said in stanza seven—

    Then did I check the tears of useless passion

—is more than *said*; it represents an active principle that informs the
poem and is there along with the plangency. We have it in the movement, in the tough prose rationality, the stating matter-of-factness of

good sense, that seems to play against the dangerous running swell. It makes us take the suggestion that some strength corresponding to 'these brown hills', which do not themselves melt, underlies the poem. And we see an obvious hint at the nature of the strength in

> Then did I learn how existence could be cherished,
> Strengthen'd and fed without the aid of joy:

the suggestion that something quite opposed to the luxury of 'memory's rapturous pain' is being 'cherished' in the poem; that a resolute strength of will, espousing the bare prose 'existence', counters the run of emotion.

Cold in the earth, then, in its strong plangency, might reasonably be judged to be a notable achievement. I say this, however, in order to go on to judge that Hardy's *After a Journey* is a much rarer and finer thing, to be placed, as a poetic achievement, decidedly higher. I approach in this way because I have not, in fact, found that those who confidently place *Cold in the earth* above *Barbara* do, as a rule, judge *After a Journey* to be obviously superior to *Cold in the earth*, and yet, for such readers, the superiority can, I think, be demonstrated; that is, established to their satisfaction.

The difficulties, or conditions, that explain the failure of response on the part of intelligent readers lie largely, it would seem, in the nature of the superiority itself, though no doubt some stylistic oddities—what there is some excuse for seeing as such—play their part. Here is the poem:[1]

> Hereto I come to view a voiceless ghost;
>   Whither, O whither will its whim now draw me?
> Up the cliff, down, till I'm lonely, lost,
>   And the unseen waters' ejaculations awe me.
> Where you will next be there's no knowing,
> Facing round about me everywhere,
>   With your nut-coloured hair,
> And gray eyes, and rose-flush coming and going.
>
> Yes; I have re-entered your olden haunts at last;
>   Through the years, through the dead scenes I have tracked you;
> What have you now found to say of our past—
>   Scanned across the dark space wherein I lacked you?
> Summer gave us sweets, but autumn wrought division?
>   Things were not lastly as firstly well
>   With us twain, you tell?
> But all's closed now, despite Time's derision.

[1] Reprinted from *Collected Poems* by Thomas Hardy, by kind permission of the Trustees of the Hardy Estate and of Messrs Macmillan and Co. Ltd.

I see what you are doing: you are leading me on
    To the spots we knew when we haunted here together,
The waterfall, above which the mist-bow shone
    At the then fair hour in the then fair weather,
And the cave just under, with a voice still so hollow
    That it seems to call out to me from forty years ago,
        When you were all aglow,
And not the thin ghost that I now fraily follow!

Ignorant of what there is flitting here to see,
    The waked birds preen and the seals flop lazily,
Soon you will have, Dear, to vanish from me,
    For the stars close their shutters, and the dawn whitens hazily.
Trust me, I mind not, though Life lours,
    The bringing me here; nay, bring me here again!
        I am just the same as when
Our days were a joy, and our paths through flowers.

A difference in manner and tone between Hardy's poem and the
other two will have been observed at once: unlike them it is not
declamatory. The point should in justice lead on to a positive formulation, and this may not come as readily; certain stylistic characteristics
that may at first strike the reader as oddities and clumsinesses tend to
delay the recognition of the convincing intimate naturalness. It turns
out, however, that the essential ethos of the manner is given in

Where you will next be there's no knowing

This intimacy we are at first inclined to describe as 'conversational',
only to replace that adjective by 'self-communing' when we have
recognized that, even when Hardy (and it is significant that we say
'Hardy') addresses the 'ghost' he is still addressing himself. And it
shouldn't take long to recognize that the marked idiosyncrasy of idiom
and diction going with the intimacy of tone achieves some striking
precisions and felicities. Consider, for instance, the verb in

Facing round about me everywhere...

There is nothing that strikes us as odd in that 'facing', but it is a use
created for the occasion, and when we look into its unobtrusive
naturalness it turns out to have a positive and 'inevitable' rightness
the analysis of which involves a precise account of the 'ghost's' status—
which in its turn involves a precise account of the highly specific
situation defined by the poem.

Then again, there is that noun in the fourth line which (I can testify)
has offended readers not incapable of recognizing its felicity:

And the unseen waters' ejaculations awe me.

'Ejaculations' gives with vivid precision that sound that 'awes' Hardy: the slap of the waves on the rocky walls; the slap with its prolonging reverberant syllables—the hollow voice, in fact, that, in stanza three, 'seems to call out to me from forty years ago' (and the hollowness rings significantly through the poem).

In fact, the difference first presenting itself as an absence of declamatory manner and tone, examined, leads to the perception of positive characteristics—precisions of concrete realization, specificities, complexities—that justify the judgment I now advance: Hardy's poem, put side by side with Emily Brontë's, is seen to have a great advantage in *reality*. This term, of course, has to be given its due force by the analysis yet to be done—the analysis it sums up; but it provides the right pointer. And to invoke another term, more inescapably one to which a critic must try and give some useful force by appropriate and careful use, if he can contrive that: to say that Hardy's poem has an advantage in reality is to say (it will turn out) that is represents a profounder and completer sincerity.

Emily Brontë's poem is a striking one, but when we go back to it from Hardy's the contrast precipitates the judgment that, in it, she is dramatizing herself in a situation such as she has clearly not known in actual experience: what she offers is betrayingly less real. We find that we have declamatory generality—talking *about*—in contrast to Hardy's quiet presentment of specific fact and concrete circumstance; in contrast, that is, to detailed complexity evoking a total situation that, as merely evoked, carries its power and meaning in itself. Glancing back at Alexander Smith we can say that whereas in postulating the situation of *Barbara* (he can hardly be said to imagine it) he is seeking a licence for an emotional debauch, Emily Brontë conceives a situation in order to have the satisfaction of a disciplined imaginative exercise: the satisfaction of dramatizing herself in a tragic role—an attitude, nobly impressive, of sternly controlled passionate desolation.

The marks of the imaginative self-projection that is insufficiently informed by experience are there in the poem, and (especially with the aid of the contrast with Hardy) a duly perceptive reader could discern and describe them, without knowing the biographical fact. They are there in the noble (and, given the intimate offer of the theme, paradoxical) declamation, and in the accompanying generality, the absence of any convincing concreteness of a presented situation that speaks for itself. Locally we can put a finger on the significance of the declamatory mode in, for example, the last line of the first stanza:

Sever'd at last by Time's all-severing wave.

The imagery there, or the suggestion of it, is essentially rhetorical; the noble declamation, the impressive *saying*, provides the impressiveness, and when we consider the impressiveness critically we recognize that to respond to the declamatory mode *is* to be unexacting in respect of offered imagery: the unrealized rhetorical-verbal will receive a deference that cannot be critically justified. Time's 'wave' is of the order of cliché; prompted, it would seem, by 'grave', it makes as rime— and the closing rime of the stanza—a claim to strength that it certainly cannot sustain.

Turning back to *After a Journey* we may now look at the words in the first line that have made it (strange as that must seem when one has taken the poem) characteristic of Hardy's clumsiness. Actually it is characteristic of the supreme Hardy achievement, the poem in which what at first may look like clumsiness turns out, once the approach to the poem has been found, to be something very different—something supremely right. The vindication of the questioned details in the first line must be, then, in terms of what follows, and of the whole effect in which they have their part. Of 'hereto', the archaism that (in such a use) looks like a Hardy coinage, we need say little more than that it comes to look like one of those Hardy coinages which, in the great poems, cease to be anything but natural and inevitable. Its balanced slowness is precisely what was needed—as appears when we consider 'view', which, again, has been challenged as a perversity, one characteristically settled on by Hardy, it would seem, for the sake of a perverse alliteration with 'voiceless'.

But we cannot judge 'view' until we have realized just what is the nature of the 'ghost'. This should have been sufficiently established by the time we have come to the opening of the second stanza:

> Yes; I have re-entered your olden haunts at last;
>   Through the years, through the dead scenes, I have tracked you.

Prompted by these lines we are at first inclined to say that the journey has also been a journey through time. But an essential effect of the poem is to constate, with a sharp and full realization, that we *cannot* go back in time. The dimension of time dominates the poem; we feel it in the hollowness of the 'waters' ejaculations'— the voice of the 'cave just under', a voice that has more than a hollowness of here and now; 'it seems to call out to me from forty years ago.' It calls out here and now; but here and now it calls out from forty years ago. The dimension of time, the 'dark space', is in the voice itself, so startling in its immediacy, and, with the paradoxical duality of the experience, so annunciatory that the forty years ago from which it seems to call out is not, all the same, here and now, but forty years away. And memory, having 'tracked' the woman 'through the years, through the dead scenes', attains only a presence that is at the same time the absence felt more acutely. The reference to the time 'when we haunted here together' contains an implicit recognition of the different kind of 'haunting' represented by such presence as she has for him now, when their togetherness is so illusory. And by this point in the poem we know that the 'ghost', if an evanescent and impalpable thing, is in no ordinary sense a ghost.

We can now go back to the opening lines of the poem and judge fairly what it offers, and, having done that, tell how it demands to be read. 'View', we recognize, is no insensitive perversity; it is the word compelled by the intensely realized situation, and we feel it imposing itself on Hardy (and so on us) as right and irreplaceable: the seeing that memory will do (given success in its 'tracking') will be an intent dwelling of contemplation upon the object. And the object will be— again the word is, with a poised recognizing endorsement, accepted when it comes—a 'voiceless' (it will be a one-sided meeting, and the voice will be the cave's) 'ghost': on this word, again after a kind of judicially recognizing pause, the reader's voice descends and rests, as on a kind of summing-up close to the sentence.

It will be seen, then, that to recognize the rightness of 'view' and 'voiceless' and give them their due value is to recognize the kind of rendering demanded by the line: a slow and deliberate 'Hereto I come', followed by judicial discovering and accepting rests on 'view' and 'voiceless', and the concluding tone for 'ghost' that makes it plain that no literal ghost is in question—so that the 'nut-coloured hair and gray eyes and rose-flush' should bring no disconcerting surprise. Once the deliberate stock-taking poise of the opening line has been appreciated, the rest of the poem is safe against the kind of misreading that would give the movement a jaunty sing-song.

The self-communing tone is established in the first four lines, and there is no change when Hardy passes from the 'its' of the second line to the 'you' of the fifth. He remains 'lonely, lost' throughout the poem; that is not a state which is altered by his communion (if that is the word) with the 'ghost'. The loneliness and the desolation are far from being mitigated by the 'viewing' in memory; for the condition of the 'viewing' is Hardy's full realizing contemplation of the woman's irremediable absence—of the fact that she is dead.

There are two places in the poem where a difficulty of interpretation has been found. One of them is the last line of the second stanza:

But all's closed now, despite Time's derision.

The last line doesn't mean: 'All's closed now, in spite of Time, or Time's derision, standing in the way of its being closed.' It isn't a simple, direct statement of fact. It conveys a quite complex attitude that entails a weighing of considerations against one another and leaves them in a kind of poise. The effect is: 'Well, anyway, all that's over now, the suffering of division, things not being firstly as lastly well—I recognize that, though what, of course, I find myself contemplating now is the mockery of time; it's Time's derision I'm left with.' There is certainly no simple, and no preponderant, consolation. In the 'all's closed now' there is an irony, to be registered in a kind of sigh. '*All's* closed', not only the suffering, though that, Hardy recognizes, is of course included. But the last word is with Time's derision; and the rendering of the closing phrase, 'despite Time's derision', makes a testing demand on the reader: the phrase must be spoken with a certain flatness of inflection —an absence of clinching effect, or of any suggestion of a sum worked out.

The other place is at the fourth line from the end of the poem:

> Trust me, I mind not, though life lours,
> The bringing me here...

Not to take the significance of that 'Trust me, I mind not' is to have failed to respond to the complexity of the total attitude, and to have failed to realize the rare kind of integrity the poem achieves. It is to miss the suggestion of paradoxical insistence, the intensity of directed feeling and will, in 'Nay, bring me here again'. For what, in the bringing him here, he may be supposed to mind is not the arduousness, for an old man, of the long journey and the ramble by night. 'To bring me here', says Hardy, 'is to make me experience to the full the desolation and the pang—to give a sharp edge to the fact of Time's derision. But I don't mind—I more than don't mind: bring me here again! I hold to life, even though life as a total fact lours. The *real* for me, the focus of my affirmation, is the remembered realest thing, though to remember vividly is at the same time, inescapably, to embrace the utterness of loss.'

The rare integrity appears in the way in which the two aspects, the affirmation and the void, affect us as equal presences in the poem. Vacancy is evoked as an intensity of *absence* with a power that sends us for comparison to that other poem of the same years (1911–13), *The Voice* ('Woman much missed'); but vacancy, we find, in the other poem prevails, setting off by contrast the astonishing way in which in this poem it does not. *After a Journey* closes on the affirmation. But if 'affirmation' is the word (and it seems to be a necessary one), it mustn't suggest anything rhetorical; the affirmation is dramatic in a quite other sense. The opposite of the rhetorical has its very observable manifestation in the opening of the stanza:

> Ignorant of what there is flitting here to see,
>   The waked birds preen and the seals flop lazily,
> Soon you will have, Dear, to vanish from me,
>   For the stars close their shutters, and the dawn whitens hazily.

No one who has responded perceptively to the mode established at the beginning of the poem would read this as a trivial sing-song, but it clearly doesn't lend itself to noble plangency. 'Flitting' and 'flop' are key words—and 'flop', while being so decidedly the reverse of noble, has at the same time a felicity of poetic strength: rendering the sound, as it does, with matter-of-fact precision and immediacy (there is no plangency about the resonance), it conveys both the emptiness and the quotidian ordinariness that are essential notes of the ethos with which the poem leaves us at the end. And 'the stars close their shutters' gives the right defining touch to Hardy's attitude towards the woman—to the spirit of his cult of memory. This spirit is manifested in the stars suggesting to him, and to us, as they disappear, not sublimities and the vault of heaven, but lamplit cottage windows—associations in key with his recollections of 'forty years ago'. The note is intimate—with the touch of humorous fancy, it is tenderly familiar and matter-of-fact. No alchemy of idealization, no suggestion of the transcendental, no nobly imaginative self-deceiving, attends on this devotion to the memory of a woman. It is the remembered as it was that Hardy is intent on. '*I* am just the same': that is the final stress. *She* is a 'thin ghost'—mattering only because she matters to *him*. It is astonishing how the peculiar reality of the remembered but non-existent is conveyed: vivid—

> nut-coloured hair,
> And gray eyes, and rose-flush

—and real enough to be addressed; yet at the same time 'flitting', a 'thin ghost'; never, that is, more than something recalled in memory, so that the address is never anything other than self-communing. It is the purest fidelity, the sincerest tribute to the actual woman. Hardy, with the subtlest and completest integrity, is intent on recapturing what *can* be recaptured of that which, with all his being, he judges to have been the supreme experience of life, the realest thing, the centre of value and meaning.

> The sense in which, though he now frailly follows, he is
>   just the same as when
> Our days were a joy, and our paths through flowers

has been, when the poem reaches this close, precisely defined, and his right to affirm it established beyond questioning. It is a poem that we recognize to have come directly out of life; it could, that is, have been written only by a man who had the experience of a life to remember back through. And recognizing that, we recognize the rare quality of the man who can say with that truth 'I am just the same', and the rare integrity that can so put the truth beyond question. It is a case in which we know from the art what the man was like; we can be sure, that is, what personal qualities we should have found to admire in Hardy if we could have known him.

8

CRITICS

ARNOLD AS CRITIC

F. R. LEAVIS (1938)

'And I do not like your calling Matthew Arnold Mr Kidglove Cocksure. I have more reason than you for disagreeing with him and thinking him very wrong, but nevertheless I am sure he is a rare genius and a great critic.'[1]

The note of animus that Hopkins here rebukes in Bridges is a familiar one where Arnold is concerned: it characterizes a large part of recorded comment on him. Raleigh's essay in *Some Authors* is (if we can grant this very representative *littérateur* so much distinction) a convenient *locus classicus* for it and for the kind of critical injustice it goes with. But one may be quite free from such animus or from any temptation to it—may welcome rather than resent that in Arnold by which the Raleighs are most antagonized—and yet find critical justice towards him oddly difficult to arrive at. He seems to present to the appraising reader a peculiarly elusive quantity. At least, that is my experience as an admirer, and I am encouraged in generalizing by the fact that the experience of the most important literary critic of our time appears to have been much the same.

In *The Sacred Wood*, speaking of Arnold with great respect, Mr Eliot calls him 'rather a propagandist for criticism than a critic', and I must confess that for years the formula seemed to me unquestionably just. Is Arnold's critical achievement after all a very impressive one? His weaknesses and his irritating tricks one remembers very well. Is it, in fact, possible to protest with any conviction when we are told (in the later essay, *Arnold and Pater*)?—

Arnold had little gift for consistency or for definition. Nor had he the power of connected reasoning at any length: his flights are either short flights or circular flights. Nothing in his prose works, therefore, will stand very close analysis, and we may very well feel that the positive content of many words is very small.

And yet, if the truth is so, how is it that we open our Arnold so often, relatively? For it is just the oddity of Arnold's case that, while we are

[1] *The Letters of Gerard Manley Hopkins to Robert Bridges*, XCVII.

apt to feel undeniable force in such judgments as the above, we nevertheless think of him as one of the most lively and profitable of the
accepted critics. Let us at any rate seize on the agreement that as a
propagandist for criticism he is distinguished. On the view that has been
quoted, the first two essays in *Essays in Criticism: First Series* would
be the texts to stress as exhibiting Arnold at his strongest, and they have,
indeed, seemed to me such. And re-reading confirms the claim of *The
Function of Criticism at the Present Time* and *The Literary Influence of
Academies* to be remembered as classical presentments of their themes.
The plea for critical intelligence and critical standards and the statement
of the idea of centrality (the antithesis of 'provinciality') are made in
memorable formulations of classical rightness:

Whoever sets himself to see things as they are will find himself one of a very
small circle; but it is only by this small circle resolutely doing its own work
that adequate ideas will ever get current at all.

All the world has, or proposes to have, this conscience in moral matters...
And a like deference to a standard higher than one's own habitual standard in
intellectual matters, a like respectful recognition of a superior ideal, is caused
in the intellectual sphere, by sensitiveness of intelligence.

...not being checked in England by any centre of intelligent and urbane
spirit...

M. Planche's advantage is...that there is a force of cultivated opinion for
him to appeal to.

...a serious, settled, fierce, narrow, provincial misconception of the whole
relative value of one's own things and the things of others.

—Arnold's distinction as a propagandist for criticism cannot be questioned. At the same time, perhaps, it must be admitted that these essays
do not involve any very taut or subtle development of an argument or
any rigour of definition. They are pamphleteering—higher pamphleteering that has lost little of its force and relevance with the passage of time.

Yet it must surely be apparent that the propaganda could hardly
have had its virtue if the pamphleteer had not had notable qualifications
in criticism. The literary critic, in fact, makes a direct appearance, a very
impressive one, in the judgment on the Romantics, which, in its time,
remarks Mr Eliot[1] (who elsewhere justly pronounces it incontrovertible),
'must have appeared startlingly independent'. It seems plain that the
peculiar distinction, the strength, represented by the extracts given
above is inseparable from the critical qualifications manifested in that
judgment: the sensitiveness and sure tact are essentially those of a fine
literary critic.

But does any actual performance of Arnold's in set literary criticism

[1] *The Use of Poetry and the Use of Criticism*, p. 104.

bear out the suggestion at all convincingly? Again it is characteristic of his case that one should be able to entertain the doubt. How many of his admirers retain very strongly favourable impressions of the other series of *Essays in Criticism?*—for it is to this, and to the opening essay in particular, *The Study of Poetry*, that the challenge sends one back. For myself, I must confess to having been surprised, on a recent re-reading of that essay, at the injustice of my recollection of it. The references to Dryden and Pope tend (in my experience) to bulk unfairly, and, for that reason and others, there is a temptation to talk too easily of the essay as being chiefly memorable for having standardized Victorian taste and established authoritatively what, in the academic world, has hardly ceased to be the accepted perspective of poetic history. And it is, actually, as a review of the past from the given period angle that the essay claims its classical status. But it is classical—for it truly is— because it performs its undertaking so consummately. Its representative quality is of the highest kind, that which can be achieved only by the vigorously independent intelligence. If it is fair to say that Arnold, in his dismissal of Dryden and Pope by the criterion of 'soul' and his curious exaltation of Gray, is the voice of the Romantic tradition in his time, we must note, too, that he is the same Arnold who passed the 'startlingly independent' judgment on the Romantics. And with what-ever reservations, protests and irritations we read *The Sudy of Poetry*, it is impossible in reading it (I find) not to recognize that we have to do with an extraordinarily distinguished mind in complete possession of its purpose and pursuing it with easy mastery—that, in fact, we are reading a great critic. Moreover, I find that in this inconsequence I am paralleled by Mr Eliot. He writes in *The Use of Poetry and the Use of Criticism* (p. 118), in the mainly depreciatory chapter on Arnold: 'But you cannot read his essay on *The Study of Poetry* without being convinced by the felicity of his quotations: to be able to quote as Arnold could is the best evidence of taste. The essay is a classic in English criticism: so much is said in so little space, with such economy and with such authority.'

How is this curious inconsistency of impression—this discrepancy of report which, I am convinced, many readers of Arnold could parallel from their own experience of him—to be explained? Partly it is, I think, that, taking critical stock at a remove from the actual reading, one tends to apply inappropriate criteria of logical rigour and 'definition'. And it is partly (a not altogether separable consideration) that the essay 'dates' in various ways; allowances have certainly to be made with reference to the age to which it was addressed, certain things 'date' in the most damaging sense, and it is easy to let these things infect one's general impression of the 'period' quality of the essay.

The element that 'dates' in the worst sense is that represented by the famous opening in which Arnold suggests that religion is going to be replaced by poetry. Few now would care to endorse the unqualified intention of that passage, and Arnold as a theological or philosophical thinker had better be abandoned explicitly at once. Yet the value of the essay does not depend on our accepting without reservation the particular terms in which Arnold stresses the importance of poetry in those introductory sentences, and he is not disposed of as a literary critic by pointing out that he was no theologian or philosopher; nor is it proved that he was incapable of consistency and vigour of thought. Many who deplore Arnold's way with religion will agree that, as the other traditions relax and social forms disintegrate, it becomes correspondingly more important to preserve the literary tradition. When things are as already they were in Arnold's time, they make necessary, whatever else may be necessary too, the kind of work that Arnold undertook for 'Culture'—work that couldn't have been done by a theologian as such. No doubt Arnold might have been able to do it even better if he had had the qualifications that actually he hadn't; he would at any rate have known his limits better, and wouldn't have produced those writings of his which have proved most ephemeral and which constitute the grounds on which Mr Eliot charges him with responsibility for Pater.[1] But his actual qualifications were sufficiently remarkable and had their appropriate use. His best work is that of a literary critic, even when it is not literary criticism: it comes from an intelligence that, even if not trained to some kinds of rigour, had its own discipline; an intelligence that is informed by a mature and delicate sense of the humane values and can manifest itself directly as a fine sensibility. That the specific qualifications of the literary critic have an important function some who most disapprove of Arnold's religious position readily grant.[2] Failure to recognize—or to recognize unequivocally—an admirable performance of the function in *The Study of Poetry* may be partly explained by that opening of the essay: Arnold, after all, issues the distracting challenge, however unnecessarily.

The seriousness with which he conceived the function and the importance he ascribed to poetry are more legitimately expressed in the phrase, the best-known tag from the essay, 'criticism of life'. That it is not altogether satisfactory, the animadversion it has been the object of must perhaps be taken to prove: at best we must admit that

[1] See the essay 'Arnold and Pater' in *Selected Essays*.
[2] See e.g., *Poetry and Crisis* by Martin Turnell (Sands: The Paladin Press). With what reservations Mr Turnell, writing as a Catholic, grants it, a perusal of his extremely interesting book will show. But the book, which thus comes out opportunely for my purpose, bears on my argument, I think, in the way I suggest.

the intention it expresses hasn't, to a great many readers, made itself satisfactorily clear. Nevertheless, Arnold leaves us with little excuse for supposing—as some of his most eminent critics have appeared to suppose—that he is demanding doctrine or moral commentary on life or explicit criticism. Nor should it be necessary to point out that all censure passed on him for having, in calling poetry 'criticism of life', produced a bad definition is beside the mark.[1] For it should be obvious to anyone who reads the phrase in its context that Arnold intends, not to define poetry, but, while insisting (a main concern of the essay) that there are different degrees of importance in poetry, to remind us of the nature of the criteria by which comparative judgments are made.

Why Arnold should have thought the insistence and the reminder worth while and should have hit on the given phrase as appropriate for his purpose is not difficult to understand if we think of that Pater with whom, as noted above, he has been associated: '"Art for Art's sake" is the offspring of Arnold's culture; and we can hardly venture to say that it is even a perversion of Arnold's doctrine, considering how very vague and ambiguous that doctrine is.' At any rate, we can certainly not say that 'Art for Art's sake' is the offspring of Arnold's 'criticism of life'. In fact, Arnold's phrase is sufficiently explained—and, I think vindicated—as expressing an intention directly counter to the tendency that finds its consummation in 'Art for Art's sake'. Aestheticism was not a sudden development: the nature of the trend from Keats through Tennyson and Dante Gabriel Rossetti was, even in Arnold's mid career, not unapparent to the critic who passed the judgment on the great Romantics. The insistence that poetry must be judged as 'criticism of life' is the same critic's reaction to the later Romantic tradition; it puts the stress where it seemed to him that it most needed to be put.

In so far as Arnold ever attempts to explain the phrase, it is in such terms as those in which, in the essay on Wordsworth, he explains why it is that Wordsworth must be held to be a greater poet than the 'perfect' Gautier. But with no more explanation than is given in *The Study of Poetry* the intention seems to me plain enough for Arnold's purposes. To define the criteria he was concerned with, those by which we make the more serious kind of comparative judgment, was not necessary, and I cannot see that anything would have been gained by his attempting to define them. His business was to evoke them effectively (can we really hope for anything better?) and that, I think, he must be allowed to have done. We may, when, for example, he tells us why

[1] See, e.g. J. M. Robertson's curious performance in *Modern Humanists Reconsidered*, referred to by Mr Eliot.

Chaucer is not among the very greatest poets, find him questionable and provoking, but the questions are profitable and the provocations stimulate us to get clear in our own minds. We understand well enough the nature of his approach; the grounds of his criticism are sufficiently present. Pressed for an account of the intention behind the famous phrase, we have to say something like this: we make (Arnold insists) our major judgments about poetry by bringing to bear the completest and profoundest sense of relative value that, aided by the work judged, we can focus from our total experience of life (which includes literature), and our judgment has intimate bearings on the most serious choices we have to make thereafter in our living. We don't ordinarily ask of the critic that he shall tell us anything like this, or shall attempt to define the criteria by which he makes his major judgments of value. But Arnold appears to challenge the demand and so earns reprobation for not satisfying it. By considering the age to which he was addressing himself we are able to do him justice; but if in this way he may be said to 'date,' it is not in any discreditable sense.

There is still to be met the pretty general suspicion to which Mr Eliot gives voice when he says[1] that Arnold 'was apt to think of the greatness of poetry rather than of its genuineness'. It is a suspicion that is the harder to lay because, with a slight shift of accent, it turns into an unexceptionable observation :'The best of Arnold's criticism is an illustration of his ethical views, and contributes to his discrimination of the values and relations of the components of the good life.'[2] This very fairly accords due praise while suggesting limitations. We have, nevertheless, to insist that, but for Arnold's gifts as a literary critic, that criticism would not have had its excellence. And when the suspicion takes such form as the following,[3] some answer must clearly be attempted:

Yet he was so conscious of what, for him, poetry was *for*, that he could not altogether see it for what it is. And I am not sure that he was highly sensitive to the musical qualities of verse. His own occasional bad lapses arouse the suspicion; and so far as I can recollect he never emphasizes this virtue of poetic style, this fundamental, in his criticism.

Whatever degree of justice there may be in these suggestions, one point can be made at once: some pages of *The Study of Poetry* are explicitly devoted to considering 'genuineness'—the problem of how the critic makes those prior kinds of judgment, those initial recognitions of life and quality, which must precede, inform and control all profitable discussion of poetry and any evaluation of it as 'criticism of life'. Towards the close of the essay we read:

[1] *The Use of Poetry*, p. 110. [2] *Criterion*, Vol. III, p. 162.
[3] *The Use of Poetry*, p. 118.

'To make a happy fireside clime
　　To weans and wife,
That's the true pathos and sublime
　　Of human life.'

There is criticism of life for you, the admirers of Burns will say to us; there is the application of ideas to life! There is undoubtedly.

And Arnold goes on to insist (in terms that would invite the charge of circularity if we were being offered a definition, as we are not) that the evaluation of poetry as 'criticism of life' is inseparable from its evaluation as poetry; that the moral judgment that concerns us as critics must be at the same time a delicately relevant response of sensibility; that, in short, we cannot separate the consideration of 'greatness' from the consideration of 'genuineness'. The test for 'genuineness' Arnold indicates in this way:

Those laws [of poetic truth and poetic beauty] fix as an essential condition, in the poet's treatment of such matters as are here in question, high seriousness —the high seriousness which comes from absolute sincerity. The accent of high seriousness, born of absolute sincerity, is what gives to such verse as

'In la sua volontade è nostra pace...'

to such criticism of life as Dante's, its power. Is this accent felt in the passages which I have been quoting from Burns? Surely not; surely, if our sense is quick, we must perceive that we have not in those passages a voice from the very inmost soul of the genuine Burns; he is not speaking to us from these depths, he is more or less preaching.

This passage is old-fashioned in its idiom,[1] and perhaps 'high seriousness' should be dismissed as a mere nuisance.[2] But 'absolute sincerity', a quality belonging to the 'inmost soul' and manifested in an 'accent', an 'accent that we feel if our sense is quick'—this

---

[1] Comparison with a passage in a more modern idiom may prove interesting:

> But unless the ordering of the words sprang, not from knowledge of the technique of poetry added to a desire to write some, but from an actual supreme ordering of *experience*, a closer approach to his work will betray it. Characteristically its rhythm will give it away. For rhythm is no matter of tricks with syllables, but directly reflects personality. It is not separable from the words to which it belongs. Moving rhythm in poetry arises only from genuinely stirred impulses, and is a more subtle index than any other to the order of the interests.　　　　I. A. Richards, *Science and Poetry*, p. 40.

Arnold's 'accent,' it will be shown, is intended to do much the same work as 'rhythm' in this passage.

[2] It is an insistent nuisance in the whole essay. But the suspicion that Arnold is demanding with it a Victorian nobility of *tenue* should have been disposed of by his remarks on Burns.

phrasing, in the context, seems to me suggestive in a wholly creditable and profitable way. And actually it has a force behind it that doesn't appear in the quotation: it is strengthened decisively by what has come earlier in the essay.

The place in question is that in which Arnold brings out his critical tip, the 'touchstone'. Whatever that tip may be worth, its intention should be plain.[1] It is a tip for mobilizing our sensibility; for focusing our relevant experience in a sensitive point; for reminding us vividly of what the best is like.

Of course we are not to require this other poetry to resemble them; it may be very dissimilar.

The specimens I have quoted differ widely from one another, but they have in common this: the possession of the very highest poetical quality.

It is only by bringing our experience to bear on it that we can judge the new thing, yet the expectations that we bring, more or less unconsciously, may get in the way; and some readers may feel that Arnold doesn't allow enough for the danger. But that he means to allow for it and envisages the problem with the delicate assurance of a fine critic is plain.

What, however, we have particularly to mark—the main point of turning back to this place in the essay—is what follows. Arnold, while protesting that 'it is much better simply to have recourse to concrete examples', ventures, nevertheless, to give some critical account, 'not indeed how and why' the characters of a high quality of poetry arise, 'but where and in what they arise'. The account is characteristic in its method and, I think, notably justifies it. 'They are in the matter and substance of the poetry and they are in its manner and style. Both of these, the substance and matter on the one hand, the style and manner on the other, have a mark, an accent of high beauty, worth and power.' And the succeeding couple of pages might seem to be mainly a matter of irritating repetition that implicitly admits an inability to get any further. Nevertheless, there is development, and the varied reiteration of associated terms, which is certainly what we have, has a critical purpose:

We may add yet further, what is in itself evident, that to the style and manner of the best poetry their special character, their accent, is given by their diction, and, even yet more, by their movement. And though we distinguish between the two characters, the two accents, of superiority, yet they are nevertheless vitally connected one with the other. The superior character of

[1] For a striking example of the kind of misinterpretation from which Arnold has suffered, the reader should turn up Raleigh's comments on the 'touchstone'.

truth and seriousness, in the matter and substance of the best poetry, is inseparable from the superiority of diction and manner marking its style and movement.

It is plain that, in this insistent association of 'accent', 'diction' and 'movement' in the equally insistent context, Arnold is offering his equivalent of Mr Eliot's 'musical qualities of verse' and of the 'rhythm' of the footnote to page 264. His procedure is a way of intimating that he doesn't suppose himself to have said anything very precise. But he seems to me, all the same, to have done the appropriate directing of attention upon poetry—and that was the problem—not less effectively than the other two critics.[1]

Inquiry, then, into the main criticisms that have been brought against *The Study of Poetry* yields reports decidedly in Arnold's favour. If he speaks in that essay with economy and authority, it is because his critical position is firmly based, because he knows what he is setting out to do, and because he is master of the appropriate method. The lack of the 'gift for consistency or for definition' turns out to be compensated, at his best, by certain positive virtues: tact and delicacy, a habit of keeping in sensitive touch with the concrete, and an accompanying gift for implicit definition—virtues that prove adequate to the sure and easy management of a sustained argument and are, as we see them in Arnold, essentially those of a literary critic.

However, it must be confessed that none of the other essays in that volume can be called a classic in English criticism. The *Milton* is a mere ceremonial address. (But it may be noted at this point that the reader who supposes Arnold to have been an orthodox idolator of Milton will be surprised if he turns up in *Mixed Essays* the essay called *A French Critic on Milton*.) The *Gray* dates most of all the essays in the series—dates in the most damaging sense; though it may be said to have gained in that way a classical status as a document in the history of taste. Neither the *Keats* nor the *Shelley* makes any show of being a model critique of poetry; but nevertheless the rarely gifted literary critic is apparent in them. It is apparent in his relative placing of the two poets. 'Shelley', he says, 'is not a classic, whose various readings are to be noted with earnest attention.' And the reasons he gives for his low valuation, though they are not backed with particular criticism,

[1] As a way of bringing home the difficulty of achieving anything more precise in the treatment of this problem, the reader may profitably compare with one another Arnold's passages, the footnote above from *Science and Poetry*, Mr Eliot's account of the 'auditory imagination' (*The Use of Poetry*, pp. 118–19), and Coleridge's remarks on 'the sense of musical delight' in chapter xv (head 1) of *Biographia Literaria*.

Arnold's comparative adequacy will be apparent.

seem to me unanswerable. On Keats he is extraordinarily just, in appreciation both of the achievement and of the potentiality—extraordinarily just, if we think of the bias that 'criticism of life' is supposed to imply. The critic's quality comes out in some notable phrases:

But indeed nothing is more remarkable in Keats than his clear-sightedness, his lucidity; and lucidity is in itself akin to character and to high and severe work.

Even in his pursuit of 'the pleasures of song', however, there is that stamp of high work which is akin to character, which is character passing into intellectual production.

The *Wordsworth*, with all its limitations, is at any rate a distinguished personal estimate, and though by a Wordsworthian, and by the critic who spoke of poetry as the 'application of ideas to life', exhibits its salutary firmness about the 'philosophy'.

But what has to be stressed is his relative valuation of the great Romantics: Wordsworth he put first, then Byron (and for the right reasons), then Keats, and last Shelley. It is, in its independence and its soundness, a more remarkable critical achievement than we easily recognize to-day. (The passage on the Romantics in the *Heine* essay should not be overlooked.)

If any other particular work of his is to be mentioned, it must be the long essay *On Translating Homer*. It was, as Saintsbury points out,[1] an extraordinarily original undertaking at the time, and it was carried out with such spirit and intelligence that it is still profitable reading.

The actual achievement in producible criticism may not seem a very impressive one. But we had better inquire where a more impressive is to be found. As soon as we start to apply any serious standard of what good criticism should be, we are led towards the conclusion that there is very little. If Arnold is not one of the great critics, who are they? Which do we approach with a greater expectation of profit? Mr Eliot himself—yes; and not only because his preoccupations are of our time: his best critical writing has a higher critical intensity than any of Arnold's. Coleridge's pre-eminence we all recognize. Johnson?—that Johnson is a living writer no one will dispute, and his greatness is certainly apparent in his criticism. Yet that he imposes himself there as a more considerable power than Arnold isn't plain to me, and strictly as a critic—a critic offering critical value—he seems to me to

[1] Almost for the first time, too, we have ancient literature treated more or less like modern—neither from the merely philological point of view, nor with reference to the stock platitudes and traditions about it.' G. Saintsbury, *Matthew Arnold*, p. 68.

matter a good deal less to us. As for Dryden, important as he is historically, I have always thought the intrinsic interest of his criticism much
overrated: he showed strength and distinction in independent judgment,
but I cannot believe that his discussion of any topic has much to offer
us. We read him (if we do) because of his place in literary history,
whereas we read Arnold's critical writing because for anyone who is
interested in literature it is compellingly alive. I can think of no other
English critic who asks to be considered here, so I will say finally that,
whatever his limitations, Arnold seems to me decidedly more of a
critic than the Sainte-Beuve to whom he so deferred.

COLERIDGE IN CRITICISM

F. R. LEAVIS (1940)

That Coleridge was a rarely gifted mind is a commonplace. It is
perhaps equally a commonplace that what he actually accomplished with
his gifts, the producible achievement, appears, when we come to
stocktaking, disappointingly incommensurate. That 'perhaps' registers
a hesitation: judges qualified in the religious and intellectual history of
the past century might, I think, reply that actually Coleridge was a
great power, exercising influence in ways that must be credited to him
for very notable achievement, and that we cannot judge him merely by
reading what is extant of him in print.[1] My concern, however, is with
the field of literary criticism. That his performance there justifies some
disappointment is, I believe, generally recognized. But I believe, too,
that this recognition stresses, in intention, rather the superlativeness of
the gifts than shortcoming in the performance. The full disparity, in
fact, doesn't get clear recognition very readily; there are peculiar
difficulties in the way—at least, these are the conclusions to which,
after reconsidering the body of Coleridge's work in criticism, I find
myself brought.

The spirit of that reconsideration had better be made plain at once.
Let me start, then, by reminding the reader of the introduction to the

---

[1] Cf. J. S. Mill's witness in 1840: 'The name of Coleridge is one of the few
English names of our time which are likely to be oftener pronounced, and to
become symbolical of more important things, in proportion as the inward
workings of the age manifest themselves more and more in outward facts.
Bentham excepted, no Englishman of recent date has left his impress so deeply
in the opinions and mental tendencies of those who attempt to enlighten their
practice by philosophical meditation.' *Dissertations and Discussions*, Vol. I,
'Coleridge'.

standard scholarly edition of *Biographia Literaria*. The ninety pages or so are devoted almost wholly to discussing Coleridge's relation to Kant and other German philosophers. Now it seems clear to me that no head of study that involves discussions of Coleridge's indebtedness to, or independence of, Kant, Schelling, the Schlegels or Fichte has any claims on the attention of the literary student; it is from his point of view a solicitation to unprofitable expenditures. If in a work recommended to him as directly relevant to the problems of literary criticism any such solicitations seem likely to engage or confuse him, he had better be warned against them. It follows then, if this is so, and if J. Shawcross's introduction is relevant to the work it precedes, that the docile student ought certainly to be warned against a large part of *Biographia Literaria*. It may be that, as Shawcross suggests, 'Coleridge's philosophy of art' has not 'received in England the consideration which it deserves'. But Coleridge's philosophy of art is Coleridge's philosophy, and though no doubt he has an important place in the history of English thought, not even the student of philosophy, I imagine, is commonly sent to Coleridge for initiations into key problems, or for classical examples of distinguished thinking. And the literary student who goes to Coleridge in the expectation of bringing away an improved capacity and equipment for dealing critically with works of literature will, if he spends much time on the 'philosophy of art', have been sadly misled.

It is by way of defining the spirit of my approach that I assert this proposition, the truth of which seems to me evident. Actually, of course, its evidence gets substantial recognition in established academic practice: the student usually starts his reading—or at least his serious reading—of *Biographia Literaria* at chapter XIV. Nevertheless, since the appropriate distinction is not formulated and no sharp separation can be made in the text, the common effect of the perusal can hardly be clarity—or clear profit. It is certain, on the other hand, that Coleridge's prestige owes a great deal to the transcendental aura; his acceptance as a master of 'theoretical criticism' is largely an awed vagueness about the philosophy—a matter of confused response to such things as:

The primary IMAGINATION then, I consider, to be the living power and prime agent of all human Perception, and as a repetition in the finite mind of the eternal act of creation in the infinite I AM.

The essential distinction ought to be plain enough to us, but that Coleridge himself should not have made it sharply and have held firmly to it cannot, given the nature of his genius, surprise us; on the contrary, even if he had been a much more orderly and disciplined worker than he was, we still couldn't have expected in his work a clear separation between what properly claims the attention of the literary critic and what does not. 'Metaphysics, poetry and facts of mind', he wrote, 'are my darling studies.' The collocation of the last two heads suggest the sense in which Shelley's phrase for him, 'a subtle-souled psychologist', must often, when he impresses us favourably in the literary-critical field, seem to us an apt one, and, on the other hand, it is difficult not to think of the first head as a nuisance. Yet we can hardly suppose that we could have had the psychologist without the metaphysician; that the gift of subtle analysis could have been developed, at that date, by a mind that shouldn't also have exhibited something like the Coleridgean philosophic bent. But that makes it not less, but more, necessary to be firm about the distinction that concerns us here.

I had better at this point indicate more fully the specific equipment that might seem to have qualified Coleridge for great achievements in literary criticism—to be, indeed, its modern instaurator. The 'subtle-souled psychologist', it seems not superfluous to emphasize, was intensely interested in literature. He was, of course, a poet, and the suggestion seems to be taken very seriously that he indulged the habit of analytic introspection to the extent of damaging the creative gift he turned it upon. However that may be, it is reasonable to suppose that the critic, at any rate, profited. The psychological bent was associated with an interest in language that expresses itself in observations such as lend colour to I. A. Richards's enlistment of Coleridge for Semasiology. But, as in reviewing in these pages *Coleridge on Imagination* I had occasion to remind Dr Richards, who lays stress on those of Coleridge's interests which might seem to fall outside the compass of the literary critic, these interests went, in Coleridge, with a constant wide and intense cultivation of literature:

O! when I think of the inexhaustible mine of virgin treasure in our Shakespeare, that I have been almost daily reading him since I was ten years old— that the thirty intervening years have been unintermittingly and not fruitlessly employed in the study of the Greek, Latin, English, Italian, Spanish and German *belle lettrists*, and the last fifteen years in addition, far more intensively in the analysis of the laws of life and reason as they exist in man—and that upon every step I have made forward in taste, in acquisition of facts from history or my own observation, and in knowledge of the different laws of being and their apparent exceptions from accidental collision of disturbing forces,—that at every new accession of information, after every successful exercise of meditation, and every fresh presentation of experience, I have unfailingly discovered a proportionate increase of wisdom and intuition in Shakespeare... '[1]

[1] I quote from the Everyman volume, *Essays and Lectures on Shakespeare*, but see T. H. Raysor, *Coleridge's Shakespearean Criticism*, vol. I, p. 210.

The 'analysis' and the 'laws' mentioned hardly belong to literary criticism, but it is easy to assemble an impressive array of characteristic utterances and formulas that promise the literary critic's own concern with principle:

The ultimate end of criticism is much more to establish the principles of writing than to furnish *rules* how to pass judgment on what has been written by others; if indeed it were possible that the two should be separated. [*Biographia Lit.* ch. XVIII.]

You will see, by the terms of my prospectus, that I intend my lectures to be, not only 'in illustration of the principles of poetry', but to include a statement of the application of those principles, 'as grounds of criticism on the most popular works of later English poets, those of the living included'. [*Coleridge's Shakespearean Criticism*, vol. II, p. 63.]

It is a painful truth that not only individuals, but even whole nations, are ofttimes so enslaved to the habits of their education and immediate circumstances, as not to judge disinterestedly even on those subjects, the very pleasure arising from which consists in its disinterestedness, namely, on subjects of taste and polite literature. Instead of deciding concerning their own modes and customs by any rule of reason, nothing appears rational, becoming, or beautiful to them, but what coincides with the peculiarities of their education. In this narrow circle, individuals may attain to exquisite discrimination, as the French critics have done in their own literature; but a true critic can no more be such without placing himself on some central point, from which he may command the whole, that is, some general rule, which, founded in reason, or the faculties common to all men, must therefore apply to each—than an astronomer can explain the movements of the solar system, without taking his stand in the sun. And let me remark, that this will not tend to produce despotism, but, on the contrary, true tolerance, in the critic. [*Coleridge's Shakespearean Criticism*, vol. I, p. 221.]

These things seem the more significant for being thrown out by the way, suggesting a radical habit of mind, the literary critic's concern to 'ériger en lois'—his proper concern with the formulation of principle. They add greatly to the impressiveness of the account that can be elaborated of Coleridge's qualifications for a great achievement in criticism. My own experience is that one can easily fill a lecture on Coleridge with such an account, and that the impressiveness of the qualifications has a large part in one's impression of a great achievement. The qualifications are obvious, but the achievement isn't readily sized up.

What, in fact, can be said of it after a resolute critical survey? Asked to point to a place that could be regarded as at the centre of Coleridge's achievement and indicative of its nature, most admirers would probably point to the famous passage on imagination at the end of chapter XIV of *Biographia Literaria*:

The poet, described in *ideal* perfection, brings the whole soul of man into activity, with the subordination of its faculties to each other, according to their relative worth and dignity. He diffuses a tone and spirit of unity, that blends, and (as it were) *fuses*, each into each, by that synthetic and magical power, to which we have exclusively appropriated the name of imagination. This power, first put into action by the will and understanding, and retained under their irremissive, though gentle and unnoticed, control (*laxis effertur habenis*) reveals itself in the balance or reconciliation of opposite or discordant qualities: of sameness, with difference; of the general, with the concrete; the idea, with the image; the individual, with the representative; the sense of novelty and freshness, with old and familiar objects; a more than usual state of emotion with more than usual order; judgment ever awake and steady self possession, with enthusiasm and feeling profound or vehement; and while it blends and harmonizes the natural and the artificial, still subordinates art to nature; the manner to the matter; and our admiration of the poet to our sympathy with the poetry.

It is an impressive passage—perhaps too impressive; for it has more often, perhaps, caused an excited sense of enlightenment than it has led to improved critical practice or understanding. The value we set on it must depend on the development and illustration the account of imagination gets in such context as we can find for it elsewhere in Coleridge and especially in his own critical practice. The appropriate commentary according to general acceptance would, I suppose, bear on the substitution by Coleridge of an understanding of literature in terms of organism, an understanding operating through an inward critical analysis, for the external mechanical approach of the Neo-classic eighteenth century. That Coleridge has a place in literary history to be indicated in some such terms is no doubt true. And yet we ought hardly to acquiesce happily in any suggestion that the subsequent century exhibits a general improvement in criticism. What in fact this view— the academically accepted one, I believe—of Coleridge amounts to is that, of the decisive change in taste and literary tradition that resulted from the Romantic movement, Coleridge is to be regarded as the supreme critical representative.[1]

And it has to be recognized that, in effect, his 'imagination' does seem to have amounted to the Romantic 'creative imagination'. This much, at any rate, must be conceded: that, though justice insists that

[1] Cf. Mill: 'The healthier taste and more intelligent canons of poetic criticism, which he was himself mainly instrumental in diffusing, have at length assigned to him his proper rank, as one among the great, and (if we look to the powers shown rather than to the amount of actual achievement) amongst the greater names in our literature.'

Coleridge's account of the creative process is not that given by Shelley in his *Defence of Poetry*, nevertheless Coleridge's influence did not, in the subsequent century, avail to make the Romantic tradition, of which he was an acclaimed founding father, aware of the difference. From whom, for instance, does that 'soul' descend in which, according to Arnold (who—and it is one of his claims to honour—was much less satisfied than Coleridge with the notion of poetry as the product of the inspired individual), 'genuine poetry' was 'conceived and composed'? Arnold can hardly be said to have favoured Shelleyan notions, and yet, if we conclude that it descends from the soul 'brought into activity' by the poet who is described in chapter XIV of *Biographia Literaria*, we are hardly recommending Coleridge.

In any case, Coleridge's historical importance isn't at the centre of my concern. My concern is with the intrinsic interest of his extant critical work—with his achievement in that sense. A critic may have an important place in history and yet not be very interesting in his writings: Dryden seems to me a case in point. Coleridge, on the other hand, may be more interesting than the claims made for him as an influence suggest. What credit we give him for the interesting possibilities of that passage on imagination depends, as has been said, on the way the account is developed and illustrated.

The Fancy–Imagination contrast hardly takes us any further. Coleridge does little with it beyond the brief exemplification that cannot be said to justify the stress he lays on the two faculties he distinguishes. I. A. Richards's attempt in *Coleridge on Imagination* to develop the distinction is a tribute not to Coleridge but to Bentham. The best that can be said for Coleridge is that, though he was undoubtedly serious in positing the two faculties, actually the distinction as he illustrates it is a way of calling attention to the organic complexities of verbal life, metaphorical and other, in which Imagination manifests itself locally: Fancy is merely an ancillary concept. And Coleridge certainly gives evidence of a gift for critical analysis:

> 'Look! how a bright star shooteth from the sky;
> So glides he in the night from Venus' eye!'

How many images and feelings are here brought together without effort and without discord, in the beauty of Adonis, the rapidity of his flight, the yearning, yet hopelessness, of the enamoured gazer, while a shadowy ideal character is thrown over the whole. [*Coleridge's Shakespearean Criticism*, vol. I, p. 213.]

A good many passages of this kind could be quoted, showing a capacity for a kind of sensitive analytic penetration such as will hardly be found in any earlier critic.

But 'capacity'—again it is evidence of qualifications we are adducing. What corresponding achievement is there to point to? The work on Shakespeare constitutes the nearest thing to an impressive body of criticism, and everyone who has tried to read it through knows how disappointing it is. Coleridge didn't inaugurate what may be called the Bradley approach but he lends his prestige to it. Of course, his psychologizing is pursued with nothing of Bradley's system—he never carries through anything with system. On the other hand, he has things to offer that are beyond Bradley's range. The subtle-souled psychologist appears to advantage, for example, in the analysis, if not of Hamlet's character, of the effects, at once poetic and dramatic, of the opening of the play. There are various notes of that kind and a good many acute observations about points in the verse. In short, when we take stock of what there is to be said in favour of the Shakespeare criticism, we again find ourselves considering, not achievement, but evidence of a critical endowment that *ought* to have achieved something remarkable. Even those who rate it more highly would, I imagine, never think of proposing the work on Shakespeare to the student as a classical body of criticism calculated to make much difference to his powers of appreciation or understanding.

What is, I suppose, a classical document is the group of chapters on Wordsworth in *Biographia Literaria*. But if they are that, it is at least partly for reasons of historical interest, because Coleridge on Wordsworth is Coleridge on Wordsworth, and not because of achieved criticism of a high order contained in them. The treatment of the poetry, however interesting, hardly amounts to a profound or very illuminating critique. The discussion of poetic diction provides, of course, more evidence of Coleridge's peculiar gifts, especially in the argument about metre in chapter XVIII. That Coleridge perceives certain essential truths about poetic rhythm and metre—truths that are not yet commonplaces, at any rate in academic literary study—is plain. But anything approaching the satisfactory treatment of them that he seems preeminently qualified to have written he certainly doesn't provide. His virtue is represented by this:

Secondly, I argue from the EFFECTS of metre. As far as metre acts in and for itself, it tends to increase the vivacity and susceptibility both of the general feelings and of the attention. This effect it produces by the continued excitement of surprise, and by the quick reciprocations of curiosity still gratified and still re-excited, which are too slight indeed to be at any one moment objects of distinct consciousness, yet become considerable in their aggregate influence. As a medicated atmosphere, or as wine during animated conversation; they act powerfully, though themselves unnoticed. Where, therefore, correspondent food and appropriate matter are not provided for the attention and feelings thus aroused, there must needs be a disappointment felt; like that of leaping in the dark from the last step of a staircase, when we had prepared our muscles for a leap of three or four.

This fairly earns the tribute that I. A. Richards pays Coleridge in *Principles of Literary Criticism*, in the chapter on 'Rhythm and Metre' (one of the useful parts of that book). But though the paragraph quoted tends to confer credit upon the context of technical-looking analysis, it doesn't really gain anything from that context, the rigorously and ambitiously analytic air of which doesn't justify itself, despite an element of interesting suggestion.

And this seems the moment to make the point that Coleridge's unsatisfactoriness isn't merely what stares at us in the synopsis of *Biographia Literaria*—the disorderliness, the lack of all organization or sustained development: locally too, even in the best places, he fails to bring his thought to a sharp edge and seems too content with easy expression. Expression came, in fact, too easily to him; for a man of his deep constitutional disinclination to brace himself to sustained work at any given undertaking, his articulateness was fatal. He could go down to the lecture-hall at the last minute with a marked copy of Shakespeare and talk—talk much as he talked anywhere and at any time. And what we read as Coleridge's writings comes from that inveterate talker, even when the text that we have is something he actually wrote, and not reported discourse.

Perhaps the habit of the lecture-hall accounts for such things as the definition of a poem in chapter XIV of *Biographia Literaria*:

The final definition then, so deduced, may be thus worded. A poem is that species of composition, which is opposed to works of science, by proposing for its immediate object pleasure, not truth; and from all other species (having *this* object in common with it) it is discriminated by proposing to itself such delight from the *whole*, as is compatible with a distinct gratification from each component *part*.

That, I am afraid, is representative of a good deal in Coleridge, though it seems to me quite unprofitable. And at the end of the same chapter is this well-known pronouncement:

Finally, GOOD SENSE is the BODY of poetic genius, FANCY is its DRAPERY, MOTION its LIFE, and IMAGINATION the SOUL that is everywhere, and in each; and forms all into one graceful and intelligent whole.

It comes, characteristically enough, just after the famous passage on imagination, which is of another order altogether.

The immediately succeeding chapter (XV) seems to me to show Coleridge at his best. It is headed, 'The specific symptoms of poetic power elucidated in a critical analysis of Shakespeare's Venus and Adonis and Lucrece', and this heading is significant: it suggests with some felicity the nature of Coleridge's peculiar distinction, or what should have been his peculiar distinction, as a critic. He speaks in his first sentence, referring no doubt mainly to the passage on imagination, of 'the application of these principles to purposes of practical criticism'. Actually, principle as we are aware of it here appears to emerge from practice; we are made to realize that the 'master of theoretical criticism' who matters is the completion of a practical critic. The theory of which he is master (in so far as he is) doesn't lead us to discuss his debt to Kant or any other philosopher; it comes too evidently from the English critic who has devoted his finest powers of sensibility and intelligence to the poetry of his own language.

This commentary is prompted by, specifically, the second head of the chapter:

A second promise of genius is the choice of subjects very remote from the private interests and circumstances of the writer himself. At least I have found that, where the subject is taken immediately from the author's personal sensations and experiences, the excellence of a particular poem is but an equivocal mark, and often a fallacious pledge, of genuine poetic power.

The general considerations raised are immediately relevant to that central theme of T. S. Eliot's criticism, impersonality. But they are presented in terms of particular analysis, and the whole passage is a fine piece of practical criticism:

In the 'Venus and Adonis' this proof of poetic power exists even to excess. It is throughout as if a superior spirit more intuitive, more intimately conscious, even than the characters themselves, not only of every outward look and act, but of the flux and reflux of the mind in all its subtlest thoughts and feelings, were placing the whole before our view; himself meanwhile unparticipating in the passions, and actuated only by that pleasurable excitement, which had resulted from the energetic fervour of his own spirit in so vividly exhibiting, what it had so accurately and profoundly contemplated. I think, I should have conjectured from these poems, that even then the great instinct, which impelled the poet to the drama, was secretly working in him, prompting him by a series and never broken chain of imagery always vivid and, because unbroken, often minute; by the highest effort of the picturesque in words, of which words are capable, higher perhaps than was ever realized by any other poet, even Dante not excepted; to provide a substitute for that visual language, that constant intervention and running comment by tone, look and gesture, which in his dramatic works he was entitled to expect from the players. His 'Venus and Adonis' seem at once the characters themselves, and the whole representation of those characters by the most consummate actors. You seem to be told nothing but to see and hear everything. Hence it is, that from the perpetual activity of attention required on the part of the reader; from the rapid flow, the quick change, and the playful nature of the thoughts and images; and above all from the alienation, and, if I may hazard such an expression, the utter *aloofness* of the poet's own feelings from those of which he is at once the painter and the analyst; that though the very subject cannot but detract from the pleasure of a delicate mind, yet never was poem less dangerous on a moral account. Instead of doing as Ariosto, and as, still more offensively, Wieland has done, instead of degrading and deforming passion into appetite, the trials of love into the struggles of concupiscence; Shakespeare has here represented the animal impulse itself, so as to preclude all sympathy with it, by dissipating the reader's notice among the thousand outward images, and now beautiful, now fanciful circumstances, which form its dresses and its scenery; or by diverting our attention from the main subject by those frequent witty or profound reflections, which the poet's ever active mind had deduced from, or connected with, the imagery and the incidents. The reader is forced into too much action to sympathize with the merely passive of our nature. As little can a mind thus roused and awakened be brooded on by mean and indistinct emotion, as the low, lazy mist can creep upon the surface of a lake, while a strong gale is driving it onward in waves and billows.

It will have been seen that, incidentally, in the sentence about 'the perpetual activity of attention required on the part of the reader' and the further observations about the 'action' into which the reader is forced, Coleridge has given an account of the element of 'wit' that is in *Venus and Adonis*.

Though the other heads of the chapter contain nothing as striking, we tend to give full credit to what is best in them. In the first and third, for instance, Coleridge makes it plain (as he has already done in practical criticism) that the 'imagery' that matters cannot be dealt with in terms of 'images' conceived as standing to the verse as plums to cake; but that its analysis is the analysis of complex verbal organization:

It has therefore been observed that images, however beautiful, though faithfully copied from nature, and as accurately represented in words, do not of themselves characterize the poet. They become proofs of original genius only as far as they are modified by a predominant passion; or by associated thoughts or images awakened by that passion; or when they have the effect of reducing multitude to unity, or succession to an instant; or lastly, when a human and intellectual life is transferred to them from the poet's own spirit.

But there would be little point in further quotations of this kind. Such imperfectly formulated things hardly deserve to be remembered as classical statements, and nothing more is to be adduced by way of justifying achievement than the preceding long quotation. And there is nowhere in Coleridge anything more impressive to be found than that. We are left, then, with the conclusion that what we bring from the re-survey of his critical work is impressive evidence of what he might have done.

A great deal more space, of course, could be occupied with this evidence. Some of the most interesting is to be found in *Coleridge's Miscellaneous Criticism* (T. H. Raysor's collection) where, in the form of marginalia, odd notes, table talk and so on, there are many striking judgments and observations. There are, for instance, the pages (131 ff.) on Donne—pages that incline one to comment that if Coleridge had had real influence the vogue of Donne would have started a century earlier than it did. (Of Satire III, e.g., he says: 'If you would teach a scholar in the highest form how to *read*, take Donne, and of Donne this satire.') He is sound on Beaumont and Fletcher: 'Beaumont and Fletcher write as if virtue or goodness were a sort of talisman or strange something that might be lost without the least fault on the part of the owner'— and he refers to 'the too poematic-minus-dramatic nature' of Fletcher's versification. He is good on Swift: 'In short, critics in general complain of the Yahoos; I complain of the Houyhnhnms.' He is acutely severe on Scott. In fact, the volume as a whole repays exploration. Elsewhere there are the various notes on dramatic and poetic illusion, of which those in *Coleridge's Shakespearean Criticism*, vol. I (pp. 199 ff.) should be looked up, though the best-known formulation, 'that willing suspension of disbelief for the moment, which constitutes poetic faith', occurs in *Biographia Literaria* (ch. XIV).

But to revert to the depressing conclusion: Coleridge's prestige is very understandable, but his currency as an academic classic is something of a scandal. Where he is prescribed and recommended it should be with far more by way of reservation and caveat (I have come tardily to realize) than most students can report to have received along with him. He was very much more brilliantly gifted than Arnold, but nothing of his deserves the classical status of Arnold's best work.

I. A. RICHARDS

D. W. HARDING (1933)

Conversational comments on Richards's work, favourable or unfavourable, seldom express opinions about his actual views; they seem more often than not to be reactions to the general tone of his writing. Nor can this aspect of his work be neglected in an attempt to formulate a more precise opinion: some peculiarity of tone, or some prevailing attitude, undoubtedly distinguishes him from most scientific and critical writers. It would be laborious to analyse this attitude in detail. As a handy label for it, the term 'amateur' (with some of its implications) will perhaps do. It is suggested, for one thing, by the slight acerbity with which so many 'professionals'—literary critics, psychologists, metaphysicians—dismiss him, together with the slight awe that he inspires in the virginally lay. But it has more important justification than this in two essential features of his work, namely in his insistence upon the significance for 'normal practical life' of his special interests, and in the buoyancy with which he rides over difficulties of detail by means of general principles.

Take, for instance, his basic hypotheses for criticism, and consider the difficulty and labour that would be involved in proving them. Only the spirit of the amateur could enable Richards to express them with as little inhibition as he does. 'The first point to be made is that poetic experiences are valuable (when they are) in the same way as any Other experiences. They are to be judged by the same standards' (*Science and Poetry*, p. 28). 'The greatest difference between the artist or poet and the ordinary person is found, as has often been pointed out, in the range, delicacy and freedom of the connections he is able to make between different elements of his experience' (*Principles of Literary Criticism*, p. 181). 'The ways then in which the artist will differ from the average will as a rule presuppose an immense degree of similarity. They will be further developments of organizations already well advanced in the majority. His variations will be confined to the newest, the most plastic, the least fixed part of the mind, the parts for which reorganization is most easy' (*Principles of Literary Criticism*, p. 196). 'It is in terms of attitudes, the resolution, inter-inanimation, and balancing of impulses . . . that all the most valuable effects of poetry must be described' (*Principles of Literary Criticism*, p. 113). Nor has his confidence waned with time. He is still ready to assert (see *The Criterion* of October, 1932) that the explanation of the difference between good and less good experiences 'is inevitably in terms of that order or disorder among "impulses" (or however else you care to describe the elementary processes on which consciousness depends) . . .'. Contrast the more 'professional' attitude towards similar problems. 'Personally I do not think the problem of ethical valuation [of different cultures] is hopeless, but it need not necessarily be undertaken in a purely sociological inquiry' (M. Ginsberg in *Studies in Sociology*). 'Moreover, in humanity as it exists at present it is not easy to decide that one physical type is better adapted than another, and, when it comes to deciding which emotional and intelligent types are better or worse, the situation becomes far too complicated to handle with any probability of success'

(T. H. Morgan in a paper in *The Foundations of Experimental Psychology*). These quotations, I think, fairly represent the attitude of qualified specialists when they refer to ethical questions: not hopeless but.... The contrast with Richards need not be stressed.

Three hypotheses, distinct although closely related, are expressed by Richards in the passages quoted. They are, roughly, (*a*) that art and the rest of human activity are continuous, not contrasting; (*b*) that art is the most valuable form of activity; and (*c*) that the value of any activity depends on the degree to which it allows of a balancing or ordering among one's impulses. It is the third which is fundamental and upon which the other two depend, and our attitude to his work in general must depend to a great extent upon the view we take of this account of value. The practical purpose of his account must not be overlooked: he is attempting to discover 'a defensible position for those who believe that the arts are of value', and it is clear from the context that he intends primarily a position that can be defended against all those who regard art as something other than one of the practical affairs of life. He attempts in effect to meet the friendly and intelligent Philistine on his own ground. Hence his account of value is best regarded as a systematization based on certain assumptions which are not questioned by the people whom he has in mind. He assumes first that living activity is its own satisfaction and that any questioning of its 'value' is bogus questioning. Next he implies a conception of quantity in living activity and assumes that a further unquestionable satisfaction arises as one becomes *more* alive; he takes as the unit of living activity the satisfied impulse, so that the value of an activity or attitude can be measured, hypothetically, in terms of the number of impulses it satisfies. Further, he adopts the view that in all living organisms there is an unquestionable effort after greater and greater differentiation and integration of experience.

The necessary limitations of such an account of value have to be recognized before its usefulness for particular purposes can be judged. It is clear that it cannot, even hypothetically, give us grounds for judgment when a difference of opinion rests on a fundamental constitutional difference between two people. Richards, for instance, condemns swindling and bullying because they lead to a thwarting of important social impulses: the implicit assumption is that the swindler and bully in question possess the 'normal' social impulses. If they do not, then they cannot be condemned on these lines. You might as well try to convince a tiger of its misfortune in not being a buffalo. The numerical treatment of impulses will not help here; it would be flat dogma to assert that the man without social needs must achieve a lower total ouptut of satisfied 'impulses' than the man with them. And according to Richards it is the total number that matters, for the 'importance' of an impulse is only another term for the number of other impulses that depend upon it. It is difficult to suppose that the tiger, given equal strength and good health, satisfies fewer 'impulses' (fewer of 'the elementary processes on which consciousness depends') than the buffalo. This is only to point out that Richards's systematizing of value judgments cannot, even in theory, lead to agreement in evaluations unless the parties concerned have the same fundamental constitution. In point of fact, Richards keeps his numerical conception in the background, and implies that greater ordering or integration will of itself lead to the satisfying of more impulses. 'At the other extreme are those fortunate people who have achieved an ordered life, whose systems have developed clearing-houses by which the varying claims of different impulses are adjusted. Their free untrammelled activity gains for them a maximum of varied satisfactions and involves a minimum of suppression and sacrifice' (*Principles of Literary Criticism*, p. 53). Similarly, in the much finer discussion of development in *Practical Criticism*, where he relates the sayings of Confucius on sincerity to modern biological views, it is the ordering alone that is insisted on. The implication here and throughout his work is that everyone begins with the same fundamental impulses, but that they and the secondary impulses dependent on them get muddled and disorganized, thwarting each other unnecessarily. He is profoundly convinced that the function of the arts is to bring back order. In the discussion of sincerity, more-over, he brings forward, perhaps not explicitly enough, the idea that art is not merely remedial (restoring an original order) but that it aids in positive development; aids, that is, the assumed effort of the living organism to become more finely differentiated in its parts and simul-taneously more integrated. 'Being more at one within itself the mind thereby becomes more appropriately responsive to the outer world.' Fundamental difficulties confront anyone who attempts to grasp the full meaning of this integration and this appropriateness. But the essential feature of Richards's attitude to art is clear: he pins his faith to the possibility of its being shown to be a means of further progress along the lines of what we regard as biological advance. This is the essence of his defensible position for the arts. Its significance rests perhaps less on the usefulness of its contentions than on the fact that it was formulated by a writer who is genuinely sensitive to poetry, not by one with convictions of its uplift value, nor by a philosopher who felt that he 'ought' somehow to provide art with a pedestal in his exhibition of the universe.

The practical usefulness of Richards's account of value in convincing the plain man of the value of poetry or in helping us to reach agreement over disputed points is doubtful. After outlining the theory Richards writes (*Principles of Literary Criticism*, p. 51), 'We can now take our next step forward and inquire into the relative merits of different systematizations.' This step remains to be taken, unless it consisted in the brief discussion which follows, on the importance of the social virtues. In practice, of course, Richards is able to give us no more help in making these judgments than, for instance, T. H. Morgan offers, in the passage quoted. One might innocently suppose that we should judge a work of art by assessing the number of impulses it satisfied. It is needless to point out that Richards has nowhere done this, nor even pointed out what main impulses any one work of art has satisfied in him. It is of course quite clear that 'the impulse' will not serve in practice as a unit of measurement. Who can say what this smallest impulse is in terms of which the importance of the others must be expressed? There is obviously a vast gap between Richards's theory of value and any actual judgment one may make. To say that 'it is in terms of attitudes, the resolution, inter-inanimation, and balancing of impulses...that all the most valuable effects of poetry must be described' is perhaps as true, and just as helpful, as to say that it is in terms of the combination and disintegration of molecules that all the effects of modern warfare must be described. Even the difference between a pleasing and an irritating variation of rhythm is 'a matter of the combination and resolution of impulses too subtle for our present means of investigation' (*Principles of Literary Criticism*, p. 138). And in making up our minds about a poem 'we have to gather millions of fleeting semi-independent impulses into a momentary structure of fabulous complexity, whose core or germ only is given us in the words' (*Practical Criticism*, p. 317). And if his account of the basis of valuable experience has little practical significance for literary judgments, as a means of judging other arts it is more remote still. The greater part of his chapters on painting, sculpture, and music must be regarded as something very close to psychological eyewash; he hardly makes the gesture of applying his main theory to these subjects. We have to conclude that this attempt to provide a conception (of a balance of impulses) which will establish continuity between the everyday standards of a civilization advanced enough to condemn the bully and swindler and the standards of its art critics, fails through the remoteness and elusiveness of the common denominator chosen—the impulse.

This conclusion does not affect the significance of Richards's profound conviction of the value of poetry and his belief that this value is of the same kind as that implicitly recognized by the civilized Philistine. The significance lies in the fact that such a writer should have felt the need to meet the outside world of common sense and science on its own ground and justify his position by current standards. It is one sign of the uneasiness that those with special qualifications in the arts are experiencing. They cannot now confidently remain specialists, secure in the knowledge of fulfilling a recognized function. They have to become amateurs, looking at the matter from the point of view of the majority and attempting to prove that their function does exist before they can attack their own more specialized problems. This consideration may account for the kind of use to which Richards puts psychology. In the first place, it is a means of shaking the complacency of practical people, who are more uneasy at the hints of psycho-analysts than they are at the gibes or fury of artists. 'Human conditions and possibilities have altered more in a hundred years than they had in the previous ten thousand, and the next fifty may overwhelm us, unless we can devise a more adaptable morality. The view that what we need in this tempestuous turmoil of change is a Rock to shelter under or to cling to, rather than an efficient aeroplane in which to ride it, is comprehensible but mistaken' (*Principles of Literary Criticism*, p. 57). Secondly, psychology as Richards uses it seems to help him in repudiating the pseudo-mystical monopolists of aesthetic theory whose ideas do more harm than good to his demand for the recognition of poetry as a practical assistance in living. It seems to confer authority on such a statement as ' . . . the experience of "seeing stars" after a bang on the nose is just as "unique" as any act of musical appreciation and shares any exalted quality which such uniqueness may be supposed to confer' (*Principles of Literary Criticism*, p. 171). On the other hand, the work of psychologists on aesthetics has not been of the kind he has any use for; it has usually implied other standards than his in its approach to works of art, and it has done nothing to show the practical value of such art as it has dealt with. Hence his care to dissociate himself from the professional psychologists. 'Such more complex objects as have been examined have yielded very uncertain results, for reasons which anyone who has ever *both* looked at a picture or read a poem *and* been inside a psychological laboratory or conversed with a representative psychologist will understand' (*Principles of Literary Criticism*, p. 8). And rather than be committed to existing psychological methods he draws still further on the already heavily mortgaged future of neurology. Musical effects, for instance,' . . . belong to a branch of psychology for which we have as yet no methods of investigation. It seems likely that we shall have to wait a long while, and that very great advances must first be made in neurology before these problems can profitably be attacked' (*Principles of Literary Criticism*, p. 170). But there is a marked change of tone in *Practical Criticism*. After reiterating his dissatisfaction with much of the psychological work on aesthetics he goes on, 'The general reader, whose ideas as to the methods and endeavours of psychologists derive more from the popularizers of Freud or from the Behaviourists than from students of Stout or Ward, needs perhaps some assurance that it is possible to combine an interest and faith in psychological inquiries with a due appreciation of the complexity of poetry. Yet a psychologist who belongs to this main body is perhaps the last person in the world to underrate this complexity' (*Practical Criticism*, p. 322). Again, speaking of the harm done by the cruder psychologies, 'But the remedy of putting the clock back is impracticable. Inquiry cannot be stopped now. The only possible course is to hasten, so far as we can, the development of a psychology which will ignore none of the facts and yet demolish none of the values that human experience has shown to be necessary. An account of poetry will be a pivotal point in such a psychology.' His attitude here seems to be one of willingness to leave professional psychology to make its contribution to the problem in its own way, whereas the tendency before was to short-circuit psychological methods by dogmatizing about the essentials of the conclusions they must reach. The change may perhaps be related to the fact that in *Practical Criticism* Richards has a much more demonstrable function that he had in the earlier work. For one thing he can offer work as a contribution to academic psychology: '...to find something to investigate that is accessible and detachable is one of the chief difficulties of psychology. I believe the chief merit of the experiment here made is that it gives us this' (*Practical Criticism*, p. 10). Further, he offers his work as a contribution to education, and is able to show that even by existing educational standards such work as he has done here has an important and undeniable function. 'This, then, may be made a positive recommendation, that an inquiry into language...be recognized as a vital branch of research, and treated no longer as the peculiar province of the whimsical amateur' (*Practical Criticism*, p. 337).

It is undoubtedly in dealing with problems of communication that Richards comes most closely to grips with his material and least shows the characteristics of the amateur. But to say this ought not to suggest that his work falls into two isolated compartments, one concerned with evaluation and the other with communication, and that they can be appraised separately. It is in fact through a consideration of his theory of value and its limitations that the importance of his work on communication can best be seen.

The conclusion that his account of value gives a basis for agreement only when 'normality' (or identical abnormality) is assumed, might seem to leave us no defence against an endless variety of critical opinions, each justified by an appeal to a fundamental constitutional peculiarity in the critic. Since innate differences do of course exist, we

must perhaps admit that in the end we shall have to recognize distinguish-
able 'types' of critical opinion founded on psycho-physiological
differences in the critics, and irreconcilable. But this is too remote a
consideration to give 'type' psychologists any excuse for extending
their literary labelling. It is still possible to show that differences of
opinion in literary matters frequently arise from errors of approach
which even those who make them can be brought to recognize. With
people who assert that they know what they like, the one hope is to
demonstrate to them that in point of fact they *don't*, that according to
standards they themselves recognize elsewhere their judgment here is
mistaken. As these inconsistencies are faced and abandoned, the
possibility of agreement with other people grows greater. We cannot
tell how far this principle may be pushed, but undoubtedly we have a
very long way to go before innate psycho-physiological differences
are the sole cause of disagreement between us. The most important part
of Richards's work consists in extending the possibility of agreement.
From one point of view it is work on problems of communication;
from another it offers us exercise in attaining self-consistency in
literary judgments, and remotely approaching the 'self-completion'
that Richards sees as the ultimate form of valuable experience.

In this part of his work there are so many distinct contributions—
close, fully illustrated discussions of actual instances—that little
general comment is in place. Many of them offer a starting point for
further investigation; sometimes there seems a possibility of fresh
preliminary discussion, where, as for instance in his treatment of
intellectual truth in poetry and of rhythm, Richards does not seem free
from ambiguities and shifts of ground; all draw attention to serious
possibilities of misreading and misjudging, and all go towards stress-
ing the same main theme, that the adequate reading of poetry is a
discipline and not a relaxation.

The relation between the two aspects of his work is well set out by
Richards himself. 'The whole apparatus of critical rules and principles
is a means to the attainment of finer, more precise, more discriminating
communication. There is, it is true, a valuation side to criticism. When
we have solved, completely, the communication problem, when we
have got, perfectly, the experience, *the mental condition* relevant to the
poem, we have still to judge it, still to decide upon its worth. But the
later question nearly always settles itself; or rather, our own inmost
nature and the nature of the world in which we live decide it for us.
Our prime endeavour must be to get the relevant mental condition and
then see what happens. If we cannot then decide whether it is good or
bad, it is doubtful whether any principles, however refined and subtle,
can help us much. Without the capacity to get the experience they

cannot help us at all. This is still clearer if we consider the use of critical maxims in teaching. Value cannot be demonstrated except through the communication of what is valuable.' The difficulty of demonstrating the rightness of an opinion even on these lines ought not to be underrated; over the Longfellow poem, for instance, it seems only to have been a drawn battle between Richards and the protocols. But a reliance on improved methods of reading as the most hopeful way of reaching agreement in literary judgments undoubtedly grows out of Richards's practice more naturally than does his explicit theory of value. The suspicion is left, however, that in making practical judgments he is assuming more principles of evaluation than one would expect from the passage just quoted. One weakness of Yeats's transcendental poetry, for instance, is a 'deliberate reversal of the natural relations of thought and feeling...' (*Science and Poetry*, p. 74). His charge against Lawrence is rather similar. But *natural relations...* Lawrence might have detected a principle of criticism here. The fact is that principles of evaluation remain a necessity for the practising critic even when interpretation and understanding have been carried to their hypothetical limit. How large is the highest common factor in human natures, and how far it can be formulated into agreed ethical principles, are questions that will not be answered in the near future. Yet guesses have to be made: 'To set up as a critic is to set up as a judge of values.' This is a fact that receives less prominence in Richards's later work than it did in his earlier, and it is not surprising to find Father D'Arcy reminding him (in *The Criterion*, January 1933) that we have to set out 'both to understand the meaning of others *and* the truth of what they say'.

The importance of Richards's work on communication is unfortunately obscured for many people by their annoyance at a too frequent outcropping of the amateur spirit. This shows itself particularly as a romantic inflation of the significance of the topic, in the form of dark hints at the extent of our ignorance and the cataclysm that awaits us as the Theory of Interpretation is pushed further. Exploitation of the Tremendous Idea makes a peculiarly strong appeal to one side of the amateur: for one thing, every professional immediately has the ground cut from under his feet. No matter what a man's standing, and no matter how impressive the substance of his views, you can still regard him from an unassailable vantage-ground if only you happen to observe that he isn't capable of understanding what's said to him. This, according to Richards (in *The Criterion*, October 1932) is the weak place in the armour of Max Eastman, T. S. Eliot, and Irving Babbitt. They are all 'untrained in the technique of interpretation...this is not their fault since the proper training has not yet been provided...you must *understand* before you argue . . . When the right training has been provided, our three champions here will be seen to be each journeying through and battling with his own set of mirages.' So much for Irving Babbitt, T. S. Eliot, and Max Eastman. The earlier work, too, occasionally betrays this anxiety to cut the ground from under the feet of those who might otherwise seem qualified to express an opinion: 'Neither the professional psychologist whose interest in poetry is frequently not intense, nor the man of letters, who as a rule has no adequate ideas of the mind as a whole, has been equipped for the investigation [into the nature of poetry]. Both a passionate knowledge of poetry and a capacity for dispassionate psychological analysis are required if it is to be satisfactorily prosecuted.

It will be best to begin by . . .' (*Science and Poetry*, p. 9). It is probably, too, as an aspect of the amateur that we must interpret the curiously romantic tone that sometimes appears in Richards's writing. *Science and Poetry*, for example, leaves a strong impression of a thrilled responsiveness to the difficulties and hazards of 'the contemporary situation', and also of some failure to get at grips with any definite problems that concern people. The latter is a serious failing here, for it prevents him from clinching his argument that poetry is of supreme value as a means of re-orientation. The nearest he comes to specifying more closely 'the contemporary situation' of which one may be 'agonizingly aware' is in his discussion of the neutrality of nature and the impossibility of beliefs. But the former is surely not a concern of fundamental importance to most informed people nowadays, though in some moods they may feel chilled by it. And the impossibility of beliefs—except in some quite limited sense—seems itself to be impossible. Certainly T. S. Eliot has repudiated Richards's suggestion that *The Waste Land* is without beliefs; but apart from this repudiation it is impossible to see how any living activity can go on without beliefs in some sense, and we must suppose that Richards is speaking only of a special sort of belief. Indeed he seems only to mean that most people have ceased to believe in the possibility of supernatural sanctions or aids. If this is all, the excitement apparent in his tone seems naïve. 'It is very probable that the Hindenburg line to which the defence of our traditions retired as a result of the onslaughts of the last century will be blown up in the near future. If this should happen a mental chaos such as man has never experienced may be expected' (*Science and Poetry*, p. 82). 'Consider the probable effects upon love poetry in the near future of the kind of inquiry into basic human constitution exemplified by psycho-analysis.' These are very bourgeois bogies. Their worst feature is the way they play into the hands of the would-be emancipated, those whom L. H. Myers has described in *Prince Jali*: 'They depended basically upon a solid, shockable world of decorum and common sense. They had to believe that a great ox-like eye was fixed upon them in horror.'

These defects of tone in Richards's writing cannot be passed over. In the first place they tend to attract the least desirable kind of audience, though the astringency and discipline of Richards's best work should be a sufficient safeguard against this. A more serious consideration is that they offer a needless obstacle to an appreciation by better readers of Richards' real significance. To sum up this significance one may indicate the two points of view from which Richards sees poetry: he sees it both as the practised reader who has acquired his standards of culture imperceptibly, and as the plain man of common sense and faith in science who needs *convincing*, without a gradual process of education, that poetry might be of some importance to him. A large part of Richards's work can be regarded as an attempt to find common ground for these two points of view; to find a set of standards recognized by the second man which will lead logically to the position of the first. He sets to work in two ways: first by an explicit theory of value, second by showing up the kind of mistakes that are likely to lead to an underestimation of poetry. The second method really consists in making explicit, and at the same time telescoping, the steps which those who adequately value poetry must at some time have taken, normally without having analysed them. This second method is obviously of enormous value to people already prepared to take poetry seriously; it may well divert university students, for instance, from their otherwise almost inevitable progress towards the point from which they regard 'the time when they read poetry' with slightly more wistful feelings than they have for 'the time when they played Red Indians'. But whether Richards's methods would be effective in convincing the intelligent and friendly Philistine is another matter. It may be that his work fulfils its purpose by giving those who already value poetry a new assurance that their concern for it is a development, and not a distortion, of 'ordinary practical living'. If this is one of its functions it bears witness to the growing need of those with minority views to justify themselves at the bar of the main community. The main community may not be convinced; perhaps the fundamental need is that the minority should be.

F. R. LEAVIS (1933)

The Christian Renaissance, by G. Wilson Knight (Macmillan)

As reviewer of *The Christian Renaissance* I am disqualified, if what Professor Knight says of a part applies to the whole and the book does not 'aim to convince the unsympathetic'. I confess to have approached with strong prejudices against the whole undertaking; and my prejudices were confirmed by the assemblage of influences acknowledged in the Preface: Mr T. S. Eliot, Mr Aldous Huxley, Mr Middleton Murry, M. Henri Bergson, Mr G. K. Chesterton, William James, Mr Max Plowman, Canon Streeter, Oscar Wilde and others. Mr Eliot, I imagine, wonders how he got into this company. I am further disqualified by being no theologian, though a theological equipment is clearly indispensable if Professor Knight's enterprise is to be properly judged. On the other hand, I think it likely that a trained theologian would be no more sympathetic than myself, and unlikely that he would have the competence in literary criticism that is in any case also necessary.

So, pretending only to this last, and writing from the point of view of one who is grateful to Professor Knight for his services to literary criticism, I ask: How can so much original talent, energy and rare disinterestedness be prevented from spending themselves—as more and more since *The Wheel of Fire* they seem to me to have been doing—to no commensurate end? And I find the answer in a dictum of Professor Knight's own: 'To the true adept and initiate, nothing about poetry will appear more important than poetry itself.' He has spent a large part of his book endeavouring to forestall the criticisms that his method of interpretation might seem to invite, but he never squarely faces the important one: that is, that he has preposterously underrated the difficulty of relevance; indeed, that relevance might be—and, in such an enterprise as his, must be—a matter of difficult achievement never seems to have occurred to him. 'Therefore the poet's sources or supposed intentions must never be allowed to interrupt or modify our interpretations'—this is a characteristic defence, but it does not meet the charge, which is, to adapt to him one that he himself brings, that what he 'will not do is to face the literary product'. So when he complains that 'we go on refusing to face the creative visions of poetry', we reply that it is a question, rather, of asking who, in this kind of interpretation, the predominating poet is—the original, or the interpreter?

He explicitly exempts himself from critical discipline, the plea being that to analyse and check scrupulously would baulk and hamper the swift play of intuition, the immediate sensitive response, on which the virtue of his work depends. And one must admit that, in *The Wheel of Fire*, all qualifications being made, he is justified. But the plea is a dangerous one. Shakespeare's text he knows intimately, and it is a text potent enough to keep the interpreter's 'romantic consciousness' under some control. But with other texts he pays little heed to the 'poetry itself': it becomes quickly plain that the 'creative vision' we are most concerned with is rarely to be that of the poet specified.

It is significant that he should not question his ability to approach Dante and Goethe on the same easy terms as Shakespeare. Something of them, of course, will get through in translation, but Professor Knight shows not the least sign of uneasiness at having to rely on Cary's *Divine Comedy* and Professor Latham's *Faust*. In the poetry of his own language his procedure is truly shocking: any text will do so long as it yields a congenial or convenient explicit 'content'; 'exactly the same experience', he will say, quoting from *Paradise Lost*, 'is being transmitted', when the passage he quotes (p. 132) proves, to anyone concerned with *poetry*, that Milton was incapable of the kind of experience in question. Worse than that, he seems to rely entirely on the conventional valuations, and will cap Dante and Shakespeare not merely with Shelley, but with the Browning of *Abt Vogler* and the Tennyson of *In Memoriam*—worse, he actually quotes for the sake of the 'content' some stanzas from the disastrously bad part of *The Palace of Art*.

He seems, in fact, completely indifferent about quality—realized value: the general paraphrasable meaning, if it fits the argument, is good enough. On page 40 we read, incredulously, ' . . . Kent in *Lear*, Horatio in *Hamlet*, Osborne in *Journey's End*'. On page 115 he speaks of 'Webster, who reached a poetic intensity and sombre magic comparable with Shakespeare's'. On page 116 we find: 'The Augustan period is, as a whole, clearly less intense, the imagination here is more relaxed: and its finest works in Dryden, Pope, or Swift tend toward satire, *a mode which* [my italics] . . . But when intensity returns, we have Gray meditating on a Country Graveyard . . . ' Wordsworth's Immortality Ode is repeatedly appealed to, though the factitiousness betrayed in the style disqualifies the document as evidence.

I do not adduce all this for fun, but in shocked exasperation, for even in this book Professor Knight shows that he is potentially a fine critic of the kind that all along he has refused to be. Refused? I venture to ask him if it has ever occurred to him that there is not a paragraph of criticism in all the six volumes of Dr Elton's *Survey of English Literature*. And myself I remind that the age of Professor Whitehead, Canon Streeter and Mr Middleton Murry is an age unfavourable to the development of critics, as it is of poets. *The Christian Renaissance* is neither criticism nor poetry—Professor Knight, I suspect, will say it is some third thing, combining them, perhaps, and I can only reply that it has the disadvantages of abstract writing without the virtues. One cannot miss the genuine excitement that thrills in it, but, however intensely Professor Knight may feel, there is little that is intense in the book. One guesses that in another age he might have been a poet; but to be a poet he would have to make himself more of a critic. In his

Preface he invokes Mr T. S. Eliot: let him read the essay in *The Sacred Wood* on Mr Arthur Symons.

Yet there is something admirable about the very extravagance of Professor Knight's ambition. One cannot imagine Mr Symons proposing to regard 'the whole New Testament as a single art-form of Shakespearian quality' or prophesying the 'advent of a newly Christianized literature and a newly poetic Christianity'. The courage and the energy are magnificent: is refusal of discipline their essential condition?

HARDY AND CRITICISM

Q. D. LEAVIS (1943)

Thomas Hardy (English Men of Letters), by Edmund Blunden (Macmillan)
Hardy the Novelist, by Lord David Cecil (Constable)
The Southern Review, Thomas Hardy Centennial Issue, Summer 1940

'No, I think I shall do much better to be allusive and charming and rather subtle, you know the sort of thing, and tender. I think one ought to *see* a book before one starts it. Well, I see this rather like a portrait by Van Dyck, with a good deal of atmosphere, you know, and a certain gravity, and with a sort of aristocratic distinction. Do you know what I mean? About eighty thousand words.'

He was absorbed for a moment in the ecstasy of aesthetic contemplation. In his mind's eye he saw a book, in royal octavo, slim and light in the hand, printed with large margins on handsome paper in a type that was both clear and comely, and I think he saw a binding in smooth black cloth with a decoration in gold and gilt lettering.

So the man of letters in Mr Somerset Maugham's little masterpiece, *Cakes and Ale*, explains his intention of writing a critical biography of that novelist whose works so curiously resemble those of Thomas Hardy. And now (though of course you can't have large margins in war-time) the thing has been done, or at least one cannot avoid the suspicion that when Lord David Cecil was invited to give the Clark Lectures at Cambridge he started with very nearly that intention. No one can suppose he was impelled by a sense of urgent critical work to be done. Take a fair specimen:

Hardy's books do not always end thus on a crashing major chord. He is also master of the dying fall, the Miltonic close in calm of mind, all passion spent, the fading echoing music that, when soft voices die, vibrates in the memory. *Under the Greenwood Tree* presents us with an example.

This is the kind of prose in which much of *Hardy the Novelist* is written. I should have thought that to anyone it was obviously a style in which literary criticism cannot be conveyed; it is certainly a style which undergraduates are discouraged from using in their first term at the university to which these lectures were addressed. Yet the publisher informs us that 'the aim of this book is—while taking advantage of the greater extent of modern knowledge—to return to the true critical path'. And besides its sub-title, 'An Essay in Criticism', there is an opening section explaining how all criticism is wrong which is not purely aesthetic. It is solely the critic's function, we are told, 'to illuminate our appreciation of them [books], to define the nature of the satisfaction they give, to analyse the circumstances conditioning their production and the arts by which they make their impression'. Lord David makes it clear that he intends this to be understood in the narrowest sense.

Those interested in the criticism of novels—or perhaps in this connection one should say of The Novel, for to the aesthete the Novel, the Epic, the Lyric, are profitable abstractions—will recollect that the doyen of this school of novel-critics was Mr Percy Lubbock with his *Craft of Fiction*. I must say that I have never been able to see that the *Craft of Fiction* approach to novels ever justifies itself, and it seems a criticism of this method that it produces in all the instances I have seen only a succession of commonplace observations put across in fine writing at tiresome length, and that when the aesthetic critic tries to go further he dries up in a desert of meaningless phrases such as shallow modelling, narrative and visual art, and unreal distinctions between form and content, and even sets up such concepts as the Comic Spirit and Tragic Feeling to be permanent stumbling-blocks in the way of the young. It is not thus that criticism can come to grips with a work of art. In fact, the conclusions, that the approach Lord David favours provides, seem to have little connection with the experience of the sensitive reader—e.g. he says '*Under the Greenwood Tree* is one of Hardy's most faultless works', whereas the facetious tone of the book and its being made entirely out of Hardy's comic-relief material without anything to be relieved, anything (that is) which comes from the deeper and more vital sources of his experiences and interests, must strike any critical reader, I should have thought, and mark it as the novel in the canon (excluding the hopeless failures such as *The Well-Beloved*) least likely ever to be noted for re-reading. Again, 'No one describes love more impressively than Hardy...' I should have thought no one did less so in his novels, for it is a mere counter and convention in all Hardy's, being one of three stock varieties—either the grand-passion convention, or the faithful love of the worthy man or woman, or the philandering motions executed by the other sort. No, to be a critic it is necessary to bring more pressure to bear on the undertaking than the aesthete can; he is a lazy fellow: without bothering to verify he slaps down his first impressions, and doesn't notice whether he is expressing conventional judgments or contradictions or other people's ideas misunderstood, or what mess of clichés, fine writing and empty phrases he is making on the paper. In so far as the method may have an incidental usefulness when properly practised, it is felt to be impertinent, for what can it do at best but point to the mechanism of a novel?—the part played by the characters in forwarding the plot and the part played by the plot in shaping the work of art, where is the author's viewpoint and mouthpiece, which parts of the narrative are dramatic or descriptive and why, and similar pieces of elementary surface observation, the kind of thing any intelligent reader can and should do for himself at second reading if he hasn't mechanically done so during the first. If he cannot do it for himself he cannot be said to read at all. I don't see how Lord David can think he has fulfilled a mission by telling a university audience:

The creative gift, the power to apprehend his material aesthetically, he possessed in the highest degree; but, for complete success a writer cannot rely on the aesthetic qualities alone. He must know how to present his imaginative conceptions to best advantage. Hardy was a great artist, but not a great craftsman.

I must repeat—Hardy's novels are visual novels. It is in his ability to make us 'see' that his greatest strength lies... Hardy's creative power also shows itself in his characters...

Lord David in short violates the first law of literary criticism, whether aesthetic or otherwise, which is, when you have nothing to say, don't say it.

As a revelation of the pretensions of the lecturer I should like to make one more quotation:

Indeed, it is the inevitable defect of a spontaneous genius like Hardy's that it is impervious to education. No amount of painstaking study got him within sight of achieving that intuitive good taste, that instinctive grasp of the laws of literature, which is the native heritage of one bred from childhood in the atmosphere of a high culture.

Hardy, we may justly reply, had a good Victorian education, was further equipped in the special arts and crafts of music and architecture, was generally well read and thoroughly understood what he read, as his notebooks show, had a remarkably acute grasp of literary theory and a most intelligent response to its practice;[1] that if his style was often

[1] E.g. in 1883 he remarked of Mark Twain. 'Why don't people understand that Mark Twain is not merely a great humourist? He's a very remarkable fellow in

bad in the sense of being gauche, pedantic and so on, it was at least his own style and succeeded in expressing something real and personal; and that he had a heritage more valuable than that of 'one bred from childhood in the atmosphere of a high culture' (whatever that may be, for the implication that Hardy's cultural *milieu* was a low one is preposterous).

I am not carping because I disagree with Lord David's valuation of Hardy the novelist, in fact it would be hard to do so because his book leaks all kinds of opinions and ideas that have been current about Hardy and his novels, without any attempt to distinguish critically or to formulate them incisively, so that anyone else may. I am registering a protest against his critical theory and practice. When Mr Somerset Maugham (to whom we may turn to take the taste of elegant aestheticism out of our mouths) writes of his fictitious novelist:

He was for long thought to write very bad English, and indeed he gave you the impression of writing with the stub of a blunt pencil; his style was laboured, an uneasy mixture of the classical and the slangy, and his dialogue was such as could never have issued from the mouth of a human being... His prime belonged to a period when the purple patch was in vogue, and there are descriptive passages in his works that have found their way into all the anthologies of English prose... It should be a mortification to me that I cannot read them without discomfort... My own heart sank when he led me into the forecastle of a ship or the taproom of a public-house, and I knew I was in for half-a-dozen pages of facetious comment on life, ethics, and immortality. But, I admit, I have always thought the Shakespearean clowns tedious, and their innumerable progeny insupportable... His women hardly come to life. But here again I must add that this is only my own opinion; the world at large and the most eminent critics have agreed that they are very winsome types of English womanhood, spirited, gallant, high-souled, and they have been often compared with the heroines of Shakespeare. We know of course that women are habitually constipated, but to represent them in fiction as being altogether devoid of a back passage seems to me really an excess of chivalry. I am surprised that they should care to see themselves thus limned' [*Cakes and Ale*].

—then, though as it stands it is not literary criticism (neither is Lord David's[1]), yet it presents incisively a critical attitude, and a response to certain elements in the work that cannot be ignored by the critic, and

a very different way'; and specified *Life on the Mississippi*. His notebooks, quoted by Florence Hardy in the two volumes of her husband's life, show a constant preoccupation with the theory and practice of novel-writing, and a very critical response to reviews of his works.

[1] I should perhaps in fairness add that *The Times Literary Supplement*, however, describes *Hardy the Novelist* as 'criticism of the first rank', 'a wise and gracious book'.

is therefore useful, as good sense and first-hand judgment always are. When one of the contributors to the Hardy Centennial number of the *Southern Review* writes:

Only the disenchanted sophomore can be deeply impressed by Hardy's view of life. Although it was an outcome of the new scientific views, it now seems like a simple variant of supernaturalism...And although Hardy properly objected to treating his fiction as a 'scientific system of philosophy', the trouble is that he often wrote as if it were. The scheme of his novels is typically all too rigid and diagrammatic, their argument all too formal and explicit...The serious objection, at any rate, is not to his philosophy *per se*, the dismal generalizations he illogically induces from the extraordinary actions he invents. It is to his artistry, the inventions themselves.

—then one sees that critical argument is being advanced by someone with a central grasp of the subject. In this case, the critic (Herbert J. Muller, 'The Novels of Hardy Today') is actually citing the serious faults of his subject before disposing of these objections by advancing his own account of the greatness of Hardy the novelist. I mention this in order to make it clear that I do not object to some people's criticism of Hardy because I disagree with their verdict, like the supervisor who failed a paper I once produced on Shelley because she admired that poet so fervently that no adverse criticism of *Prometheus Unbound*, however plausibly argued and substantially supported, could be allowed merit. I am merely expressing a preference for criticism that comes from some kind of a mind, instead of no kind.

Hardy criticism has even in our time passed through several phases. To his contemporaries, as Mr Edmund Blunden abundantly demonstrates in his volume on Hardy in the English Men of Letters series, he was just another Victorian novelist. They were not deep enough in the machine age to ecstasize over the glimpses of pastoral England his novels afford, and they had enough good models current in fiction to recognize how awkward his style was, how limited his conception of characterization, and (when they were not, as with the last novels, provoked by his moral unconventionality) the imperfect relation between the moral feeling and the fable he found for embodying it. One can sympathize with the Saturday Reviewer who complained of *Tess* that 'few people would deny the terrible dreariness of this tale, which, except during a few hours spent with the cows, has not a gleam of sunshine anywhere'. One sees what he meant about the gratuitous nature of the tragic action, and is grateful for the degrading of the dairy-idyll passages to 'a few hours spent among the cows', when so much since has been written rapturously about the novel largely on the strength of those descriptions.

The next phase, recognizing Hardy both as a beautiful writer of descriptive passages about rural England and as a creator of Sophoclean tragedy, came about, I suppose, when the knowledge of writers like George Eliot and Richard Jefferies faded. With Meredith, the then current comparison, he could of course only be compared to his advantage in every respect. In *Thomas Hardy: A Critical Study* by Lascelles Abercrombie (1912) this very solemn acceptance of Hardy's novels is well expressed. If you want an analytic account of Hardy's novels in such terms, this remains the best work of the kind, unencumbered by other material (if you ignore the account of the poems and *The Dynasts*). Lionel Johnson's six essays, *The Art of Thomas Hardy* (1892), are in the same direction, but too pervaded by Lionel Johnson.

It was Hardy himself who claimed for his novels an Aeschylean intention and a Sophoclean unity and grandeur. But even examination papers have ceased on the whole to demand comparisons between *Tess* (and the other 'great' tragic novels) and Greek Tragedy. A more sober rate of admiration has been given to the Hardy novels since, for there have been exasperated debunking efforts by unsympathetic writers with quite other kinds of demands from fiction (such as Mr Somerset Maugham), and the growing acceptance of the greater art of Conrad and Henry James, who unlike Hardy are in no respect shown up by time as old-fashioned, has probably helped to put the Hardy novels in juster perspective.[1] It would be well if it were recognized that the novelist who can be most profitably employed for 'placing' Hardy is George Eliot, from whom he derives (Lord David couples him with Scott and the academic world with Meredith); a useful critical exercise is to recommend for reading *Silas Marner* after *Under the Greenwood Tree*.

George Eliot in her novels and stories (except *Romola*) shows a corresponding seriousness of outlook and purpose embodied in similar fictional forms, but, it seems to me, she excels Hardy in every respect. She is the finer artist with wider capacities, the sounder thinker in her account of the relation of man to environment, people to the community and personalities to each other, the wiser moralist, the more efficient writer, and gives us a more interesting and sensitive apprehension of character. She is equally sincere without being so simple. She has a vein of wit whereas he has only rustic humour, and her irony is real where his is merely the tragic brand. And though she, too, is saddened she is not morbid. But Hardy's superior appeal has lain in something like morbidity combined with the overpoweringly dramatic impression left by his conceptions. It is a fact that his novels have for at least a

[1] One contributor to the *Southern Review* remarks that he wouldn't have known Hardy to be a great novelist if he hadn't been told.

generation provided something that no other body of work could or at any rate did. In spite of the critic whom I have quoted as saying that 'only the disenchanted sophomore can be deeply impressed by Hardy's view of life', there is always a generation of such readers, and few people can re-examine dispassionately writings which have impressed them deeply at so critical a stage in their emotional development. Mr E. L. Woodward the Oxford historian in his most interesting autobiography *Short Journey* (Faber, 1942) is representative when he writes: 'During my last year at school and my first two years at Oxford, the poems and novels of Thomas Hardy influenced my mind far more than the work of any other English writer...The book (*Tess*) moved me so deeply that I could not read more than a chapter at a time...So I read on until I had come to the end of everything which Hardy had published. I have read these novels and poems over and over again. They are part of my life.' Whether some other novelist will ever replace Hardy for this purpose is a matter for speculation. But we need not speculate on the ultimate effect of reading Hardy at any phase of development. We can only be grateful for having a body of fiction that proceeds from so honest, worthy and compassionate a nature, so sensitive to human misery and so powerful to record its distresses at the spectacle of suffering, so disinterested, unworldly and unfailingly tender.

Mr Edmund Blunden's biography is an index of current judgment. He is extremely cautious of making high claims, confines himself in the critical field to countering adverse criticism of the less radical kind, and gives a surprising proportion of his book to extracts from the contemporary reviews. While conveying the peculiarities of Hardy's character as it appeared in old age, with some interesting reminiscences by men of letters of the impression his personality made on them, he does not give us the essential anecdotes and reminiscences about Hardy's youth which provide a clue in his morbid sensitiveness to suffering or even the appearance of it in nature (such as his weeping at seeing the leaves fall). Perhaps he wished to avoid overlapping with Mrs Hardy's *Early Life* and *Later Life of Thomas Hardy*, which remain indispensable although written in the most unfortunate style of standard biography. Nobody tells us the facts, which are only vaguely known, about his emotional history and its reactions on his writings—for instance, the estrangement from his first wife which produced the attacks on marriage and the marriage laws in his writings at that time (*Jude, The Woodlanders*). The really useful critical biography of Hardy has not yet been written. But in a quiet way, and leaving the reader to read between the lines, Mr Blunden has gone some way towards producing it.

As a start there are some stimulating and constructive essays in Hardy criticism in the Hardy centenary issue of an American periodical

I have referred to, nearly all by Americans. Some of the contributions are, inevitably, academic in the derogatory sense, but, to point out the live wood, I should like to specify Mr Zabel's 'Hardy in Defense of his Art: The Aesthetic of Incongruity' (perhaps I am biased by his specifying the *Scrutiny* evaluation of Hardy in June 1934 as still one of the best essays written on the novels); the valuable analysis of '*Jude the Obscure* as a Tragedy' by Arthur Mizener—such a really fundamental analysis of one novel done with intelligence and critical method, and by someone in possession of a great deal of parallel information about Hardy's mentality and outlook, is more illuminating than a library of 'aesthetic' flounderings; and the final essay on 'The Novels of Hardy Today' by Herbert J. Muller. These really are essays in criticism which it would be enlightening instead of insulting to present to a university audience. One is glad, too, to have a spirited, able and critically demolishing essay by the distinguished short-story writer Miss Katherine Anne Porter, 'Notes on a Criticism of Thomas Hardy', in reply to the outrageous account of Hardy's work in *After Strange Gods*. One understands why Henry James in a letter about *Tess* permits himself to refer to Hardy the novelist as 'the good little Thomas Hardy'—he was in a position to employ the patronising 'little', though we aren't, and the attribution of innocence and moral worth in the combined adjectives is just right in contrast to Mr Eliot's criticism of the novelist, which could hardly be more wrong in tone, intention and expression. There are also a number of essays on Hardy's poems in the memorial number of this periodical, but I have been concerned here with the criticism of Hardy's fiction. What really warms one's heart is the complete absence of the belletristic approach or of any aesthetic posturing in this collective enterprise. Could one believe that any similar undertaking on this side of the Atlantic, even before the War, would have been so profitable or even harmless? It is certainly the most helpful critical work on Hardy I know, and since the best essays in it are by tough-minded critics with a corresponding tightness of argument and idiom, who raise many debatable critical problems, it could be recommended for teething purposes at the university. Unfortunately the *Southern Review* has become a war fatality, and back numbers are probably unobtainable.

EDMUND WILSON OF 'THE NEW YORKER'

JOHN FARRELLY (1951)

Classics and Commercials, by Edmund Wilson (W. H. Allen)

Several years ago the critical reputation of Mr Edmund Wilson in America was consigned to history by Mr Stanley Edgar Hyman. Mr Hyman acted in his capacity of Inquisitor for an emergent literary-critical dogma with pretensions to an inclusive science. This dogma was largely formulated by academics and loosely called 'new', although the 'new' orthodoxy now possessed a history, a hagiology, and a 'Summa' in Mr Hyman's book, *The Armed Vision*. In this book his account of the qualifications of the ideal technician read like a description of Mr Kenneth Burke. An 'amateur' like Edmund Wilson patently belonged to the old dispensation. Ironically, he had given some credence to Mr Hyman's performance by anticipating these obsequies with his own obituary on the occasion of 'being bibliographed' by the library of his old university, Princeton, in 1943.

At this time, Mr Wilson reviewed his undergraduate life at Princeton, his formative influences as a writer, his mission as critic, his career, his milieu. He includes these remarks in the present volume and they seem to me (in ways it is beyond my purpose to detail here) a remarkably compressed and revealing document. He was at the university just before the first World War. For anyone concerned with literature these were lively and exciting years in America, years to which Mr Wilson nostalgically hearkens. Ezra Pound, that archetypal Yankee, had already escaped to England where he was making his high intransigent claims for the Artist, but he was shouting back exhortation and encouragement across the water. At home, the magazine *Poetry* was a revolutionary paper; James Huneker was instructing the provincial Philistine in what he had missed of European music and literature of the past fifty years; Mencken was shocking the 'Booboisie' into an elementary awareness of other than purely mercantile values. And the young Edmund Wilson was editing the 'Lit' (a college paper) and aspiring to the vocation of 'writer'. 'You read Shakespeare, Shelley, George Meredith, Dostoevsky, Ibsen, and you wanted, however imperfectly and on however infinitesimal a scale, to learn their trade and have the freedom of their company.' To the young Wilson, after the war and after Huneker and Mencken, there were 'two roads still to be broken' in pushing forward the 'Enlightenment': 'the road to the understanding of the most recent literary events in the larger international world—Joyce, Eliot, Proust, etc.—which were already out of the range of readers the limits of whose taste had been fixed by *Egoists* and *The Quintessence of Ibsenism*; and to bring home to the "bourgeois" intellectual world the most recent developments of Marxism in connection with the Russian Revolution'. However grandiose (or general) a description, the first was the concern which was to occupy Wilson, as popularizer and publicist, during the most fruitful period of his life, a period of real distinction in its way. By the time he came to review his career (still a comparatively young man) the atmosphere had changed, an age had ended. The ideals had either been discredited (Marxism) or achieved (in established reputations). Or such is Wilson's view of it (and it is indicative of his idea of the critic-champion), for the 'blood-heating crises that have been recurring periodically in literature since the first night of *Hernani* in 1830: howls of denunciation, defiant applause and defence, final vindication in triumph' seemed unlikely to recur for Edmund Wilson. *Finnegans Wake*, which he feels should have been an occasion 'for young men to wear the red vest of Gautier . . . was received with incurious calm . . . [The book] went straight from the hands of Joyce into the hands of the college professors, and is to-day not a literary issue but a subject of academic research'. 'And what', asked Mr Wilson, in closing this review of his life and times, 'is the next logical step?'

The 'next' step (if it was 'logical' it must have been the logic of an ironic historic instinct) for the 'old-red-waistcoat-wearer', the Communist, the publicist of the avant-garde, was to join the *New Yorker* as a staff reviewer—the *New Yorker*, that 'humorous' magazine that teaches the frazzled denizens of Megalopolis and its garden suburbs to discount themselves as a bitter-sweet joke.

Classics and Commercials is largely made up of the reviews Mr Wilson has written for that magazine during the past eight years and they aren't likely to persuade the reader that he has enjoyed his work. He appears to have succumbed to a virulent and communicable boredom. It is true that the limitations of space might explain the often cursory and superficial account of his subject, and the exigencies of regular reviewing excuse the fatigue. But an uncomfortable restriction is revealed in Mr Wilson's relation to his average reader. For this person, 'Enlightenment' has *occurred*. He is not the illiterate Mencken was cajoling or insulting: he is *semi*-literate. He has probably been to 'college' where a smattering of 'culture' was part of the routine. He may well have paid his tribute to literature in an undergraduate enthusiasm. In effect he is case-hardened; he is not susceptible. But he is substantially the type in whose image the *New Yorker* was founded and on whose patronage it depends. He is to be amused above all, confirmed in his complacency incidentally, and titillated (not aroused) by the well-insulated jibes at his expense.

Mr Wilson can make do most of the time by relying on his skill as a summarizer for a synopsis of a book, or he can exploit his ingenuity as a literary 'private eye' to dig up biographical gossip, or he can supply his readers with 'instruction' in the form of 'background' notes from the literary text-books. More rarely, he finds occasion for a completely deflating attack on Somerset Maugham or a sensible and persuasive corrective to the cult of Kafka. But should the advocate of serious writing be tempted to break new roads, the timidity of the proffered simplification is nothing less than astonishing. *Finnegans Wake*, as has been suggested, is one of his pet cults, but it is a cult to which he offers the barest initiation, and that usually in the nature of encomiums for the book ('one of the top works of literature of our times'; 'one of the few great intellectual and aesthetic treats'; 'it is an exciting, a unique experience to find pages that have seemed to us meaningless start into vivid life, full of energy, brilliance, passion'). But granting Mr Wilson's genuine (if uncommunicated) enthusiasm, of what persuasive force is such a compromise as this, dangled, perhaps, before the addicts of detective fiction and crossword puzzles? 'For people who do like to solve puzzles, the puzzles are fun to solve. To-day, when we are getting so many books in which the style is perfectly clear but the meaning non-existent or equivocal, it affords a certain satisfaction to read something that looks like nonsense on the surface but underneath makes perfect sense.' Invest the price of the book, is Mr Wilson's tip to the customers: 'If you have not tried *Finnegans Wake*, you cannot do better than get it and get the Campbell-Robinson key [constructed by a "folklore scholar" and an editor of *Reader's Digest*] and prepare to have them around for years.' Mr Wilson is too perspicacious for that! Surely he recognizes the original of that appeal to the customers—it is the appeal of the Book Clubs which press on subscribers, as 'bonuses', such ornaments to the 'library' as a 'de luxe' edition of Proust or a volume of the now modish Dr Schweitzer.

This, one might claim with sympathy, is Edmund Wilson of the *New Yorker* making his wry best of a distasteful situation. But there are other persistent notes in these reviews disturbing to anyone inclined to respect the writer's more substantial work. They hint that Mr Wilson's attitude to literature may not be incompatible, after all, with the apathy of his *New Yorker* public, for they remind us that a man may be busy about books without a lively concern for, or appreciation of, the writing itself. 'Style' is a key word in Mr Wilson's critical vocabulary, and one comes to suspect that it means to him much the same thing as to the young aspirant to fine writing on the 'Lit', or, for that matter, to that young man's 'English' instructor. (There is Mr Wilson's habit of going through his subject's 'compositions' with a blue pencil, alert for cliché and grammatical errors.) 'Style' in this sense may be a mere correctness, or a decorative excrescence, or an engaging idiosyncrasy—in almost every case something detachable from the matter to hand and to be savoured for itself. In Samuel Johnson's style he relishes 'the phrases, the sentences, the paragraphs, that one can feel between one's teeth'. Well, pass that, but when we come to Mr Cyril Connolly (that 'personality of some courage and distinction' who may 'turn out to stick' as a classic of the language) we stop short. When Mr Wilson describes Mr Connolly's writing as 'delicious and crisp, like good food to the taste, fresh and bright, like new sights to the eye', we suspect that his is going for his sensations rather beyond anything the writer could pretend to offer. Max Beerbohm is another candidate for classic status, and Ronald Firbank, too, is 'likely to become a classic'. In the latter's style our attention is called (and alerted, one might add,) to 'the tension behind it of the effort to find the felicitous or the witty phrase which will render the essence of something'. Yes, but of what? He evidences Firbank's 'artistic seriousness', which is true enough as far as it goes, but it is characteristic of Mr Wilson's somewhat ingenuous respect for the artist's calling that the 'dedication' (for 'Art was his only sainthood') assures a rewarding 'seriousness' for the reader. What it comes to is that Mr Wilson's fortuitous notion of 'style' often bewitches him and traps him in disproportionate evaluation of writers who are only curious or frivolous, at best, and at worst vapid.

But then it occurs to one that evaluation of a given writer is not Mr Wilson's concern as a critic. His interest is usually peripheral to the work at hand, and his instinct for 'obsessions which recur in [a writer's] work and to which we can find the key in his life'. It is true that Mr Wilson has made some of his most ingenious discoveries turning over stones in the literary graveyard. But some questions on this kind of activity are provoked by his comments on a not dissimilar writer, Van Wyck Brooks. He is talking of Brooks's attempt (in *The World of Washington Irving*) to convey Fenimore Cooper's quality through his own incantatory paraphrase of the novelist's prose: 'The creation is not Cooper's but Brooks's; he has sifted out the images from [one of Cooper's stories] and made out of them something quite new...With anybody like Cooper Mr Brooks has a field almost like that of the artist who deals directly with crude experience. And how many inferior or tedious writers he must have transmuted in this book...We are amazed at the skill with which Brooks has been turning the old carriage springs, spectacle frames and pickaxes of 1800–1840 into a fine-beaten kind of white gold.' The point being that Mr Wilson instances this kind of criticism with applause, and if Brooks's performance isn't criticism (of a kind), what is it? But no; Brooks is not a critic, we are told; he is a cultural historian. 'The paradox of Brooks's career is that he has himself been able to develop into one of the first-rate American writers of his time without achieving any commensurate development of his appreciation of other writers save as material for cultural history.' It is behind that word 'paradox' that Mr Wilson escapes what is a real contradiction: how can a man write 'cultural history' without the discernment to appreciate the writers who so largely record and make accessible to a people its culture? And what are we to make of one who finds such a defective critic (for, I repeat, if Brooks is not a critic he's nothing worth the effort of naming) a 'first-rate' writer?

These questions seeem to me all the more pertinent because if Brooks the cultural historian is also, willy-nilly, a critic, Wilson the critic is also, in his most valuable work and with his tangential interest in literature, something we may call for lack of another term a 'cultural historian', and it is interesting to have Mr Wilson's views on the qualifications for such work. But besides critical insight and discrimination these qualifications, it seems to me, should include at the very least a disinterested comprehension of a people's sentiments and beliefs. And if this is so, Mr Wilson is occasionally handicapped by what can be most suggestively termed his cranks. His anglophobia is an instance. Another is implied in his naïve and invidious reference to 'the obedient Catholic [who] swallows the priest's doctine'. But these cranks can be more serious, and then 'handicapped' is scarcely the description of Mr Wilson's limitations: *disqualified*, rather. In a note, printed in this volume, on Mr Evelyn Waugh's *The Loved One*, Mr Wilson has this to say on the author's satire of 'those de luxe California cemeteries that attempt to render death less unpleasant by exploiting all the resources of landscape-gardening and Hollywood mummery. To the non-religious reader...the patrons and proprietors of Whispering Glades [the cemetery in the book] seem more sensible and less absurd than the priest-guided Evelyn Waugh. What the former are trying to do is, after all, merely to gloss over physical death with smooth lawns and soothing rites; but, for the Catholic, the fact of death is not to be faced at all: he is solaced with the fantasy of another world in which everyone who has died in the flesh is somehow supposed to be still alive and in which it is supposed to be possible to help souls advance themselves by buying candles to burn in churches. The trappings invented for this other world by imaginative believers in the Christian myth...beat anything concocted by Whispering Glades.' It is true that Mr Waugh is a convert to the Roman Catholic Church, but he doesn't find it necessary in his book to invoke dogma or to appeal to any specific religious belief to condemn a morbid preoccupation with physical dissolution in death. It is Mr Waugh's point that this vulgarization of death by grotesque mortuary art and the magic of cosmetics parallels a shrivelled and vulgar attitude to *life*. If Mr Wilson finds the attitude to life implicit in Whispering Glades more congenial than that explicit in the traditional 'Christian myth', that should prove 'disturbing', as I said above, 'to anyone inclined to respect' etc. Rather, 'depressing' would be the more sympathetic term.

THE NEW SCHOLARSHIP?

R. G. COX (1952)

A Reading of George Herbert, by Rosemond Tuve (Faber & Faber)
Elizabethan and Metaphysical Imagery, by Rosemond Tuve (U.S.A.: University of Chicago Press; U.K.: C.U.P. 1947)

Whatever may be lacking in American criticism, it is not variety any more than it is thoroughness or conviction. We have become accustomed to a heterogeneous assortment of 'New Critics' loosely ranged over against the academic Old Guard, and to a large number of individuals and groups whose positions are governed by different philosophical, psychological or sociological preconceptions. Professor Tuve does not seem to fit into any of these categories: she comes nearest, perhaps, to the Historians of Ideas, and she stands squarely for the control of criticism by scholarly information, but in the preface to her latest book she declines to consider herself at war with 'The New Criticism' 'except where it asks what-is-truth? and will not stay for an answer'. What this means in practice and how far it is significant that Professor Tuve's work should have been highly praised in this country by those not particularly sympathetic to modern critical methods it is the business of this review to consider.

The immediate occasion is her recent book on George Herbert, finely produced by Faber and embellished with seventeen plates (two coloured) illustrating mediaeval iconography. The chief aim is to show that Herbert worked deliberately and consciously within a tradition of symbolism and scriptural interpretation, going right back through mediaeval liturgy and devotional and expository literature to the beginnings of the Christian Church, that this raises special problems for criticism, and that in particular much of his imagery which has been seen as quaint or startling is in fact thoroughly conventional and can only be properly appreciated by a mind aware of the tradition. The book falls into two parts, an essay on '"The Sacrifice"' and modern criticism', starting from Mr Empson's analytical pages in *Seven Types of Ambiguity*, and a general section discussing 'images as language', wit, the interpretation of some obscure passages, and the significance of the 'Jordan' poems.

A fundamental issue is raised on p. 42, apropos 'the wilful modern divorce between "scholarship" and "criticism"':

I should like to speak out for willingness to repair our ignorances, despite the current fear (not least current among 'academic' critics) that we may somehow substitute knowledge 'about' poem and author for response to poetry. This *substitution*, which I admit to be deplorable, is far less frequent than the losses we sustain by the modern necessity to avoid any noticeable use of the helps furnished by literary scholarship *in case* [*sc. if*] *criticism is one's end*. Revolt against the abuses of the former may have been necessary. But criticism may not longer decline to face the problems created by the fact that recognition of the richest and deepest meanings of poems sometimes depends about equally upon the knowledge and upon the sensibility of a reader. The fact operates as truly in the case of early poems as with those of Eliot and Yeats: there it has been recognized and valiantly met.

General statements of this kind are slippery things to handle: one does not quite know who or what is really under fire. There may be excesses and errors of 'new critics' to justify this feeling that ignorant criticism does more harm than scholarly irrelevance, but Professor Tuve's optimism hardly allows for the many instances of scholarship used to support critical prejudices which remain unconscious or unacknowledged. In any case, I am not sure who advocates 'divorce': what we want is informed criticism and scholarship which answers genuine critical questions. But response to the deepest meaning of a poem is not absolutely the same thing as *recognition* of it, and even where Eliot and Yeats are concerned it is worth noting that exposition and exegesis sometimes permit an interest in underlying doctrines and systems in general forms to replace the response to their particular embodiment in the poems.

A major question here, and one relevant to all Professor Tuve's writing, is how far, where works of the past are concerned, we ought to try to turn ourselves into contemporary readers (bearing in mind that we can obviously never do so completely)? To say that this question is not so easy to answer as it may appear at first sight is not to assert the contrary extreme: that we may find in a work of the past anything we can—may consider ourselves free, in fact, to re-make it entirely. But it has always been generally assumed that the greater works were precisely those with the power to speak to other ages than their own, and it might therefore be argued that the more exactly we succeed in reconstructing in ourselves the mind of a past age the greater the danger that we shall merely endorse the age's own critical values and blur our perception of the more lasting vitality. Clearly there must be compromise, adjustment and critical choice at every point: we start from where we are and what experience and information we possess: we correct continually by the acquisition of any knowledge that seems relevant, including that of the first readers' mental habits and the author's probable intention. But we should not forget that achievement may exceed as well as fall short of intention, and we are not bound to restrict ourselves to the conscious interpretations possible to contemporaries, since it would be unreasonable to suppose that *all* other meanings discovered by subsequent generations were simply anachronistic and not in some sense implicit from the start.

When, therefore, Professor Tuve asserts that we misinterpret Herbert through inadequate knowledge of the symbolic tradition governing his imagery, we are perhaps more ready to be impressed by her claims of what the knowledge will add to our understanding than by her notions of what it ought to exclude, though we shall examine both critically. It must be said that in Mr Empson's account of *The Sacrifice* in *Seven Types of Ambiguity* she chose a handy stick with which to beat modern criticism: its lapses of tone and its patches of irresponsible ingenuity would be acknowledged by most critics, New or otherwise, without any special equipment or learning. The analysis has nevertheless merits which she acknowledges fairly, and Mr Empson, while admitting some faults and errors, has defended himself to some effect in a letter to the *Kenyon Review* for Autumn 1950 (XII, 735). Professor Tuve is mainly concerned to show that the poem derives from the liturgical office for Holy Week and belongs with the Complaints of Christ to his People, a large group of mediaeval religious lyrics. Its statement of conflicts, its ironical juxtapositions and its symbols, she says, are not Herbert's, but are prescribed by tradition, and she reinforces her point with a mass of parallels including MS illuminations and stained glass windows. Some of these are enlightening locally and all have general interest, though it is not clear that anything essential in the poem is likely to be missed by a reader normally familiar with the Bible and the Anglican prayer-book. To suggest that without these learned annotations we are lost is, I think, to ignore the extent to which a successful poem may embody and perpetuate a tradition, carrying it over with new life into a different age. Is there not also an opposite danger, especially where religious belief is concerned, that the reader too thoroughly saturated in a given tradition may tend to take the will for the deed, to distinguish insufficiently between conventional repetition and true re-embodiment? Since Professor Tuve recognizes that Herbert's originality lay in the way he used traditional thought, making new connections to sharpen existing and inherent ironies and to 'reawaken into new life whole complexes of meaning', it is not easy to see why she denies the presence of new connotations in the imagery as part of the process. It would seem, for one thing, to be a normal method of the popular preacher to bring home conventional symbols to the imagination by giving them a touch of homely concreteness. Professor Tuve says that when in *The Agonie* Herbert says 'Sinne is that presse and vice...' he is using the conventional metaphor of the winepress of the Passion. 'He is not the daring Metaphysical innovator wittily joining the lowly press to the exalted idea of Christ, but the poet choosing familiar and moving language...' But if the addition 'and vice' is not there to revivify the symbol, bringing the properties of 'presse' more concretely to our imaginations (with a hint also of thumbscrews and torture) it is difficult to see why it is there at all, however many woodcuts and windows may depict as a type of Christ the bunch of grapes stolen by the Israelite spies. It is the same with other examples: in the anagram poem *Mary: Army* how can we be certain that Herbert would not have expected some of the common associations of 'pitch his tent' to occur to the reader, if only as stimulant of attention, whatever familiarity he may have counted on with the symbol of the Virgin as 'tabernacle of the Deity'? Even 'Man stole the fruit, but I must climbe the tree' seems to depend for *part* of the force of its antithesis on a connection between 'fruit' and 'tree' which is *not* purely symbolic, though we do not need to follow Mr Empson's suggestions all the way, or even, necessarily, to believe that the connotations are completely under control. Professor Tuve seldom seems to admit the possibility that the poet might miscalculate. Is there, one wonders, a traditional justification for the 'grave-clothes'–'handkerchief' conceit?

Perhaps the real point to make, however, is that scholarship, however thorough, cannot completely prove these points: it is a critical judgment that is in question, and there is room for disagreement. Professor Tuve claims that when we understand the symbolic language and exclude 'irrelevancies' the poems she analyses are transformed: I can only say that many of them do not seem to me to become all that much more effective. Not all readers, I think, will agree that the answer to rebellious protest in *The Bunch of Grapes* becomes 'as moving, once we grasp the symbolism, as the end of *The Collar*'. It may be significant that not very much is said about the best and most well-known poems: perhaps they have been able to make their impact in spite of our ignorance. In some cases Professor Tuve is able to clear up obscurities (the references, for example, to Joseph's coat and Solomon's 'sea of brass', which involve rather more than a knowledge of the Bible) but sometimes the obscurity which she seeks to illuminate, and the eccentric tone which she claims to remove by explanation appear to exist for her alone, or to be much exaggerated. In *Whitsunday*, for instance, the symbolism of light and life-giving water explains itself, and the image of the apostles as 'pipes of gold' works sufficiently well without the additional help of recognizing the source in Zechariah iv (though we are naturally grateful for Hutchinson's note). The most difficult lines seem to be those describing the pipes as

> cut and martyr'd by the fault
> Of those who did themselves through their side wound

and here Professor Tuve has nothing to offer that we could not work out for ourselves. Incidentally, she is silent on the earlier image in the poem about the stars coming down 'to know If they might mend their wages, and serve here': it would be interesting to know if any traditional symbolism can remove from this the connotation of servants bettering themselves (not that it matters). On other occasions, for example, the note on 'God help poore Kings' in *Church-musick*, the offered explanation seems no more adequate than any other excogitated gloss, unless one grants the assumption that an allusion, even without much point, is inherently more likely than a fanciful thought. As a matter of fact, there is considerable evidence that Professor Tuve is fascinated by the scholarly processes in themselves: her enthusiasm often seems to be the pleasure of the chase. This would not matter at all if one were not haunted by the vision of a literary world divided between New Critics ranging ever more widely in techniques of free association and scholars insisting on the necessity of an ever-increasing burden of knowledge, with the common reader, if he still exists, distracted between them.

Many of the general qualities of Professor Tuve's comparatively short book on Herbert appear in her monumental study of imagery, which came out five years ago, and received some discussion in an exchange between Mr Bewley and Mr Donald Davie in *Scrutiny* for September 1949 (XVI, p. 234). Bearing the sub-title 'Renaissance Poetic and Twentieth-Century Critics', its main thesis is that all post-seventeenth-century criticism has been wrong in its account of Metaphysical poetry, whether favourably or unfavourably disposed, and in particular that all modern attempts to distinguish Metaphysical from Elizabethan poetry largely in terms of its use of imagery have been wrong-headed and misleading. Professor Tuve argues that Renaissance critical theory, on the other hand, has been misunderstood and therefore underestimated, and that it provides a much more useful basis for discussion of all poetry down to the Restoration. The book is divided into two parts: 'Sensuousness and Significancy as Functions of Images' and 'The

Logical Functions of Imagery'. The first begins by dealing with the effect upon imagery of the Renaissance doctrines of Imitation (conceived as the author's ordered interpretation of nature expressed through deliberate artifice and a conscious attempt at the artistic statement of truth), '*ut pictura poesis*' (a desire for something like significant form rather than external ornament) and 'style as a garment' (in the sense that the flesh is the garment of the soul). It goes on to consider in turn various criteria for the use of images which may be derived from these general principles—sensuous vividness, delightfulness (including 'varying' and 'beautifying' as more than mere multiplication or elaboration), significancy (contribution to the expression of the poet's coherent ordering of nature), rhetorical efficacy, and the various types of decorum, especially according to the three levels of style and the different literary 'kinds'. The last chapter ascribes to decorum more importance than distinctions of schools or individuals, replacing the idea of a Metaphysical 'revolt' by a simple choice of certain 'kinds' to which the 'middle' and the 'low' style were appropriate, but which were well within the bounds permitted by contemporary theory. The second part discusses images according to their logical bases and logical functions, rejecting as useless the present tendency to class them according to 'the area from whence comparisons are drawn, because of personal predilections of the author'. It relates Renaissance imagery to Renaissance logical method, suggesting in particular that the rise of the new Ramist logic with its emphasis on dialectic, not merely for disputing or proving but as a means of investigating the nature of things, of intellectual probing, may have been the main influence towards that emphasis on certain kinds of poetic method, especially in the use of imagery, that we are accustomed to call Metaphysical. Professor Tuve, however, does not choose to press this point (perhaps her most interesting general conclusion) because the English poetic tradition seems to her 'so much of a piece from Marlowe (or Wyatt) to Marvell'.

Professor Tuve is a formidable scholar, as well as an energetic and ingenious controversialist: she presents this comprehensive argument with a tireless industry in multiplying distinctions, qualifications and examples which makes it very difficult for the critical reader to penetrate her defences, however much he may feel that something is going wrong. The most effective answer that I have yet seen deals mainly with her treatment of Donne, and is once more by Mr Empson, in an article on *Donne and the Rhetorical Tradition* in the *Kenyon Review* for Autumn 1949 (XI, 571). Perhaps the first point to consider is that here again far too exclusive an importance seems to be attached to intention—to what the writer thought that he was doing and what the reader thought had been done, as deduced from evidence of current theory. Professor Tuve appears to abandon the possibility of any critical theory or method which could be applied equally to any poetry from the Renaissance onwards, though at times she seems to suggest that modern poetry can be fitted rather better into Renaissance categories than vice versa. Elsewhere, however, she says explicitly that she doesn't know whether Renaissance theory is true, only that it fits Renaissance poetry. She certainly succeds in interpreting the theory to us as rather less naïve than has sometimes been assumed, but hardly, I think, as covering all the complexities with which modern criticism finds it necessary to deal, and, which as Mr Empson points out, have always existed as practical problems for writers.

This focusing on intention and theory has the obvious danger of deflecting attention from the actual experience of and response to poetry. Professor Tuve has a logical acuteness which enables her in numerous instances to show that modern criticism has pointed to the wrong quality as the differentiating factor between an Elizabethan and a Metaphysical poem (frequently that differences ascribed to imagery really depend on other things). But she is more concerned to demonstrate the relevance of Renaissance theory to the common use of imagery than to point to the true *differentia*; the possibility that behind the inadequate modern analysis lay a genuine perception is forgotten or minimized, so that there seems to be often an implicit suggestion, without direct statement, that the perception was false. At the beginning of the book Professor Tuve urbanely claims to share modern tastes, to prefer seventeenth- to sixteenth-century poets, and to be dissatisfied merely with 'the *reasons why* so far advanced'. This, it must be said, does not altogether square with the general trend of the discussion, and as we have seen, when she does produce, in the influence of Ramist logic, something that might suggest from her point of view more adequate reasons, she soft-pedals the argument in the interests of a feeling that Renaissance poetry is all of a piece. Are we not justified in suspecting here a critical assumption masquerading as a disinterested conclusion from evidence? Granting for a moment that all the many examples of imagery used for similar purposes in Spenser and Donne, Drayton and Marvell, can be accepted as convincing, we are still left with the plain fact that poems by Spenser and Drayton do not look like poems by Donne and Marvell (nor even do those of the Ramist, Sidney) and that this is important for criticism and even for literary history.[1]

---

[1] A typical example is the comparison between *Amoretti* XLVI and *The Definition of Love* on pp. 325–6. Differences in pace or verse form, it is said, should not lead to false antitheses regarding the nature of *images*. But the similar logical

At this point Professor Tuve refers us to 'decorum', the careful discrimination of 'kinds' and their appropriate styles. Decorum has perhaps been underestimated in the past, though there are a good many signs that it is coming into its own now, especially as a means of undermining theories of stylistic development (e.g. in Shakespeare). Here it is argued that Donne and the Metaphysicals simply chose to write in short forms favouring concentration and in kinds demanding those middle and lower styles whose legitimacy for certain purposes had always been recognized. This, of course, is only to push the problem further back, as Miss Bradbrook[1] and others have noted: it remains significant that at this time a number of writers became particularly interested in the opportunities offered by these kinds and styles. To imply that if Sidney and Spenser had had Donne's 'causes' (a term covering both 'poet's intention' and 'poetic subject') they would have written like Donne simply gets us nowhere: to have had exactly Donne's 'causes' they would have had to be Donne. Professor Tuve seems to suggest that because the deliberate expression of personality was not a characteristic of Elizabethan poetry, personal differences count for little in the total effect—a *non-sequitur* if there ever was one.

Or perhaps she would say that here she is speaking particularly of imagery, and that personal differences of style come out in subtler matters of tone and rhythm. The whole tendency of her argument, of course, is to assert that imagery cannot be properly considered apart from its function in a controlling context. The point is sound enough, if not original, and undoubtedly modern criticism shows a number of excesses which make the reminder timely. But too narrow a concentration on imagery is ascribed to too many critics: Professor Tuve talks of 'Imagist theory' and 'Symbolist poetic' as if most modern criticism could be fitted quite simply into these categories. Not many modern critics demand 'vivid sensuous particularity' in quite the naïve way she suggests, nor can their demands be so easily connected with Romanticism. Speaking of the Elizabethan 'refusal to narrow the task of images to that of a truthful report of experience' on p. 42, she points out that Donne apostrophizes the personified universal even in Elegy XIX: *Going to Bed*. But this, of course, doesn't make the total effect of the poem less dramatic and concrete, and I don't know who wants to restrict images to 'truthful report of experience' in such a narrow sense. Often it seems to be missed that statements made by modern critics of

function of the images here seems a trivial matter beside the contrast in total effect, the so much greater force and concentration of the Marvell than the Spenser passage. Even if it is 'the formal patterns which give the two images their character', that difference of character remains the important thing.

[1] See her *Shakespeare and Elizabethan Poetry*, p. 248, note 12.

the Metaphysicals refer to whole poems and passages, and that discussion of images is only a pointer to the main effect. Mr Eliot's famous phrases, for example, about 'sensuous apprehension of thought' and the rest were *not* merely descriptions of imagery (see the subtle over-simplification of the summary on pp. 165–6) and it is not likely that the list of critics in the footnote to p. 164 would all subscribe without reserve to Professor Tuve's account of their common notions.

It would be possible to pursue Professor Tuve through discussion of particular examples to the extent of almost her own four hundred pages, but perhaps enough has been said to show her aim and method and the nature of the disagreements she provokes. It is only fair to say that the book contains many incidental discussions of considerable interest, and that she has certainly made some kinds of glibness about imagery impossible in future. To provoke more careful thought about the relation between Metaphysical and Elizabethan poetry is a service. Most of the critical rehabilitation of the Metaphysicals was accomplished against a background of conventional taste inherited from the nine-teenth century: the main task was to break down Romantic prejudices against wit, conceits, and metrical irregularity. Less careful attention, perhaps, was paid to what differentiated the Metaphysicals from their predecessors, and something of the older conception of the Elizabethan age as romantic in the nineteenth-century way, only more youthful and naïve, may have survived in some recent criticism. It will hardly, I think, be found in Mr Eliot's essay, or in Sir Herbert Grierson's famous introduction, where the definition of 'Metaphysical' neither ignores the presence of wit and conceits in earlier poetry nor concentrates narrowly on imagery. Whether a recognition of the conscious art, the philosophical, moral, and practical ends, and the intellectual qualities of Elizabethan poetry will lead us to find as much in common between Sidney, Spenser, Drayton, or Daniel and Donne, Herbert, King, or Marvell as Professor Tuve does is another matter.